Conflict and Compromise
Volume I

CONFLICT AND COMPROMISE

VOLUME I
PRE-CONFEDERATION CANADA

Raymond B. Blake

Jeffrey A. Keshen

Norman J. Knowles

Barbara J. Messamore

UNIVERSITY OF TORONTO PRESS

Copyright © University of Toronto Press 2017

Higher Education Division

www.utppublishing.com

Library and Archives Canada Cataloguing in Publication

Blake, Raymond B. (Raymond Benjamin), author

Conflict and compromise / Raymond B. Blake, Jeffrey Keshen, Norman Knowles, Barbara Messamore.

Includes index.

Contents: v. 1. Pre-confederation.

Issued in print and electronic formats.

ISBN 978-1-4426-3553-1 (volume 1: paperback).—ISBN 978-1-4426-3554-8 (volume 1: hardback).—ISBN 978-1-4426-3555-5 (volume 1: html).—ISBN 978-1-4426-3556-2 (volume 1: pdf).

1. Canada—History. 2. Cultural pluralism—Canada—History. I. Keshen, Jeff, 1962–, author II. Knowles, Norman James, 1963–, author III. Messamore, Barbara Jane, 1959–, author IV. Title.

FC165.B54 2017 971 C2016-905201-X C2016-905202-8

We welcome comments and suggestions regarding any aspect of our publications—please feel free to contact us at news@utphighereducation.com or visit our Internet site at www.utppublishing.com.

North America

5201 Dufferin Street

North York, Ontario, Canada, M3H 5T8

2250 Military Road

Tonawanda, New York, USA, 14150

ORDERS PHONE: 1–800–565–9523

ORDERS FAX: 1–800–221–9985

ORDERS E-MAIL: utpbooks@utpress.utoronto.ca

UK, Ireland, and continental Europe

NBN International

Estover Road, Plymouth, PL6 7PY, UK

ORDERS PHONE: 44 (0) 1752 202301

ORDERS FAX: 44 (0) 1752 202333

ORDERS E-MAIL: enquiries@nbninternational.com

Every effort has been made to contact copyright holders; in the event of an error or omission, please notify the publisher.

This book is printed on paper containing 100% post-consumer fibre.

The University of Toronto Press acknowledges the financial support for its publishing activities of the Government of Canada through the Canada Book Fund.

Printed in the Canada.

CONTENTS

PREFACE

istory offers a way to make sense of the world. If we wish to understand the Arab–Israeli conflict, why Taiwan calls itself the Republic of China, why one-third of Canada's Supreme Court appointees are from Quebec, or why New Brunswick has more senators than British Columbia, history is the key. Even in our day-to-day interactions, most people instinctively look to history as a means of understanding: if we meet someone new, our questions turn to history. Where you have come from and what you have experienced will have written the story of who you are. Similarly, a nation's history explains what it has become.

As a fundamental component of a liberal arts education, the study of history builds general knowledge, but also helps to inform our judgment and reason. In 1914, John Alexander Smith, an Oxford professor of moral philosophy, stated to his incoming class: "Nothing that you will learn in the course of your studies will be of the slightest possible use to you in after life—save only this—that if you work hard and intelligently you should be able to detect when a man is talking rot, and that, in my view, is the main, if not the sole, purpose of education."[1] Wide exposure to ideas and events of the past can offer us the means by which we can judge new schemes. Everyone learns from experience; history offers a way to broaden these lessons, to learn from the experience of others.

Historical study enables us to enter into the minds of those who differ from us. And, sometimes, learning just a little can be enough to topple the preconceived ideas that

---

1   John Alexander Smith, as quoted in Andrew Delbanco, *College: What It Was, Is, and Should Be* (Princeton, NJ: Princeton University Press, 2012), 29.

prevent us from being open to fresh insights. Condemnation is easy; empathetic understanding is more difficult to achieve. Empathy does not necessarily imply full agreement, but it is a route to a more nuanced view of other perspectives. Too often, when we do not simply condemn those in the past, we attempt to excuse them for actions we disapprove of by explaining that they lived in a different age, with different values. The implication is that they would have behaved differently, were they as wise as we are. The English historian E.P. Thompson complained of "the enormous condescension of posterity."[2] Before we reach for that all too ready explanation—that everyone in the past was hopelessly benighted—we should investigate a little more deeply.

Conflict and Compromise is organized chronologically. Rather than devoting discrete chapters to themes, geographical areas, or some combination of those—for example, "industrialization in the Maritimes"—it follows a narrative pattern, shifting location to explore concurrent events. For historians, context is everything, and the only way to fully understand events is to situate them in their time. And, although the focus of *Conflict and Compromise* is on Canada's history, events that happened here were often informed by a wider world context. The outcome of the Seven Years' War (1756–63), for example, only makes sense in a global perspective; North American battles were important, but do not provide the whole story. The 1791 *Constitutional Act*—our first written constitution—can only be fully appreciated by considering the events that would have been on the minds of British parliamentarians as they contemplated this legislation. Just across the channel, the French Revolution was providing a very powerful, and immediate, demonstration to Britain's policy makers of the excesses they wished to avoid. The debate over Canada's constitution was the occasion for debate in Britain over the nature of its own constitution and political traditions, and the essential result was, political scientist Janet Ajzenstat asserts, the famous British unwritten constitution in written form. In the form of the 1791 document, we can see the "bones" of our modern constitution.[3] In a similar vein, it is important to remember the context in which the "Fathers" of Confederation met at Charlottetown in 1864. The American Civil War (1861–65) raging across the border heightened anxieties about defence, adding urgency to the plan for federation. And the outbreak of the Civil War itself provided an object lesson in the need for a satisfactory division of powers between a nation's component parts.

In university study, learning history implies more than simply building a sequential timeline of events. It is, of course, important to know some objective facts, to know when and where pivotal events unfolded, but it is also important to recognize that the

---

2 E.P. Thompson, *The Making of the English Working Class* (Harmondsworth: Penguin Books, 1968), 13.

3 Janet Ajzenstat, "Celebrating 1791: Two Hundred Years of Representative Government," *Canadian Parliamentary Review* 14, no. 1 (Spring 1991): 30.

very decision about which events are studied is a subjective one. We select the events we study because we believe that they marked great turning points or demonstrate important ideas. The facts we choose to include are, by necessity, selected, and the facts are always in the service of a larger idea. The historian E.H. Carr recalled the observation that a fact is like a sack—it won't stand up until you put something in it.[4] The ideas and events that we deem most important change over time and are inevitably a function of our own circumstances. University-level historical study must therefore include some consideration of historiography—the writing of history. We do not merely study the past, but also how that history has been written, and what changing interpretations can tell us about the age in which the history was produced.

New crises and new developments can suddenly invest old events with new significance. For example, the 9-11 attacks in 2001 sparked an understandable wish to investigate the roots of Islamic fundamentalism, a topic that had attracted little scholarly interest beforehand. Even the 1683 defeat of the Islamic Ottoman Empire by a coalition of Christian armies at the siege of Vienna suddenly seemed more significant; some even speculated that the timing of the 2001 attacks was linked to the September 11, 1683, commencement of the final, decisive battle in which the Ottoman Turks were defeated. Did the end of an era of Islamic expansionism in Europe leave a bitter legacy to be avenged? In Canadian historical study, the Royal Proclamation of 1763 was once of interest primarily because it set out a plan for British governance of the newly acquired colony of Quebec. Today, however, the proclamation is under-stood to be a fundamental document in the legal recognition of what we now call "Aboriginal title," and there are frequent references to that 1763 document in the courts and the news media; the 1982 Charter of Rights and Freedoms makes specific mention of it. While students may insist that they want to study what is relevant, it is important to remember that relevance is a moving target. The historian Ged Martin offers a reminder that an insistence on "relevance" in historical study can be "a blind alley, a present-centred approach that naturally privileges the near past."[5] Pre-Confederation history may seem hopelessly distant, but it is well to remember that the importance of events is not determined by how recently they occurred.

In the past several decades, our definition of history has broadened. Where historical study once focused almost exclusively on politics, governance, warfare, and economic matters, historians now investigate social arrangements, family life, and the quiet daily rhythms of work. Research into such questions can only broaden our understanding of the past. We are now mindful about writing history that is more

4   E.H. Carr, *What Is History?* (Harmondsworth: Penguin, 1984 ed.), 11.

5   Ged Martin, *Past Futures: The Impossible Necessity of History* (Toronto: University of Toronto Press, 2004), 191.

inclusive, spurning an exclusive focus on "dead, white males," and seeking to include the stories of those who have been marginalized. This laudable goal, however, can itself produce distortion, and we must be faithful to the past even if it does not tell us what we hope it will. Canadians celebrate Laura Secord, who risked her life to deliver a warning to British troops during the War of 1812, but our eagerness to discover heroines may lead us to attach more historical significance to her deeds than is warranted. When a story appeals to us, we want it to be meaningful. On the other hand, the stories of other prominent women in history have receded in our consciousness. Marie de l'Incarnation, the dynamic founder of the Roman Catholic Ursuline order who came to Quebec in 1639, was indisputably an important figure in the early life of New France, but pervasive secular values today make us less inclined to celebrate such a figure.

While *Conflict and Compromise* incorporates aspects of new historical scholarship, in some respects the approach is traditional. It aims to provide a coherent narrative and always seeks to ground events in a clear understanding of the political circumstances. Most of our readers will be Canadians, and one of our key goals is to enhance our readers' understanding of the political traditions of their country. As citizens and voters, we have an obligation to be well informed. Canada's history, as we demonstrate, was not without conflict, but, more often, has been a story of peaceful gradualism, and this history has yielded a nation founded upon compromise. "Unity" may sound like an admirable goal, but a successful nation must accommodate heterogeneity, disagreement, and conflicting visions, rather than seeking to stifle them.

The American historian Gertrude Himmelfarb argues that it is not in the household or the village that humans exercise their highest faculties for reason, but in the public realm, in the polis, where they act as citizens. She recalls Aristotle's observation that "bees or any other gregarious animals" also "inhabit households…eat, play, copulate, rear their young…[and] have social relations." "What they do not have," she explains, "is a polity, a government of laws and institutions by means of which…man consciously, rationally tries to establish a just regime and pursue the good life."[6] It is in the political realm that we can often see individuals shaping their circumstances, and it is especially striking to see that some of the most prominent individuals we study were highly flawed people. Robert Baldwin, in partnership with fellow reformer Louis-Hippolyte La Fontaine, worked to achieve self-government in Canada in 1848, but was far from a natural politician: he loathed public life and frequently was mired in depression, especially after he lost his beloved Eliza, the first cousin whom he married

6   Gertrude Himmelfarb, *The New History and the Old* (Cambridge, MA: Belknap Press of Harvard University Press, 1987), 25.

over family objections. Conservative Prime Minister John A. Macdonald dominated post-Confederation Canadian politics despite his frequently debilitating spates of drunkenness. These important actors did not wait until they were perfect before they sought to make their mark on events, and it can inspire us to remember that our own inevitable flaws do not preclude big aspirations.

It is our hope that this story of Canada will help readers to see their own country more clearly, to gain greater understanding of its complexity and its place in a wider world, and to appreciate the struggles of those in the past to achieve fairness and justice.

1 FIRST PEOPLES AND FIRST CONTACTS

The history of Canada's Indigenous inhabitants prior to the arrival of Europeans is a dynamic one, as the First Peoples responded to environmental change, new technologies evolved, and social and cultural beliefs and practices developed. With the arrival of Europeans, this process of change and adaptation continued. For both Indigenous peoples and Europeans, the story that unfolded was one of cultural persistence and accommodation, conflict and cooperation, as the needs and expectations of both Indigenous peoples and Europeans changed as they encountered each other and contributed to making what would become a "new world" for both.

FIRST PEOPLES

Prehistory—the thousands of years in the human past before the advent of writing and written records—poses a tremendous challenge to historians. By drawing upon the tools and resources of other disciplines, however, historians are able to gain insight into many aspects of the dynamic past of Indigenous North Americans prior to European contact. Indigenous oral traditions passed on from generation to generation offer insight into Indigenous worldviews and understanding of the past. Archaeology provides evidence of past human behaviour through the careful examination of material remains. Through the study of the nature and structure of language, linguistics enables scholars to reconstruct the linguistic history of the continent and the movement of culturally related peoples. Using the tools of DNA analysis, physical anthropologists are able to study the diffusion of biological characteristics over time, and the interrelationships between different groups. Scientists who study the human impact on the environment and the effects of environmental changes on human ways of life have revealed a great deal about shifts in settlement and subsistence patterns. Ethno-historians use the evidence generated by scholars of many disciplines, as well as traditional written sources, to reconstruct Indigenous society and culture. The result has been a growing understanding of the complex history of Canada's First Peoples before the arrival of Europeans.

Like most peoples, the earliest inhabitants of North America have their own creation stories explaining their origins. Although these stories differ in detail, they all place Indigenous peoples in North America "when the world began." These oral traditions assert that there were no migrations resulting in the peopling of the Americas; rather, Indigenous peoples originated on the American continents. Archaeologists and palaeo-anthropologists, however, do not think that human life gradually evolved in the Americas as in other parts of the world. Because remains of early humans, such as those discovered in Africa, Asia, and Europe, have never been found in the Western Hemisphere, they are convinced that the First Peoples must have arrived in the Americas as the result of migrations from other continents. Convinced of the historical veracity of their own traditions, many Indigenous persons have charged that such migration theories have more to do with politics than science. They argue that it is easier to justify the dispossession of Indigenous peoples by Europeans if it can be demonstrated that they were just the first of several waves of migrants to colonize the Americas.[1] Such debates raise important questions about the very nature of history and its uses.

Most palaeo-anthropologists and archaeologists believe that North America was first populated by nomadic peoples from Siberia. DNA studies demonstrate a close genetic relationship between the peoples of northeast Asia and the Indigenous peoples of the Americas. During the last Ice Age, huge volumes of water were locked up in massive glaciers, lowering sea levels by as much as 100 metres and creating a land bridge between Siberia and North America. This treeless grassland, which geologists refer to as Beringia, provided an ideal habitat for large grazing mammals such as mammoth, bison, horse, and camel. Nomadic hunter-gatherers followed game across the land bridge from Siberia into present-day Alaska and Yukon. These migrants do not appear to have settled but to have seasonally occupied the region. A massive ice sheet separated Beringia from the rest of North America, preventing migration further south. With the passing of the Ice Age, the climate began to warm, creating an ice-free corridor along the eastern slopes of the Rockies that allowed both people and game to migrate south, eventually populating both North and South America. While there is general agreement that nomadic

1 Vine de Loria, *Red Earth, White Lies: Native Americans and the Myth of Scientific Fact* (Golden, CO: Fulcrum, 1997).

hunter-gatherers from northern Asia crossed a land bridge to North America and travelled south along a narrow, ice-free corridor, questions remain about when and in what numbers these palaeo-Indians migrated.

Until the 1920s it was generally accepted that the land bridge migration had taken place between 4000 and 6000 BCE. The discovery of stone spear points embedded in the rib cage of a species of bison extinct for nearly 10,000 years, by a cowboy in Folsom, New Mexico, in 1926, proved that the human occupation of North America began at a far earlier date. Ten years later, in Clovis, New Mexico, stone spear points were found in the remains of a mammoth discovered in a layer of earth that was deeper than those at the Folsom site, indicating that they came from an even earlier age. The older spear points, which came to be known as Clovis points, were radiocarbon-dated and found to be about 11,500 years old. After the first of these

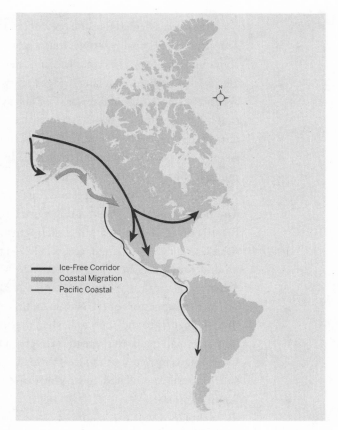

Map 1.1 Possible migration routes to North America at the end of the last Ice Age.

spear points was found, many more Clovis points were discovered throughout North and Central America. For several decades most scientists thought that the Clovis points signalled the earliest period of human life in the Americas. Then, in 1977, archaeologist Tom Dillehay began digging at a site at Monte Verde in south-central Chile. Dillehay discovered the remains of an ancient village preserved under a peat bog. Extensive testing showed the artifacts at the Monte Verde site pre-dated the Clovis culture. Convinced that Clovis humans had been the first in the Americas, many within the archaeological community remained skeptical and contested the Monte Verde findings until other sites in North and South America yielded artifacts dating back before the Clovis period. Excavations at Pendejo Cave in New Mexico and at Pedra Furada in Brazil have provided evidence of human habitation as early as 30,000 years ago.[2]

---

2   Brian M. Fagan, *Ancient North America: The Archaeology of a Continent* (New York: Thames and Hudson, 2000).

Having confirmed that the previously accepted dates for the peopling of the Americas were probably wrong, many scholars have gone on to develop new theories about human life on the American continents before the Clovis era and presented alternatives to the Bering land bridge theory of migration. Seaworthy boats have been around in some parts of the world for at least 40,000 years. Many experts now believe that migrants from northeast Asia may have travelled by boat along the coast of Asia during the Great Ice Age and then sailed south along the Pacific coast of the Americas as early as 30,000 years ago.[3] It is thus likely that North America was populated by multiple migrations using both land and sea routes.

Linguistic evidence suggests at least two subsequent migrations to North America. Most of the known Indigenous languages are believed to be descended from the first set of migrations. A second linguistic group, represented by the Na-Dene or Athapascan family of languages, is believed to have been carried to North America around 7000 BCE. The Na-Dene settled in Alaska and northwestern Canada. Some Athapascan-speaking people later migrated to the American Southwest where they became the ancestors of the Navajo and the Apache. A third migration is believed to have begun around 3000 BCE when maritime hunting peoples crossed the Bering Strait in small boats and spread throughout the Far North.[4] Whether by land or by sea, humans moved south to ice-free areas of North America. By 12,000 years ago the Americas were populated, to varying degrees of density, from the Arctic to the tip of South America.

Scholars divide the history of North America's Indigenous peoples following the initial migrations and prior to European contact into distinct periods based on technological developments. The first of these periods, the Palaeo, extends from 30,000 to 9000 BCE. During this period, Palaeo peoples spread throughout much of North America, establishing a base from which most regional cultures later developed. These peoples, who are identified by their skillfully crafted stone spearheads, were nomadic hunter-gatherers who subsisted on big game such as mammoth and mastodon, and prehistoric caribou and bison. Archaeological evidence indicates that Palaeo peoples travelled in small groups of extended family numbering between 20 and 50, and that social and political relations were likely highly egalitarian. Men hunted while women gathered nuts, berries, and other food and cared for children. Much of the archaeological evidence suggests that Palaeo hunting methods involved the mass extermination of prey, and it was once thought that these methods

---

3 Herbert S. Klein and Daniel C. Schiffner, "The Current Debate about the Origins of the Paleoindians of America," *Journal of Social History* 37, no. 2 (Winter 2003): 486–88.

4 Ibid., 486.

contributed to the extinction of many species of large mammals. Many now question this overkill hypothesis. It seems more likely that changes in climate and vegetation at the end of the last Ice Age led to the extinction of many of these prehistoric mammals. The discovery of stone spear points and other tools far from the stone's original source suggests that Palaeo peoples travelled over large territories and probably engaged in trading or exchange relationships with other groups.

The climate and environment of North America changed significantly between 10,000 and 8000 BCE. Large lakes, fed by melting glaciers, formed as the ice retreated; sea levels rose rapidly, flooding the Bering land bridge; and vegetation regions shifted north. During this period, humans spread across much of North America. Because of the distinctive fluted projectile points that these people left behind, they are known as the Fluted Point people. By 8000 BCE the climate had stabilized and the Fluted Point people gradually adapted to different environments. This gave rise to distinctive regional cultures: Plano culture in the west and Archaic culture in the woodlands of the east. To compensate for the disappearance of many large mammals, Indigenous peoples developed new survival strategies and learned to hunt smaller game and waterfowl, to fish, and to forage for wild plants. On the western plains, the Plano peoples developed a subsistence technology and way of life that specialized in bison hunting. Plano culture eventually expanded into the northern forests and adopted a new hunting regime that depended upon caribou. There is also evidence that by 4000 BCE Plano culture had penetrated the Interior Plateau of British Columbia. In the eastern woodlands, Archaic culture developed out of the earlier Fluted Point culture. Here Indigenous peoples adopted new means of subsistence and diversified their food base. As Archaic peoples became more efficient in hunting and gathering, their numbers grew and their societies probably became less egalitarian.

REGIONAL CULTURES

As they adapted to particular environments, Plano and Archaic peoples developed specialized skills and tools to exploit local resources. By classifying these technological innovations, archaeologists and anthropologists have identified a number of distinct regional cultures or culture complexes across what is today Canada. The major culture complexes are Maritime, Great Lakes–St. Lawrence, Shield, Plains, Plateau, Pacific Northwest, and Arctic. These cultures are further divided into early (8000–4000 BCE), middle (4000–1000 BCE), and late (1000 BCE–500 CE) periods to account for ongoing innovation and adaptation. Cultural change occurred through the diffusion of technology, beliefs, and practices, and adaptation to particular local ecological needs. By the time of sustained European contact in the sixteenth century, Canada was occupied by peoples who spoke many different languages and belonged to distinct cultures suited to their diverse environments.[5]

MARITIME CULTURE

In Atlantic Canada, archaeologists have unearthed evidence of an early Maritime culture dating from 6,000 to 8,000 years ago. A maritime- and riverine-adapted people who drew upon the resources of both land and sea occupied the Atlantic coastal plain. Small in number, they may have moved northward during the spring and summer months in search of particular resources and returned south for the winter. As the climate warmed, people remained within the region and their numbers increased. Small family groups appear to have converged into larger bands on the coast during the late spring to exploit the resources of the sea, and then divided as they returned to the interior for the winter. Marriages were probably contracted when bands came together to form a broad social network of blood-related families. As the population grew, early Maritime people spread north into Labrador and down the St. Lawrence. The introduction of ritual practices and degrees of social rank is suggested by the distinctive mortuary practices that appeared 5,000 to 6,000 years ago. Excavations of burial sites have revealed human remains smeared with red ochre, and both functional and ornamental artifacts. Trade with neighbouring peoples is evident in the discovery of copper tools at many coastal sites, and walrus ivory in the Great Lakes–St. Lawrence region.

Sometime after 2000 BCE, Maritime culture retreated from Labrador, Newfoundland, and the north shore of the St. Lawrence. A number of factors probably contributed to this disappearance. Cooler weather may have made these areas less suitable to the adaptations of Maritime culture. Around the same time, new peoples migrated into the region. Palaeo-Eskimos began to penetrate Labrador, and hunters of the Shield culture began to appear seasonally on the north shore.

The appearance of pottery vessels around 500 BCE marks the beginning of late Maritime culture. Archaeologists and anthropologists also refer to this as the Woodland period in eastern North America. In the past, the introduction of pottery was associated with the advent of a new stage of development characterized by a much more complex society and sophisticated culture. It is now believed that pottery was simply an introduced technology that did not significantly alter Maritime life-ways. Maritime peoples moved between cold weather camps located on tidal estuaries and salt-water lagoons with abundant shellfish and waterfowl resources, and interior river sites, where

---

5 On regional culture complexes, see Olive Patricia Dickason, *Canada's First Nations: A History of Founding Peoples from Earliest Times* (Toronto: Oxford University Press, 1997); Alan D. McMillan and Eldon Yellowhorn, *First Peoples in Canada* (Vancouver: Douglas & McIntyre, 2004).

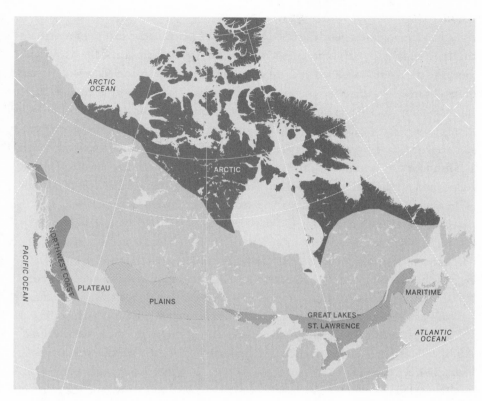

Map 1.2 Regional Indigenous cultural complexes.

spawning salmon and eels were harvested in the spring and summer. The appearance of burial mounds similar to those found in the Ohio Valley marked the introduction of Adena mortuary customs into Maritime culture. The origin of these mounds dating from 400 to 300 BCE remains a mystery. Their introduction may have been a product of an expanding network of trade. The presence of such mounds suggests that a priest-shaman class had been introduced into Maritime culture, at least in some localities.

At the time of first European contact in the fifteenth century, the Maritime region is estimated to have had a population of between 5,000 and 6,000 people. This population was divided into two distinct groups: the Mi'kmaq, numbering about 4,000 and occupying present-day Nova Scotia, Prince Edward Island, the Gaspé, and the northeastern part of New Brunswick; and the Maliseet-Passamaquody, numbering about 1,000 and inhabiting western and southern New Brunswick.

GREAT LAKES–ST. LAWRENCE CULTURE

The Great Lakes–St. Lawrence lowlands were initially occupied shortly after the glaciers retreated around 11,000 years ago. Although the development of early Archaic culture in this region is poorly defined, by 5000 BCE a distinctive Laurentian Archaic culture is evident. By this time, climatic conditions had stabilized and the hardwood forests of the region sustained a mixed economy based on deer and elk, a wide variety of small game, fish, nuts, and berries. Laurentian Archaic people gathered together in summer camps located on the shorelines of lakes and rivers and dispersed into smaller family groups during the winter months. They manufactured spear throwers, chipped stone dart heads, knives and scrapers, polished stone axes and adzes for woodworking, and fishhooks, awls, pendants, and beads made from native copper. The use of native copper and the discovery of exotic shells among burial goods indicate that the people of the Great Lakes–St. Lawrence participated in an extensive trading network with the peoples to their north and south.

Burial sites provide a glimpse into Laurentian beliefs and religious practices. The placement of personal goods in graves and the sprinkling of red ochre on bodies suggest that the people of the Laurentian Archaic engaged in some form of ceremonial burial based on a belief in an afterlife. Over time, burial goods became more extensive, indicating both rising levels of prosperity and increased notions of social hierarchy. The discovery of human remains with projectile points lodged in the bone, fractured skulls, and instances of decapitation, testifies that violence and warfare were part of Laurentian Archaic society.

The introduction of pottery cooking vessels, the bow and arrow, and the construction of burial mounds around 1000 BCE mark the beginning of the Woodland period in the Great Lakes–St. Lawrence lowlands. These developments entered the region from the south and reflected the influence of the Adena and Hopewell cultures of the Ohio Valley. The increased number of archaeological sites from this period suggests a significant increase in population, although Woodland peoples continued to live as hunter-gatherers who moved between seasonal camps.

More sedentary life-ways developed following the introduction of agriculture to the Great Lakes–St. Lawrence lowlands around 500 CE. Maize was the first plant to be cultivated by the Indigenous peoples in the region. Maize was first domesticated in Meso-America sometime between 4000 and 3000 BCE, and was vital to the emergence of the Mayan, Toltec, and Aztec civilizations. In the Great Lakes–St. Lawrence lowlands, the introduction of maize marked the beginnings of Iroquoian culture. Other crops followed, with sunflowers in evidence by 1100 CE and beans by 1300 CE. The addition of cultivated crops to an earlier hunting and gathering society resulted in a significant increase in the population, changed settlement patterns, and altered social organization and belief.

By the eighth century, the peoples of the Great Lakes–St. Lawrence lowlands lived in multi-family longhouses in small, palisaded villages. By the fifteenth century, these villages had grown to an average of more than three hectares in size and were occupied by as many as 2,000 people. Villages were palisaded for defence, indicating that warfare was common. The increase in warfare may have reflected changing gender roles. Women appear to have become the main food producers. The depletion of local game due to population increase and the ability to store food may have deprived men of their traditional role as hunters, leaving warfare as the principal means for men to acquire and assert status. Remains of broken and charred human bones, and ornaments and tools made from bone, further suggest that warfare and possibly ritual cannibalism were not uncommon. At the time of European contact in the sixteenth century, Iroquoian culture had spread up the St. Lawrence as far as Quebec.

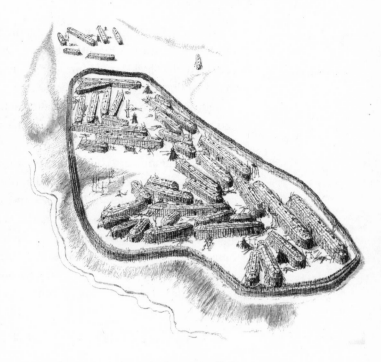

Figure 1.1 Artistic recreation of Iroquois village.

SHIELD CULTURE

The vast Canadian Shield was occupied slowly between 8000 and 4000 BCE as glacial ice retreated and water levels subsided. Because the population appears to have moved from west to east, many archaeologists believe that Shield culture developed out of the Plano culture of the northern plains and parkland. Dependent upon the caribou, small bands of Shield people ranged over a large territory. The Canadian Shield's extensive network of rivers and lakes facilitated this movement and brought different bands into contact with one another. Inter-band marriages seem to have been common and to have promoted a flexible social system with wide-ranging relationships. This interconnectedness promoted a certain cultural similarity among the peoples who lived in this vast region. The location of archaeological sites on islands and along waterways suggests that the birch-bark canoe was widely in use at an early date.

Shield peoples lived in family-sized semi-subterranean dwellings with hearths and stone-lined pits. Subsistence depended on an annual cycle of hunting, fishing, and plant collecting. Wild rice was especially important in some areas. Some groups along the southern Shield grew corn and squash in their summer camps, but poor soils and short growing seasons meant that they could not rely on these crops. The Algonquian peoples of the Shield traded furs, copper, and stone for food with the Iroquoian farmers to the south. Copper from Lake Superior was in use by 4000 BCE and was being widely traded. Some archaeologists speculate that the development of technology to process and store wild rice may have made certain bands in this area wealthy and more sedentary. Pottery and the bow-and-arrow were introduced into southern parts of the Canadian Shield around 1000 BCE, but no great cultural break is evident except along the present-day Minnesota–Ontario border, where large burial mounds and multi-family dwellings have been found. The appearance of prominent burial mounds—generally absent in the Shield region—and large band gathering sites suggests a level of authority and social organization not found elsewhere among the Shield peoples. Pictographs of humans, animals, and mythological beings suggest that the peoples of the Shield ascribed spiritual power to all nature. Shield culture was long-lived and provided the basis for the Ojibwe (Ojibwa or Ojibway), Cree, Algonquin, and Montagnais peoples.

PLAINS CULTURE

In the west, Plano culture gave way to early Plains culture around 6000 BCE. This shift corresponded with the advent of a long period of warmer and drier climate (the Altithermal) that resulted in the expansion of prairie grasslands and the retreat of parkland and forest farther north. These conditions supported smaller numbers of bison and humans. Early Plains peoples developed new hunting technologies, such as the spear thrower (or atlatl) to exploit the bison, and diversified their food resources to include smaller game, fish, and wild berries. With the end of the Altithermal dry period around 3000 BCE, moister conditions returned to the plains and the population of bison and humans apparently grew considerably.

The bison dominated life on the plains. Bison meat was consumed fresh and dried for winter consumption and trade. Hides were made into clothing and shelters, bone into tools, and sinew into bowstrings and thread. Dried buffalo dung was burned as fuel, and bladders were used as containers for storing and boiling water. The Plains people produced pemmican by pounding dried bison meat, mixing it with fat rendered from bones and marrow, and packing it into large bladder sacks. Not surprisingly, bison came to be viewed as the provider and a link between the Creator and humans, and the bison hunt came to be surrounded by ritual. A bison skull was often placed on a large rock at the centre of medicine wheels—circular patterns of rocks laid out on prominent hilltops—to communicate with the spirits who brought rain, good forage, and large herds of bison. The hilltops were also burial sites for the Plains people. In early Plains culture, the bison were stalked by small groups of hunters. The introduction of the buffalo jump and the buffalo pound required greater communal cooperation and solidarity in order to coordinate the efforts of the many people needed to stage a successful hunt. The result was a more complex social and political structure, with bands coming together for the spring hunt. The Sun Dance, an important cultural ritual, which varied in content between nations, followed a successful hunt and took place before bands dispersed for the winter.

Mobility was essential to life on the plains, and dogs were used as draft animals. Both the bow-and-arrow and pottery entered into the tool kit of Plains culture around 500 BCE. Contact with peoples to the south and east resulted in the introduction of burial mounds in what is today southern Manitoba. New peoples also migrated onto the plains. The Athapascan-speaking Beaver, Sekani, and Sarcee appear to have migrated into northern Alberta and adopted a Plains way of life after 500 CE. The Siouan-speaking Assiniboine migrated to the eastern Canadian Plains from what would later be central Minnesota early in the seventeenth century. Horses were brought to the Canadian plains early in the eighteenth century through the extensive network of trade that linked Indigenous peoples across the continent and preceded any significant European penetration of the region. Within a short period, the peoples of the plains became skilled equestrians. The horse transformed the buffalo hunt. It also enabled peoples to range over wider areas, bringing them in contact with other groups, often sparking conflict. Since horses could transport more personal goods than dogs, the accumulation of wealth was facilitated and a more stratified society resulted. The northwestern plains were sparsely populated. It is estimated that at the time of European contact there was only one person for every 26 square kilometres.

PLATEAU CULTURE

The origins of the Plateau culture of the British Columbia Interior are debated among scholars. Some archaeologists believe the region was penetrated by elements of Coastal culture 9,000 years ago. Others find evidence of early Plains culture, especially in the southeastern part of the Interior Plateau. Still others suggest Plateau culture resulted when elements of an as yet ill-defined Northwest Interior culture moved south. It is likely that multiple migrations occurred and account for what is one of the most culturally and linguistically complex regions of Indigenous Canada.

By 4000 BCE a seasonal subsistence-settlement pattern based upon salmon had emerged on the southern Plateau. People lived and worked in small mobile bands from spring to fall and came together in larger villages for the winter months. By 2500 BCE there is evidence of large pit-house villages in the river valleys that indicate more settled village life. Salmon provided the major food source for most peoples of the Interior Plateau, and large quantities were dried and stored for winter consumption. The most sedentary and culturally complex of the Plateau peoples were found along the Fraser River, where large salmon runs sustained villages of perhaps a thousand people. The peoples of the Plateau participated in an extensive trade network, exchanging dried salmon and desirable carving stone for copper, obsidian, and turquoise. These materials were used to produce ornamental items that probably conveyed status, suggesting that social distinction was an important element of Plateau society. Rank may also be indicated by variations in house size. While the average pit house was 7 metres in diameter, others were as large 20 metres. Such large homes may have belonged to chiefs or have been used for ceremonial functions.

Rock art depicting humans, animals, supernatural creatures, and abstract symbols indicates that the peoples of the Interior possessed a rich cosmology. The rock paintings may record the dreams adolescent males received during their vision quests. Cut off by the Rocky Mountains to the east and the Coast Mountains to the west, the Plateau peoples of the Interior were among the last to make contact with Europeans. It was not until 1793 that North West Company explorer Alexander Mackenzie passed through Chilcotin territory on his way to the Pacific.

PACIFIC NORTHWEST CULTURE

On the Pacific coast, mobile hunting and fishing bands exploited the resources of both land and sea. Sea-level fluctuations and tectonic forces appear to have delayed the development of the more sedentary lifestyle that later developed on the west coast. Evidence that these peoples hunted large sea mammals suggests that they must have possessed seaworthy watercraft. Archaeologists and anthropologists distinguish between Southwestern and Northwestern Coastal cultures. It is now believed that the peoples of the Southwestern Coast evolved from Palaeo peoples of the Columbia plateau to the south who migrated northward. Northwestern Coastal culture is thought to have been of Palaeo-Arctic origin. The two cultures eventually met and merged along the central coast. By 4000 BCE, the stabilization of sea levels supported the development of an increasingly complex culture that exploited the rich resources of the coastal and riverine ecosystems.

Two resources—salmon and red cedar—were vital to the development of Pacific Northwest culture. Salmon were not only abundant, they appeared at the same places at the same time each year and were easy to catch and easily preserved. Lightweight, strong, and rot resistant, red cedar was an ideal building and carving material. Red cedar was used to construct the large plank homes, dugout canoes, monumental carvings, and decorated storage boxes that are emblematic of Northwest Coast culture. Red cedar bark was used to weave baskets, hats, and clothing. The abundant resources of the west coast sustained the densest human population and the most complex cultures in Indigenous Canada. The peoples of the west coast lived in permanent waterfront villages during the winter months, some exceeding 1,000 persons. During the summer, smaller groups dispersed to summer camps to exploit seasonal resources.

The plentiful resources of the Pacific Northwest supported a complex of social ranks, customs, and artistic expression not found elsewhere in Indigenous Canada. Archaeological evidence indicates that highly ranked societies had developed on the Northwest coast by 1000 BCE. Large quantities of status items such as beads, copper, and shell ornaments have been found in some gravesites. Status differences appear to have been inherited. Skeletal remains reveal that the skulls of some infants were flattened, probably as a sign of noble birth. Social position was sustained and validated through the ritual of giving away large quantities of food and goods at potlatches, elaborate festivals that could last for weeks. Besides asserting status, potlatches contributed to social unity and welfare through the distribution of wealth.

The peoples of the Pacific Northwest possessed a rich spiritual life. Success in fishing, hunting, warfare, and potlatching required supernatural aid. Cleansing rituals were common, and individuals with special ability to control supernatural forces became shamans and were believed to possess special healing powers. It was widely believed that humans and animals had once been part of the same people and that animals could transform from one realm to another. Because salmon were so vital, the first salmon caught each season were ceremonially welcomed and honoured, their bones returned to the river to be resurrected the next year.

Warfare appears to have been common among the peoples of the Pacific Northwest. Many villages were defended by earthworks, and some human remains display signs of injury likely sustained during combat. Conflict probably arose to assert status, to acquire property and slaves, and to control access to resources and trade. The peoples of the Pacific Northwest traded extensively among themselves and with peoples to the east. At the time of European contact, almost half of Canada's Indigenous peoples lived in the Pacific Northwest, and some 30 different languages were spoken there.[6]

ARCTIC CULTURE

The Arctic was the last part of Canada to be settled by Indigenous peoples. Palaeo-Eskimo culture spread rapidly across the Arctic from Alaska to Greenland around

---

6   On the culture of the peoples of the Pacific Northwest, see Olive Patricia Dickason, *Canada's First Nations: A History*.

2000 BCE. While the origins of these peoples are obscure, it is widely believed that they were originally of Siberian stock. Although this was a period of warmer climate and expanded open water, conditions were still harsh. Palaeo-Eskimo culture was adapted to the challenges presented by severe cold, the seasonal migration of game, the lack of plant foods, and the scarcity of fuel and other raw materials. Circular clearings surrounded by rings of stone suggest that the earliest inhabitants of the Arctic were a highly mobile people who lived year-round in tents. The Palaeo-Eskimos survived by hunting caribou and muskoxen with spears and bows and arrows, and seals with harpoons. Life in the Arctic was precarious, and the archaeological evidence indicates that changes in climate or scarcity of game caused some areas to be abandoned, or those living there to die out.

Significant innovations, such as stone lamps used to burn oil from the blubber of sea mammals, large bone knives used to cut snow blocks for constructing igloos, and ivory sled shoes, were introduced into the Arctic around 1000 BCE. These mark the beginnings of what archaeologists term Dorset culture. Dorset culture spread beyond the Arctic down the Labrador coast and into Newfoundland. Little is known about the spiritual world of the Dorset culture, although sculptures fashioned from bone, antler, ivory, and soapstone depicting humans and animals, as well as masks, suggest shamanic activity.

Around 900 CE new peoples appeared in the Canadian Arctic. Norse explorers from Greenland ventured to Baffin Island and northern Labrador but do not appear to have settled or to have had a significant impact on Dorset culture. However, the Dorset may have traded ivory from walrus tusks in return for metal and other goods from the Norse. Depictions of men with European faces and beards on Dorset antler wands provide evidence for interactions with the Norse. Much more momentous was the arrival of the Thule in the twelfth and thirteenth centuries. The Thule migrated eastwards from Alaska and quickly established a presence throughout the region, displacing the Dorset, possibly drawn by the allure of Norse goods.

The fate of the Dorset people is a matter of considerable speculation. Some scholars believe they were largely exterminated by the Thule. Others maintain that they were simply absorbed into a culture that possessed a superior technology. It has also been questioned whether contact even occurred between the two cultures and whether assimilation of Dorset technology by the Thule was merely the result of the Thule finding artifacts that had been left behind. However, the descendants of the Thule, the Inuit, recall in their oral histories encountering a people who, despite their larger stature and strength, were unskilled at fighting and whose weapons were no match for the recurved bows of the invaders. Unable to withstand the encroachment of the Thule, the Dorset people either perished or scattered. Whatever the reasons, the Dorset subsequently disappeared from the Canadian Arctic, except for a few isolated pockets on the eastern shore of Hudson Bay in northern Quebec, where they survived for a few more centuries.[7] Ancestors of the historic Inuit, the Thule lived in semi-subterranean stone and sod houses with whalebone supports for roofs, and erected stone cairns to channel caribou to prime hunting locations. Innovations introduced by the Thule included the kayak, used to hunt whales in summer, and the dog sled, used to travel across the ice in winter. For a time, the Thule manufactured pottery oil lamps, but abandoned the practice because clay was difficult to find and of poor quality. The discovery of smelted iron, bronze, and copper artifacts suggests that the Thule traded with the Norse of Greenland.

By the time of sustained European contact in the sixteenth century, most of what is now Canada had been inhabited for thousands of years by peoples who spoke many different languages and who belonged to many distinct cultures. These peoples possessed technologies well-suited to the environments in which they lived. The Indigenous peoples of Canada participated in extensive trade networks that crossed the continent. Some lived in small bands of hunter-gatherers. Others lived in large villages of several thousand. All possessed spiritual belief systems that helped them comprehend the world in which they lived and political structures adapted to their needs and way of life. Indigenous Canadians belonged to dynamic societies that were constantly evolving in response to ecological and social change. That these diverse peoples came to be subsumed by the single name "Indian" reveals far more about the values and worldviews of Europeans than it does about the reality of Indigenous societies and cultures. By classifying all these many peoples as "Indians," Europeans betrayed not only an inability or an unwillingness to appreciate or to understand the Indigenous peoples of North America but a set of assumptions that were used to justify the occupation and possession of what was for them a new world.

Estimates of the Indigenous population of the Americas at the time of European contact at the end of the fifteenth century range from a low of 30 to 40 million to as high as 100 million or more. Most Indigenous Americans lived in southern areas with warm climates. There were probably no more than half a million persons in the territory now called Canada at the time of contact. Scholars estimate that there were between 150,000 to 200,000 persons on the west coast; 100,000 to 150,000 persons in the Great Lakes–St. Lawrence lowlands; and no more than 100,000 in the rest of the country. It is very likely that the Indigenous population had already been reduced substantially by the introduction of European diseases for which they had no immunity. These diseases were likely carried on trade goods from the south and earlier contact with European whalers and fishers.

---

7 Robert McGhee, *The Last Imaginary Place: A Human History of the Arctic World* (Toronto: Key Porter Books, 2004), 53.

FIRST ENCOUNTERS: THE NORSE

The first Europeans to arrive in North America—at least the first for whom there is solid evidence—were Norse, travelling west from Greenland, where Erik the Red had founded a settlement around the year 985 CE. Shortly after the establishment of the Greenland settlement, a trading ship blown off course sighted land further to the west and, around the year 1000 CE, Eric the Red's son, Leif, launched an exploratory expedition. Leif Ericsson explored the coasts of Helluland, Markland, and Vinland, thought to be present-day Baffin Island, Labrador, and Newfoundland, respectively. After camping at Vinland for the winter, he returned to Greenland in the spring with a shipload of timber and stories of a warm and fruitful land. Several attempts to colonize Vinland followed. One of these settlements was at L'Anse aux Meadows on the tip of Newfoundland's Great Northern Peninsula. There, in 1960, archaeologists unearthed the remains of three large Norse dwellings, a kiln, a forge, and a bathhouse dating to approximately 1000 CE. Conflict with the Indigenous population, isolation from other Norse settlements, and the impracticability of pursuing a pastoral way of life in a heavily forested landscape eventually convinced the Norse to abandon their efforts to settle in Vinland.

Figure 1.2 Norse sod houses at L'Anse aux Meadows.

Although no further attempts at colonization seem to have been made, the Norse continued to voyage to North America for several centuries to trade and to acquire resources. Markland provided Greenland with timber, and Helluland supplied the white falcons and polar bears prized in the courts of medieval European monarchs. The discovery of Norse metal artifacts throughout the eastern Arctic testifies to ongoing trade with the Indigenous peoples of the area. By the twelfth century, a dozen parish churches, a monastery, and a convent had been established on Greenland, but the Norse do not appear to have attempted to introduce Christianity to the Indigenous peoples with whom they traded. A prolonged period of climatic cooling, the Little Ice Age, began in the middle of the twelfth century and continued for at least the next three centuries. As the climate deteriorated, the Greenland settlements declined, disappearing by around 1500 CE.

THE AGE OF EXPLORATION

Intermittent voyages to North America's Atlantic coast by fishers and others probably continued, but sustained European contact was not renewed until late in the fifteenth century. A number of forces combined at that time to propel Europe into a great age of expansion and discovery. Improvements in navigation and shipbuilding allowed Europeans to travel further from their shores. Without this navigational revolution, European exploration and expansion would have been impossible. Renewed economic and population growth increased demands for new sources of raw materials and foodstuffs. Societies throughout Europe were in transition: a social order character-ized by agricultural self-sufficiency and rigid hierarchies was giving way to a new order in which trade and market-based relationships were becoming increasingly important. Although a land-owning aristocracy continued to dominate society, in cities and towns new leaders emerged whose wealth derived from commerce. The rise of commerce slowly eroded the medieval feudal system with its interlocking rights and obligations between lords, vassals, and serfs. As towns grew and trade expanded, a new class of individualistic and profit-seeking merchants and bankers appeared, and money increasingly was substituted for payments in goods and services. The new middle classes that emerged from these developments were increasingly dissatisfied with the limitations of local control that the feudal system sustained and began to support strong leaders who could exercise control over larger areas.

In time, Europe's small feudal states gave way to larger nation states. The displace-ment of medieval feudal structures by centralized monarchies supported by competent bureaucracies and well-equipped armies provided the means needed to support overseas exploration. By the second half of the fifteenth century, European monarchs had increased both their power and authority and were in a position to turn their energies beyond their borders. As Europeans competed for access to resources and commercial advantage, they projected their power overseas. Cut off from traditional overland trading routes to Asia by the Ottoman Turks and the fall of Constantinople in 1453, Europeans began to seek an alternative route to the spices, metals, and other riches of Asia.

Underlying Europe's outward thrust was a new outlook on humanity and the world produced by the intellectual and religious awakenings that accompanied the Renaissance and the Reformation. The Renaissance produced a confidence in human-ity's ability to control nature and stoked a curiosity in the peoples and cultures that existed beyond Europe. The religious divisions produced by the Reformation gave rise to a period of intense missionary zeal as Roman Catholics and Protestants sought to spread the "true faith" and competed for converts around the globe. The discovery of "new" worlds affirmed Europe's sense of being at the heroic frontier of civilized history.

Convinced that Asia could be reached by sailing westward, Christopher Columbus persuaded the Spanish court to sponsor an expedition. After Bartholomew Dias rounded the Cape of Good Hope in 1487, the Spanish feared Portuguese control over direct trade with Asia and were eager to find an alternate route. In 1492, Columbus explored the coast of Cuba and Haiti and returned to Spain certain that he had reached the Indies. Columbus's reports of the lands and peoples he encountered captured the European imagination. The term "Indian" as a general designation for the inhabitants of the Americas stems from the erroneous geography of Christopher Columbus. Under the impression that he had landed among the islands of Asia off the coast of India, he called the peoples he met "los Indios."

Columbus described the people he encountered as naked, primitive, idolatrous, and ignorant. Although he characterized one group as ferocious and cannibalistic savages, he found most of the people he encountered to be generous, content, easily pleased, attractive, and well-proportioned. Using the twin criteria of Christianity and civilization, the Spanish found the "Indian" wanting in a long list of attributes: letters, laws, government, clothing, arts, trade, agriculture, marriage, morals, and above all religion. Because they had no scriptures, the Spanish assumed they lacked religion. Indigenous beliefs were dismissed as irrational, superstitious, and idolatrous, and the peoples themselves were seen as immoral because of their nakedness. Eurocentrism prevented the Spanish from appreciating Indigenous culture and society on its own terms. Judging by European standards, the Spanish were not able to recognize that the peoples of North America possessed their own forms of government and social organization and a rich system of cultural and religious beliefs that made sense of the world in which they lived. Convinced of their own superiority and the rightness of their cause, the Spanish proceeded to take possession of America. Wild America, the Spanish believed, needed to be tamed and domesticated. The Indigenous peoples were simply part of the American environment, an environment the Spanish believed they had a God-given mandate to civilize and make productive.

STAKING CLAIMS

Fearing that rivals would encroach upon their discoveries, the Spanish appealed to the Vatican to recognize their sovereignty over the new territories. The Pope claimed the right to grant sovereignty over any lands not possessed by a Christian ruler, and had already granted the Portuguese title over the lands they had explored along the coast of Africa. In 1493 Pope Alexander VI defined a dividing line through the North Atlantic 100 leagues west of the Azores, running south to the Cape Verde Islands. All lands west of this line he granted to Spain; all lands east were conferred on Portugal. As a condition of this grant, the Pope required the Spanish Crown to bring the inhabitants of these territories to the profession of the Catholic faith. In 1494, Spain and Portugal negotiated an agreement, the Treaty of Tordesillas, moving the line 270 leagues further west and thus giving Portugal a claim to Brazil and a foothold in the Americas.

Henry VII of England ignored the exclusive claims of Spain and Portugal and commissioned the Venetian navigator Giovanni Caboto, known to the English as John Cabot, to seek out a northwest passage to Asia. With financial backing from the wealthy merchants of Bristol, Cabot explored the Atlantic coast of Canada in 1497 and claimed Newfoundland and Nova Scotia for England. He led a second expedition of five vessels the following year, but Cabot himself is believed to have perished on the voyage and never returned. Although Cabot did not succeed in finding a northern passage to Asia, he did report on the impressive cod stocks of the Grand Banks. There was a huge demand for cod in Catholic Europe, and Portuguese, Spanish, French, Basque, and English fishers were soon making annual trips to the Grand Banks. The fishery grew rapidly and by 1570 there were as many as 400 ships travelling to Newfoundland each spring to harvest cod. Others came to hunt whales. Whale oil was a valuable commodity, used for lamp oil, the manufacture of soap and pharmaceuticals, and for fabric treatments. Red Bay, Labrador, became the centre of whaling operations. Situated on the narrow Strait of Belle Isle that separated Newfoundland and the Labrador coast, Red Bay was an ideal location from which to capture migrating Right and Bowhead whales. The whales were harpooned, their flippers and tails removed to make the carcass more manoeuvrable, and the blubber taken to onshore "tryworks" where the fat could be rendered in copper cauldrons. The oil was then transported in barrels. It is estimated that some 20,000 whales were taken within a 50-year period before the industry declined because of over-harvesting and shifting whale migration patterns.

While on shore to dry their catch of cod or to process whale blubber, Europeans established contact and began to trade with the local Indigenous peoples, providing them with durable goods, but also introducing European diseases against which they had no immunity. The result was a significant weakening of Indigenous populations long before the establishment of permanent European settlements. Frequently displaced from their summer fishing camps by European fishers, and desirous of European trade goods, the Indigenous peoples of the Atlantic coast became increasingly preoccupied with trapping furs and grew dependent on the resources of the interior. As the local supply of furs became depleted, Indigenous groups expanded beyond their traditional territories, and conflict between Indigenous peoples appears to have intensified significantly. Important changes in Indigenous ways of life were already evident decades before the arrival of settlers and missionaries.

Although Cabot had laid claim to this "newe founde lande" in 1497, the English did little to exercise their dominion beyond the fishery, and Portugal soon launched a more direct challenge. In 1500, Gaspar Corte-Real was commissioned by King Manuel I of Portugal to discover and claim lands in the new world and to search for the Northwest Passage. He left that summer and appears to have journeyed around Newfoundland. A second expedition the following year with three ships returned to Portugal with 60 Indigenous captives, but without the ship bearing Corte-Real himself. Gaspar's brother, Miguel, attempted to find him in 1502 but was also lost. A Portuguese attempt to establish a settlement on Cape Breton Island around 1520 proved to be ill-fated.

Preoccupied by European conflicts, the French did not send out an expedition to North America until 1524. In that year the French King, Francis I, hired an Italian navigator, Giovanni da Verrazano, to explore the eastern coast of North America for a passage to Asia and to search out gold and silver. War with the Habsburgs prevented the French from launching a second voyage until 1534. This expedition was led by Jacques Cartier, an experienced seaman from Saint-Malo, Brittany. Setting out on April 20, 1534, Cartier's two ships, crewed by 61 men and guided by favourable winds, crossed the Atlantic in only 20 days and entered the Strait of Belle Isle at the northern tip of Newfoundland. Cartier was not impressed by the land he encountered on the coast of Labrador, noting in his journal that he "did not see one cartload of earth" in any of the places he landed, but only rock. This territory, he suggested, "should not be called the New Land" but, rather, "the land God gave to Cain." This bleak initial impression gave way to enthusiasm when Cartier journeyed south into the Gulf of St. Lawrence, where one island won his particular favour: it was "covered with fine trees and meadows, fields of wild oats, and of pease in flower, as thick and fine as ever I saw in Brittany."[8]

Cartier was less enthusiastic about the Indigenous peoples he encountered. Late in July 1534, he encountered a group of St. Lawrence Iroquois making their annual fishing expedition from Stadacona (present-day Quebec City) to the Gaspé. "This people," he wrote in his journal, "may well be called savage; for they are the sorriest folk there can be in the world, and the whole lot of them had not anything above the value of five sous, their canoes and fishing-nets excepted." Cartier was shocked that they went about "quite naked, except for a small skin, with which they cover their privy parts." Seeing no signs of a settlement, he concluded that these people had "no other dwelling but their canoes, which they turn upside down and sleep on the ground underneath." Cartier's account reveals the difficulty of using European sources as a means to access the world of Indigenous Americans. Seemingly unaware that he had encountered an itinerant fishing party, he assumed that they were poor and lacked possessions and dwellings. Offended

8   Ramsay Cook (ed.), *The Voyages of Jacques Cartier* (Toronto: University of Toronto Press, 1993), 10–14.

by their lack of dress, he concluded that they were "savages" bereft of morals and culture. While such judgments reveal much about French scruples and expectations, they display little understanding of Indigenous society. Ignorant of the importance attached to sharing in Indigenous culture, for example, Cartier concluded that they "are wonderful thieves" who "steal everything they can carry off."[9] Convinced that they were an inferior people without government, religion or culture, Cartier saw no reason to seek their permission before exploring and claiming their lands.

On July 24, 1534, Cartier erected a large cross at Gaspé Harbour and claimed the territory for France. Donnacona, a Stadaconan chief, objected strongly to the action. "Donnacona," Cartier wrote, "made us a long harangue, making the sign of the cross with two of his fingers, and then he pointed to the land all about, as if he wished to say that all this region belonged to him, and that we ought not to have set up this cross without his permission." Unimpressed, Cartier ordered his men to seize Donnacona and his sons and forced them aboard his ship. There Cartier offered Donnacona trade goods, feasted him, and assured him that the cross was merely a navigational aid. As a sign of trust, Donnacona permitted two of his sons, Domagaya and Taignoagny, to return to France with Cartier where they were to be instructed in French so that they might act as interpreters when Cartier returned. To ensure their return to Canada, Domagaya and Taignoagny told Cartier fabulous stories of a kingdom located far in the interior and rich with precious metals.[10]

The following year, Domagaya and Taignoagny guided Cartier's three ships up the St. Lawrence to Stadacona where they were reunited with their father. Cartier was eager to travel farther upriver to discover the "kingdom of the Saguenay." Anxious to maintain control over access to the interior and French trade goods, Donnacona did his best to dissuade Cartier from making the trip. Undeterred, Cartier proceeded upriver to Hochelaga (present-day Montreal) where he was enthusiastically greeted by the village's 1,000 residents. While at Hochelaga, Cartier ascended Mont Royal where he erected another cross and viewed the rapids that blocked any further progress into the interior and prevented him from reaching the riches of the fabled kingdom. Disappointed, Cartier returned to Stadacona where he received a cool reception from Donnacona. Suspicious of Donnacona and his people, Cartier instructed his men to construct a fort for the winter. The winter was a severe one, and 25 of Cartier's men succumbed to scurvy before Domagaya provided a recipe for a curative infusion made from the bark of white cedar. When spring returned, relations between Cartier and Donnacona remained tense and were marked by mutual distrust. When Taignoagny

9   Ibid., 24.
10 Ibid., 26–27, 43.

asked Cartier's help in removing a rival headman, Agona, Cartier saw an opportunity to break Donnacona's power and to eliminate opposition to his plans. Feigning co-operation with the plot against Agona, Cartier invited Donnacona and his supporters to a celebration of the feast of the Holy Cross. At the feast, Cartier ordered his men to seize Donnacona, his two sons, and two other headmen. To appease Donnacona's people, Cartier promised he would return in 12 months with their chief and gifts from the French king. On May 6, 1536, Cartier sailed for France with his Native captives. When they arrived in France, Cartier's Natives were paraded through the streets as exotic novelties from the "new world." Donnacona appeared before a notary for questioning and met with Francis I to whom he related tales of the kingdom of the Saguenay and its marvellous riches. None of the captives ever returned to Canada.

Although Francis I was impressed by Donnacona's stories, war between France and Spain delayed Cartier's return to Canada until 1541. This time, Cartier served under Jean-François de la Rocque, Sieur de Roberval, a Huguenot nobleman mandated by the Crown to establish a colony and to locate the intriguing kingdom of the Saguenay. Cartier sailed from France in May 1541 as Roberval's representative. For his part, Roberval was to join Cartier in Canada once he had raised an army to defend the new colony. Cartier returned to Stadacona in August where he was warmly received by Agona. Cartier explained that Donnacona had died and that his other "guests" lived like lords in France and did not wish to return to Canada. Although this news initially pleased Agona, he soon feared that he might suffer a similar fate and relations between Cartier and the Stadaconans soured. As relations deteriorated, Cartier thought it best to relocate to a more defensible position at the mouth of the Cap Rouge River where they established the tiny settlement of Charlesbourg-Royal. In September, Cartier sailed upriver to Hochelaga but, lacking interpreters, he gained little new knowledge of the interior. He entrusted two French boys to the Hochelagans in the hope that they would learn the local language and gather intelligence about the kingdom of the Saguenay. Cartier returned to the outpost at Charlesbourg-Royal where the band of French settlers suffered through a miserable winter. Many appear to have died of scurvy, or to have been killed by the local Indigenous peoples. Anxious to return to France, Cartier abandoned the settlement in the spring with a load of iron pyrite and quartz he mistook for gold and diamonds. He met up with Roberval at the port of St. John's, Newfoundland. Roberval ordered Cartier to sail with him to Charlesbourg-Royal but Cartier absconded under cover of darkness and hastened to France with his cargo of "Canadian diamonds."

Despite Cartier's desertion, Roberval carried on and his small company of men and women settled at Charlesbourg-Royal. Roberval journeyed upriver and unsuc-cessfully attempted to navigate the Lachine rapids. An expedition up the Saguenay in search of gold and precious stones proved no more successful. During the winter, the ill-fated company endured cold, famine, and sickness. A strict Calvinist, Roberval was a demanding taskmaster who severely punished anyone who failed to follow his commands. Not surprisingly, some of the colonists rose up to challenge Roberval's authority. Determined to maintain order, Roberval had six of the dissidents hanged. In the spring of 1543, Roberval dispatched a ship to France for help. When help arrived, Roberval and his entire company abandoned Charlesbourg-Royal and returned to France. A fortune-seeking nobleman with a cruel temperament, Roberval was ill-suited to found a colony, as was the strange mixture of courtiers, gentlemen, society ladies, and criminals that accompanied him on the misadventure. Wracked by internal religious warfare and disillusioned by Roberval's and Cartier's failures, France lost interest in North America.

As French interest in Canada waned, English interest revived. To Protestant England, the great wealth that flowed to Catholic Spain from its "new world" colonies and its southern routes to Asia made Spanish power a growing threat that had to be challenged. Under Elizabeth I, England was determined to find an alternative route to the riches of the Orient and to establish overseas colonies of her own. In 1576, a group of London merchants commissioned the sometime mariner, privateer, and explorer Martin Frobisher to lead an expedition to find a northwest passage to Asia across the top of North America. Frobisher sailed from London with a tiny armada of three ships that June. During the hazardous north Atlantic crossing, one of Frobisher's ships sank and another turned back. On July 28, Frobisher sighted land (probably Resolution Island), which he named Queen Elizabeth's Foreland. He continued westward and entered what he thought was a great strait, which he named after himself. The strait was in fact Baffin Island's Frobisher Bay. There he met Inuit who came out to his ship to trade. Frobisher persuaded one of the Inuit to pilot his ship into the "west sea." Frobisher sent the Inuit pilot, accompanied by five of his sailors, ashore to prepare for the journey. None of the men was seen again. Frobisher sailed nearby for several days firing canons and blowing trumpets to summon his men. When they failed to appear, he decided to take an Inuit hostage in the hope that he might be ransomed for the return of his own men. With only 13 tired and sick crew remaining and the weather worsening, Frobisher called off the search and set sail for England where his Inuit captive would prove that he had reached a far and strange land. London was captivated by the Inuit man and his kayak but he died shortly after reaching England. Frobisher also brought back with him some black rock as a token of "Christian possession" of the land.

When a London assayer declared that the rock contained gold, gold fever swept England. Investors in Frobisher's first voyage joined with others to form the Cathay Company to finance a second voyage, not to discover the Northwest Passage but to search for gold. In July 1577, Frobisher returned to the small island where he had landed the previous summer. There he erected a cross on a high hill and claimed the land in the name of God and the English Crown. Shortly after this ritual, Inuit came to trade, but relations soured when Frobisher decided to capture an Inuit man to use as an interpreter. A skirmish followed in which Frobisher was wounded by an Inuit arrow. Matters worsened when Frobisher's crew discovered a few items of European clothing, which they assumed must have belonged to the men lost the previous summer. Determined to find the men, Frobisher launched a raid against a nearby village, killing several Inuit and taking a man, woman, and child captive. Frobisher returned to England with his Inuit prisoners and 200 tonnes of black rock. The three captives were a great attraction when they landed at Bristol, but all three died within a few weeks of their arrival. The real attraction, however, was the black rock. Thrilled by the haul, Elizabeth I named the new land *Meta Incognita*, or the unknown limits. Although assayers gave widely differing estimates of the value of the ore brought back by Frobisher, investors chose to believe the most hopeful reports and began to organize a third, more ambitious expedition. In the spring of 1578 a fleet of 15 ships carrying some 400 men departed to mine gold and to establish a colony. The expedition was plagued with problems from the start. Poor weather delayed the fleet's arrival, one ship was crushed in the ice, and another turned around and returned to England. Inuit hunters, who had provided fresh meat in the past, now avoided the English and did not come to trade. Spoilage of provisions and the loss of the timber that was to be used to construct barracks for the men who were to remain behind over the winter to mine convinced Frobisher to abandon any plans of establishing a settlement. Despite these difficulties, Frobisher returned to England with 1,200 tonnes of what he believed to be gold-bearing ore. Although efforts to refine the ore continued for several years, it was ultimately proven to be worthless.

That same year, Sir Humphrey Gilbert, a confidant of Elizabeth I, received a royal patent to claim for the English Crown "heathen and barbarous landes, countries and territories not actually possessed of any Christian prince or people."[11] After several false starts, Gilbert set out in 1583 on an expedition to claim lands for England in North America. He arrived at St. John's, Newfoundland, on August 3 but found the harbour filled with Portuguese, Basque, French, and English ships that denied him entry. Gilbert flourished his royal commission and the English ships at least made way. He went ashore, and with the fishers of different nations assembled before him read his commission and formally took possession of Newfoundland for the English Crown. To assert English sovereignty he issued fishing licences to each of the ships in the harbour, collected a levy in kind to resupply his poorly provisioned fleet, assigned drying stages or racks in perpetuity to certain fishers, outlawed the public exercise of religion apart

---

11 "The Letters Patent Graunted to Sir Humfrey Gilbert knight, for the inhabiting and planting of our people in America" in Richard Hakluyt, *The Principal Navigations, Voyages, Traffiques and Discoveries of the English Nation*, vol. 3 (London: Hakluyt Society, 1847–1852), 1691–92.

from the Church of England, and erected
a wooden pillar bearing the royal coat
of arms. Having established England's
first overseas colony, Gilbert sailed south
to claim more territory for the Crown.
However, it was late in the season and
when one of his ships foundered on a sand
bar off Sable Island, Gilbert decided to
return home. He perished at sea when his
flagship, the *Squirrel*, was lost in a storm.
Little was done to follow up on Gilbert's
claim to Newfoundland as English
attention returned to the search for a
northern route to Asia free of Spanish
and Portuguese interference. With the
patronage of the Queen's secretary, Sir
Francis Walsingham, and financial support from wealthy merchants in London
and Devon, John Davis conducted three
expeditions in search of the Northwest

Figure 1.3 Catching, curing, and drying code in the early
eighteenth century. The fishery attracted fishers from many
nations to the coast of Newfoundland.

Passage between 1585 and 1587. Davis charted much of the coasts of Greenland, Labrador,
and Baffin Island but did not succeed in finding the illusive Northwest Passage.

In 1610 a company of Bristol and London merchants received a charter to colonize
Newfoundland. John Guy was named governor of the colony and set out with a group
of 39 colonists. The colonists settled at Cuper's Cove on Conception Bay, where they
erected dwellings and fortifications, cleared the land, and put in crops. Although they
experienced a mild first winter and suffered few losses, the spring brought harassment
from pirates and hostility from the seasonal fishers accustomed to coming ashore
to dry their catch and repair their gear. Appeals to London for help fell on deaf ears.
Despite these setbacks, Guy was eager to scout out the area for future settlement sites
and to make contact with the local Indigenous people, the Beothuk. Although the
Beothuk tended to avoid the Europeans who occupied many of their summer fishing
camps, Guy convinced them that he came in friendship. At Bull's Arm, Guy and the
Beothuk exchanged gifts, feasted, and traded, but these friendly relations did not last.
Unable to use many of their traditional coastal fishing camps, the Beothuk had come
to rely on salmon, which they harvested upstream away from the European interlopers. When the English planters, as the colonists were called, began to string nets across
the mouths of the salmon rivers, the Beothuk cut the nets and began to plunder the

settlers' supplies. The colonists retaliated. Historian and archaeologist Ralph Pastore has questioned sensationalist stories that assert that the Beothuk were systematically exterminated by European newcomers, who shot them on sight and paid a bounty for Beothuk heads. The Beothuk did indeed become an extinct people by early in the nineteenth century, and retaliations for thefts were not uncommon, but Pastore maintained that loss of traditional access to resources was a more likely cause.[12]

The colony at Cuper's Cove struggled: the weather was harsh and the soil poor. Nonetheless, additional settlers, including 16 women, arrived in 1612. Although Guy had been appointed governor, his attempts to regulate the fishery failed. Relations with the company of merchants financing the colony soured when the venture failed to turn a quick profit. Frustrated, Guy returned to England in 1615. Although he never came back to Newfoundland, Guy continued to champion the interests of its settlers. Determined to ensure that the colonists had access to the rich resources of the sea, Guy opposed a bill introduced into the British Parliament in 1622 allowing British-based fishers virtually unrestricted access to the Newfoundland fishery. His protests failed, and so began a long history of outsiders reaping most of the benefits of Newfoundland's resources, while its residents struggled for subsistence.

CONCLUSION

Although contact between Europeans and Indigenous peoples prior to the seventeenth century in what is now Canada was often intermittent, and only a tiny number of new-comers occupied the first settlements, the impact on Indigenous societies was profound. The introduction of European diseases had already begun to take its grim toll, a devastating process that would recur in cataclysmic waves right up to the early twentieth century and which would all but annihilate some communities. At the same time, Indigenous peoples established trade networks with Europeans. In return for food and furs, Native Americans received useful, labour-saving European-made products. Already, competing European claims to the land betrayed imperialist ambitions and began to complicate traditional alliances and rivalries among Indigenous nations. That Europeans gained a foothold in what is now Canada, however, could not have happened without the coopera-tion and assistance of Indigenous peoples. It was from them that Europeans learned how to survive in North America. In the decades to come, the relationships between Indigenous peoples and the European newcomers became closer and more complicated and to a considerable degree defined the course of Canada's development.

---

12 Ralph Pastore, *Shanawdithit's People: The Archeology of the Beothuks* (St. John's, NL: Atlantic Archeology, 1992); Ingeborg C.L. Marshall, *A History and Ethnography of the Beothuk* (Montreal and Kingston: McGill-Queen's University Press, 1996).

2 FURS AND FAITH: NEW FRANCE, 1603–1663

S hortly after the English proclaimed their first North American colony in Newfoundland, the French developed a renewed interest in Canada. The proclamation of the Edict of Nantes in 1598 ended France's long civil war between Protestants and Catholics. With peace, France could once again look beyond its own borders. Although Canada lacked the gold and silver of New Spain, the French monarch, Henri IV, was anxious not to be shut out of the Americas and sought to promote colonization by granting wealthy merchants an exclusive right to trade in return for establishing French settlements and bringing Christianity to the Indigenous peoples. Canada's furs promised to supply the French fashion industry with the felt used to make hats while the establishment of Christian missions provided an outlet for the religious fervour that swept France during the Catholic Reformation that followed the emergence of Protestantism.

THE FOUNDING OF ACADIA AND QUEBEC

After several failed ventures, the Crown granted a trading monopoly in 1603 to Pierre du Gua de Monts, a Protestant soldier and administrator. The terms of his commission required that de Monts settle 60 colonists a year and that he "lead the natives to the profession of the Christian faith, to civilization of manners, an ordered life, practice and intercourse with the French for the gain of their commerce; and finally their recognition and submission to the authority of the Crown of France."[1] Rather than establish a colony along the St. Lawrence, de Monts searched out a location with a more temperate climate along the Atlantic coast. The French called the region Acadia and in 1604 a fledgling settlement was established on a small island in the middle of the Sainte-Croix River. Included among the 80 colonists were assorted artisans, tradesmen, soldiers, vagabonds, noblemen, clergy (both Catholic and Protestant), and an experienced soldier, accomplished navigator and map maker— Samuel de Champlain. It was Champlain who designed the fort-like "habitation" in which the colonists spent an unusually cold and snowy winter. Confined to an island with little fresh food or water, most of the men succumbed to scurvy and nearly half of them died. Although de Monts feared attack, it was the local Maliseet who relieved the colonists' misery when they arrived in the spring with fresh meat to trade. The spring also brought supply ships from France and 40 additional men to augment the colonists. The new arrivals informed de Monts that his trading monopoly was in jeopardy and he resolved to return to France to protect his interests. Before leaving, de Monts ordered the structures erected the previous year dismantled and relocated to a new site, Port-Royal, across the Bay of Fundy.

At Port-Royal, the French established good relations with the local Mi'kmaq and their chief Membertou. These friendly relations caused Champlain to conclude optimistically that the Indigenous peoples "would be speedily brought to be good Christians, if their country were colonised, which most of them would like."[2] During the summer of 1605, Champlain explored the region farther south for a permanent settlement site but found none to his liking. With the prospects of another long and hard winter, Champlain formed a social club, the Order of Good Cheer, to lift the spirits of the men. However, just as the colony seemed capable of sustaining itself, de Monts's monopoly was revoked. The colonists returned to France in the fall of 1607, entrusting Port-Royal to Membertou.

In 1608 de Monts persuaded French authorities to renew his monopoly for a year with the promise that he would found a trading post and settlement on the St. Lawrence. De Monts called upon his faithful navigator, Champlain, to find a suitable site. On June 30 Champlain selected a strategic location at the point where the river narrowed, which the local Indigenous peoples called Kébec. From this position, Champlain hoped to control access to the interior and prevent clandestine traders from challenging de Monts's monopoly. The new settlement at Quebec was located close to where the Iroquois village of Stadacona, visited by Jacques Cartier in 1535, had

---

1   Quoted in Cornelius Jaenan, "Problems of Assimilation in New France, 1604–1645," *French Historical Review* 4, no. 3 (Spring 1966): 267.

2   H.P. Biggar (ed.), *The Works of Samuel de Champlain*, vol. 1 (Toronto: The Champlain Society, 1922–36), 117.

A Logemens des artifans.
B Plate forme où eſtoit le ca-
 non.
C Le magaſin.
D Logement du ſieur de Pont-
 graué & Champlain.
E La forge.

F Paliſſade de pieux.
G Le four.
H La cuiſine.
O Petite maiſonnette où l'on
 retiroit les vtanſiles de nos
 barques ; que depuis le
 ſieur de Poitrincourt fit

rebaſtir, & y logea le ſieur
 Boulay quand le ſieur du
 Pont s'en reuint en France.
P (1) La porte de l'abitation.
Q (2) Le cemetiere.
R (3) La riuiere.

(1) Cette lettre manque dans le deſſin ; mais la porte est bien reconnaiſſable tant par ſa figure que par l'avenue qui y aboutit. — (2) K, dans le deſſin. — (3) L, dans le deſſin.

Figure 2.1 The habitation at Port-Royal.

once stood. The disappearance of the St. Lawrence Iroquois is one of the great mysteries of Canadian history. Although there is no certain explanation, various theories have been proposed. It may be that European diseases diminished the population. Others have suggested that crop failure could be to blame: the area is at the northern limit for crops such as corn and beans and the site may have been abandoned in favour of more promising agricultural land. Or perhaps the St. Lawrence Iroquois succumbed to the powerful military force created by the formation of the Iroquois League or nations further inland, such as the Huron, who resented the efforts of the Stadaconans to control access to European trade goods.

Determined to ensure a plentiful supply of high-quality furs for Quebec, Champlain felt compelled to agree to a military alliance with a party of Montagnais, Algonquin, and Huron that sought his support for a raid against their Iroquoian enemies to the southwest. On July 30, 1609, the war party confronted a band of

Figure 2.2 Sketch showing Champlain and Indigenous allies in battle with the Iroquois. Champlain's alliances set the pattern for ongoing conflict in North America.

Mohawk at Ticonderoga on Lake Champlain. A few shots from French arquebuses easily scattered the enemy war party, who had never seen guns before. About the time that Champlain joined in the raid on the Iroquois at Ticonderoga, Henry Hudson sailed up the Hudson River just to the south. Hudson had been commissioned by the Dutch East India Company to find a route to Asia. Although that endeavour failed, the voyage alerted the Dutch to the opportunities the region offered for trade and agriculture. Anxious to establish their own foothold in North America, the Dutch quickly formed an alliance with the Iroquois, setting in play the prolonged conflict that pitted rival European powers and their Indigenous allies against one another.

Determined to solidify his alliances, Champlain participated in another raid on the Iroquois in 1610, demonstrating his personal courage by canoeing down the treacherous Lachine Rapids with a group of Algonquin warriors. As an expression of trust and goodwill, the allies agreed to send representatives to live with their trade and military partners. Champlain entrusted 17-year-old Étienne Brûlé into the care of Iroquet, an Algonquin chief, and in turn received a Huron youth, Savignon. After visiting France with Champlain, Savignon returned to his people and gave a good report of his experiences. Brûlé spent more than 20 years among the Huron, learning their language and customs, and exploring territory never before seen by Europeans.

Although French interest had shifted to the St. Lawrence, a close associate of de Monts, Jean de Biencourt de Poutrincourt, returned to Port-Royal in 1610 with 20 colonists and re-established a profitable trade in furs. A devout Catholic, Poutrincourt was accompanied by a priest, Jessé Fléchée, who baptized Membertou and his family. News of the baptisms piqued the interests of French Jesuits who dispatched two priests, Pierre Biard and Énemond Massé, to Acadia the following year to minister to the fledgling settlement at Port-Royal and to convert the Mi'kmaq to Christianity. Funds for their mission were raised by Madame de Geurcheville, the devout wife of the governor of Paris and the first of several wealthy French women to sponsor religious activities in New France. Upon their arrival, the Jesuits were shocked to learn that Fléchée did not speak Mi'kmaq and had not provided instruction to Membertou and his family. Determined not to repeat Fléchée's errors, Massé went to live among the Mi'kmaq to learn their language and something of their ways. In 1611, Poutrincourt returned to Paris and entrusted Port-Royal to his son, Charles. Tensions soon developed between the younger Poutrincourt and the Jesuit missionaries, who removed themselves from Port-Royal and established a new post at Saint-Sauveur on the Penobscot River. Disturbed by the spread of French settlements, the governor of the fledgling English colony at Jamestown commissioned the privateer and adventurer, Samuel Argall, to attack Acadia. When the elder Poutrincourt returned in 1612, he found Port-Royal had been sacked and burned and the Jesuits taken prisoner. He returned to France with most of the colonists, leaving only his son, his cousin Charles de Saint-Étienne de La Tour, and a few others behind.

Back at Quebec, Champlain's success at establishing alliances and expanding the fur trade was rewarded in 1612 when he was given vice-regal powers to administer justice, uphold the Crown's laws, and oversee relations with the Indigenous peoples. Champlain sought to use his new powers to make New France more than a fur trade colony and increasingly devoted himself to colonization and economic diversification. This shift in priorities had a significant impact on Champlain's relations with New France's Indigenous military and trading partners. Determined to convince the Indigenous peoples to abandon their traditional ways, take up farming, accept French culture, and embrace Christianity, Champlain was confident that "in the course of time and through association with others" they would "acquire a French heart and spirit."[3] Ultimately, he hoped the French and Indigenous Christians would intermarry and form a single people.

A man of his times, Champlain was deeply influenced by the religious enthusiasm generated by the Catholic Reformation and the prevailing assumptions that the

---

3   W.L. Grant (ed.), *The Voyages of Samuel de Champlain, 1604–1618*, vol. 1 (New York: C. Scribner, 1917), 264, 323.

Indigenous peoples had no religion of their own. Convinced that the "New World" was a resource to be conquered and exploited, and driven by a deep sense of mission, the French believed that they had a God-given duty to bring Catholic Christianity and French "civilization" to these peoples. Although contact with Indigenous Americans confirmed their belief that Europeans were at the pinnacle of civilization, the French did not look upon them as "savages" beyond redemption, but rather, as persons created, like themselves, in the image of God. Indigenous peoples were thus not innately inferior, but were like children who required French guardianship in order to realize their full capacities and potential—a potential that would only be achieved by accepting French culture and the Catholic faith.

Champlain took the first tangible steps toward conversion and acculturation in 1614 when he enlisted the services of four Récollet missionaries to convince the Montagnais to abandon "their filthy habits, loose morals, and uncivilized ways," "to render them sedentary," and "to bring them up in our manner and laws."[4] A reformed Franciscan order founded in Paris at the end of the sixteenth century and active in social work among the poor, the Récollets appeared to Champlain to be well suited to the work among the nomadic hunter-gathers who came down to Quebec to trade. Convinced that the Montagnais must first be rendered sedentary before they could to become Christians, the Récollets established a number of agricultural mission stations around Quebec where they hoped to teach the Montagnais how to farm and expose them to French manners and customs.

Champlain's changed relationship with New France's Indigenous allies was evident when he joined a Huron war party in a raid against the Iroquois in 1615. The Huron were farmers, strategically located between the nomadic Algonkian peoples to the north who collected furs for the French, and the Iroquois to the south who were allied with the Dutch. Now that he was the representative of the French Crown, Champlain assumed that the Huron had invited him to command the expedition. For their part, the Huron viewed Champlain as an ally, who, like any other, had the right to be consulted and to express an opinion. Champlain's concept of European command had no meaning among the Huron, who were moved by one's powers of persuasion and example, not by any abstract notion of authority. Not only did Champlain misjudge his position, he misconstrued the purpose of the raid itself. The objective was not the total destruction of the Iroquois village, as Champlain assumed, but simply to force the Iroquois to engage in traditional hand-to-hand combat so that a few prisoners might be secured as compensation for Huron warriors lost in similar raids. Ignorant of these aims, Champlain berated the Huron warriors for what he considered their lack of courage and concerted

---

4   Biggar, *The Works of Samuel de Champlain*, vol. 4, 321.

action. The Huron were appalled by such unseemly behaviour and compelled Champlain, who had been wounded during the battle, to spend the winter at Huronia in the hope that they could instruct him in their ways and manners while he recuperated. There is little evidence to suggest that Champlain's time among the Huron changed his attitudes. If anything, Champlain returned to Quebec in the spring of 1616 more convinced of their need to be "civilized."

In 1616, the Récollets abandoned their work among the Montagnais and established a mission close to the Huron village of Carhagouha. Frustrated by the unwillingness of the Montagnais to abandon their nomadic way of life, the Récollets were attracted by the more settled life of the Huron. The Récollets were impressed by the hospitality and generosity of the Huron people, but repelled by the relative power of women, the permissive upbringing of children, and the sexual freedom that existed among youth. The mission to the Huron was not a great success. Unable to master their language and unwilling to live among non-Christians, the Récollets failed to understand the Huron or win their trust. For their part, the Huron appear to have tolerated the Récollets simply as a means of cementing their alliance with the French and protecting their position within the fur trade. One of the missionaries, Gabriel Sagard, complained that the Huron were content to "leave everyone to his own belief" and refused to embrace Christianity.[5]

Figure 2.3 Title page of Gabriel Sagard's account of his voyage to the Huron. The Récollet missionaries were succeeded by the Jesuits.

From 1616 until his death in 1635, chronic misunderstanding plagued Champlain's relations with France's Indigenous allies. In 1616 and again in 1629, Champlain refused gifts offered by the Montagnais as compensation for the murder of two French traders and insisted that the Montagnais turn the perpetrators of the crime over to him for trial. Champlain relented only when the significance of the blood feud in Montagnais society was impressed upon him. When Miristou sought Champlain's support to become headman of his band in 1622, Champlain assumed that this was recognition of his own authority over the Montagnais. In fact, Miristou was simply following a traditional courtesy. Champlain later insisted that a council of headmen of his own choosing be established to regulate relations between the Montagnais and the French. To the disapproval

5   Gabriel Sagard, in George Wrong (ed.), *The Long Journey to the Country of the Hurons* (Toronto: The Champlain Society, 1939), 133.

of all, Champlain appointed Chomina to the council, a man who had close ties with the French but whose trustworthiness was suspect among the Natives. Such callous behaviour threatened to destroy the alliances Champlain had successfully built over the years.

Colonies Lost and Recovered

Meanwhile in Acadia, Charles de Biencourt de Poutrincourt and his cousin, Charles de Saint-Étienne de La Tour, maintained friendly relations with the Mi'kmaq and succeeded in establishing a profitable enterprise in fish and fur. When Poutrincourt died in 1623, responsibility for the colony fell to La Tour, who strengthened his ties to the local Natives when he took a Mi'kmaq wife. The French claim to Acadia was challenged in 1621 when James I of Britain renamed the territory Nova Scotia and granted it to his Scottish friend and courtier, Sir William Alexander. Attempts to establish a British colony proved difficult. In 1624, Alexander convinced the King to institute 150 new knights-baronet, who, in return for a title and land grant, agreed to bring colonists out to Nova Scotia. The scheme generated little interest, however, and only a small number of Scots ever settled in the colony.

In 1626, Champlain's quest to establish a viable colony took him back to France, where he met with Cardinal Richelieu, Louis XIII's chief minister. Convinced by Champlain of New France's vast potential and of the necessity of colonization, Richelieu chartered the Company of One Hundred Associates the following year. In return for a monopoly in the fur trade, the company was required to provide New France with several hundred settlers a year. Determined to avoid the religious tensions that beset France, the charter stipulated that only Catholics were to be settled in New France and that a suitable number of priests were to accompany the colonists. With the formation of the Company of One Hundred Associates, it seemed as if Champlain's vision of colonization was about to be realized.

That very same year, however, France's position in North America became precarious when war broke out with England. Determined to profit from the conflict, a company of London merchants sought to establish a trading post on the St. Lawrence and to reassert the British claim to Canada laid by John Cabot in 1497. A fleet of three ships was dispatched to the area in 1628 under the command of a privateer, David Kirke. Kirke, a Huguenot, had been born in Dieppe, and his family had business ties on both sides of the English Channel. His brothers, Lewis, Thomas, John, and James, accompanied him on his expedition. The Kirke brothers easily captured Tadoussac in 1628 and found a warm reception from the Montagnais who, dissatisfied with the French, saw an opportunity to exploit French–English rivalry to gain advantages in trade. Kirke next turned his attention to Quebec and sent a dispatch to Champlain demanding its surrender. Expecting relief to arrive shortly from France, Champlain rejected the demand. Kirke decided not to press on to Quebec that season, but as the returning fleet reached the open water off the coast of Gaspé, another opportunity presented itself. Champlain's eagerly awaited supply fleet was just arriving, and Kirke captured the vessels as prizes of war. On board the French vessels were the first 400 settlers sent by the Company of One Hundred Associates; these hapless victims of the war found themselves carried to England as prisoners.

Inspired by the Kirke brothers' impressive victory, a group of English and Scottish merchants commissioned a second, larger expedition the following year to take Quebec itself. A French traitor, the Huguenot fur trader Jacques Michel, aided the English cause by piloting the invading fleet down the St. Lawrence to Quebec. When reinforcements failed to arrive, Champlain had little choice but to surrender Quebec to the Kirke brothers on July 19, 1629.

When Champlain surrendered to the Kirkes, New France was inhabited by fewer than 100 French traders, fishers, artisans, and missionaries and could claim only one settled farm family, that of Louis and Marie Hébert. France's colonization efforts compared poorly to those of the Dutch and English to the south. The Dutch West India Company established Fort Orange on the Hudson River in 1624 to trade for furs. Although New Netherland grew slowly, it could claim a population three times that of New France by 1629 and constituted a serious rival to the French in the competition for furs.

Despite the comparatively slow progress of its North American colonies, France was eager to regain control of the St. Lawrence and Acadia. The fur trade had proved profitable, and France was not willing to concede the North American continent to its English and Dutch rivals. After lengthy negotiations, the treaty of St-Germain-en-Laye restored Canada and Acadia to France in 1632. Unable to raise funds through a recalcitrant Parliament, the cash strapped Charles I of England relinquished New France in return for a payment of 1 million *livres*. Upon his return in 1633, Champlain found a Quebec that had been razed to the ground by the departing Kirke brothers. Undaunted, Champlain persevered and set about rebuilding New France.

THE "BEAVER WARS"

When the Company of One Hundred Associates resumed trading activities, its prospects appeared extremely promising at first. The Algonquian and Huron had continued to travel to Quebec to trade during the English occupation, but, not enjoying the same good relations they had with the French, held back large quantities of fur. When trade with the French recommenced, they brought this great bounty to Quebec, rewarding their old allies with windfall profits. However, this encouraging beginning concealed ominous developments that threatened the company's future. The company was still mired in debt, and the English interregnum had impressed upon the Algonquians and the Huron that the French were not alone in desiring to trade. The Dutch and their Iroquois allies launched a dangerous challenge to New France's supply of furs and sought to redirect trade south to the Dutch Fort Orange. To Champlain, the solution lay in eliminating the Iroquois threat once and for all, and forcing the Dutch and the English to abandon the fur trade.

The Iroquois were a formidable foe. Sometime before the arrival of Europeans, five warring nations—the Seneca, Mohawk, Cayuga, Oneida, and Onondaga—had been brought together in a sophisticated confederacy, the Great League of Peace, by Dekanawidah and Hiawatha. The chronology of this event is disputed: it may have been as early as the twelfth century or as late as the sixteenth. According to Iroquois tradition, Dekanawidah, a Huron, was a supernaturally gifted individual who received the Great Law of Peace in a vision. With the assistance of Hiawatha, an Onondaga, Dekanawidah convinced the warriors of all five nations to bury their weapons under a great white pine, the Tree of Peace. The Iroquois visualized the League as a longhouse, with the Mohawk the guardians of the eastern door and the Seneca the guardians of the western door. The centrally located Onondaga were keepers of the fire who called council meetings. The council consisted of 50 chiefs chosen by the female clan elders. Decision making was by persuasion and consensus, with wampum belts made of clam shells used as tangible chronicles of significant events and agreements. Although each nation reserved the right to pursue its own interests and to act independently whenever debate failed to produce a common agreement, the Great League of Peace ensured security. For the French, however, the presence of this powerful confederacy to the south of their fledgling colony produced a constant sense of menace.

The "beaver wars" between New France and the Iroquois have often been interpreted as a product of competing economic interests. Historian José Brandão has challenged this view, asserting that status in Iroquois society did not depend on the accumulation of wealth in the form of material goods, but rather, the honour and glory gained in warfare. The blood feud was a defining feature of Iroquois society, and warfare provided a means to avenge an injury or wrong through the taking of captives. Captives might be tortured, a public spectacle meant to strike fear into enemies that appears also to have had a religious significance; alternatively, they might be adopted into families who had lost relatives in war. The latter practice seems to have become increasingly common as warfare and disease depleted the Iroquois population. Allied with the longstanding enemies of the Iroquois, the French were unavoidably drawn into the Iroquois system of honour and blood feuding. According to Brandão, Iroquois interest in the fur trade was essentially an extension of Iroquois military policy. The

Iroquois did not seek to dominate the fur trade but simply to use it to acquire weapons needed to defeat their enemies. French ambitions to control the fur trade and extend their influence into lands the Iroquois considered within their sphere of influence "turned them into a direct threat and thus the focus of Iroquois hostilities."[6]

BROKEN PROMISES: THE CHALLENGES OF COLONIZATION

As the fortunes of the fur trade faltered, so too did the prospects for the colonization of Canada. In return for its monopoly from the French Crown, the Company of One Hundred Associates had promised to settle 300 Catholic colonists a year in New France, but settling colonists was an expensive business and cut into company profits. Every new colonist represented a potential free trader and competition to the company. New arrivals frequently found the prospects of a free and adventurous life in the fur trade more appealing than the backbreaking work of clearing land and eking out an existence tilling the soil.

The Company of One Hundred Associates adopted an amended version of the old world's land tenure system, the seigneurial system of medieval France. Large tracts of land called *seigneuries* were granted to individuals and religious orders. Those occupying the individual holdings that made up the *seigneurie* were called *habitants* or *censitaires*. Because responsibility for settling colonists now rested with the recipients of these land grants, the seigneurs, the system also enabled the company to offload the costs of colonization.

Robert Giffard, Quebec's first physician, was one of the earliest seigneurs, receiving a land grant in 1634. Giffard energetically recruited *engagés*, or indentured servants, in France, and set them to work constructing a manor house and clearing the land. *Engagés* typically laboured for a seigneur for three to five years, receiving a token wage as well as food and lodging. At the end of their terms of service, *engagés* could choose either to return to France or to remain in the colony as *habitants*. The 43 *engagés* recruited by Giffard represented a significant addition to Canada's population. Father Paul le Jeune was impressed by the progress made by Giffard: "His lordship Giffard, who has only been clearing his land for two years and has still left many tree stumps, hopes this year, if the amount of grain lives up to its present showing, to harvest enough to feed twenty people. Already last year he garnered eight puncheons [barrels] of wheat, two of peas and three of corn."[7]

---

6 José Antonio Brandão, *"Your Fyre Shall Burn No More": Iroquois Policy toward New France and Its Native Allies to 1701* (Lincoln: University of Nebraska Press, 1997), 8–11.

7 "Letter from Father Paul Le Jeune to the Reverend Father Provincial of France, at Paris," in Reuben Gold Thwaites (ed.), *The Jesuit Relations and Allied Documents: Travels and Explorations of the Jesuit Missionaries in New France, 1610–1791*, vol. 6 (Cleveland: Burrows, 1896–1901), 61.

Despite his success, Giffard had few imitators. New France suffered from an acute labour shortage and it was difficult to keep *habitants* fixed to the land. Such conditions limited seigneurial revenues and discouraged most seigneurs from putting much effort into recruiting colonists. While lords of the manor lived in grand style in France, seigneurs in the colony found that revenues were slim and did not allow them to maintain so elevated a social position. As a result, many held their *seigneuries* for speculative purposes, the land remaining devoid of settlers for many years. Growth of an agricultural population in New France continued to be very slow.

Champlain's determination to rebuild the colony after the English occupation took a heavy toll on his health. He developed paralysis in October 1635. No longer able to apply himself to colonial affairs, Champlain focused on his own spiritual welfare. During his illness, Champlain amended his will, making the Virgin Mary his heir: all his possessions and shares in the Company of One Hundred Associates were bequeathed to the church of Notre Dame de la Recouvrance, a church he had erected in Quebec in 1633 to celebrate the colony's restoration. His final wishes attested to the central place both New France and his faith had occupied in his life.

The Catholic Reformation, the Society of Jesus, and the Mission to the Huron

While the fur trade dominated the economic life of New France, religion played an equally important role in the colony's development. New France was founded at a juncture in European history when a revitalized Catholicism was emerging to meet the challenge of the Protestant Reformation. Through the Council of Trent (1543–63) called by Pope Paul III, the Roman Catholic Church sought to reform itself by clarifying its teachings and doctrines, educating the clergy, restoring discipline, and eliminating abuses. In the wake of the council, a reinvigorated Catholicism emerged: charitable works increased, new religious orders of men and women were formed and older ones expanded, devotional literature flourished, lay devotional societies were founded, and missionary efforts intensified.

The fervency of this reformed Catholicism was carried from France to New France by the Society of Jesus. Founded in 1540 by Basque nobleman Ignatius Loyola, the Jesuits were ideally suited to conditions in New France. Loyola had been a military officer who once dreamed of winning glory through warfare. Fighting for the Spanish against the French at Pamplona in 1521, Loyola was struck by a cannon blast that broke his legs. While convalescing, a bored Loyola turned to religious tracts and soon was gripped by a profound spiritual crisis. Resolving to turn his back on his past life, he vowed to devote himself to serving Christ and his Church: if he could not be a real soldier, he would become a soldier of God. Loyola organized the Society of Jesus along military lines, insisting upon absolute obedience to superiors, strict discipline, and a clear sense of purpose. The Jesuits proved to be a formidable instrument of the Catholic Reformation in Europe and effective missionaries overseas. The Jesuits had already established a track record of winning converts in the Far East. When Canada was restored to France in 1632, it was natural that the Jesuits, with their impressive record and missionary experience, should be granted a monopoly by the Crown to the Canadian mission field.

In 1634 the Jesuits, under the leadership of Jean de Brébeuf, established their first mission among the Huron at the village of Ihonatiria (Saint-Joseph). The Huron, a prosperous agricultural people who were firmly allied with the French as intermediaries in the fur trade, had the advantage of being removed from the corrupting vices of the French trading posts and settlements on the St Lawrence. To the Jesuits, the Huron were seen not only as human beings capable of salvation but as "*les bons sauvages.*" Unspoiled by the sins of Europe, the Huron offered the prospect of a return to a pristine Christianity. For their part, the Huron reluctantly accepted the Jesuits into their midst, fearing that a refusal to do so would jeopardize their relations with the French and position within the fur trade.

Life among the Huron proved a difficult adjustment for the Jesuits. The missionaries described the smoky and crowded conditions that existed within the Huron longhouses as a type of "martyrdom." The priests were appalled by the lack of discipline parents exercised over children and husbands over wives. Premarital sexual intercourse and the casualness of marriage and divorce offended their Catholic sensibilities. For their part, the Huron considered the Jesuits' celibacy unnatural and condemned the greed of the French, their cruelty toward others, and especially the corporal punishment of children. It was the Huron disinclination to abandon their own beliefs and embrace Christianity, however, that most frustrated the missionaries. "When we preach to them of one God, Creator of Heaven and Earth, and of all things, and even when we talk to them of Hell and Paradise and of our other mysteries," Jean de Brébeuf complained, "the headstrong reply that this is good for our Country and not for theirs; that every Country has its own fashion."[8] Despite opposition, the Jesuits persisted by learning the Huron language and trying to adapt themselves to Huron ways. "As God made himself man in order to make men God's," one superior remarked, "a Missionary does not fear to make himself Savage, so to speak, in order to make them Christians." "We must," the missionary continued, "follow them to their homes and adapt ourselves to their ways, however ridiculous they may appear,

8 *Jesuit Relations*, vol. 33, 143.

in order to draw them to ours."[9] Whenever possible, the Jesuits attempted to use Huron images and rituals, reinterpreting them in accordance with Christian belief and practice. The Jesuits attempted to impress the Huron with clocks and other pieces of European technology and the rich and colourful ceremony of Catholic liturgy. Initially the missionaries focused their efforts upon the young but, recognizing the esteem in which elders were held, redirected their efforts from children to adult men. The Jesuits were sustained in their work by the conviction that they had been called by God to save a people who were otherwise doomed to damnation, and by the belief that suffering and self-sacrifice were necessary to secure oneself a place in Paradise after death. "Truly," Jean de Brébeuf observed, "to come here, much faith and patience are needed; and he who thinks of coming here for any other than God, will have made a sad mistake."[10]

Deadly epidemics of smallpox and influenza swept through Huronia in 1634 and again during the winter of 1636–37. Huronia's population—estimated to have been as high as 35,000—fell by more than half. Traditional Huron medicine proved powerless against these scourges, and their shamans began to suspect witchcraft. The Jesuits' celibacy, their own sound health, and their ability to predict eclipses led many Huron to believe they possessed supernatural powers. Even more alarming, the Jesuits were apt to baptize those on the brink of death—an apparent cause-and-effect relationship that seemed to confirm Huron suspicions. Opinion turned sharply against the priests. Doors were shut against them, children pelted them with stones, and a Huron council met to contemplate putting them to death. By late October 1637, the missionaries prepared what they believed would be their final report to their superiors and called their Huron hosts to a farewell feast, warning them that they would have to answer for all eternity for their treatment of Christ's messengers. Whether the message struck a chord with the Huron, or whether the more prosaic need to avoid alienating French trading partners prevailed, the Jesuits were spared.

This difficult period past, Jesuit persistence appeared to bear fruit. Some Huron sought out Christian baptism in the hope that this would cure them or protect them from disease. Others converted to Christianity to gain access to firearms or trade advantages. No doubt a few were sincere in their decision to embrace Christianity. These conversions, genuine or not, deeply divided Huron society between Christians and traditionalists. Threatened by the divisions among the Huron, the Jesuits built a fortified mission headquarters at Sainte-Marie in 1639 as a refuge for themselves and their converts. With livestock imported from Quebec and a growing community of

9   Ibid., vol. 51, 266.
10 Ibid., vol. 88, 99.

priests, lay brothers, *engagés*, and *donnés*—laymen who took limited term vows to work with the Jesuits—Sainte-Marie Among the Hurons soon became a self-sufficient community.

RELIGIOUS WOMEN AND INSTITUTION BUILDING

During its early years, New France was predominantly a colony of male traders, administrators and missionaries. A small number of women, however, crossed the Atlantic to serve God in the Canadian wilderness. Caught up in the religious zeal that defined seventeenth-century Catholicism, significant numbers of French women joined religious orders, performed acts of charity, or used their influence and wealth to support religious causes. One of these women was Marie Guyart. Born at Tours in 1599, Guyart began to have visions at a young age and felt a deep calling to religious life. Her desire to enter a convent, however, was thwarted by her parents' insistence that she take a husband. Guyart acceded to her family's wishes and married, but her husband died just two years later after his business failed. Now a destitute 19-year-old single mother, Guyart went to live with her sister and assumed an active role in her brother-in-law's cartage business. Despite these worldly concerns, her life continued to be one of prayer and mystical experiences. She wore hair shirts and engaged in self-flagellation to purge herself of sin and prove her worthiness to serve God. In 1626, resolved to resist the call no longer, Guyart became a novice in the Ursuline order, leaving her eight-year-old son in her sister's charge and adopting the name Marie de l'Incarnation.

Shortly after she made her life profession in 1633, Marie de l'Incarnation dreamed that God called her to go to Canada to spread the gospel among the "heathen." The idea of sending religious women to the wilds of New France met with many objections from the male church hierarchy, but with financial backing from two wealthy noblewomen, a small group of Ursulines and Augustinian Hospitalières were finally permitted to set sail for Canada in 1639. Under Marie's direction, the Ursulines built a convent and opened a school for Indigenous girls at Quebec. Marie began her work among these children with tremendous zeal and hope. "These girls love us more than they love their parents, showing no desire to accompany them," she enthusiastically wrote to her son. "They model themselves

Figure 2.4 Marie de l'Incarnation, 1677. Marie de l'Incarnation was one of several influential religious women who established institutions in New France.

upon us as much as their age and condition can permit."[11] This initial optimism proved short lived. Many of their young pupils, separated from their families and culture and thrown into an alien environment, fell into despair and depression. Some became ill and died. Others tried to escape the regimented life and strict discipline of the school and return to their families. "It is a very difficult thing, not to say impossible, to make the little Savages French or civilized," a discouraged Marie later wrote. "We have observed that of a hundred that have passed through our hands we have scarcely civilized one. We find docility and intelligence in these girls but, when we are least expecting it, they clamber over our wall and go off to run with their kinsmen in the woods."[12] Frustrated by their lack of success with Indigenous children, the Ursulines redirected their efforts toward educating the daughters of the colony's official and commercial classes. Marie's talents as a businesswoman and fundraiser proved indispensable in her religious endeavours. She successfully cultivated wealthy patrons in France who lent support to her mission and oversaw the creation of a vibrant community of women.

Women also played a vital role in the founding of Montreal. The idea for a new settlement on the island of Montreal originated in France with the Compagnie du Saint-Sacrament, a secret devotional society dedicated to evangelization, good works, and the defence of public morality. The company created an auxiliary, the Société de Notre Dame de Montréal pour la Conversion des Sauvages de la Nouvelle-France, to raise subscriptions for the founding of a new settlement dedicated to its godly ideals. Ville Marie, as the settlement was then known, was founded on May 17, 1642. It was to be "a Jerusalem blessed by God and composed of citizens destined for Heaven."[13] Residents of Ville Marie lived by a strict religious code and were subject to severe punishment or ostracism if they violated its terms. Among its first residents was a 35-year-old nurse, Jeanne Mance. Although not a member of a religious order, Mance was a woman of intense personal piety and energy who devoted her life to religious and charitable work. Upon her arrival at Ville Marie, Mance immediately established a medical dispensary. This would later become the colony's first hospital, the Hôtel-Dieu. An outstanding administrator and entrepreneur, Mance returned to France on three occasions to raise funds, to search out an order of nuns to staff her medical mission, and to recruit settlers for Ville Marie.

The governor of the new settlement at Ville Marie, Paul de Chomedey de Maisonneuve, arrived shortly after Jeanne Mance. Like Mance, Maisonneuve had strong religious convictions. An experienced military officer, Maisonneuve resolved

---

11 "Marie de l'Incarnation to a Lady of Rank, Quebec, 3 September 1640," in Joyce Marshall (ed.), *Word from New France: The Selected Letters of Marie de l'Incarnation* (Toronto: Oxford University Press, 1967), 74.

12 "Marie de l'Incarnation to Her Son, Quebec, 1 September 1668," in *Word from New France*, 341.

13 *Jesuit Relations*, vol. 7, 273.

to serve in New France after reading some of the published accounts of the Jesuits' ordeals in North America. When colonial authorities at Quebec attempted to dissuade Maisonneuve from establishing a settlement on the island of Montreal, so near the hostile Iroquois, he responded: "my honour is at stake, and you will agree that I must go up there to start a colony, even if all the trees on that island were to change to so many Iroquois."[14] The defence of the vulnerable settlement occupied most of Maisonneuve's energies during the 25 years he spent at Montreal. As governor, he formed the Militia of the Holy Family and instituted a system of flying camps, or temporary outposts, to keep enemy Iroquois at a distance.

Maisonneuve's sister, Louise de Chomedey de Sainte-Marie, was the mother superior of the Congregation de Notre Dame at Troyes in the French province of Champagne. She shared her brother's stories of New France with other women within her order, and one of these, Marguerite Bourgeoys, resolved to dedicate her life to the service of God in Canada. Born into a prosperous commercial family, Bourgeoys was inspired by a mystical vision of the Virgin Mary to join a teaching community associated with the Congregation de Notre Dame. After meeting Bourgeoys in 1652, Maisonneuve invited her to come to New France to establish a school.

Bourgeoys arrived at Ville Marie the following year but found no school age children. A high rate of infant mortality, disease, and attack from the Iroquois all contributed to the settlement's lack of children. Unperturbed, she carried out social work among the settlers and oversaw the construction of the chapel of Notre Dame de Bon Secours, Ville Marie's first stone church. In 1657, she finally opened a school in a donated stable. She later acted as a chaperone for single female immigrants to New France, instructing them in domestic arts and helping them to select suitable husbands. To further her educational and social work, Bourgeoys founded the Soeurs de la Congregation de Notre Dame. Unlike most other female religious communities, Bourgeoys's congregation of sisters was not cloistered and did not wear the traditional nun's habit. This was an innovative and even radical action that caused some consternation among the colony's male religious authorities. Bourgeoys invoked the example of the Blessed Virgin Mary to justify her extraordinary actions. "The Holy Virgin," she insisted, "was not cloistered, but she everywhere preserved an internal solitude, and she never refused to be where charity or necessity required."[15]

Each of these women embodied the religious fervour and piety characteristic of Early Modern Catholicism. Theirs was a deeply mystical faith of dreams and visions

---

14 Marie-Claire Daveluy, "Paul de Chomedey de Maisonneuve," *Dictionary of Canadian Biography* (DCB), http://www.biographi.ca.

15 Hélène Bernier, "Marguerite Bourgeoys," DCB, http://www.biographi.ca.

that idealized suffering and demanded a life of strict discipline directed to the service of others and to the problems that afflicted society. Each of these formidable women had a gift for leadership and demonstrated a talent for administration and business. As the founders and managers of hospitals, schools, poorhouses, and orphanages, they played a central role in the life of New France.

WAR WITH THE IROQUOIS AND THE FALL OF HURONIA

While missionaries and nuns worked to plant the faith in New France, Champlain's successor, Charles Jacques Huault de Montmagny, set out to secure the colony from the Iroquois threat. A Knight of Malta who had considerable military experience fighting the Turks and chasing pirates in the Mediterranean, Montmagny seemed well suited to the task of defending the colony. After attempts in 1641 to negotiate a peace treaty with the Iroquois failed, Montmagny organized a naval patrol of the St. Lawrence and built a fort at the mouth of the Richelieu River to blockade the routes the Iroquois used to intercept Huron and Algonquian trading parties. These efforts proved futile. The Iroquois destroyed Fort Richelieu in a daring raid and intensified their attacks against New France and its Indigenous partners. By 1645 the number of furs had dwindled and the Company of One Hundred Associates faced bankruptcy. Determined to cut their losses, French investors in the company decided to turn the fur trade over to a subsidiary made up of traders resident in Canada, the Compagnie des Habitants. The prospects of the new company brightened when Montmagny succeeded in negotiating a peace treaty with the Mohawk and the fur trade resumed. The peace was short lived, however, and by 1647 the Iroquois began an all-out offensive against the French and their Huron allies.

Divided between traditionalists and Christian converts, and their population greatly reduced by disease, the Huron were especially vulnerable to Iroquois attack. In the tense summer of 1647, no Huron canoes dared to bring furs to Quebec or Trois-Rivières. At Saint-Joseph, a substantial palisaded Huron village of about 2,000, Father Antoine Daniel had just finished saying mass on the morning of July 4, 1648, when some 700 Iroquois warriors descended upon the town. Daniel was killed in a volley of arrows and musket fire. Some Huron managed to escape to Sillery, a reserve for Christian Natives outside Quebec, while hundreds were taken as prisoner. Others in the besieged town had long resented the presence of the black robes and opted to join forces with the attackers. The Iroquois set the town afire, and the bulwark of Huronia was razed to the ground.

The following spring, a second, even larger, Iroquois force fell upon Huronia. Just before daybreak on the morning of March 16, 1649, 1,200 Iroquois struck the village of Saint-Ignace. Startled from their sleep, the Huron tried to flee the slaughter but only three managed to escape. The alarm was raised at the neighbouring village of Saint-Louis, where most of the 700 Huron residents took to the woods in panic. Only 80 warriors and 2 Jesuit priests, Jean de Brébeuf and Gabriel Lalemant, remained to mount a defence and to minister to those too weak to flee. When the besieging Iroquois broke through the defences, they torched the town. Brébeuf and Lalemant were taken captive and carried back to Saint-Ignace where they were tortured and killed. Desperate and dispirited, the Huron abandoned Ossossane, and the Jesuit mission at Sainte-Marie was burned to the ground to prevent it from desecration. Many of the remaining Huron sought refuge on Christian Island in Georgian Bay. After enduring a winter fraught with disease and starvation, they dispersed, some to Manitoulin Island, others to the western shore of Lake Huron where they became known as the Wyandot.

For the French, the gruesome deaths of Brébeuf and Lalemant marked the end of the dream of establishing an enclave of Christian allies in the wilderness. More than that, the destruction of Huronia cut off the supply of furs from the interior and put the very life of New France at risk. No furs came down to Quebec at all in 1653. A Jesuit missionary observed that "the Huron flotillas have ceased to come for the trade; the Algonquins are depopulated and the remote Nations have withdrawn ever further in fear of the Iroquois. The Montréal store had not purchased a single beaver from the Natives in the past year. At Trois-Rivières, the few Natives that came were employed to defend the place where the enemy is expected. The store in Québec is the image of poverty."[16] Canada found itself in a state of siege, with Montreal, Trois-Rivières, and even Quebec itself vulnerable to Iroquois attack. With little support from France, Canada had to rely on its own small population and meagre resources to defend itself. It would take a new commitment from metropolitan France to ensure the survival of the colony.

The Acadian "Civil War"

Although far removed from Iroquois attacks, Acadia fared little better than Canada during the decades of the mid-seventeenth century. The 1632 Treaty of Saint-Germain-en-Laye put an end to the claims of William Alexander and the British Crown to Nova Scotia. After the restoration, French authorities divided Acadia between two ambitious men, Charles de La Tour and Charles de Menou d'Aulnay. Both men soon clashed over the precise boundaries and trading rights granted to each. Of humble origin, the Protestant

16 *Jesuit Relations*, vol. 40, 211.

La Tour arrived in Acadia in 1610, quickly established an interest in the fur trade, emerged as a leader in the tiny settlement, and was awarded a commission as governor while the colony was still under British control in 1631. La Tour had commercial ties with the powerful Companie de la Nouvelle France. With the company's help, he established a fort and settlement at the mouth of the Saint John River, the gateway to prime fur country. By contrast, the aristocratic d'Aulnay first set foot in Acadia in 1632 as an advisor to the newly appointed lieutenant-general of Acadia, his cousin, Isaac de Razilly. When Razilly died in 1636, d'Aulnay assumed his position. A Catholic, d'Aulnay enjoyed the support of Louis XIII's chief minister, Cardinal Richelieu. It was d'Aulnay's hope that Acadia would become agriculturally self-sufficient. To this end, d'Aulnay recruited colonists from his French estates and relocated Acadian settlers to the fertile lands around Port-Royal. There he built a new fort and oversaw the construction of dikes to drain the salt marshes to create thousands of acres of rich, arable farmland. To support the local fishery and eliminate the need for expensive imported salt, d'Aulnay recruited French salt makers to create evaporative salt pans. The rivalry between La Tour and d'Aulnay threatened to engulf all of Acadia and derail the fragile colonization experiment.

Determined to exercise complete control over Acadia and its trade, d'Aulnay challenged La Tour's commission and trading rights. When La Tour arrived at Port-Royal in 1640 to pick up furs and supplies, d'Aulnay ordered his cannon to open fire on La Tour's ship. Forced to retreat, La Tour sailed to Boston for necessary supplies. This apparent collusion with the English gave d'Aulnay further ammunition, and he claimed that the Huguenot La Tour was a traitor to French interests in Acadia. Using his connections at the French court, d'Aulnay obtained an order from the King ordering La Tour's arrest and return to France. Convinced that d'Aulnay had deceived French authorities and knowing that abandoning his interests to defend his reputation in France would play into the hands of his enemy, La Tour sent his wife, Françoise Marie Jacquelin, to make his case before the King. She was evidently persuasive and won consent for the Companie de la Nouvelle France to send soldiers and supplies to Fort La Tour. When she returned in April 1643, Lady La Tour found d'Aulnay's forces had blockaded the mouth of the Saint John River and access to Fort La Tour, and was forced to turn back.

The conflict between the two men culminated in April 1645. When d'Aulnay learned that his rival was absent in Boston, he seized the opportunity to launch an assault on Fort La Tour. The redoubtable Lady La Tour, who now had an infant son, led a valiant defence of the fort, with a garrison reduced by desertion to a mere 45 soldiers. At last, on Easter Sunday, after the fort had withstood bombardment for three days and more than half the defenders had fallen, a traitor opened the gates to d'Aulnay's invaders. Lady La Tour surrendered, securing a promise that her soldiers would be spared. Instead, Lady la Tour was forced to watch, with a rope around her neck, as they were hanged. When she was caught attempting to smuggle a note to her husband through an Indigenous trader, Lady La Tour herself was thrown into prison. She died a few days later at the age of 24. La Tour learned the sad news as he prepared to launch a relief expedition from Boston. Defeated, he moved to Quebec to start over.

The dream of a thriving colony in Acadia had been consumed in the fires of personal ambition. Yet by the spring of 1650, the victorious d'Aulnay was dead, having drowned in a canoeing accident. La Tour took the opportunity to reassert his case in France. After an inquiry he was restored to royal favour, and his property and commission as governor returned to him. La Tour set out once again for Port-Royal in the summer of 1653, bringing several families of colonists with him. Impoverished by the protracted conflict, d'Aulnay's widow, Jeanne Motin, was willing to put past acrimony behind her "for the peace and tranquility of the country and concord and union between the two families," and accepted La Tour's offer of marriage.[17]

This surprising end to the enmity between the two rival claimants did not, unfortunately, usher in an era of peaceful security for Acadia. One of d'Aulnay's French creditors, Emmanuel Le Borgne, laid claim to d'Aulnay's rights and assets in Acadia. Leading a large force, Le Borgne arrived in Acadia in 1654 to assert his rights. Determined to take control of the colony, Le Borgne's men seized property belonging to La Tour and captured forts throughout the region. Le Borgne's military campaign was interrupted by a threat from outside. In July 1654, a fleet from New England arrived led by Robert Sedgwick. Sedgwick acted on orders from England's Lord Protector, Oliver Cromwell. While the struggle between La Tour and d'Aulnay had been raging, and while Canada had been at war with the Iroquois, a bigger cataclysm had shaken England. The long and bitter conflict between King Charles I and his Parliament over their respective rights and privileges had culminated in civil war by 1642. Charles was beheaded on January 30, 1649, and the Puritan Oliver Cromwell, who had led the parliamentarians to victory over the royalists, assumed the role of Lord Protector in December 1653. When the First Anglo-Dutch War broke out between England and the Netherlands in 1652, largely over maritime trade, Cromwell commissioned Robert Sedgwick to lead a campaign to subdue the Dutch in New Netherland. Cromwell added that Sedgwick should feel free to look for other chances to expand English power in North America as well. Acadia offered such an opportunity.

Although England and France were not at war, the actions of French privateers had plagued English merchants in North America, and New England had long coveted access to the rich fishery off Acadia's coasts. A devout Puritan, Sedgwick no

17 From the marriage contract cited in Marcel Trudel, *The Beginnings of New France, 1524–1663* (Toronto: McClelland & Stewart, 1973), 204.

doubt relished the opportunity to strike a blow against "popery" in the name of "true religion." Weakened by internal dissension, Acadia fell quickly. La Tour surrendered after a three-day battle at Saint John and le Borgne followed suit after a brief resistance at Port-Royal. Acadia's French residents were allowed to remain on their land, and Catholic missionaries continued to minister to the local population. Intent on eking out a living and having witnessed Acadia change hands twice in their lifetimes, Acadians were becoming indifferent to questions of loyalty and readily diverted the produce of the fur trade and fisheries to New England. The Treaty of Breda restored Acadia to France in 1667.

COUREURS DES BOIS AND THE IMPACT OF THE FUR TRADE

The 1649 defeat and dispersal of the Huron disrupted old fur-trading patterns. Instead of flotillas of canoes laden with furs making their way down to Quebec and Trois-Rivières each year, fleets of *coureurs des bois* (literally, "runners of the woods") travelled far into the interior carrying trade goods. To ensure that the season's pelts were not lost to the Dutch or the English, French traders wintered among their Indigenous suppliers and carried the furs back from the *pays-d'en-haut* (upper country) themselves. These changes required a liberalization of trading regulations. In the past, only the clerks employed by the authorized trading company could procure furs. With the relaxation of the rules, trading fever swept the colony. "All our young Frenchmen," a Jesuit missionary observed in 1653, "are planning on a trading expedition, to find the Nations who are scattered here and there; and they hope to come back laden with the beaver skins of several years' accumulation."[18] The rush of young men to the upper country concerned the governor of New France, Jean de Lauson. In 1654 he decreed that no one could go trading "with the Huron or other Nations without our previous written consent, under penalty of a fine." The governor explained that he simply wanted to know "the number and quality of the individuals who wish to embark on these voyages," but the introduction of trading permits provided him with a powerful tool of patronage that aroused considerable resentment.[19]

As competition with the Dutch and the English increased, firearms and alcohol were increasingly used to secure supplies of fur. Although Champlain had outlawed the use of brandy as an item of trade in 1633, traders now insisted that it was essential if the French were to remain competitive. Alcohol was initially valued by Indigenous peoples for its

18 *Jesuit Relations*, vol. 40, 215.
19 Order of April 28, 1654, cited in Trudel, *Beginnings of New France*, 225.

Figure 2.5 *Coureurs de bois*. The fur trade offered an appealing alternative to settled life.

hallucinogenic properties and viewed as a means of communicating with the supernatural. The fact that alcohol could be consumed on site and did not have to be transported back home added to its appeal for migratory Indigenous traders who did not accumulate many material possessions. Missionaries and visitors to New France frequently commented on the negative impact of alcohol. "Liquors," observed Marie de l'Incarnation, "destroys all these poor people—the men, the women, the boys and even the girls."[20]

The destructive effect of alcohol has sometimes been interpreted as part of a larger pattern of exploitation, growing Indigenous dependence, and cultural degeneration. According to this interpretation, credulous Indigenous traders were cheated by wily Europeans, sacrificing valuable furs for worthless trinkets. More recently, historians such as Arthur Ray have challenged this idea, pointing out that Indigenous traders actively sought to trade and became "good comparison shoppers" who quickly learned to discern quality goods.[21] Indigenous traders sought out European trade goods as durable alternatives to traditional tools and utensils painstakingly produced from wood, stone, and bone. While European goods were relatively rare, furs were abundant and Indigenous traders readily took advantage of European competition to ensure the best terms of trade. A Montagnais man observed: "The Beaver does everything perfectly well, it makes kettles, hatchets, swords, knives, bread" and "The English have no sense; they give us twenty knives like this for one Beaver skin."[22] While European goods were incorporated

20 "Marie de l'Incarnation to Her Son, 10 August 1662," *Word from New France*, 273.

21 Arthur Ray, "Fur Trade Histories as an Aspect of Native History" in Ian A.L. Getty and Donald B. Smith (eds.), *One Century Later: Western Canadian Reserve Indians since Treaty 7* (Vancouver: University of British Columbia Press, 1978), 12.

22 Ibid., 9.

into Indigenous economies, the collective self-sufficiency of Indigenous society was not replaced by a helpless dependence on imported trade goods. Indigenous peoples tenaciously held on to their cultures and lifestyles. Their traditionalism, however, was neither blind nor passive, and they readily accepted innovations that made life easier.

Acculturation, of course, could cut both ways: French fur traders happily adopted items of Indigenous dress and swiftly accustomed themselves to the use of canoes and snowshoes. There was much in Indigenous society that appealed to French traders. With few French women in the colony, *coureurs des bois* appreciated the less restrictive attitudes about sexual relations found within Indigenous society. Many French traders took Indigenous women as companions or wives *à la façon du pays*—according to the custom of the country. These alliances, both casual and long lasting, bound the French more closely to their Indigenous hosts and enabled them to better understand Native society and culture. The egalitarian relations that characterized Indigenous society also appealed to many *coureurs des bois*, most of whom were men of humble backgrounds and modest means who enjoyed little status or influence within their own society.

The journey west was a long and costly one and traders began to seek out a less arduous way to access the rich beaver country surrounding Lake Superior. In 1657, Jean Bourdon, the head clerk for the Companie des Habitants, unsuccessfully attempted to reach the northwest via Hudson Bay in 1657. The need to find an alternative trade route became more urgent with the resumption of Iroquois hostilities in 1658. Despite the rising level of violence, officials and merchants based at Quebec opposed efforts to access the interior via Hudson Bay, and for good reason: a maritime-based fur trade would divert activity away from the St. Lawrence and effectively destroy their ability to control and profit from the fur trade. Frustrated by favouritism, regulation, and taxation, many *coureurs des bois* began to trade illegally with the Iroquois, the Dutch, and the English.

Whereas the English and Dutch colonies to the south enjoyed relatively stable government, New France suffered from administrative confusion. With the creation of a council in 1647, an attempt had been made to provide the colony with an effective administration, but ongoing rivalries and competing interests limited its effectiveness. Even the Church, which had provided one of the few examples of efficient organization, found itself afflicted with dissension. The appointment of François de Laval as Vicar Apostolic for New France in 1659 aroused considerable dissent. Determined to assert the Church's supremacy over all aspects of life in New France, the strong-willed Laval frequently found himself in conflict with the governor, the religious orders, and fur traders. Especially problematic was Laval's attitude to the brandy trade. Convinced that alcohol had a destructive impact upon the Indigenous peoples and the Church's missionary efforts, Laval threatened to excommunicate anyone found to be trading spirits. Squabbles even erupted over the symbolic issue of who should take precedence in religious ceremonies and public events—the governor or the bishop. While such disputes may seem petty, they assumed great significance in a hierarchical society preoccupied by honours and proved a distraction from more important matters. The struggle between Laval and the governor was symptomatic of the larger problems afflicting Canada. With the constant threat of Iroquois attack, a small population, a precarious economy, and beset by internal tensions and rivalries, the future of New France appeared bleak.

In 1660, a small party led by a young French soldier and trader, Adam Dollard des Ormeaux, set out from Montreal to ambush what they thought was a small band of Iroquois traders and seize their furs. They were dismayed to discover that these were only the advance scouts of a much larger war party intent on attacking Montreal. Dollard and his men took shelter in an abandoned palisade at Long Sault in a desperate attempt to defend themselves, surviving for a hellish week with limited water and provisions. When a keg of gunpowder accidentally exploded and destroyed the makeshift fort, the Iroquois swarmed over the crumbled defences and slaughtered or captured those within. In the nineteenth century Dollard was transformed into a brave "martyr of the faith" who nobly went out from Montreal to intercept the Iroquois and save the settlement. While the truth is less heroic, the battle at Long Sault so weakened the Iroquois that they returned home rather than continue with their planned attack.

"DISASTERS AND PORTENTS"

To many, the "massacre" at Long Sault was just one of a series of events that bode ill for the future of Canada. Portents of impending disaster seemed everywhere. In a September 1661 letter to her son, Marie de l'Incarnation reported strange signs in the sky that "terrified many people" and that an unborn child was heard to cry in her mother's womb. Charges of sorcery were levelled against several persons said to have cast evil spells and to have conjured up phantoms. Many attributed the appearance of a new and deadly malady that swept through the colony to witchcraft. To Marie de l'Incarnation, these occurrences were signs of God's wrath and impending judgment. Such fears seemed to be confirmed when a massive earthquake shook New France in February of 1663.[23] Beset by dark omens, the residents of New France desperately appealed to the mother country for help. Remarkably, after years of neglect and indifference, French authorities began to pay attention to the pleas issuing forth from their beleaguered North American colony. Although few could have believed it at the time, New France stood on the threshold of a new era.

---

23 "Marie de l'Incarnation to Her Son, September 1660 and 20 August 1663," *Word from New France*, 260–65, 287–95.

3 CONSOLIDATION AND CONFLICT: CANADA, 1663–1748

I n 1663, the monopoly of the Company of One Hundred Associates was revoked, and New France was made a royal province under the direct control of the Crown. After decades of neglect and indifference, French authorities began to invest in the defence, administration, settlement, and economic diversification of their North American colonies. While this ambitious plan proved difficult to implement, the distinctive French society planted in Canada over the previous difficult decades became more firmly established and even began to flourish. A whirlwind of external events beyond its control, however, threatened to erode these gains and increasingly cast an ominous shadow over the very future of New France.

COLBERT'S VISION

Why did French authorities assume control over the affairs of New France in 1663? There is no doubt that the sorry state of New France demanded action. With the colony vulnerable to Iroquois attack, suffering from a divided administration, under-populated, economically weak, and dependent on a single industry, its survival required intervention from the mother country. The Crown's renewed interest in the fate of the colony, however, owed as much to developments at home as to the precarious state of its North American possessions. With the death of Louis XIII in 1643, France found itself beset by internal dynastic struggles and the threat posed by external rivals. Ruled by an infant king and female regent, Anne of Austria, members of the nobility rose to challenge the authority of the Crown. This contest between the

Crown and the nobility weakened France in its struggle with the Habsburgs during the Thirty Years' War. Preoccupied by domestic concerns and foreign threats, France could devote little attention and few resources to New France. France's prospects improved with the signing of the Peace of Westphalia that ended the Thirty Years' War in 1648. Over the next few years, the Crown solidified its power and gradually reasserted its control over rebellious nobles and the common people, ushering a new age of royal absolutism. By 1663, Louis XIV was firmly ensconced upon the throne and could confidently proclaim: "L'état c'est moi" (I am the state).

France's "Sun King" surrounded himself with capable advisors and lieutenants who created a competent bureaucracy to administer state affairs. Chief among these was Jean-Baptiste Colbert. To protect France's commercial interests and to further her imperial ambitions, Colbert built up the navy and reorganized the army, making it one of best trained in Europe. He reformed the taxation and budget systems and placed France upon a sound financial foundation. Through these actions, Colbert provided France with the means to manage and support its overseas colonies. A dedicated follower of mercantilism, Colbert strove to replicate the success of the English and Dutch and transform France's colonies into secure sources of raw materials and ready markets for French manufactured goods. Long overlooked, New France now became a vital part of Colbert's grand imperial plan.

To execute his vision, Colbert imposed a new form of government upon New France that reflected the absolutist ideas of the King. As a royal colony, New France was governed by a Sovereign Council that included the governor general, intendant, bishop and other officials appointed by the Crown. The number of councillors varied over time but never exceeded 12 persons. The Sovereign Council acted as a legislative, administrative, and judicial body. It served as a court of appeal in civil and criminal matters, exercised control over spending, and was responsible for the maintenance of order, public security, supply and services for towns. Appointed directly by the King, the governor general embodied the power of the Crown. He was responsible for the defence of the colony, diplomatic affairs, and relations with the Native peoples. Most governors of New France were members of the nobility and professional soldiers. While the governor general represented the authority of the King and chaired the Sovereign Council, the day-to-day civil administration of the colony rested with the intendant. Well-educated and trained in the law, the intendant epitomized the rise of a modern bureaucracy. Appointed by a royal commission and subject to recall at will, the intendant reported to the Minister of Marine. The intendant ensured that the King's will was implemented and attended to the colony's settlement, economic development, and administration of justice. The final member of this ruling triumvirate was the bishop. The bishop represented the interests of the established Church and the desire to maintain spiritual order and moral stability by disseminating an ethic calculated to remind each person of his or her allotted place in the social order and duty to demonstrate "humility, obedience, purity, meekness, modesty, simplicity, chastity, charity and an ardent love of Jesus and his holy Mother."[1]

Overlapping responsibilities among the governor general, intendant, and bishop, and the distinct personalities of the office holders, ensured that tensions frequently developed. The bishop of Quebec, François de Laval, clashed almost immediately with the first governor appointed under the new regime, Augustine de Saffray de Mézy. The bishop and the governor held differing views of the relationship between church and state. A staunch ultramontanist, Laval insisted that the Pope was the final authority in all matters, religious and secular. De Mézy shared the Gallican views of the King, which placed the monarch, who ruled by divine right, in a position of authority over the Church. The governor and the bishop soon found themselves involved in a noisy quarrel over the governor's salary and allowances, appointments to the Sovereign Council, and the implementation of the tithe. In September 1664, Laval directed the clergy to read a letter from the pulpit denouncing the governor. Saffray de Mézy responded by having notices posted throughout the colony condemning the bishop. The residents of New France were spared the spectacle of a protracted public feud between the colony's temporal and spiritual leaders by the governor's early death in May 1665. The tensions between Laval and Saffray de Mézy might have been mitigated by the presence of an intendant, but the first appointee to this office, Louis Robert de Fortel, never made it to Canada. The office of intendant was not taken up until the arrival of Jean Talon in 1665. An experienced civil servant who enjoyed the confidence of Colbert, Talon soon became the dominant figure on the Sovereign Council, presiding over its meetings and dispensing justice. Convinced that the establishment of a sound justice system was essential to New France's development, Talon set out to rationalize the colony's courts. Intent on putting an end to costly and time-consuming civil cases, Talon prohibited lawyers from practising in the colony, assumed the right to hear all cases where less than 100 *livres* were involved, and encouraged out-of-court settlements. The end result was a highly paternalistic legal system, but one that ensured that justice was both expeditious and inexpensive.

New France's new governor, Daniel de Rémy de Courcelle, resented Talon's control of the legal system, and the two frequently clashed. Talon also came into conflict with bishop Laval. Colbert had directed Talon to be assertive with the imperious bishop and to restore a proper balance between temporal and spiritual authorities. Laval and the Jesuits, Colbert warned, "have acquired an authority that goes beyond

---

1   Archives de Séminaire de Québec, MS-179, *Rulebook for Boarders of the Petit Séminaire.*

the limits of their true profession, which must be concerned only with consciences."[2] To Laval's consternation, Talon reduced the tithe and exempted new colonists from the church tax for five years. Talon further alienated Laval when he expropriated part of one of the Church's seigneuries, Notre-Dames-des-Anges. For Talon, the Church's vast and largely undeveloped landholdings impeded economic progress by depriving settlers of some of the best land in the colony, and compromised New France's security by leaving large unpopulated gaps on the landscape that facilitated Iroquois attack. Even more vexing to Laval was Talon's decision to repeal the edict that outlawed the trade in alcohol. The alcohol trade, Talon concluded, was essential to combat Dutch and English competition for furs and to maintain influence among New France's Indigenous allies. Laval responded by declaring it a sin to get Indigenous persons drunk. Talon accused the bishop of interfering in temporal affairs and "tormenting people's consciences."[3] To counterbalance the power of Laval and the Jesuits, Talon invited the Récollets to return to New France and supported the work of another religious order, the Sulpicians.

Committed to implementing Colbert's "grand plan" for New France, Talon systematically set out to improve the beleaguered colony's defences. In 1665, French authorities dispatched some 1,200 soldiers of the Carignan-Salières Regiment to defend the colony against the Iroquois. The regiment was warmly received by colonists, who craved peace and security, but the presence of such a large number of troops in the colony brought on social problems such as drunkenness, prostitution, rape, and other crimes that strained relations between the soldiers and the civilian population. Responsibility for provisioning the troops fell to Talon, who directed his considerable energy and talent to procuring shelter, food, and clothing for the winter months, and to making preparations for an attack on the Iroquois. In January 1666, some 300 soldiers of the regiment, along with 200 Canadians, set out on foot for Iroquois territory under the command of Governor Courcelle. This campaign, launched in the dead of winter and contrary to Talon's advice, proved disastrous. Poorly guided, Courcelle found himself in the Dutch settlement of Schenectady and confronted by a British delegation incensed by the French incursion into lands recently acquired by the English Crown. After a few skirmishes with the Mohawk, the French forces returned to Quebec, exhausted and close to starvation. Having learned some important lessons during this first failed expedition, the French undertook another campaign during the summer and fall, razing villages, burning crops, and destroying stores of food throughout Iroquois country. This achieved the desired effect, and the Iroquois opted

2 Library and Archives Canada, MG 1, SeriesC11A, vol. 1, Colbert, Instructions to Talon, 25 March 1665, 50–51.

3 André Vachon, "Jean Talon," *Dictionary of Canadian Biography* (*DCB*), http://biographi.ca.

for peace the following year. Although he did not accompany the expedition, its success owed a great deal to Talon's organizational abilities.

With the Iroquois threat temporarily contained, Talon convinced several officers and nearly 450 men of the Carignan-Salières Regiment to remain in the colony and to settle along the Richelieu River, providing an important defence against future Iroquois attacks. Some 30 officers were granted seigneuries, and discharged soldiers received both land and livestock. Although this constituted a significant addition to the colony's population, many of the soldiers were not suited to farming and left their farms to pursue the freer life offered by the fur trade. With the demobilization of the Carignan-Salières Regiment, a colonial militia was created in 1669. Every able-bodied man between the ages of 16 and 60 was required to take part in regular training drills. The militia was organized by parish, and each company of 50 men was commanded by a local captain of militia appointed by the governor. Although militia captains were unpaid, the position carried considerable prestige. Militia captains were entitled to wear a sword like a nobleman, to sit in a prominent place in church, and to take a position of precedence, following the seigneur in religious processions.

SETTLEMENT AND THE SEIGNEURIAL SYSTEM

New France now enjoyed the peace that was essential for settlement. Although the seigneurial system was well established, it had developed haphazardly. Many seigneuries were under-populated and underdeveloped, and there remained large stretches of wilderness along the St. Lawrence. Talon began a major reorganization of the entire system, registering all land holdings in the colony and requiring seigneurs to declare the extent of their property, the amount of land that had been cleared, and the number of tenants that had been settled. After gathering this information, Talon withdrew the rights of seigneurs who had neglected their obligations and granted new seigneuries to those committed to settling and developing their land. Talon required seigneurs and settlers to take up residence within a year and to clear and cultivate at least two acres (about 0.8 hectare) of land, or forfeit their property. He also sought to create a more compact colony that would enable settlers to better assist each other, support the development of industry and commerce, and provide protection against attacks. Three model villages—Bourg-Royal, Bourg-la-Reine, and Bourg-Talon—were laid out on lands expropriated from the Jesuits near Quebec. Triangular land grants radiated out from a central village where all dwellings and services were located. Despite its merits, the experiment was not repeated.

Land grants varied widely in size and depended on the rank, merit, wealth, and connections of the seigneur. The average seigneurie was 16 kilometres deep and 8 kilometres across; the largest grants were up to 100 kilometres deep and 30 to 40 kilometres across.

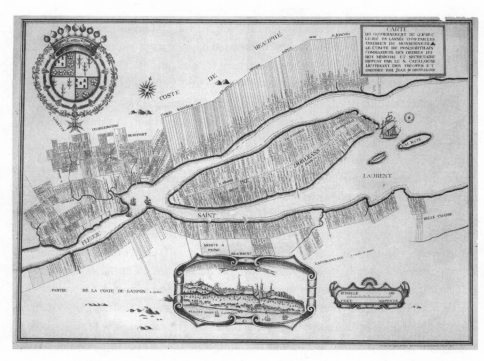

Figure 3.1 Seigneurial landscape: Ile d'Orléans and the north and south shore of the St. Lawrence, 1709.

Convinced that such large grants were less likely to be developed, Talon favoured more modest grants. Seigneurs were required to settle their seigneuries, conceding parcels of land (*censives*) to individuals (*censitaires*) who requested it. The typical *censive* was between 14 to 68 hectares and consisted of a narrow rectangular strip that ran back from the river. River frontage provided *censitaires* with access to the main transportation corridors within New France and to good fishing areas. This pattern of land distribution was easily and cheaply surveyed, allowed *censitaires* to live close to their neighbours, and often provided access to a variety of soils and vegetation. Long daily treks were required, however, to feed livestock and milk the cows that were kept on the poorer-quality soils far back from the river. *Censitaires* were not merely tenants in the modern sense. Initially, they received a temporary deed, a *billet de concession*. Once a *censitaire* had fulfilled his settlement duties by occupying his concession, clearing the land, and planting crops, he received a final deed of possession entitling him to enjoy the use of his land in perpetuity and enabling him to sell or bequeath his property. French inheritance law required that a widow retain half of her husband's estate, with the other half to be divided equally among his children. Such fragmentation threatened the viability of farms, and means were found to keep estates intact. In some cases, parents granted land to a single child in return for a promise to maintain them in their old age and to make payments to their siblings. In other cases, additional *censives* were acquired to maintain a viable operation.

Much like the French feudal system, the seigneurial system sought to create an authoritarian and hierarchical society that rested on a series of mutual obligations. The Crown granted lands to seigneurs in return for obligations of settlement and service. Seigneurs were required to render homage and fealty to the King and his representatives, acknowledge the Crown's claim to all mineral rights, build a manor house, cede land to settlers, render justice to tenants, and maintain a mill, bake oven, and chapel for the use of *censitaires*. The *censitaires* who received land owed rents and services to their seigneur. These obligations included the *cens*, nominal dues that symbolized the *censitaires*' dependence on the seigneur, and the *rentes*, a more substantial fee paid each year in money or in kind. *Censitaires* were also obliged to perform three days of unpaid labour, the *corvée*, each year, to provide the seigneur with a share of any fish caught or wood cut on the seigneurie, and to take their grain to the seigneur's mill, paying him one-fourteenth of the flour milled. These monopoly rights and obligations were known as the *banalités*. *Censitaires* could sell their land concession, but seigneurs were entitled to a transfer tax, the *lods et ventes*, that amounted to one-twelfth of the value of the sale. In France, this system of mutual obligations could be oppressive. Such was not the case in New France where seigneurial dues were governed by contract and could not be arbitrarily changed. As a result, the burdens of seigneurial dues were significantly less onerous than those that fell upon the French peasantry. Seigneurial power was further weakened in New France by the concessions needed to attract *censitaires* in a society in which land was widely available, labour scarce, and the lure of the fur trade ever present. Aware of the differences between Canada and the mother country, the French-Canadian farmer preferred to be known as an *habitant* rather than by the legal feudal title of *censitaire*. French-Canadian *habitants* frequently challenged the actions of government officials and their seigneurs. "There is no doubt," one official complained, that "the people of this country, neither docile nor easy to govern, are very difficult to constrain, for they like freedom and no domination at all."[4]

WOMEN AND THE FORMATION OF FAMILIES

Jean Talon actively recruited colonists for New France, promising land, farm animals, seeds, and implements, and some 1,500 settlers and indentured servants arrived during his tenure as intendant. Opposition from the French court, however, limited the number of colonists sent to Canada. "His Majesty cannot agree," Colbert admonished

---

4   Richard Colebrook Harris, *The Seigneurial System in Early Canada: A Geographical Survey* (Montreal and Kingston: McGill-Queen's University Press, 1984), 181.

Talon, "with the arguments you make on the means of making of Canada a great and mighty state....It would not be prudent to depopulate his Realm, which would be required in order to have Canada populated."[5] Nevertheless, Talon and Colbert cooperated in addressing another issue critical to the growth of the colony: the shortage of women. Some 1,200 marriageable young women known as *filles du roi*, or "daughters of the king," were recruited for New France. *Filles du roi* were to be in no way "disgraced by nature" or have anything "repulsive about their exterior person." They were to be "healthy and strong" and to have some "inclination to work with their hands."[6] As an incentive, the Crown provided substantial dowries to suitable women and paid for their transportation to New France. Most *filles du roi* were between the ages of 12 and 25 and came from Paris or other large urban centres. Many were recruited from the Hôpital Général in Paris, an institution that looked after the disadvantaged, including abandoned children, orphans, unwed mothers, tramps, prostitutes, and the insane. Other *filles du roi* were young women whose parents could not afford to arrange good marriages for their daughters. Taking advantage of the scarcity of single women in the colony, *filles du roi* often entered into several marriage contracts before finally settling upon a spouse and marrying in the church.

Determined to further family formation, Talon threatened to deprive bachelors of hunting, fishing, and trading privileges if they did not select a wife from among the newly arrived *filles du roi*. Fines were imposed upon fathers whose sons and daughters had not married by a suitable age. Bonuses were given to young men who married by the age of 20 and to fathers with 10 or more children. Despite these incentives, the population of New France had only grown to 7,832 by 1676. Family life in New France was governed by the *Coutume de Paris*, the French legal code of the period. According to the law, married women had a status inferior to that of their husbands. As heads of the household, husbands acted as overlords of all family property and had the right to exercise "reasonable correction" over their wives and children, including corporal punishment so long as it did not cause permanent injury or endanger life. Although the law upheld the authority of husbands and fathers, it also contained some important protections for women and children. Wives could seek legal separation from a brutal, insane, or profligate husband; husbands and fathers were obliged to provide support for wives and children; husbands could not alienate the property brought into the marriage by wives without permission; and widows were entitled to one-half of the family estate. Many noble women sought to protect themselves by insisting on written contracts before marriage.

---

5 Colbert to Talon, January 5, 1666, in *Rapport de l'Archiviste de la Province de Québec, 1922–1923* (Quebec: L.-Amable Proulx, 1923), 41.

6 Talon, quoted in *Canadian Women: A History*, 2nd ed. (Toronto: Harcourt Brace, 1996), 36.

Figure 3.2 A Canadian couple. Family formation was a priority for colonial officials.

Most women's lives revolved around the demands of family reproduction. The typical woman in New France gave birth to nine children, six of whom survived to adulthood, a better survival rate than in the mother country. Children remained legally dependent on their parents until reaching the age of majority, 25, and could not leave their father's house without his consent. Fathers had the right to approve the choice of a child's marriage partner before the age of majority and could exercise considerable control over their daughters beyond that age by threatening to withhold a dowry. Children owed their parents honour and respect, whatever their age, and were bound to care for them if they should be in want or become infirm. Viewed as an economic asset, children were put to work at an early age. Older children cared for younger children, girls helped in the household and the fields, and sons assisted their fathers. To help with family finances, children were often bound out to others as domestic servants, labourers, or apprentices. Women spent much of their time with the production of food: butchering, curing, and drying meat; caring for dairy cattle, swine, and poultry; tending vegetable gardens and orchards; and preserving food for the long winter months. Women frequently kept the household accounts and would often take charge of the household entirely when husbands left to participate in the fur trade or to serve in the militia. The vital contribution that women made to the family economy tempered the patriarchal order entrenched in the law. On a visit to New France in 1749, the Swedish botanist Peter Kalm observed that men did not undertake "matters of importance without their women's advice and approval."[7] While most women's lives focused on

7   A.B. Benson (ed.), *Peter Kalm's Travels in North America*, vol. 2 (New York: 1927).

their children and households, some women became merchants and entrepreneurs. One such woman was Marie-Anne Barbel. After her husband died, Barbel took over his business, founded a successful pottery, and invested her profits in real estate. Louise de Ramezay, the daughter of the governor of Montreal, chose to pursue a highly successful career in business rather than to marry. Over the years, Ramezay profitably managed a sawmill and a brick and tile factory, invested in a tannery and a flour mill, and acquired her own seigneurie.

DIVERSIFYING THE ECONOMY

The formation of families was an important step in the creation of a stable colonial society, but the long-term success of New France demanded a more diversified economy. "Our neighbours, the English," Pierre Boucher observed in 1664, "build numbers of ships, of all sorts and sizes; they work iron mines; they have beautiful cities; they have stage-coaches and mails from one to the other; they have carriages like those in France; those who laid out money there, are now getting good returns from it."[8] Jean Talon believed that the economic progress made in New England was possible in New France. As a first step, he sought to broaden the economy of New France from its dependence on furs and make the colony less reliant on imports from France. Following Talon's reforms of the seigneurial system, the number of acres under cultivation increased significantly. While wheat was the staple crop, Talon recognized the dangers of a one-crop economy and encouraged farmers to diversify their production by planting peas, beans, and crops such as hemp, flax, and hops that could be exported or used by new domestic industries to produce rope, cloth, and beer. Talon also encouraged the importation of livestock, and within a few years the colony had become self-sufficient in pork and leather. To provide a market for agricultural produce, Talon supported the establishment of a brewery, two tanneries, and a hat factory; encouraged the importation of looms for spinning; and secured the purchase of flax and hemp harvests to prove their commercial potential. "I now have the means," Talon enthusiastically wrote to the King in 1671, "to clothe myself from head to toe."[9] Unfortunately, mercantilist-minded French authorities showed little enthusiasm for Talon's efforts to produce crops and products that replaced French imports and which might someday compete with French producers in their own market.

Colbert was more supportive of Talon's efforts to develop a lumber industry. Timber from New France was essential to Colbert's plans to construct a French navy

---

8 Pierre Bourcher, *True and Genuine Description of New France Commonly Called Canada* (Paris: Florentine Lambert, 1664) trans. E.L. Montizambert (Montreal: 1883), 73–74.

9 Vachon, "Jean Talon," DCB, http://biographi.ca.

and merchant marine that could compete with the formidable English and Dutch fleets. Canadian timber was also in demand in the French plantation colonies of the West Indies, where it was used to produce barrels and casks to carry molasses and rum. Rather than simply export raw timber, Talon sought to create value-added industries, such as sawmilling and shipbuilding, and to produce important industrial products, such as potash and tar. Despite Talon's enthusiasm, all of these industries struggled, and while trade with the French West Indies increased, it never lived up to expectations. The lack of skilled labour and expertise, the shortage of capital, the small population, the distance from larger markets, and the isolation of the colony during the long winter months when the St. Lawrence froze precluded significant industrial development. While New France did not develop the self-supporting, diversified economic base Talon envisioned, the colony was undoubtedly stronger because of his efforts. "Since he has been here as intendant," Marie de l'Incarnation observed, "the country has developed and business has progressed more than they have done since the French have been here."[10]

THE FUR TRADE AND TERRITORIAL EXPANSION

Although Talon had dedicated considerable energy to creating a strong, cohesive, and self-supporting colony centred on the St. Lawrence, the future of New France remained inextricably tied to the fortunes of the fur trade, an industry confronted by new challenges. In 1664, the English seized control of the Dutch colony of New Netherland—which was renamed New York—took up trade with the Iroquois, and began to venture westward. Recognizing the threat that English control of the Hudson Valley represented to New France, Talon advised Colbert that the French must either launch an attack to take control of New York or invest in new fortifications on Lake Ontario and the Richelieu River to protect the fur trade and New France's southern frontier. Failure to act, Talon warned, would allow the English and their Iroquois allies to harass French traders travelling to and from the west, divert trade away from the colony, and leave the colony vulnerable to a two-pronged English attack: overland from the south and by sea up the St. Lawrence.

Matters became even worse when the English established a trading presence on Hudson Bay. Ironically, two French traders, Médard Chouart des Groseilliers and his brother-in-law, Pierre Radisson, played a leading role in this development. In the summer of 1660, Radisson and Groseilliers returned to Trois-Rivières from Lake

---

10 "Marie de l'Incarnation to her Son," 1668, in Joyce Marshall (ed.), *Word from New France: The Selected Letters of Marie de l'Incarnation* (Toronto: Oxford University Press, 1967), 345.

Superior with a brigade of 50 canoes full of particularly lustrous pelts that had been collected in the lands that lay south of Hudson Bay. Rather than being rewarded for their success, Radisson and Groseilliers were fined for unlicensed trading and their cargo confiscated. Infuriated by such treatment, Groseilliers travelled to France the following year and secured financing for a ship that would carry him to Hudson Bay, bypassing officials at Quebec.

When the ship failed to appear the following spring, Radisson and Groseilliers journeyed to Boston to seek English support for such a voyage. With the recent restoration of the monarchy following the English Civil War, the King's commissioner in Boston, Sir George Cartwright, was eager to secure colonial support for the new regime of Charles II by increasing opportunities for investment and trade and encour-

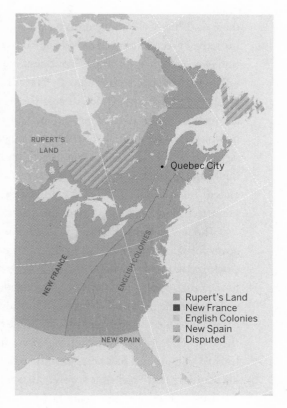

Map 3.1 Eastern North America, 1670.

aged them to travel to England. After a calamitous journey, Radisson and Groseilliers reached London in 1665, where they intrigued members of court with their accounts of the trading potential offered by the territory surrounding Hudson Bay. In 1670, Charles II granted a charter to the Company of Adventurers trading into Hudson Bay. The Hudson's Bay Company, as it soon became known, was given monopoly rights over all the territory that drained into Hudson Bay.

Disturbed by these developments, Talon acted to assert French claims to the interior of the continent and to form alliances with Natives to the north and west before they were drawn into the English sphere. In 1671, Talon directed Simon Daumont de Saint-Lusson to summon Indigenous leaders to the Jesuit mission at Sault Ste. Marie. There he proclaimed French sovereignty over all the territory stretching from Hudson Bay to the north, the Gulf of Mexico to the south, and the Pacific to the west. Talon encouraged fur trader Louis Jolliet and Jesuit priest Jacques Marquette to begin preparations to explore the Mississippi River in hopes of finding a route to the Pacific, demonstrating French possession of the interior of the continent, and securing the friendship of the Indigenous peoples. Talon's expansionist efforts and diplomatic initiatives greatly annoyed Governor Courcelle who, quite correctly, claimed jurisdiction over such matters. The achievement of peace with the Iroquois and the good relations New France enjoyed with its traditional Indigenous allies were largely due to Courcelle's efforts, and Talon's expansionism potentially threatened these hard-won accomplishments. As relations with the governor soured, Talon let it be known that he would rather be recalled to France than continue to serve under Courcelle. Talon departed New France in November 1672 and Courcelle left shortly afterwards, suffering from ill health. With their departures, an important era in the life of New France ended. Talon and Courcelle left behind a colony that was certainly more secure, better populated, and much larger than the one they had inherited.

The King delayed naming Talon's successor, but quickly replaced Courcelle as governor with Louis de Buade, the Comte de Frontenac. Frontenac was of old noble stock and had served with the French army during the Thirty Years' War and risen to the rank of colonel. After being wounded, Frontenac took up residence at the royal court where he lived and entertained lavishly and soon found himself mired in debt. Marriage to the beautiful and wealthy Anne de La Grange-Trianon offered Frontenac the appealing prospect of repairing his damaged fortunes, but when her father learned that the two had been secretly wed, he cut off her inheritance. It was to avoid his creditors that Frontenac secured his appointment as Governor of New France.

In the absence of an intendant, and accustomed from his military experience to exercising unquestioned authority, Frontenac assumed total control over the colony; he quickly alienated other members of the Sovereign Council who resented his imperious style. Intent on profiting from his position, Frontenac took an immediate interest in the fur trade and ordered the construction of a fort at the head of Lake Ontario to control access to the interior. To the consternation of Montreal merchants, he decreed that *coureurs des bois* discovered trading without a licence be publicly flogged, and that anyone doing business with them be fined and their goods confiscated. In the spring of 1673, Frontenac granted licences to a like-minded opportunist, Robert Cavalier de La Salle, to establish new trading posts at Niagara and Michilimackinac. La Salle launched the first ship on the upper Great Lakes, *Le Griffon*, to carry furs and trading goods between the newly established forts.

Fixated with extending the fur trade to the west and south, Frontenac ignored the growing English presence in the north. In 1673, the Hudson's Bay Company established Moose Factory at the southern end of James Bay, and Forts Albany and Severn a few years later. With the establishment of these trading posts, the Hudson's Bay Company began to lure away some of France's traditional Indigenous trading partners. The extension of the fur trade aggravated relations with the Iroquois, who resented the growing

French influence among the tribes south of the Great Lakes. Committed to regaining control of the fur trade for themselves and their English allies, the Iroquois began harassing French traders and attacking tribes allied to the French.

Besieged with complaints about the self-serving governor, Colbert finally filled the vacant position of intendant in 1675 with Jacques Duchesneau, an experienced civil servant. When he arrived in New France, Duchesneau bore orders from Colbert to reorganize the Sovereign Council. To curb the governor's power and ensure its independence, the Council was now to be chaired by the intendant, and all its members were to be appointed by the King rather than the governor. Incensed by this perceived assault upon the dignity of his office, Frontenac immediately found himself at odds with the new intendant and did not hesitate to resort to bully tactics to confront his critics. Frontenac's single-minded focus upon the extension of the fur trade increasingly frustrated intendant Duchesneau. In a colony with fewer than 10,000 residents, Duchesneau complained there were as many as 800 *coureurs des bois* who participated in the fur trade, men who were neglecting their farms and families and living, he was convinced, licentious and disorderly lives. Determined to reduce the number of *coureurs des bois* and to entice them back to a more settled life, Duchesneau promulgated new regulations governing the fur trade in 1681. The regulations soon became a source of conflict and recrimination between the intendant and the governor. At one point, Frontenac even ordered the arrest of Duchesneau's son. Fed up with this unseemly quarrel, Louis xiv relieved both men of their duties and recalled them to France in 1682. They left their successors a far-flung, thinly populated colony deeply divided between rival fur-trading interests, threatened by the resumption of Iroquois hostilities, and increasingly vulnerable to growing English competition on Hudson Bay.

CANADA IN AN AGE OF IMPERIAL CONFLICT

Between 1689 and 1749, New France found itself in a virtual state of siege as a series of European conflicts crossed the Atlantic and pitted North American colonies and Native peoples against each other. The troubles began in 1688 when England's Glorious Revolution deposed the Catholic James ii and put William of Orange and his wife Mary on the throne. As Stadtholder of the Netherlands, William of Orange, a devout Protestant, had fought a running conflict against the expansionist ambitions of the Catholic King of France. Under William, England took the lead in forming the League of Augsburg with Spain, the Netherlands, and the German Protestant princes against Louis xiv, who had offered James ii refuge and supported his claim to the British Crown. Fighting broke out in 1689, and the War of the League of Augsburg soon spread to North America, where it was known as King William's War.

For New France, the first inkling that war had broken out came on the early morning of August 5, 1689. Some 1,500 Iroquois warriors, with the encouragement of their English allies, launched a devastating surprise assault on the French settlement at Lachine, burning most of the houses, killing 24 *habitants*, and taking at least 70 more prisoner. Unaware that war had been declared or the size of the Iroquois force, the governor, Jacques-René de Brisay de Denonville, dispatched a small band of Canadian militia to the area. The Canadians enjoyed a small measure of revenge a few days later when they ambushed an Iroquois war party at Lac des Deux Montagnes, killing 18 and taking 3 prisoners without suffering any casualties. The Iroquois prisoners were burned alive when news reached Montreal that some of the captives taken at Lachine had succumbed to the same fate. An experienced military officer, Denonville was well aware of the vulnerability of New France. Without reinforcements, however, he could do little except encourage France's Indigenous allies to embark on the same kind of guerrilla campaign against English settlements that the Iroquois used to terrorize New France. While tribes to the west were too preoccupied with the Iroquois to respond, the Abenaki to the east did begin to torment frontier settlements in northern New England. In October, ships arrived from France with news that Denonville had been recalled to France, where his military knowledge was deemed more valuable, and carrying his replacement, the irascible Comte de Frontenac.

Although North American events were very much a sideshow to greater battles in Europe, the war did have significant consequences for New France. When Frontenac returned to New France, he found a colony that was virtually defenceless and a population demoralized by the Iroquois' relentless raids. Convinced that something needed to be done to revive morale, restore the confidence of New France's Indigenous allies, and deter the English from inciting the Iroquois, Frontenac mustered raiding parties of Canadian militia and Natives to attack English border settlements. Adopting the tactics of the Iroquois, the raiding parties descended upon the unsuspecting settlements, ruthlessly killing settlers, destroying homes, and taking prisoners. This campaign of terror succeeded in uniting the English colonies in their determination to strike a decisive blow against New France. A two-pronged attack was planned for later that year, with a large land force of English colonial militia and Iroquois striking Montreal, and a naval force taking Quebec. The English were forced to abandon the assault on Montreal, due to a smallpox epidemic that swept through the ranks of the colonial militia, allowing Frontenac to concentrate his forces at Quebec and reinforce its defences.

Preparations for the English naval assault upon Quebec were entrusted to Bostonian Sir William Phips, who successfully captured the Acadian capital of Port Royal in May of 1690. Later that summer, Phips sailed from Boston with a fleet of 32 small vessels and a force of 2,000 Massachusetts militiamen. Progress up the

St. Lawrence was slow, and the force did not reach Quebec until October 16. Phips immediately sent word to Frontenac that he had an hour to surrender. Frontenac famously replied that he would make no answer but "from the mouths of my cannon and muskets." Phips attempted a landing at the mouth of the St. Charles River, but the English forces were easily repulsed. True to his word, Frontenac's cannons bombarded Phips's armada, inflicting serious damage. Fearing that with winter approaching his ships might be caught in the ice, Phips retreated after an eight-day siege. The huge debt incurred by the expedition, the discontent that emerged among unpaid soldiers and sailors, and the loss of life to smallpox among the invading force ensured that no further attempts were made by the English colonists to launch a full-fledged invasion of Canada for the duration of the war.

Having successfully defended Quebec from Phips's attack, Frontenac resumed the guerrilla campaign against the English colonists and directed the establishment of new forts in the west. Westward expansion provoked the Ottawa. Determined to maintain their position as middlemen in the fur trade, the Ottawa entered into peace negotiations with the Iroquois. Fearing the consequences of these developments for the future of the fur trade, Frontenac initiated his own peace talks with the Iroquois against the advice of the governor of Montreal, Louis-Hector de Callière, who suspected Iroquois trickery. Callière's warning proved to be true, and the Iroquois broke off negotiations with Frontenac as soon as their alliance with the Ottawa was secured. With the survival of New France in the balance, Frontenac assembled an army of more than 2,000 regular troops, militia, and Native allies in July 1696 to strike directly at the heart of Iroquois country. Weakened by disease and years of warfare, the Iroquois retreated as the French forces advanced. When the Ottawa learned of the French offensive, they turned against the Iroquois. With the tables turned, the Iroquois now petitioned Frontenac for peace. As these shifting alliances demonstrate, Native peoples pursued their own interests and agendas in the wars of empire that beset the continent.

The war in North America was not limited to the Great Lakes–St. Lawrence region; significant battles also took place to the north on Hudson Bay and in Newfoundland. The leading figure in these events was Pierre Le Moyne d'Iberville. Born in Montreal, d'Iberville was the son of a wealthy seigneur and a partner in the Compagnie du Nord. In 1686, he led an expedition that successfully took several Hudson's Bay Company posts. After taking part in the 1690 raid on Schenectady, d'Iberville sailed to Hudson Bay, determined to capture the Hudson's Bay Company's headquarters at York Factory. With only three ships and limited men and arms, d'Iberville was not able to overtake the well-defended post. Trying again in 1694, he succeeded in capturing York Factory, but his triumph proved temporary; the English retook York Factory in 1696.

That same year, d'Iberville launched a concerted campaign to dislodge the English from Newfoundland and take control of the lucrative cod fishery. After burning St. John's, d'Iberville's men pillaged the surrounding communities. Some 36 settlements were destroyed, 200 people killed, another 700 taken prisoner, and 9 million kilograms of dried cod seized in the raids. Before the English were routed completely, however, d'Iberville was ordered to return to Hudson Bay where, after a pitched naval battle, he once again took York Factory. D'Iberville's victories in Newfoundland and Hudson Bay proved to be in vain. Shortly after his departure for Hudson Bay, an English flotilla under the command of Sir John Gibsone and Sir John Norris sailed into St. John's harbour, landed 2,000 troops, and persuaded the fishers, terrorized by the French, to return and rebuild their villages. Just a week after d'Iberville departed Hudson Bay in 1697, the Treaty of Ryswick ended the war, and what had been won in battle was subsequently lost at the treaty table: York Factory and Newfoundland were returned to the English, and France regained possession of Acadia.

Undeterred by this reversal, d'Iberville sailed for France, where he convinced the Minister of Marine to place him in charge of an expedition to establish a French colony at the mouth of the Mississippi. "If France does not seize this most beautiful part of America and set up a colony," he argued, the English "will be strong enough to take over all of America and chase away all other nations." His argument found a receptive audience in the court of Louis XIV. An expansionist policy in North America would confine the English to the Atlantic seaboard, east of the Appalachian Mountains. Travelling by sea, d'Iberville landed on Biloxi Bay, erected a garrison, and proclaimed the new colony of Louisiana in 1699. France's inland empire now stretched from the St. Lawrence to the Gulf of Mexico.

While the Treaty of Ryswick restored imperial possessions in North America to their prewar state, the war had a number of long-term effects. During the conflict, the French mastered a new style of warfare. Traditional European methods, which relied on the deployment of large numbers of infantry, cavalry, and field artillery, were impractical in the North American wilderness. Inspired by Indigenous tactics, French commanders successfully adopted *petite guerre*—or guerrilla—warfare methods, moving forces quickly in small groups, approaching the enemy without being seen, mounting surprise attacks, and then disappearing immediately. Such methods enabled the French to maintain a vast North American empire, despite having a much smaller population and fewer resources than the English colonies.

Growing French strength and military prowess, and a weakening of their own position, also led the Iroquois to re-evaluate their strategy and diplomatic goals. Prolonged conflict and disease had taken a toll on the Iroquois, who were largely forsaken by their English allies as soon as the war with France had ended. Recognizing an opportunity to open peace negotiations, the new governor of New France, Louis-Hector de Callière, invited 1,300 representatives from the Iroquois and 39 other First Nations from the Great Lakes, Acadia, and the Mississippi to a grand council at Montreal in August 1701. After prolonged discussions that adhered closely to Native customs and traditions, all parties agreed to a landmark treaty that ended nearly a century of conflict. According to the terms of the treaty, all prisoners taken captive in previous conflicts were to be returned, and the peace and security of all signatories protected. New France agreed to recognize Indigenous sovereignty and to act as a mediator whenever disputes erupted between Indigenous signatories. For their part, the Iroquois promised to remain neutral in any future conflict between the French and the English. The Great Peace of Montreal, as it became known, enabled New France to expand its commercial and military presence in the interior and to establish new posts such as Detroit, founded in 1701 by Antoine de la Mothe Cadillac. The terms of the peace also benefited the Iroquois, whose neutrality and strategic position allowed them to pursue their own interests in the fur trade and profit from the competition between European rivals.

It was not long before the Great Peace of Montreal was tested. Dynastic struggles once again led to war in Europe. In 1700, the last of the Spanish Habsburgs, Charles II, died without heirs. Spain's crown passed to Philip of Anjou, the grandson of France's Louis XIV. A Bourbon power bloc uniting France and Spain raised the spectre of a profound upheaval in Europe's balance of power. Further provocations were added when Britain's exiled king, James II, died in 1701. When Louis XIV recognized his son, James Edward, as Britain's legitimate monarch, William III organized a new coalition to oppose French ambitions. When William died early in 1702, his sister-in-law and successor, Queen Anne, continued the fight, which is known as Queen Anne's War in North America.

The war in Europe proved a costly one for France, and few resources could be spared for the colonies. Fortunately for New France, New Yorkers were weary of war and the Iroquois adhered to the Great Peace of Montreal, remaining neutral through-out most of the war. With the St. Lawrence heartland secure, most of the fighting took place in the Atlantic colonies. The governor of New France, Philippe de Rigaud de Vaudreuil, invited the Iroquois and Abenaki to join the militia in a series of border raids against New England. Although this "little war" was not of much strategic value, it enabled Vaudreuil to keep the Abenaki and the Iroquois engaged against the English.

Of even greater consequence, the raids as well as the actions of French privateers based at Port-Royal fed a growing conviction among English colonists that the French presence in North America must be destroyed if New England were to survive. In the spring of 1704, a small force of colonial militia sailed north from Boston with hopes of taking the Acadian capital of Port-Royal. Although the New Englanders burnt the small settlement of Grand-Pré and took a number of prisoners, they failed to take their key objective. A second attempt on Port-Royal in 1707 by a larger force was also repulsed, thanks to the quick thinking and deceptive tactics of Acadia's governor, Daniel d'Auger de Subercase, who skillfully deployed the few settlers and Mi'kmaq allies at hand to harass the English colonists as they attempted to land advance parties. Convinced that they faced a large number of settlers, and fearful of being taken prisoner by the Natives, the New Englanders retreated, but not before burning homes and killing livestock. With two failed attempts behind them, the New England governors appealed to England for reinforcements to launch a full-scale invasion. English preoccupation with the war in Europe delayed assistance until 1710. In that year, Colonel Francis Nicholson led a naval force of almost 2,000 and finally succeeded in capturing Port-Royal, which he renamed Annapolis Royal, in honour of the Queen.

With the conquest of Acadia, New Englanders were determined to take Quebec itself. On July 30, 1711, an armada of 69 ships carrying 7,500 soldiers and 4,500 sailors sailed north from Boston under the command of Sir Hovenden Walker. At the same time, Nicholson proceeded to Albany to take charge of a colonial militia force of nearly 2,300 men that was to invade Canada from the south, diverting French forces from Quebec. Unfavourable winds and heavy fog threw the convoy into confusion. When eight transport vessels carrying hundreds of soldiers struck a reef off Anticosti Island in the Gulf of St. Lawrence, Walker abandoned the mission and sailed back to England. Nicholson was preparing to move up Lake Champlain toward Montreal when he received news of the British fleet's misfortune. With his men already suffering from fatigue, disease, and shortages of supplies, he had little choice but to disband his army and send the men home. Spared once more, New France erupted in jubilation. The celebrations were tempered in 1712 by news that some Iroquois had resumed their campaign against New France, and that warfare had broken out among the nations of the west.

Trouble had been brewing in the west for some time. With an oversupply of furs flooding into French markets, metropolitan authorities insisted that stringent measures be taken to restrict the fur trade. As a result, some trading licences were not renewed, the sale of brandy was prohibited, and the military was withdrawn from Niagara and Detroit. These measures effectively undercut the fur trade in the west and threatened to destroy New France's alliances with the region's Indigenous peoples. Emboldened by the demilitarization of Niagara and Detroit and prodded by the English, western Iroquois wavered in their commitment to the Great Peace of Montreal. To make matters worse, tensions developed among the Huron, Ottawa, and Miami, who had been encouraged to settle close to Detroit. In the absence of a garrison and with little trading taking place, there was little to prevent these traditional rivals from falling into open warfare.

The War of Spanish Succession ended in 1713 with Louis XIV's vision of continental mastery soundly defeated in Europe. Although the scale and scope of combat in

North America had been limited, the terms of the peace set out in the Treaty of Utrecht had significant consequences for France's North American empire. The treaty confirmed England's possession of Newfoundland, Acadia, and all of the lands that drained into Hudson Bay. France retained Île Royale (Cape Breton), Île St. Jean (Prince Edward Island), the St. Lawrence heartland, and much of the interior of the continent stretching from the Great Lakes to Louisiana on the Gulf of Mexico.

Although all was not lost, Governor Vaudreuil recognized that strong measures needed to be taken if France was to keep what remained of its North American empire. In a report to the Minister of Marine, Vaudreuil advised French authorities that the only way to deter future aggression was to increase the population and the number of regular troops permanently stationed in New

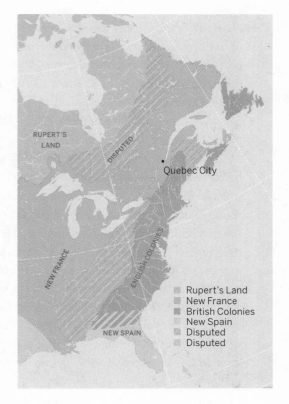

Map 3.2 Eastern North America, 1713.

France. To maintain the allegiance of its Indigenous allies and to keep them from trading with the English, Vaudreuil urged officials to reinstate the brandy trade and establish new posts in the west. With the loss of Acadia, Vaudreuil warned that it was essential to protect both land and sea approaches to the St. Lawrence by fostering the continued friendship of the Abenaki and establishing a major fortification on Île Royale to guard the entry to the Gulf of St. Lawrence and ensure French access to the lucrative fishery. Vaudreuil's program set the direction for French policy until the outbreak of the next major conflict in Europe. Additional forces were stationed in New France, while new forts were built on Lake Ontario to intercept trade before it reached the English traders at Albany and to assert French control over the region. Despite the efforts of New Englanders to lure them away, good relations were maintained with the Abenaki. And, in 1720, construction began on a massive fortress, Louisbourg, on Île Royale.

Since the Treaty of Utrecht had recognized the claims of the Hudson's Bay Company, the French fur trade had to find a way to deal with the problem of British competition. Attracted by the range, quality, and price of trade goods that the

Hudson's Bay Company was able to bring in each season by sea, increasing numbers of Indigenous traders began to divert their furs away from the French to the English posts on the Bay. Convinced that the only way to reverse this development was to reach the Natives first, the French traders began to push for a major advance of the fur trade beyond the Upper Great Lakes. With the permission of New France's new governor, Charles de Beauharnois, Pierre Gaultier de La Vérendrye set out for the west on an exploratory expedition in 1731.

Born in Trois-Rivières, La Vérendrye was the youngest of 13 children. His father had been a seigneur and governor of Trois-Rivières, but left the family destitute when he died four years after Pierre was born. La Vérendrye enlisted in the army as a young man and served in Europe during the War of the Spanish Succession, where he suffered both gunshot and sabre wounds. He returned to New France in 1712, married the daughter of a large landowner, and began farming. After a few years of trying to support his growing family by working the land, La Vérendrye abandoned his farm and entered the fur trade. His brother commanded the *poste du Nord*, headquartered at what is now Thunder Bay, which oversaw a large area north of Lake Superior, and La Vérendrye made up his mind to join him there. While he was stationed in the west, La Vérendrye became convinced that exploration of the region would lead to the discovery of a western sea flowing into the Pacific Ocean, thus enabling the French to outflank the English on Hudson Bay.

In the summer of 1731, La Vérendrye travelled beyond Lake Superior and established a chain of new posts as far west as Portage la Prairie. Ideally located to intercept Indigenous traders on their way to Hudson Bay, these far western posts soon produced half of all the furs delivered to Montreal. The Minister of Marine, the Comte de Maurepas, was not impressed, however, and accused La Vérendrye of seeking not the western sea, but the "beaver sea." Determined to restore his reputation, La Vérendrye continued what proved to be a futile search until his death in 1749.

With the signing of the Treaty of Utrecht, England controlled Acadia, which was once more known as Nova Scotia. Under the terms of the peace, the Acadians were given the choice of relocating to French territory or staying put, keeping their property and practising their Catholic faith so long as they pledged their allegiance to the British Crown. Despite the urging of French officials and missionaries to move to Île Royale, most Acadians chose to remain in Nova Scotia. Isolated from Quebec and long ignored by Versailles, the Acadians were an independent people who had established a good life for themselves. They had converted thousands of hectares of salt-soaked tidal meadow into fertile farmland protected by dikes, perfected new fishing techniques that took advantage of the Bay of Fundy's great tides to harvest the sea, and carried on a profitable trade with the local Natives and their neighbours in New England.

While British officials hoped that the Acadians would soon be outnumbered by an influx of English-speaking Protestants, no great flood of settlers arrived to transform the nature of the colony. As a result, Nova Scotia remained, as historian Barry Moody puts it, "precariously positioned at the very edge of the British empire in North America." None of the early administrators of Nova Scotia convinced the Acadians to take the oath. Each time an attempt was made to administer the oath, they objected that they had not been required to do so the last time England occupied the region. Long a pawn in the struggle between England and France, Acadians reasoned that the present situation might well prove temporary. With only a small garrison at their disposal, the early administrators of Nova Scotia did not dare to press the matter. Oath or no oath, the British Crown's agents in Nova Scotia recognized the Acadians' value. Not only did the Acadians supply food and labour for the garrison at Annapolis Royal, they provided an important buffer from the Mi'kmaq, who remained hostile to the British.

Britain showed little interest in Nova Scotia until the appointment of Richard Philipps as governor in 1717. Concerns about the growth of the French settlement on Île Royale and the mismanagement of the small garrison at Annapolis Royal prompted the British government to pay more attention to Nova Scotia's affairs. When Philipps arrived in the colony in 1720, he was determined to administer the oath of allegiance. When a delegation of 150 Acadians, led by Father Justinien Durand, protested, Philipps ordered that anyone who had not taken the oath within the next four months would have to leave the colony. Such bravado did not impress the Acadians, who knew that Philipps had few resources at his disposal to enforce his edict. The deadline passed, and all Philipps could do was appeal to Britain for more troops to enforce his authority. When he informed the home government that the Acadians would neither swear the oath nor leave, he was advised that, as they "will never become good subjects of His Majesty," they should be "removed" as soon as circumstances permitted.

A more pressing problem, however, demanded the governor's attention. Because the Mi'kmaq had been allied with the French, British authorities assumed that they too were a defeated people and required to swear an oath of loyalty as subjects of the Crown. The Mi'kmaq refused, insisting that the British were unwelcome intruders and that they were a sovereign people. In August 1720, Mi'kmaq warriors began harassing New England fishers on the disputed waters that separated mainland Nova Scotia from Île Royale. The Mi'kmaq resented this trespass upon their traditional fishing grounds, and were supported in this action by the French at Louisbourg, who feared the presence of English ships so close to their remaining colony on the Atlantic. Determined to protect the New England fishing fleet, defend Nova Scotia's frontiers, and keep watch on French activities on Île Royale, Philipps dispatched Major Lawrence Armstrong to build a fort at Canso and to begin negotiations with the Mi'kmaq. When diplomacy failed to put a stop to the attacks, Philipps sent orders to eradicate the Mi'kmaq from the area. Although the campaign succeeded in removing the immediate threat, it intensified Mi'kmaq enmity toward the English. Philipps departed for England in the fall of 1722 to persuade authorities of the impossibility of holding on to Nova Scotia without additional troops, new fortifications, and a large number of Protestant settlers, leaving Armstrong to manage Nova Scotia's affairs as best he could.

Convinced that Catholic missionaries and French agents had been dispatched from Louisbourg to stir up distrust and hostility toward the English among the Acadians and Mi'kmaq, Armstrong attempted to administer the oath to the Acadians once again in 1725. The Acadians insisted that any oath exempt them from bearing arms. Armstrong maintained that no such provision was necessary, since British law prohibited Roman Catholics from serving in the army. The Acadians persisted and, after much discussion, Armstrong agreed to write a note in the margin of the oath. The note had no official standing, but left the Acadians with the impression that they were entitled to remain neutral during times of war. Convinced that they had won an important concession, the Acadians rebuffed Armstrong's subsequent attempts to administer a more unqualified oath. Richard Philipps returned to Nova Scotia in 1729 resolved to administer the oath. The governor verbally promised the Acadians that they would be exempt from having to bear arms against the French or their Indigenous allies and appended a note to this effect to the document signed by each individual. Philipps reported triumphantly to the British government that over 4,000 Acadians had taken the oath but neglected to mention his verbal assurance that the Acadians would never be called upon to take up arms.

When the Habsburg Holy Roman Emperor and Archduke of Austria, Charles VI, died in 1740 without a male heir, a dispute erupted over the succession to the Austrian throne. Once again France and Britain were drawn into a European war in 1744 on opposing sides. As in earlier conflicts, the War of Austrian Succession soon spread to North America where it was known as King George's War. In May 1744, the governor of Louisbourg, Jean-Baptiste-Louis Le Prévost Duquesnel, directed French privateers to harass New England shipping and ordered an attack on the English fort at Canso. The fort fell easily, and Duquesnel decided to strike at the provincial capital, Annapolis Royal. An advance party of Mi'kmaq, led by the missionary priest Jean-Louis Le Loutre, laid siege to the garrison in anticipation of the arrival of a force of regular soldiers from Louisbourg and a squadron of ships from France. When the promised ships did not appear, the disgruntled Mi'kmaq departed.

Undeterred, Duquesnel dispatched a small force of troops from Louisbourg under the command of François Dupont Duvivier, a native Acadian and the great-grandson of Charles de La Tour, to take Annapolis Royal. Duvivier expected to be greeted as a liberator by his fellow Acadians. Despite urgent emotional appeals and repeated threats that they would be punished for their refusal to stand against the English, very few Acadians joined the march on Annapolis Royal. Undeterred, Duvivier pressed ahead and attacked Annapolis Royal early in September. Lacking reinforcements and with winter fast approaching, Duvivier abandoned the fight and returned to Louisbourg after a four-week siege.

The attacks of French privateers, the fall of Canso, and the siege of Annapolis Royal re-ignited old animosities in New England, where anxiety about the construction of the formidable fortress at Louisbourg had reached a fever pitch. Convinced that the future of New England was at stake, Governor William Shirley of Massachusetts commissioned prominent fish and lumber merchant William Pepperrell to organize a massive assault against Louisbourg. In late March 1745, British warships under the command of Commodore Peter Warren blockaded the harbour. A few weeks later, colonial transports brought, unopposed, an army of nearly 4,300 New England militia and 800 Royal Marines eight kilometres to the west of the fortress. Pepperrell proceeded overland and set up siege batteries on a low range of hills overlooking Louisbourg. Despite its formidable seaward defences, the fortress was vulnerable to a land attack from the rear.

To make matters worse, Governor Duquesnel died suddenly, leaving command of the fortress in the hands of Louis Du Pont Duchambon de Vergor, a career officer who lacked battle experience and inspired little confidence among the already discontented and demoralized men of the garrison. After seven weeks of bombardment, the French forces capitulated. The humiliating loss of Louisbourg constituted a major blow to French fortunes in North America, and preparations were immediately begun to assemble a large naval force to recapture the fortress. France's bid to regain Louisbourg and Acadia was entrusted to the well-connected but relatively inexperienced Jean-Baptiste Louis Frédéric de La Rochefoucauld de Roye, the duc d'Anville. The duc d'Anville set out from France in June with an armada of 56 ships and 7,000 men.

The expedition was plagued from the start. Unfavourable winds delayed the fleet's progress, and on September 13 a gale scattered the ships within sight of Acadia. Two weeks later the duc d'Anville was seized by a sudden attack of apoplexy and died; tormented by inner demons, his second in command, Constantin-Louis d'Estourmel, attempted suicide. Not surprisingly, when the third in command, the Marquis de la Jonquière, took control of the battered fleet, he abandoned the ill-fated mission. Buoyed by their success at Louisbourg, New Englanders schemed to capture Quebec and seal France's fate in North America once and for all, but nothing came of these plans. Preoccupied by Jacobite attempts to depose George II and place Charles Edward Stuart (Bonnie Prince Charlie) upon the British throne, England found that it could spare neither the ships nor troops needed for the planned conquest of Quebec.

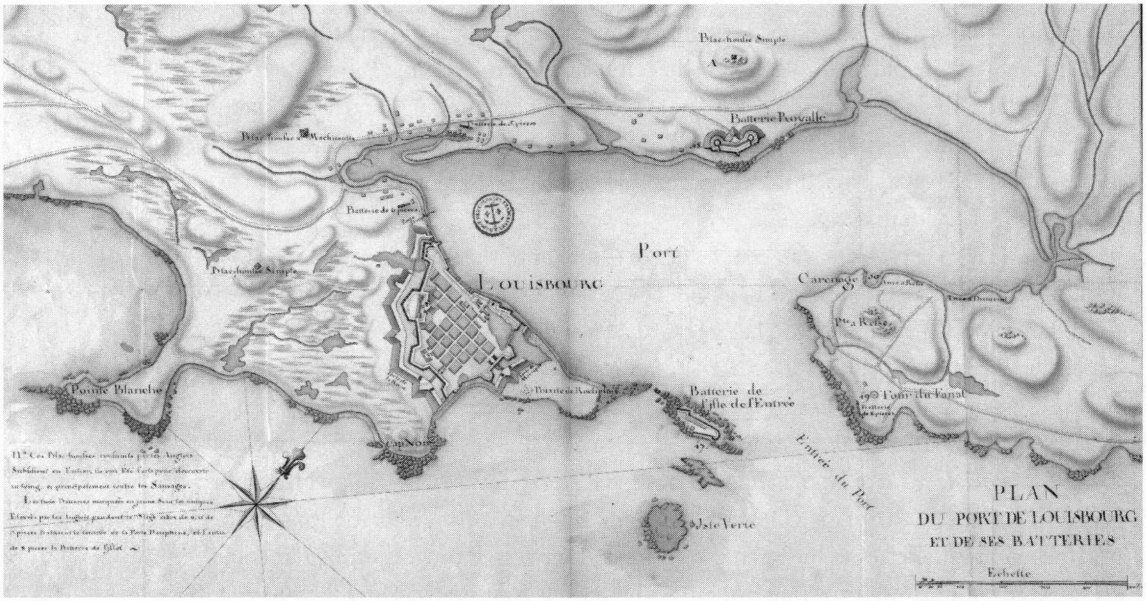

Map 3.3 Map of Louisbourg and its artillery batteries. Despite its formidable defences, Louisbourg fell to the English in 1745 and again in 1758.

Although the governor of New France, the Marquis de Beauharnois, had concerns about the rumoured invasion of Quebec, he dispatched a force of 680 Canadian militia and more than 1,000 Indigenous warriors to Acadia to join the duc d'Anville's planned offensive. When the ill-fated fleet departed, the Canadians remained in Acadia under the command of Jean-Baptiste de Ramezay.[11] After an unsuccessful siege of Annapolis Royal, Ramezay withdrew to Beaubassin on the strategic Chignecto isthmus. The presence of this large force on Nova Scotia's frontiers alarmed Governor Shirley of Massachusetts, who feared that Ramezay might rouse the Acadians and the Mi'kmaq against the English. When London failed to strengthen the British garrison in Nova Scotia, Shirley took the initiative and, in December 1746, dispatched Lieutenant-Colonel Arthur Noble and a regiment of 500 New England militiamen to occupy Grand-Pré, defeat Ramezay and deter the Acadians from supporting the Canadians. Unable to construct a garrison, Noble's forces billeted among the local population. Only a few skirmishes disturbed the peace until events took a dramatic turn on February 12, 1747. Around three in the morning, amidst a raging snowstorm, the Canadians fell upon Noble's unsuspecting forces, who quickly surrendered. Outraged New Englanders portrayed the attack as a massacre and claimed that

---

11 Barry Moody, "Making a British Nova Scotia," in *The "Conquest" of Acadia, 1710: Imperial, Colonial, and Aboriginal Constructions* (Toronto: University of Toronto Press, 2004), 128.

the traitorous Acadians were complicit. The Acadians, in fact, had alerted Noble that an assault was imminent, but refusing to believe the Canadians would attempt such a raid at the height of winter, he ignored their warnings. Far from being massacred in their beds, most of the New Englanders were permitted to withdraw to Annapolis Royal. The events at Grand-Pré nonetheless confirmed the conviction in New England that the "neutral French" were a treacherous menace that must be removed.

The War of the Austrian Succession formally ended with the Treaty of Aix-la-Chapelle in 1748. With no party victorious, gains made during the war were reversed by the treaty. France regained Louisbourg, much to the dismay of New England. Determined to counter the power of Louisbourg, the British established a fortified town and naval base of their own. On June 21, 1749, some 2,500 settlers and disbanded soldiers, led by Edward Cornwallis, landed on Chebucto Bay to found Halifax. With its protected harbour, Halifax was favourably located to defend New England shipping and, far removed from the main areas of Acadian settlement, was not dependent on "the neutral French" for supplies. The founding of Halifax and the appointment of Cornwallis as governor marked an end to England's long neglect of Nova Scotia. Resolved to increase the loyal population within the colony, Cornwallis recruited over 2,500 English and German Protestant colonists.

The founding of Halifax and the arrival of new settlers alarmed the Mi'kmaq. A Mi'kmaq chief protested:

> The ground where you stand, where you build your houses, where you build a fort, where you wish to enthrone yourself, this land of which you wish to make yourselves absolute masters, this same land belongs to me. I have grown up on it like the grass, and it is the very place of my birth and my residence. It is my land....But at the present time you force me to speak out because of the considerable theft you inflict upon me.[12]

Determined to halt encroachments upon their traditional homelands, the Mi'kmaq launched a new campaign of frontier warfare against the English. Cornwallis responded by issuing a bounty of 10 guineas for every Mi'kmaq scalp. The establishment of Halifax also disturbed the acting governor of New France, Roland-Michel de La Galissonière. In an attempt to consolidate French strength, La Galissonière appealed to the Acadians to relocate to Île Royale. When few left their farms, La Galissonière dispatched missionaries such as Abbé Jean-Louis le Loutre to the

---

12 As quoted by Abbé Maillard to Abbé Du Fau, October 18, 1749, Letter P, No. 66, Archives du Séminaire de Québec.

disputed territory north of the Bay of Fundy to remind the Acadians of their French heritage and Catholic religion. Cornwallis offered a reward of £50 for the capture, dead or alive, of that "good for nothing scoundrel" Abbé le Loutre. Growing suspicion and the construction of rival forts on the disputed frontier that separated Nova Scotia and New France threatened to overtake the Acadians and bode ill for the future.

CONCLUSION

The New France of the mid-eighteenth century was different from the beleaguered company colony taken under Crown control in 1663. By 1750, the population had grown to more than 50,000. Most of the inhabitants lived in the countryside, farmed the land, and enjoyed comfortable lives. Despite official intentions to reproduce the rigid social hierarchy of France, Canadians enjoyed a degree of social mobility and independence unheard of in the mother country. Although the fur trade continued to dominate the economy, agriculture had grown in importance, and New France now produced enough food to supply its needs and to export surplus crops to the French colonies in the West Indies. Nearly a quarter of the population lived in the principal towns—Quebec, Montreal, and Trois-Rivières. With a population of over 5,000, Quebec had emerged as a vibrant administrative, commercial, religious, and military centre. As the centre of the fur trade, Montreal had become a town of shops and ware-houses, merchants and voyageurs. New France's first highway, the King's Road, linked Montreal and Quebec, and a string of forts and trading posts stretched from the St. Lawrence to the Gulf of Mexico. Peter Kalm was impressed by the character of the Canadians. "Anyone who considers how alive, joyous, courageous, inured to fatigue the Canadiens are," Kalm concluded, "must equally foresee that Canada will, in the near future, become a very powerful country and the Rome of the English provinces."[13]

Impressive as these developments seemed, New France was not to enjoy the future Peter Kalm predicted. With over a million people, the English colonies to the south needed room to expand. The conflicts of the previous half century had begun to unite the English colonists and steeled their resolve to force a final showdown with the French for control of the continent. New France had been successful in expanding and defending its domain, but for how long could this continue, given the colony's thin defences, dependence on Indigenous allies, reliance on a civilian militia, and vulnerable supply routes? Would the tactics of frontier guerrilla warfare and the network of alliances that had effectively contained the English in the past stand up to a well-planned and concerted assault? It would not be long before New France would have to confront these questions.

---

13 Benson, *Peter Kalm's Travels in North America*, vol. 2.

4 THE FALL OF NEW FRANCE

France's long struggle to maintain a colonial presence on the North American continent ended in 1763. The conquest of New France would leave the French with only some sugar producing islands in the Caribbean and a tiny toehold in the Gulf of St. Lawrence, and left tens of thousands of French Roman Catholic subjects under the rule of an alien British Protestant power. The Seven Years' War, described by some historians as the first truly *world* war, had far-reaching implications. The enormous costs of the war—for both the victors and the vanquished—left treasuries depleted, and the resulting taxation measures helped to spark both the American Revolution in 1775 and the French Revolution in 1789. Britain's consolidation of power in India also flowed from her success in driving out her French imperial rival.

In Canada, the Conquest is often seen as a great historical wound, the beginning of English hegemony over the French. Britain's historic victory at the Plains of Abraham has been heralded as the rationale for cultural assimilation of the French. Yet historian Allan Greer sees New France not as a "conquered nation" but a "ceded colony."[1] France was ambivalent about the value of its settlement on the St. Lawrence. Preoccupied by more urgent European struggles and Britain's growing mastery of the seas, and perhaps recognizing the implications of the growth of Britain's North American colonies, France was unable to marshal enough resources to hold on to Canada.

---

1 Allan Greer, *The People of New France* (Toronto: University of Toronto Press, 1997), 115.

AUGURIES OF WAR IN THE OHIO VALLEY

On the eve of the Seven Years' War, France's claims in North America were extensive. They stretched from the Arctic to the Gulf of Mexico, including modern-day Labrador, the entire St. Lawrence and Great Lakes region, and extended south through the Ohio River Valley and Mississippi River delta. Yet actual occupation was modest: perhaps 55,000 colonists lived in New France, most of them clustered along the banks of the St. Lawrence River. By contrast, the 13 English colonies along the Atlantic sea-board—from Massachusetts to Georgia, north of Spanish-controlled Florida—boasted 1.5 million settlers. Britain also claimed Newfoundland, the vast interior territory of Rupert's Land controlled by the Hudson's Bay Company, and Nova Scotia.

The burgeoning population of the 13 colonies gave rise to much of the trouble. In 1749, the English colony of Virginia granted a charter to the Ohio Company to expand settlement west into the Ohio River Valley. The Ohio Company hoped to take advantage of the land hunger of settlers hemmed in east of the Allegheny Mountains (part of the Appalachian range). The French claimed this interior territory, but the English maintained that they held sovereignty over both the Iroquois people and their territory. While Natives living in the Ohio Valley would ultimately recognize the threat posed by the influx of settlers, in the short term a growing number of English traders offered an appealing alternative to the French traders who plied the Ohio River route. The English "give them everything very cheap," one chief explained.[2]

The task of defending France's claim fell to the Marquis de La Galissonière, a French naval officer who temporarily, and reluctantly, served as governor of New France (1747–49). La Galissonière sought to drive the British from the Ohio Valley, build a chain of French posts to link Canada to Louisiana, and cement the wavering loyalties of interior Natives. In the summer of 1749, work began on Fort de La Présentation (at present-day Ogdensburg, New York), along with improvements to Fort Detroit on the western frontier. Detroit was essential to maintain communications with the Mississippi Valley. An already established French fort at Fort Niagara was meant to control Lake Ontario. La Galissonière was especially concerned about a rival English fort on Lake Ontario's southern shore, Fort Oswego, and he urged French authorities that "nothing must be spared to destroy this dangerous post."[3] La Galissonière also dispatched an expedition that same summer to proclaim French sovereignty at the junction of the

---

2   Chief of the Wea tribe (in present-day Indiana) as quoted in William M. Fowler, Jr., *Empires at War: The Seven Years' War and the Struggle for North America, 1754–1763* (Toronto: Douglas & McIntyre, 2005), 10.

3   As quoted in Étienne Taillemite, "Barrin de La Galissonière, Roland-Michel, Marquis de La Galissonière," *Dictionary of Canadian Biography* (*DCB*), http://www.biographi.ca/en/bio/barrin_de_la_galissoniere_roland_michel_3E.html.

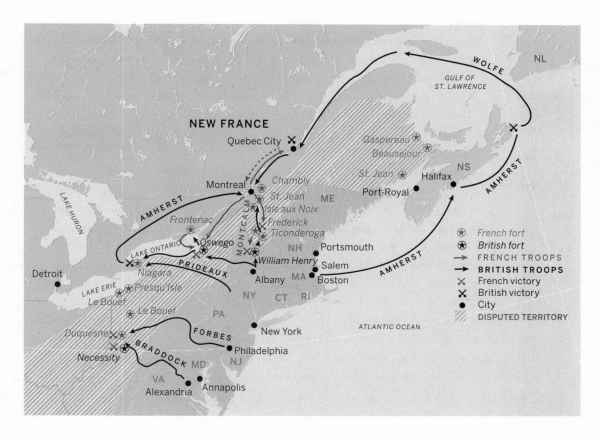

Map 4.1 North America during the Seven Years' War.

Ohio and Miami Rivers. He believed that the Ohio Valley was an essential buffer zone to keep the English from attacking the St. Lawrence colony. However, his 1749 expedition returned with the discouraging news of a growing British presence west of the Alleghenies and their flourishing trade with the Natives.

When La Galissonière returned to Paris at year's end, he was pressed into service as part of an international commission to settle British–French imperial tensions. The role was a challenging one: Louis XV's advisors downplayed the importance of France's North American possessions, and Britain rejected any compromise. Governor William Shirley of Massachusetts, advising Britain on North American affairs, confessed that his goal was to keep the French talking until the time "when it shall be thought proper to reduce 'em."[4]

That time seemed to be drawing ever nearer. Even while Britain and France were technically at peace, violence was erupting in the Ohio Valley. In 1752, the French and

---

4   Governor Shirley to the Duke of Bedford, 24 April 1749, as quoted in Fowler, *Empires at War*, 15.

allies from the Ottawa tribe attacked the Ohio Valley village of Pickawillany, capturing British traders and killing "Old Briton," a Miami chief, and others who had boldly ignored French warnings to stop trade with the British. The following year, the French built new fortifications at Fort Presque Isle on the south shore of Lake Erie, and Fort Le Boeuf on a tributary of the Allegheny. Tanaghrisson, a Seneca chief known as the Half-King, confronted the French, demanding their withdrawal, but was warned that the French would crush any opposition.

Nearby, in the British colony of Virginia, Governor Robert Dinwiddie was busy organizing a counter-move. In 1753, he dispatched 22-year-old militia officer George Washington, and a handful of companions, with a letter demanding that the French vacate Virginia's territory. Dinwiddie was a personal shareholder in the Ohio Company. Indeed, colonial critics would later complain that military action in the Ohio Valley had been launched "to serve the interest of a private company at the expense of the welfare of the public."[5] Tanaghrisson agreed to accompany Washington's party with three other warriors, although he was skeptical about how intimidating Washington and his men would be to the determined French. The French commander at Fort Le Boeuf treated Washington with courtesy when he arrived, even inviting him to dine, but instructed him to tell Dinwiddie that France's claim to the Ohio Valley was absolute and would be defended.

AN UNDECLARED WAR

The following year, at a remote stockade in the Ohio Valley, the spark was struck that would engulf the world in war. In the spring of 1754, George Washington was again marching west, leading a small militia band of 132 to reinforce Virginia's position at the site where the Allegheny and Monongahela Rivers meet to form the Ohio River. Tanaghrisson and a few Seneca warriors again accompanied this British force, but, as they neared the fort, they were disheartened to learn that the French had earlier taken possession of it, constructing Fort Duquesne on the site. Washington camped nearby at a site he called "Fort Necessity" and mulled over his next move. He learned through Native scouts that some French were bivouacked a short distance away and decided to confront them. These French were in fact emissaries, led by Ensign Joseph Coulon de Villiers de Jumonville, sent from Fort Duquesne to meet them. On the night of May 27, 1754, Jumonville's men camped in an enclosed glen, unaware that Washington and Tanaghrisson were planning an attack. At daybreak, as Jumonville's

---

5   The *New York Mercury*, January 1756, as quoted in Guy Frégault, *Canada: The War of the Conquest* (Toronto: Oxford University Press, 1969), 32.

men began to stir, the English and their allies opened fire, killing 14. Gravely wounded, Jumonville struggled to identify himself as the commander, offering Washington the message he bore. As Washington stepped away to seek a translator, Tanaghrisson moved forward and drove a hatchet into Jumonville's skull. Others set upon and killed the wounded French, scalping them, stripping the bodies, and spitting the severed head of one victim on a spike as a display. Washington managed to escort 21 French prisoners to safety at Fort Necessity, but his position was not a tenable one. News of the massacre stirred the French to launch a much larger retaliatory force from Fort Duquesne, with Jumonville's brother in command. They confronted Washington in a short skirmish near Fort Necessity on July 3, 1754, and the Virginians were forced to surrender. Washington obediently signed a document recognizing the disputed area as French territory and the killing of Jumonville as an assassination. His blundering raid—against a nation with whom Britain was at peace—had, in the words of Horace Walpole, "set the world on fire."[6]

When news of Washington's shameful surrender reached London in August of 1754, the British launched plans for an infusion of armed forces into North America, even while they remained technically at peace with France. The seasoned but inflexible Major General Edward Braddock was recalled from Gibraltar to take command. In the colonies, Britain organized the 1754 Albany Conference to bring together colonial representatives and delegates from the Iroquois Six Nations to discuss defence plans. Braddock hastened to North America, risking a stormy Atlantic passage in winter, in order to reach Virginia in February 1755, before the French could reach their own winter-locked colonial ports. As spring came, the British hoped to intercept the expected French fleet south of Newfoundland, but most French vessels managed to slip through to Louisbourg or Quebec. The *Alcide* was an exception. Lost in the fog, the captain came within hailing distance of the British *Dunkirk*. "Are we at peace, or war?" the *Alcide*'s captain called out. "La paix, la paix," came the reassuring reply, followed by a devastating volley from the *Dunkirk*'s guns.[7] This brash and provocative act—much like Washington's 1754 attack on the Jumonville party—had moved the two nations closer to open war, without offering any real military advantage to the British. Back in London, Lord Hardwicke, the lord chancellor, lamented "We have done too much or too little."[8]

---

6 As quoted in W.J. Eccles, "Joseph Coulon de Villiers de Jumonville," *DCB*, http://www.biographi.ca/en/bio/coulon_de_villiers_de_jumonville_joseph_3E.html. The account of Jumonville's death is from Fred Anderson, *Crucible of War: The Seven Years' War and the Fate of Empire in British North America, 1754–1766* (New York: Vintage Books, 2001), 5–7.

7 As quoted in Francis Parkman, *Montcalm and Wolfe* (1884; New York: Viking, 1984), 108–09.

8 As quoted in Fowler, *Empires at War*, 75.

Braddock planned a four-pronged offensive against the French: he himself would lead the assault on strategic Fort Duquesne. Once successful, he would march north to join Massachusetts governor William Shirley's attack on Fort Niagara. From there, his forces would swing east to assist Colonel William Johnson who, along with Mohawk allies, was to take Fort Saint-Frédéric at Crown Point on Lake Champlain. Lieutenant Colonel Robert Monckton, the acting governor of Nova Scotia, was to take Fort Beauséjour, located at the head of the Bay of Fundy. Unlike Fort Duquesne and Fort Beauséjour, where imperial possession was in dispute, Fort Saint-Frédéric and Fort Niagara had long been in French hands. A British assault on these positions would be a clear act of war.

Braddock confidently predicted that he would have more success expelling the French than George Washington had: "These Savages may indeed be a formidable Enemy to your raw American Militia; but, upon the King's regular and disciplined Troops…it is impossible they should make any impression."[9] However, Braddock's force of 3,000 bogged down as it advanced slowly west. Three hundred axmen led the way, trying to hack out a road passable by heavy artillery and lumbering wagons through slippery mountainous terrain, cut by deep ravines and rushing waters. Indigenous allies deserted the force, disgusted by the inefficiency of the advance. A disenchanted Oneida chief, Scarouady, complained that Braddock "looked upon us as dogs and would never hear anything what [sic] was said to him."[10] French scouts and their Indian allies skirted the British force at a distance through the shadowy forest, launching raids to pick off stragglers. Sudden alarms, real or imaginary, would set off a hair-trigger response among Braddock's demoralized force. Chief Scarouady's own son fell to friendly fire. When they learned the discouraging news that hundreds of reinforcements were en route to relieve the French at Fort Duquesne, Braddock resolved on bold action. On July 9, 1755, he set out with an advance party of 1,200 men.

The French who hoped to defend Fort Duquesne against Braddock were not optimistic either. Only 200 men, and no cannons, had been sent from Montreal to relieve the fort and they would be no match for Braddock's artillery. The French decided instead to risk an ambush. Montreal-born Captain Daniel-Hyacinthe-Marie Liénard de Beaujeu was sent to lead the assault with 250 colonial militia. Beaujeu knew that guerilla techniques of deception and stealth would be more effective in the rugged interior than European tactics of open confrontation; he also knew that Indigenous allies would be invaluable. Dressed in a fringed buckskin jacket, Beaujeu went out to

9 As quoted in John Grenier, *The First Way of War: American War Making on the Frontier* (Cambridge: Cambridge University Press, 2005), 119.
10 As quoted in Fowler, *Empires at War*, 60.

beseech the help of Natives camped near the fort: Ottawa and Delaware from the Ohio Valley, and Huron, Caughnawaga, and Abenaki from the St. Lawrence valley. The Natives were reluctant to join him in such an unequal contest, but when word reached the assembly that Braddock's force had forded the Monongahela River and were approaching the fort, Beaujeu defiantly announced that he was ready to go alone. The electric atmosphere, and Beaujeu's inspiring resolve, won his wavering allies over.

As Braddock's scarlet-clad men, marching in steady formation to the music of fife and drum, neared Fort Duquesne on July 9, 1755, Beaujeu's forces sprang the trap. Sharpshooters hidden in ravines and shielded by the dark forest opened fire. Some Virginia frontiersmen among Braddock's force emulated their enemies by attempting to take cover, but were ordered to withstand fire. Bodies of the dead and wounded littered the ground, and in the confusion, amid the smoke, the terrifying war whoops of the Indigenous warriors, and the panicked plunging of horses, the ambushed men fired blindly, even into their own ranks. Braddock frantically tried to master the situation, but snipers shot four successive horses out from under him. His secretary, Governor Shirley's son, was shot through the head. While French losses were light, Beaujeu was felled by a British volley as he waved his hat in signal to his troops. With his clothes torn by bullets, Braddock gamely mounted a fifth horse, but was at last forced to order a retreat. Having withstood three hours of fire, his men abandoned all order and fled in panic toward the ford, plunging through the water to escape. Those caught at the bank of the Monongahela were butchered, and the river ran with blood. Stores, ammunition, and wagons were set alight in the frantic retreat. For Braddock himself it was too late. A bullet entered his lung, and he collapsed into the bush, gasping for breath. Despite his orders that he should be left where he fell, Braddock's junior officers bore him away on a stretcher improvised from the general's own sash. More than 900 wounded were left behind—along with detailed plans of the four-pronged invasion. When his bearers reached Great Meadows a few days later, Braddock succumbed to his wounds. "Who would have thought it?" he murmured as he neared death.[11]

Other components of Braddock's grand plan also foundered. The untamed wilderness between Albany and Fort Oswego could not be traversed within the few weeks allotted, and Governor Shirley's objective of marching on Fort Niagara had to be abandoned for that summer. Meanwhile, the capture of Braddock's plans meant that the French commander, Baron Dieskau, expected an offensive at Fort Saint-Frédéric on Lake Champlain and was prepared. Colonel William Johnson and his Mohawk allies met him in early September 1755 in an inconclusive clash at the southern end of Lake George. The British claimed victory, and in fact captured the wounded Dieskau,

---

11 As quoted in Parkman, *Montcalm and Wolfe*, 132.

but Fort Saint-Frédéric remained in French hands. Johnson constructed Fort William Henry nearby, and the French began new fortifications at the outlet of Lake George, Fort Carillon, named for the bell-like sound of the rushing waters at the site.

The only unqualified success for the British in these earliest engagements of the still-undeclared war was at Fort Beauséjour, a star-shaped fort the French had built (in what is today New Brunswick) in response to the British construction of Fort Lawrence nearby. On June 16, 1755, a few weeks before Braddock's disaster at Fort Duquesne, Colonel Robert Monckton and a force of 2,200 New England militia and 250 British regulars captured Fort Beauséjour, renaming it Fort Cumberland. This new British military presence would have disastrous consequences for the French Acadian population.

THE ACADIAN TRAGEDY, 1755

The speedy and successful resolution of what he had feared would be a long campaign meant that the British governor of Nova Scotia, Charles Lawrence, had an opportunity. He saw a chance to deal with the threat of a potentially hostile population at the outset of what promised to be a brutal war. He had almost 2,500 paid and provisioned troops at the ready and was encouraged by the quick collapse of Fort Beauséjour. The French Acadians had lived peacefully under British rule for more than a generation—Britain's possession of Nova Scotia dated from the 1713 Treaty of Utrecht—but recent events raised concerns about their loyalty. The news that a large French fleet, en route to North America with a force of 3,000 men, had managed to elude British warships added to the sense of urgency. Lawrence grew increasingly skittish about the possibility of a French counterattack.

In the spring of 1755, before the capture of Beauséjour, the Acadian population had been asked to take an oath of allegiance as British subjects. Only a small number complied. Since most had lived their entire lives under British rule, successfully negotiating neutrality even during the previous war, they might have failed to recognize the degree to which circumstances had changed. They wavered between the wholehearted loyalty demanded by their British rulers and the loyalty to France, which that nation sought to encourage. Yet neither side could be sure of the Acadians' allegiance; some Acadians confided they would be "on the side of the strongest."[12]

Not all were neutral. Some Acadians, along with Mi'kmaq allies, had harassed the British in the days before the fall of Fort Beauséjour. One of the most troublesome of these was Joseph "Beausoleil" Brossard (or "Broussard"). In the previous war, he had aided the French cause, and the British suspected that he had led a group of 60 Natives

---

12 As quoted in John Mack Faragher, *A Great and Noble Scheme: The Tragic Story of the Expulsion of the French Acadians from Their American Homeland* (New York: Norton, 2005), 302.

Figure 4.1 The British capture of the French Fort Beauséjour, on the Isthmus of Chignecto, would have grave implications for the Acadians.

in a brutal attack in 1751 on the English colony of Dartmouth, Nova Scotia. When the French defence of Fort Beauséjour collapsed, Brossard approached Monckton with an offer to mediate with the Mi'kmaq, subject to a grant of personal amnesty, but British authorities in Nova Scotia were in no mood to be conciliatory. Brossard fled to the woods and looked for an opportunity to rejoin the resistance.

Factors beyond the military threat also dictated the British treatment of the Acadians. The growing population of the English colonies to the south looked longingly on the fertile farmland carefully diked by generations of Acadians along the Bay of Fundy and Minas Basin. As early as 1754, Governor Shirley of Massachusetts and Governor Lawrence of Nova Scotia had discussed plans for the expulsion of the Acadians from their homes. When, in July 1755, just after successful operations against Beauséjour, a small delegation of Acadians from Grand-Pré appeared before Nova Scotia's appointed council to petition for the return of some confiscated boats and arms, Governor Lawrence seized the opportunity to demand an unqualified oath of allegiance. The delegates hesitated, claiming that they needed to consult the rest of the population. Lawrence ordered them imprisoned and summoned more Acadian representatives from the Minas area and from Annapolis, warning that they must immediately take the oath "without any Reserve or else quit their lands."[13] The Acadians were determined not to take any oath that would bind them to take up arms against the French and refused. They, too, became prisoners of war. Parish priests, suspected of sowing disaffection, were rounded up and arrested.

In the summer of 1755, the British began a brutal "scorched earth" policy against the Acadians that would continue for the next three years. Acadian communities were obliterated, village by village, and an estimated 10,000 sent into exile, sometimes with less than an hour's notice to gather their belongings before being herded onto transport ships. Crops were burned, and homes and churches were put to the torch. All livestock was to be forfeited to the king: nearly 20,000 head of cattle, 30,000 sheep, 1,600 horses, and an untold number of pigs. The *Pennsylvania Gazette* rhapsodized about the benefits that would flow from the "great and noble Scheme" of ousting these "secret enemies" in favour of "some good English Farmers" who would occupy this desirable farmland.[14]

Most of the Acadians were taken to Britain's other American colonies and dispersed among a hostile and alien population, but many did not survive the process of being uprooted: nearly a third died from diseases on board the crowded ships. Some of the most troublesome Acadians, like Brossard, became prisoners of war. Ironically, the New England settlers who displaced the Acadians in the fertile lands around the Bay of Fundy found that the expertise of the former inhabitants was needed to maintain and repair the dikes; in 1760, 2,000 refugee Acadians were returned to their homeland to serve as labourers for the new proprietors. At the war's end, many Acadians, including Brossard, found new homes in Louisiana, where they became known as "Cajuns."

A WORLD WAR

Since the end of the War of the Austrian Succession in 1748, an uneasy status quo had prevailed in Europe, but the greatest tensions were arising from the imperial periphery rather than Europe itself—from continental North America, the Caribbean, and India. French influence in India was greatest on the east coast of the subcontinent, centred in Pondichéry (Puducherry), and through elaborate intrigues with Indian princes Britain and France had long jockeyed for advantage. Undeclared war was also being waged at sea, with British ships attempting to capture any vessel flying the French flag anywhere in the world, in a bid to break French commercial power. French ministers protested

13 Lt. Col. John Winslow, Journal, 5 September 1755, in Public Archives of Canada, *Report*, vol. 2 (Ottawa: King's Printer, 1905).

14 Faragher, *A Great and Noble Scheme*, 333.

impotently against these acts of piracy, but the British strategy seemed to be working, and bankruptcy loomed for a number of French merchant houses.

In May 1756, the illusion of peace was shattered and war was declared. Some alliances among world powers had shifted since the War of the Austrian Succession. During the Seven Years' War, France was allied with Saxony and Sweden as before, and would eventually also have the aid of Spain, but was now also allied with Austria and Russia. Britain, now ruled by Hanoverian George II, had the aid of the small electorate of Hanover, but, more significantly, was allied with Prussia, a nation that had emerged from the last war with new territorial gains and a reputation for military might. The impeccably trained armies of Frederick II of Prussia, "Frederick the Great," were the envy of other European powers. It was said that he sought to make his forces more afraid of their own officers than of the enemy. Prussia's forces almost tripled under Frederick's intense program: the nation of 2.5 million was able to raise an army that grew from 30,000 to 80,000 strong. These formidable troops would prove to be of enormous value to Britain by keeping the French tied down in continental European warfare. British Prime Minister William Pitt would later boast that America had been conquered in Germany. The annual drain on the British treasury of £600,000 would have to be reckoned with later.[15]

Britain's greatest strength lay with her navy, which was double the size of its French counterpart. In 1755, Britain's 42,000 sailors manned 148 first-rate ships of the line carrying 50 to 100 guns each, 103 frigates, and 80 smaller vessels. Nevertheless, the spectre of a French alliance with Spain, which possessed some 50 battleships, made the British less sanguine. Where land forces were concerned, France had the upper hand. France accordingly pinned its hopes on an invasion of the British Isles. France's north coast bristled with some 118 infantry battalions, a force almost double the size of the entire British army.[16]

MONTCALM IN NEW FRANCE

Days before the formal declaration of war, Louis-Joseph de Montcalm, the Marquis de Montcalm, arrived in Quebec to take up his new post as commander of France's forces in North America in place of the captured Baron Dieskau. A career soldier, born of a noble

15 Fowler, *Empires at War*, 21–22, 134.

16 A battalion typically numbers from several hundred to 1,000 men. More information about the respective strength of each nation may be found in Guy Frégault, *Canada: The War of the Conquest* (Toronto: Oxford University Press, 1969); Arthur Herman, *To Rule the Waves: How the British Navy Shaped the Modern World* (New York: Harper Collins, 2004), 265; and, for specifics of French naval strength, Appendix A through Appendix C in Jonathan Dull, *The French Navy and the Seven Years' War* (Lincoln: University of Nebraska Press, 2005).

Figure 4.2 Louis-Joseph de Montcalm, the Marquis de Montcalm.

family distinguished for military service, Montcalm was also a scholarly man who personally supervised his children's education during peacetime at his estate in the south of France. When duty took him overseas, he remained a devoted family man, assuring those at home that "there is not an hour in the day when I do not think of you."[17]

Montcalm exhibited some of the same failings as his late British counterpart, General Braddock; critics described him as high-handed and contemptuous of colonial ways. Montcalm was quick to clash with the new governor of New France, the Canadian-born Pierre de Rigaud de Vaudreuil de Cavagnial, the Marquis de Vaudreuil, over how France's military resources could best be deployed. As governor, Vaudreuil was Montcalm's superior in rank, but the well-connected Montcalm had friends in high places, and kept up a private channel of correspondence with the French Minister of War, the Comte d'Argenson, through which he could be as frank as he liked about Vaudreuil's shortcomings, Canadian conditions, and his increasingly pessimistic view of their prospects in the war.

The forces at France's disposal included, in theory at least, all able-bodied Canadian men between 16 and 60. This militia—citizen soldiers—amounted to about 12,000, although men might be drawn away for important competing duties like farming. These men knew local conditions but were not fully trained career soldiers. A further colonial force of 2,000, the *troupes de la marine*, consisted of colonial regulars—professional soldiers under the administration of the department of Marine. The main fighting force, the *troupes de la terre*, were regulars from France, and by 1757, eight battalions of these had been sent to New France, approximately 4,000 men. Seamen were also used as combatants ashore, although their effective numbers were limited to perhaps 1,500 men. Added to this, of course, was the formidable strength of France's Indigenous allies.

INDIGENOUS ALLIES IN THE SEVEN YEARS' WAR

Some Indigenous warriors allied with France were Canadian Iroquois who lived in seven main communities in the St. Lawrence Valley, a group distinct from the Six Nations Iroquois Confederacy. The French also drew support from the Abenaki, Algonquin, Huron, and Nipissing; in the west, the Ojibwe, Ottawa, Menominee,

---

17 As quoted in Parkman, *Montcalm and Wolfe*, 264.

Mississauga, Potawatomi, and Wyandot; in the Maritimes, the Mi'kmaq and Maliseet; and, to the south, warriors from the Delaware, Fox, Iowa, Miami, Oneida, Sauk, and Winnebago nations. At peak, perhaps 2,000 Indigenous warriors fought on the side of the French at any one time. D. Peter MacLeod has suggested that Indigenous fighters pursued "parallel warfare." They fought at the request of the French, but "in so doing they surrendered neither their independence nor their freedom to wage war in their own way."[18] Natives were loath to adopt European tactics that squandered their warriors' lives needlessly and would often refuse to attack fortified positions or face artillery fire. MacLeod also calculated that Indigenous warriors were less apt to volunteer during outbreaks of smallpox when the risk of contagion was high.[19] Alliances of individual nations could and did waver throughout the course of the war, in response to shifts in circumstances, diplomatic overtures by one European party or the other, and the Natives' simple calculation of their own interests. Indigenous warriors were a vital psychological weapon to the French, and even the prospect of confronting them could be enough to deter colonial militia from the 13 colonies. Critics condemned the brutality of Natives in battle, their refusal to respect European conventions of the rules of war, and the treatment of non-combatants. Vaudreuil admitted that atrocities were a sure way "to sicken the people of the English colonies of war."[20]

MORE EARLY SUCCESSES FOR THE FRENCH

When Montcalm arrived in the spring of 1756, he found that Vaudreuil had already launched advance operations against strategically important Fort Oswego, successfully interfering with the British garrison's supply lines. Fort Oswego, on the southern shore of Lake Ontario at the mouth of the Oswego River, had long been vital to British interests in the area. New Yorkers carried out a busy trade with Natives who travelled to this location, which was convenient to water traffic. By the early summer, Montcalm, at Vaudreuil's urging, was ready to launch the main offensive against Oswego, having carefully cultivated alliances with Oneida and Onondaga warriors. Montcalm's force of 1,300 regulars, an equal number of militia, along with 250 Indigenous allies was the largest European army to date to march into the North American wilderness.

18 D. Peter MacLeod, *The Canadian Iroquois and the Seven Years' War* (Toronto: Dundurn, 1996), 21.

19 D. Peter MacLeod, "Microbes and Muskets: Smallpox and the Participation of the Amerindian Allies of New France in the Seven Years' War," *Ethnohistory* 39, no. 1 (Winter 1992): 42–64. A list of the most significant Indigenous nations allied with the French appears in footnote 4, page 57.

20 Frégault, *Canada: The War of the Conquest*, 120; Claude Charles Le Roy, *dit* Bacqueville de La Potherie, "History of the Savage People Who Are Allies of New France" (1753) in Jon William Parmenter, "Pontiac's War: Forging New Links in the Anglo-Iroquois Covenant Chain, 1758–1766," *Ethnohistory* 44, no. 4 (Autumn 1997): 621.

Months of privation had left the British garrison at Oswego suffering from the effects of hunger, scurvy, and dysentery, and French guerilla fighters nearby kept tensions high. Montcalm's forces began siege operations against Fort Oswego on August 13, and the British commander, Lieutenant-Colonel James Mercer, felt compelled to abandon nearby Fort Ontario, which was indefensible. This left an ideal offensive position for Montcalm's forces to occupy, from which the French could train their guns upon the main fort. Under the pounding of French artillery, Mercer's garrison of some 1,800 men frantically tried to reposition their guns, none of which faced Fort Ontario. Mercer himself was beheaded by a cannon ball. At last, the British were forced to surrender.

To Montcalm's horror, his Indigenous allies swarmed into the fort and butchered some of the sick and wounded, carrying others away as prisoners, including women and children. Montcalm was appalled that even some who were Roman Catholic converts took part in the atrocities and arranged to ransom some of the captives from his own allies. Nevertheless, Vaudreuil was delighted by what he referred to as "my victory": the British had surrendered the position, along with 1,700 prisoners, several armed vessels, cannon, munitions, supplies, and currency valued at 18,000 *livres*. Moreover, from Fort Oswego, which they called Fort Chouaguen, the French could control Lake Ontario. The British colony of New York was thus exposed to attack from the northwest, and the interior waterways that linked the Great Lakes to Louisiana were secured for the French. Far from celebrating, however, Montcalm wrote an apologetic report home, explaining that his tactics had been very much at variance with accepted European rules.[21] Canadian observers speculated sourly that had it been left to Montcalm, the fort would still be in English hands.

The loss of Fort Oswego was only one of many British disasters around the globe early in the war. Several weeks earlier, a French naval force commanded by La Galissonière, New France's former governor, took the strategic British possession of Minorca in the Mediterranean. So bungled was the British attempt to relieve the garrison at Minorca that the British commander of the operation, Admiral John Byng, was executed for his failure. News of disaster in India soon followed. In June of 1756, Fort William in Calcutta, built to protect Britain's trade interests against the French, was captured by the Nawab of Bengal. A reported 146 prisoners were cast overnight into the infamous "Black Hole of Calcutta," a small, unventilated cell from which only 23 emerged alive the following morning. Inflammatory accounts of the event reached England, whipping public opinion into outraged fury. Combined with the news of North American defeats and the loss of Minorca, the blow to British prestige was profound.

---

21 W.J. Eccles, "Louis Joseph de Montcalm, Marquis de Montcalm," *DCB*, http://www.biographi.ca/en/bio/montcalm_louis_joseph_de_3E.html.

The mounting disasters toppled the British ministry led by the Duke of Newcastle, and by July 1757 George II reluctantly called upon William Pitt to form a government, a man he personally loathed. Frederick the Great cheered the news: "England has been a long time in labour but she has at last brought forth a man."[22] Pitt himself was no less grandiose in his own estimation: he proclaimed himself the only man who could save the nation. Impatient, sarcastic, arrogant, and vain, unable to accept any authority but his own, Pitt drove himself mercilessly, breaking his physical health, while being torn by such violent mood swings that many called him mad. Yet Pitt had a clear vision of how the war must be won: Britain must concentrate on the colonial prizes themselves, not Europe. The navy was the key, both to Britain's imperial possessions around the globe and to the protection and extension of British trade. Global trade funnelled wealth into the tiny island nation.

Despite a fresh infusion of forces into North America, it took time for the tide to turn in Britain's favour. Setbacks in Europe multiplied, with defeats at Hastenbeck in Hanover and a failed naval operation against the French port of Rochefort. The new British commander in North America, John Campbell, the fourth Earl of Loudoun, who had arrived in New York in the summer of 1756, seemed to pour his energies into administrative tasks, rather than striking boldly against the French; his secretary complained about working 15-hour days. In the summer of 1757, Loudoun squandered a golden opportunity. He had more than 10,000 troops, 16 ships of the line, and several frigates at his disposal to launch an attack on Louisbourg. If this fortress fell, Quebec itself would lay open to attack. However, Loudoun sailed his forces back to New York without having struck a blow, dissuaded by unfavourable winds and worrisome intelligence about the strength of the French. Only in India was the news good for Britain that year. In June, Robert Clive, the British governor of Bengal, won a decisive victory at Plassey, avenging the Black Hole of Calcutta and paving the way for the collapse of French power in India. This was a much-needed bit of encouraging news as things took an even blacker turn in North America later that summer.

In August 1757, the usually cautious Montcalm launched an offensive against Fort William Henry, at the southern tip of Lake George, from the French base at nearby Fort Carillon. The timing was propitious: Loudoun's aborted plan to attack Louisbourg had drained British manpower from the area, the French had just been reinvigorated with fresh supplies, and Indigenous support was high: 2,000 Native allies supplemented a French force of 6,000, an equal mix of regular troops and militia. The besieged British commander at Fort William Henry, Lieutenant-Colonel George Monro, sent desperate appeals for help to General Daniel Webb at nearby

22 As quoted in Charles Clive Bigham Mersey, *The Prime Ministers of Britain, 1721–1921* (London: Ayer, 1969), 79.

Fort Edward. Monro was strongly outnumbered and smallpox was raging within Fort William Henry, but no help arrived. Webb sent the discouraging reply that Monro should negotiate a surrender. To add to the humiliation, Indigenous scouts captured the British messenger, and Montcalm passed Webb's message on to Monro with his compliments. Monro had little choice but to ask for terms. Montcalm gallantly agreed to allow the defeated garrison to carry out their regimental flag in procession, with the captured force to be escorted to nearby Fort Edward to be paroled, meaning these forces could not be used for 18 months. Montcalm called a council of chiefs to explain these terms to his Indigenous allies, and the chiefs assented.

Amid the evacuation, however, Indigenous warriors descended upon the fort in search of spoils of war. They set upon the 70 sick and wounded who had been left behind. French soldiers and missionaries tried to intervene, but failed to prevent scalpings and massacres by tomahawk. Some of the thwarted warriors, after spending the night consuming rum found in the fort, gave vent to their frustration as the defeated British marched away. At the sound of blood-chilling war whoops, they attacked the retreating column. As many as 185 were killed, and up to 500 taken prisoner. By sunset, most of Montcalm's Indigenous allies were already paddling north with their plunder and captives.[23]

Outrage in the British colonies knew no bounds. They repudiated their promise of parole, swearing that they would give no quarter to any captured French. Some reflected with satisfaction that the smallpox epidemic had been carried back to the Indigenous peoples' own villages. The French, for their part, might have capitalized on the victory by capturing vulnerable Fort Edward, then sweeping forward to Albany, and even New York. To Vaudreuil's disgust, however, Montcalm refused to advance further, citing poor road conditions, the probability of British reinforcements at Fort Edward, and his militia's need to return home for the harvest.

THE TIDE BEGINS TO TURN FOR BRITAIN

Historians such as W.J. Eccles have condemned Montcalm's defeatism in the face of what should have been encouraging early successes. Montcalm's private letters to the minister of War radiated gloom, sharply criticizing both Vaudreuil and New France's Intendant, François Bigot. Bigot was notorious for lavish entertaining, staggering gambling debts, and rewarding cronies with fat government contracts. Montcalm condemned Bigot as corrupt, insisting that the intendant's focus on privateering and other sources of personal profit—the "business of plundering"—had helped to ignite the

---

23 Anderson, *Crucible of War*, 197–98.

war. At the war's end, Bigot would be made to pay with forfeiture of his property and imprisonment in the Bastille, although historians J.F. Bosher and J.-C. Dubé believed he was simply a scapegoat.[24] Montcalm also complained about runaway inflation and a growing shortage of supplies, some of which he attributed to Bigot's corruption. Lacking beef, his troops were reduced to eating horsemeat. Gifts to the Natives, essential for keeping alliances intact, began to dry up, the flow of goods hampered by Britain's mastery of the seas. Threats to French fishing vessels also curtailed the supply of cod for the colony. Even with the recent string of victories, Montcalm grimly predicted that New France would inevitably fall to the British.[25]

At home in England, William Pitt was exasperated with Loudoun's inept mishandling of the ample resources given him to secure victory in North America. Loudoun had done nothing, Pitt raged. At the end of 1757, with a string of defeats as his legacy, Loudoun was recalled in disgrace and his second-in-command, Major General James Abercromby, elevated to commander-in-chief. Pitt insisted that the plan for 1758 should call for a three-pronged assault on French positions at Louisbourg, Fort Carillon, and Fort Duquesne.

General Jeffery Amherst was given command of the planned attack on the fortress of Louisbourg on Île-Royale, the formidable guardian of the Gulf of St. Lawrence. Admiral Edward Boscawen commanded naval operations—the greatest-ever invasion by sea of North American territory. Some 157 vessels transported 27,000 troops. Throughout the winter, the British navy had enforced a punishing blockade on the fortress, and food supplies to sustain the garrison of 7,000 were dwindling. Ammunition was also in short supply; the French commander at Louisbourg, the Chevalier de Drucour, doubted if he could withstand a prolonged siege. Only six French vessels in the harbour could offer naval support; several more had been scuttled deliberately to bar entry to the British. Nevertheless, Drucour knew that every day he could hold out would better the chances that Quebec itself would not be attacked that season.

By early June 1758, Boscawen's massive fleet was anchored in Gabarus Bay to the west of Louisbourg. General Amherst made a show of courtesy—even sending a pineapple to Madame Drucour with his compliments—but he was determined to accept nothing less than unconditional surrender. Amherst's brigadier, James Wolfe, braved the pounding surf, treacherous rocks, and bombardment from the French battery to lead an advance landing party ashore. Wolfe later confessed that the operation had been rash and even reckless, succeeding only by "the greatest good fortune," a description that

24 Frégault, *Canada: The War of the Conquest*, 32–33. J.G. Bosher and J.-C. Dubé, "François Bigot," DCB, http://www.biographi.ca/en/bio/bigot_francois_1778_4E.html.
25 Eccles, "Montcalm," DCB.

might also be applied to his strategy at Quebec the following year.[26] The British invaders built a network of trenches to bring their cannon ever closer to the fort, and by July their shells were falling behind the walls. Cast iron mortar shells weighing 90 kilograms and filled with exploding charges wreaked devastation on the city. On July 6, a bomb crashed through the roof of Louisbourg's hospital, killing several, including the attending surgeon. On July 21, a British cannonball struck one of the French ships in the harbour, igniting a fire that spread to two nearby vessels. Cannons aboard one burning French ship discharged, raining more artillery fire onto Louisbourg. The fire leapt to engulf the powder magazine of another vessel, touching off a huge explosion. Dense smoke filled the harbour, spreading choking fumes through the fort. Still the defenders hung on.

On July 25, the British timed a massive bombardment to coincide with their capture of the remaining French warships. With the last shred of naval protection for the fort gone, British naval artillery could move within range of the devastated defences. At last, on July 26, Drucour ordered that a white flag of surrender be raised from the crumbling Dauphin's Bastion. For the British, the St. Lawrence route to Quebec lay open.

While Amherst lay siege to Louisbourg, Abercromby moved against Montcalm at Fort Carillon (Ticonderoga) with a force of 6,000 British regulars supplemented by 400 Six Nations warriors and 9,000 militia. Abercromby launched the offensive on July 8, 1758, impulsively deciding not to wait to bring up the heavy artillery for fear that the French garrison of 3,500 would be reinforced. Fort Carillon was surrounded by water on three sides, and the French hastily threw up a defensive *abatis* along the only viable invasion route—a crude barricade of fallen trees and branches. French marksmen coolly picked off the bottled-up British troops ineffectually storming the barricade. Some Highlanders among Abercromby's troops leapt atop the mass of timber, only to be bayoneted when they cleared it. At last, with British casualties mounting to 1,945, Abercromby recalled his forces to Fort George. The corpses of the brave dead remained entangled in the jagged branches, a reproachful reminder of the ill-conceived British tactics. The dispirited Abercromby still held a force greatly outnumbering the French in the area but launched no further offensive. That autumn, he was recalled home and Amherst promoted in his place.

The French had lost some 377 men in the defence of Fort Carillon, but their victory ensured that the French continued to hold this vital chokepoint along the Richelieu River route to the St. Lawrence settlements. Even with the British success at Louisbourg, an attack in the heart of New France was impossible for the moment. Yet Montcalm's successful defence of Carillon won little praise from Governor Vaudreuil.

---

26 Ronald J. Dale, *The Fall of New France: How the French Lost a North American Empire* (Toronto: James Lorimer, 2004), 46.

When they next met, Vaudreuil criticized Montcalm for failing to pursue Abercromby to destroy his army. Even Madame Vaudreuil chimed in to offer her own analysis. Montcalm respectfully suggested that ladies should not speak of war, stating that his own wife would no doubt have remained silent, were she present.

Montcalm remained pessimistic about France's long-term prospects in North America even after his victory at Carillon, and his gloomy outlook seemed borne out by the events that followed. On August 27, 1758, a small French garrison at Fort Frontenac (Cataraqui), at the northeast tip of Lake Ontario, was forced to surrender to a substantial British force led by Lieutenant Colonel John Bradstreet. The British burned the fort and carried off a large quantity of supplies—some of which were intended for France's Indigenous allies. The loss cost the French their route to Lake Ontario, and thus to the other Great Lakes, and the captured supplies hampered France's ability to reward its Indigenous allies. Some disillusioned Ohio Valley Natives concluded a separate peace with Britain.

The French loss of Fort Frontenac also doomed Fort Duquesne. The capture of Duquesne had been part of Pitt's three-pronged invasion plan. Brigadier-General John Forbes had set out in June of 1758 with a force of almost 7,000. By late November, they were within a day's march of Duquesne, with steady cold rain giving way to snow, and Forbes himself suffering from dysentery. Near midnight on November 24, 1758, the British camp heard a dull explosion carried through the wintry woods: when they reached their destination the next morning, passing the decomposing bodies of those who had fought for it, they found a smouldering ruin. The evacuating French knew they could not defend the position, but were determined to deny the fort to the enemy.

The British successes in gaining Louisbourg, Fort Frontenac, and Fort Duquesne (renamed Pittsburgh in honour of the prime minister) came too late in 1758 to be followed by an immediate assault on Quebec that season, but Amherst used the time to destroy communities that might lend aid to the French defence. He sent detachments to burn farms and settlements surrounding the Bay of Fundy and up the Saint John River, and along the Gulf of St. Lawrence near Gaspé and around the Baie des Chaleurs.

In the interval, a desperate Montcalm sent a subordinate officer, Louis-Antoine de Bougainville, to plead for more support for the war in New France. Bougainville was an intelligent and articulate young man—in fact, he would later gain renown as the author of calculus books—but he had had no actual combat experience before coming to North America, and his message to the French court at Versailles was tainted by Montcalm's gloomy pessimism. He likened Canada to a sick patient kept alive by stimulants and suggested that France should only send what was absolutely necessary for its defence. In any event, Bougainville speculated, Britain's naval block-ade might well prevent any aid from getting through. He also sought advice about

Figure 4.3 James Wolfe (1727–1759).

capitulation terms. Such a message was unlikely to inspire an all-out fight for France's possessions in North America. The French colonial minister responded with his own metaphor, explaining that when the house is on fire, one does not bother about the stables. All French hopes lay in a plan to invade England itself.

The court of Versailles was liberal with promotions and decorations for its officers in North America but offered little concrete aid. Montcalm's promotion to lieutenant-general meant that Governor Vaudreuil was now subordinate to him. This was little consolation, as Bougainville carried back to Canada the sobering news that a massive British fleet was en route to attack Quebec. He had also learned that one of Montcalm's daughters had died; he did not know which. Montcalm's letters home to his wife hinted at his growing despair. He lamented the price he had to pay for occasional mentions in the military gazette. He would, he vowed, renounce every honour if he could see her again. "Adieu, my heart! I believe that I love you more than ever."[27]

James Wolfe had been home that winter, too. He returned to North America with a commission as major general and commander-in-chief of the land forces for the expedition against Quebec. He would officially be under Amherst's authority, but far from any effective control. Pitt had been impressed by Wolfe's offensive zeal at Louisbourg, although doubts crept in when they dined together on the eve of Wolfe's departure: Wolfe theatrically waved his sword about, boasting of what he would accomplish. Pitt worried that he had entrusted Britain's fortunes in Quebec to a posturing braggart.

Just 32, tall and scrawny, with a pale, freckled complexion, red hair, prominent nose, and weak chin, Wolfe was not an inspiring physical specimen. He had been plagued by ill health for years, suffering from rheumatism and agonizing kidney stones that caused him to urinate blood. Hearing that his landlady's brother had died from similar symptoms, he grimly joked that at least some distant relief was at hand. Wolfe took the restorative waters at Bath before returning to North America, and there met and fell in love with a young woman named Katherine Lowther. She gave him a miniature portrait of herself to carry with him, and Wolfe wrote a will specifying that, in the event of his death, the portrait should be set in jewels valued at 500 guineas and returned to her. She also gave him a copy of Thomas Gray's "Elegy Written in a

---

27 As quoted in Parkman, *Montcalm and Wolfe*, 409.

Country Churchyard." This melancholy verse struck a chord with Wolfe as he undertook his daunting commission: he underlined the prophetic line "The paths of glory lead but to the grave."[28]

The French had been able to elude British warships to bring a supply fleet of 26 ships to Quebec in the spring of 1759. The aid was minimal—300 or 400 troops, several dozen engineers and sappers, and some arms, ammunition, and provisions—but "a little is precious to those who have nothing," Montcalm reflected philosophically.[29] Montcalm's total fighting force of 18,000 to 20,000 gave him a numerical advantage over the British force at Quebec, but the bulk of Montcalm's force were militia, not professional soldiers. He arranged to have the bulk of his supplies stored at Batiscan, 50 miles upriver from Quebec. If the fortress fell, France's honour could be preserved, he believed, with a strategic retreat to Louisiana via a fleet of canoes.

The British government was battling a budgetary crisis, racking up massive deficits with an outflow of precious currency to Germany and America. Rumours were rife of a cross-channel invasion from France, but Pitt gambled British fortunes with a strong commitment of resources to conquer the French in North America. Admiral Charles Saunders commanded a fleet of 50 armed warships and 150 transport and other vessels, nearly a quarter of the strength of the British Royal Navy. The commitment of troops was likewise unequivocal: Amherst had an army of 11,000 to secure the Champlain-Richelieu River corridor; Wolfe was entrusted with 8,500 to capture Quebec; and Brigadier-General John Prideaux was allotted 5,500 to capture Niagara, thus securing the Great Lakes route.

Amherst's plan was to "lay the axe to the root"—to attack the heart of New France at Quebec—but he knew that possession of the Champlain-Richelieu River route was essential.[30] Once he had secured this, he was to advance north to join Wolfe. On the first day of summer, June 21, 1759, Amherst arrived at the head of Lake George, at Lake Champlain's southern tip. As his forces advanced on Fort Carillon, the badly outnumbered French opted to abandon the position and destroy the fort. The British took possession of the deserted ruin, renaming it Ticonderoga, in late July, and pursued the retreating French to nearby Fort Saint-Frédéric. Again, the French pulled back, evacuating the fort and blowing it up before the British reached it on August 4. The new French line of defence had moved north to Fort Île aux Noix on the Richelieu River. Amherst ended his campaign for the season and ordered the construction of

28 As quoted in Stephen Brumwell, *Paths of Glory: The Life and Death of General James Wolfe* (Montreal and Kingston: McGill-Queen's University Press, 2006), 186. See also 185, 69, 88.

29 As quoted in Parkman, *Montcalm and Wolfe*, 407.

30 As quoted in C.P. Stacey, "Jeffery Amherst, First Baron Amherst," *DCB*, http://www.biographi.ca/en/bio/amherst_jeffery_4E.html.

elaborate fortifications at Crown Point, the site of Fort Saint-Frédéric. Aid to Wolfe at Quebec would have to wait.

In the meantime, Prideaux's British forces and 1,000 Six Nations allies besieged the French garrison at Fort Niagara. The French force of 500 held out as the artillery barrage began in mid-July, hopeful that a relieving party of French militia and Natives might reach them in time. When Prideaux fell to friendly fire, William Johnson took command and devised a strategy to ambush the relieving French force. He surprised them at La Belle Famille, a few kilometres from Niagara, winning a decisive victory. Not only did the French sustain heavy casualties, but it became apparent to the besieged garrison at Niagara that no help was coming. The French surrendered Niagara on July 26, the same day the British took possession of Ticonderoga.

THE BATTLE OF QUEBEC

These British victories, however, would count for little if Quebec remained in French hands. Britain's formidable naval fleet entered the St. Lawrence early in June 1759. Neither Montcalm nor Vaudreuil had thought it necessary to construct batteries at narrows in the river, believing that the upriver channels would be too difficult for a foreign fleet to negotiate. The high cliffs, strong currents, and high tides aided Quebec's defences, and an attack launched from Lake Champlain in the south seemed more likely, but the British used captured Canadian pilots to guide the fleet up the St. Lawrence toward Quebec, and the French scrambled to fortify the northern shoreline between the St. Charles River and the Montmorency. Alarm grew when, on June 27, Wolfe landed soldiers on Île d'Orléans.

The evening after Wolfe's landing on the Île d'Orléans, Vaudreuil made a bold move to attempt to destroy the British fleet with fire ships. Seven aging vessels were loaded with pitch, tar, and other combustibles, along with artillery and explosives, and moved under cover of a moonless night to within range of the British ships. Unfortunately for the French, the fire ships were set alight too soon, and British sentries on the Île d'Orléans took warning. Sheets of flame engulfed the masts of the fire ships, sending missiles flying through the dense smoke and glare. British sailors aboard their own vessels fended off the menacing craft; others bravely grappled the burning hulks and towed them harmlessly to safety. The British fleet remained intact, sheltering just out of range of the guns of Quebec. One French captain and several crew members who failed to escape in time were burned alive in the conflagration.

The following day, the British landed troops at Beaumont, on the south shore of the St. Lawrence, and then marched to Pointe-Lévy, across the river from Quebec. On the north side, Montcalm was sure that Beauport would be the likeliest position for an

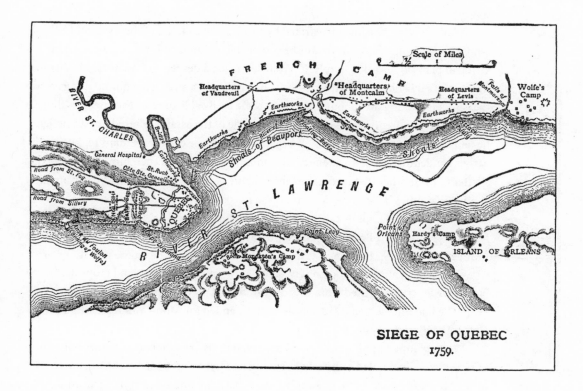

SIEGE OF QUEBEC
1759.

Figure 4.4 Siege of Quebec, 1759.

assault, and he situated the bulk of his army there, more than 12,000 men. When, on July 8, Wolfe landed a force on the north bank at the far side of the Montmorency River, separated from Beauport by a steep waterfall, Montcalm did not oppose him, convinced it was a feint. Instead, the French launched an ineffectual raid against the British encampment at Pointe-Lévy. Having held the position, the British began a massive artillery bombardment of Quebec from Pointe-Lévy on July 12. Within the first week of the two-month siege, 240 of the city's houses were destroyed. The lower town had to be evacuated and was soon half consumed by fire.

Events seemed to favour the British: they had beaten the odds to navigate their fleet up the river as far as Quebec, and they had encampments on the Île d'Orléans, at Pointe-Lévy, and on the far side of the Montmorency River. Yet time was not on Wolfe's side. He had only the summer to act, as Admiral Saunders warned him that the fleet must sail back to England by September 20 at the latest, before freeze-up.

For Montcalm, there was little urgency: if he could hold out for three months, he would have a victory without engaging the enemy. As W.J. Eccles explains, "He did not have to defeat them in a set battle, merely make sure that they did not defeat him."[31]

---

31 Eccles, "Montcalm," *DCB*.

Wolfe grew increasingly frustrated by the defensive tactics of the "wary old fellow" who opposed him.[32] He annoyed his brigadiers by making, and then abandoning, a string of plans for attack. On July 31, Wolfe launched a desperate frontal assault against Montcalm's most heavily fortified lines at Beauport. As a sweltering humid day gave way to a sudden soaking downpour, the French were easily able to repel the attack, killing 400 British. Vaudreuil crowed that the ineptitude of the assault relieved any anxieties he had about Quebec. Wolfe himself began to experience doubts, perhaps regretting his earlier condemnation of the ineffectual commanders who preceded him. He confided in a letter to his mother that he dreaded the ridicule of those at home who did not appreciate the difficulties he faced. Amid the strain, his physical symptoms worsened.

If Quebec could not be taken, Wolfe was determined to wreak as much havoc as he could. He ordered Brigadier James Murray to torch farms and villages along the south shore of the St. Lawrence. Canadians who had already faced the privations of war, with confiscation of food and livestock, now saw their homes and crops destroyed. However, Murray returned from this distasteful duty with some heartening news for Wolfe: he had intercepted a French dispatch intended for Montcalm reporting Fort Niagara's fall to the British.

Wolfe planned another raid on Beauport, but his brigadiers pleaded with him not to repeat what had failed so utterly before. Instead, they proposed an attack upriver to cut Montcalm's access to his supply base at Batiscan and sever communications with Montreal. Such a move would force the French into the open, they believed. Wolfe agreed to abandon the Beauport plan but modified the plan of his brigadiers: they would attack from l'Anse-au-Foulon, close to Quebec itself, a cove with a narrow beach leading up to a steep bank. It was so steep, in fact, that the French had done little to defend it, recognizing it as an improbable landing site. Wolfe brushed aside the misgivings of his brigadiers; if the plan was a mistake, he was sorry. There was little time to lose.

On the night of September 12, 1759, Wolfe's troops commenced operations for one of Canada's most fateful battles. The plan was a desperate one: everything depended on surprise, with no retreat possible once the British forces scaled the 173-foot cliffs to reach the Plains of Abraham outside the walled fortress of Quebec. British warships at Beauport created a diversion, and British forces in landing boats drifted in the dark from where they had been moved upriver, fortuitously mistaken by the French sentries for an expected supply fleet. When a sentry on the cliffs above called out a challenge—*Qui vive?*—a Francophone Scottish officer below answered him. "France,"

---

32 He used the phrase in a letter to his mother. As quoted in C.P. Stacey, "James Wolfe," *DCB*, http://www.biographi.ca/en/bio/wolfe_james_3E.html.

he replied, demanding imperiously that the sentry lower his voice. The sentry shrank from questioning his authority. Brigadier James Murray led the first invaders ashore and gained the heights, signalling the capture of the French guard post to those below. The way was made ready, and British troops swarmed up the cliffs in force.

As dawn broke on the rainy morning of September 13, the French were alarmed to discover the enemy on the plains outside the city. With reports of the landing at first discounted, at seven o'clock Montcalm began to march troops from Beauport, hoping that Bougainville, upriver at Cap Rouge with 3,000 men, would also be hastening to the scene. Montcalm knew that Wolfe's forces had managed to bring two artillery pieces up the embankment and feared that delay would enable them to dig in. By 10 o'clock in the morning, Bougainville not having arrived, the French commander resolved to wait no longer. He met the enemy at the time and place of their choosing, with roughly equal numbers—each side fielding some 4,500 troops. Yet historical observers have noted that Wolfe's position was a highly vulnerable one, and time alone might have handed Montcalm a victory. "Wolfe had dug a grave for his army, but Montcalm marched his own army into it," is one summation.[33]

Wolfe's combat lines, commanded by brigadiers Murray, Townshend, and Monckton, showed admirable discipline as they faced fire from the flanks by Canadian militia and their Indigenous allies. At last, Montcalm, astride a black horse and holding high his sword, led his troops into battle. His lines were ragged, surging forward unevenly, some firing out of effective range, but the disciplined British regulars held fast, awaiting orders to fire, as they endured successive French volleys. At last, a coordinated British curtain of lead and smoke thundered back in answer, and the wavering French lines broke. In less than half an hour, it was all over. Wolfe, on the right flank, felt a musket ball tear into his wrist. He bound up the wound, but the enemy's fire soon found him again. Hit in the stomach and the chest, he fell. As his life ebbed away, Wolfe was conscious of a nearby officer's voice: "They run, see how they run!" "Who runs?" he murmured. "The enemy, Sir; Egad! They give way everywhere!" Wolfe brushed aside offers to fetch a surgeon—"It is needless; it is all over with me"—but ordered that a force be sent to the Charles River to cut off the French retreat. "Now, God be praised, I will die in peace."[34] Montcalm followed his retreating troops into the city on horseback, and was just about to enter the Saint-Louis gate, when he, too, received mortal wounds. He lived until the following day, long enough to take the sacrament and to dictate a letter of farewell to his beloved family, but not so long as to have to witness the entry of the British army into Quebec.

---

33 As quoted in Fowler, *Empires at War*, 198.
34 As quoted in C.P. Stacey, *Quebec, 1759: The Siege and the Battle* (Toronto: Macmillan, 1959), 150.

THE FRENCH STRIKE BACK

The dramatic Battle of the Plains of Abraham has come to symbolize the final defeat of French power in North America, but it is only in retrospect that this battle was decisive. In the immediate aftermath of the battle, Vaudreuil was obliged to surrender Quebec. The British entered the ruined city, marching past smouldering rubble and empty storehouses. James Murray was entrusted with command, becoming military governor of Quebec. General François-Gaston de Lévis took command of the French forces, still hopeful that he could reverse the effects of Montcalm's rash action—an action that Lévis congratulated himself for having no part in. With the British holding the fortified city of Quebec, and the French on the outside, positions had changed, but hostilities had not ended. The looming onset of winter meant that the British fleet had to depart, and Lévis was able to slip a small number of French vessels out to sea late in the season to carry with them his pleas for help to the royal court of Versailles. Fresh troops, artillery, and supplies could enable him to retake Quebec, he urged.

Yet Lévis knew that the spring would bring succour to his enemies. In late April 1760, the St. Lawrence still locked with ice, Lévis made a bold move against British-controlled Quebec. Murray's garrison, now reduced to approximately 3,800, had endured a hungry winter. Lévis marched a force of 7,000 men to nearby Ste. Foy to challenge the British, and on April 28, 1760, Murray confronted them there, hoping to dislodge the French before they could become established—a rationale that parallels Montcalm's idea of the previous autumn. Murray was forced in the end to retreat back behind the city walls, having lost some 20 pieces of field artillery and 1,104 casualties, 259 of them fatal. Lévis's losses amounted to 833, of whom 193 were killed. The 1760 Battle of Ste. Foy, all but forgotten in the shadow of the famous 1759 battle, was thus a far bloodier conflict than that fought over much the same ground the previous September. Losses in the 1759 battle have been estimated at 658 on the British side, and approximately 650 on the side of the French.[35]

NAVAL DEFEAT DOOMS NEW FRANCE

Lévis's victory at Ste. Foy could not preserve French power in North America. Unknown to him, a distant naval battle late the previous autumn had already dashed French hopes. On storm-tossed seas on November 20, 1759, the British Royal Navy foiled France's long-cherished dream of an invasion of the British Isles. The British fleet, under the command of Sir Edward Hawke, intercepted a French squadron of

---

35 Ibid., 164, 152.

21 ships off France's coast at Quiberon Bay. The British boldly chased their quarry under full sail into dangerous waters, where the French were sunk, run aground, or captured. The bells of London rang out in celebration. Historian Fred Anderson identifies the Ohio Valley as the "crucible" of the Seven Years' War, but points to these far-distant events as the critical determinant of the outcome: "The Battle of Quiberon Bay, and not the more celebrated Battle of Quebec, was the decisive military event of 1759."[36]

On May 15, 1760, the French in North America learned that their fate was sealed. That evening, the first relieving ships of the season sailed into the port of Quebec: three British vessels. Murray's garrison in Quebec, seeing the flags flying from the masts, cheered joyously. A dejected Lévis was forced to confront the truth that France had abandoned its North American colony.

Montreal remained in French hands, but in early September, three British armies—a combined force of 17,000—converged upon the city. Vaudreuil and Lévis, with a mere 2,000 defenders, were compelled to surrender on September 8, 1760. Amherst refused the French the honours of war, blaming them for the acts of their Indigenous allies, and the defeated French regiments burned their colours rather than relinquish them to the British.

THE END OF THE WAR AND THE TREATY OF PARIS, 1763

For New France, the war had ended. Yet events elsewhere kept the great powers at war, bringing Spain into an alliance with France against Britain in January 1762. The British navy struck at Spain's colonial possessions around the globe, capturing Havana late that summer and Manila in the Philippines a few weeks later. The French Caribbean colonies of Martinique and Guadeloupe also fell into British hands. In fact, the British used their commanding control of the oceans to take millions of pounds in prizes of war throughout 1762, helping to redress the financial drain of several years of war. The French, for their part, embarrassed General Amherst by capturing St John's, Newfoundland, in June 1762. Amherst dispatched his brother William to recover it, and, in the September 15, 1762, Battle of Signal Hill, the British regained possession of St John's.

The Caribbean islands proved to be a lucrative bargaining chip for Britain in the peace talks. More value was attached to the tiny sugar-producing islands than to the vast Canadian wilderness. In the negotiation of the February 1763 Treaty of Paris ending the war, Spain regained Cuba and Manila, and France bargained for Guadeloupe, Martinique, St. Lucia, and the island of Gorée off the coast of Senegal,

---

36 Anderson, *Crucible of War*, 383.

a centre of the African slave trade. France also won continued rights to the "French shore" of Newfoundland to serve their Grand Banks fishery and recognition of France's claim to the islands of St. Pierre and Miquelon in the Gulf of St. Lawrence. Spain was compelled to surrender Florida to the British, but was rewarded by her French allies with possession of Louisiana. While the Canadians may have been dismayed thus to be handed over to British rule, France evidently recognized that the steady growth of Britain's American colonies would deny any rival nation a foothold on the continent. Indeed, the Duc de Choiseul, negotiating for the French, presciently foresaw that the very size and power of those American colonies made Britain vulnerable to their loss. If they attempted to throw off British rule, France might just be able to help them.

CONCLUSION

The end of the French colonial regime in Canada was thus part of a much larger picture. Forces of global competition had originally prompted colonization in North America, but hard-headed calculation and other exigencies forced France to withdraw from the contest. For the people living on the North American continent, the war wrought great changes. Indigenous nations had calculated the risks and opportunities of allying with warring powers, and were now confronted with a changed landscape as French power collapsed. The Acadians had suffered permanent upheaval, and the Canadians would be forced to now accept governance by a once-hostile power. Nevertheless, the Seven Years' War had set in motion forces whose impact would only be fully felt years later.

5 EVOLUTION AND REVOLUTION: BRITISH NORTH AMERICA, 1763–1784

With the end of the Seven Years' War in 1763, Britain acquired the new colony of Quebec, once the heart of New France. However, British mastery of the North American continent was not as complete as it seemed. Britain confronted the challenge of governing an alien French Roman Catholic population in Quebec. Even more pressing, immediately on the heels of the Treaty of Paris, strong Indigenous resistance in the continent's interior revealed the fragile nature of British control. There was also the question of costs: the all-out commitment Britain had made to win the war had almost doubled the country's national debt. Since the war had been fought to guarantee the security of Britain's American colonies, it seemed only fitting to British policy makers that those colonists should bear some of the costs. The colonists, however, vigorously resisted attempts by Britain's remote Parliament to tax them, contributing to a crisis-filled era in which Britain's responses played a determinative role in shaping the course of history. British policy to address Indigenous grievances, in the form of the 1763 Royal Proclamation, laid the ground-work for Native–newcomer relations for subsequent centuries. The compromise of the 1774 *Quebec Act* contributed to both the persistence of a distinct Canadian culture and society in Quebec and the outbreak of the Revolutionary War. The British colonies of Quebec and Nova Scotia opted not to join their rebellious neighbours, and in the aftermath of the war received a flood of refugee Loyalists. These much-mythologized

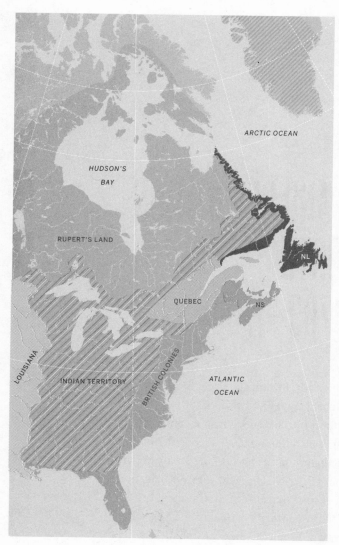

Map 5.1 North America after the Treaty of Paris.

newcomers swelled the populations of Quebec and Nova Scotia and led to the creation of new British colonies in North America.

BRITISH POLICY AND "PONTIAC'S WAR"

The long negotiations that followed the capitulation of New France ended with the ratification of the Treaty of Paris on February 10, 1763. Important parties, however, had been excluded from the peace talks that reshaped North America—the Indigenous peoples. Most nations of the Great Lakes and Ohio country had allied themselves with the French during the Seven Years' War and were confused and angered by its outcome. Undefeated in the interior, and hopeful that the French would return to reclaim their lost empire, the Indigenous peoples of the northwest continued to harass the British who now occupied the former French forts of the region, and the American settlers who began to sweep into the Ohio country. As traders and soldiers, the French had used the lands of the interior on a seasonal and nomadic basis, much like the Indigenous peoples themselves. In contrast, the settlers from the seaboard colonies attempted to divide, clear, and cultivate traditional Indigenous territory. Whereas the French maintained an extensive system of alliances through gift giving, the British viewed the Indigenous peoples of the northwest as conquered and abandoned the practice as an unnecessary expense.

Sir William Johnson, whose long friendship with the Mohawk gave him valuable insights, warned that Indigenous peoples would interpret the sudden withdrawal of presents as a clear sign of "contempt, dislike, and an inclination to reduce them so low as to facilitate designs of extirpating them."[1] The Ojibwe war chief Minweweh spoke for many when he warned Alexander Henry, one of the first English traders to venture into the interior:

> Englishman, although you have conquered the French you have not yet conquered us! We are not your slaves. These lakes, these woods, and mountains were left us by our ancestors. They are our inheritance; and we will part with them to none....Englishman, your king has not sent us any presents, nor entered into any treaty with us, therefore he and we are still at war.[2]

In 1762, an Ottawa war chief, Pontiac, began to meet with the leaders of other Indigenous nations, encouraging them to join together in a confederacy to resist British domination. His cause was strengthened by the visions of Neolin, a charismatic Delaware prophet, who preached a return to traditional ways and the annihilation of the English intruders. "Wherefore do you suffer the whites to dwell in your lands?" Neolin asked. "Drive them away; wage war against them."[3] His words were echoed by Pontiac: "And as for the English—these dogs dressed in red, who have come to rob you of your hunting grounds, and drive away the game—you must lift the hatchet against them. Wipe them from the face of the earth....The children of your great father, the King of France, are not like the English."[4]

In May 1763, Pontiac and a diverse group of warriors laid siege to Fort Detroit. The conflict then spread rapidly throughout the Ohio country and Great Lakes region, with eight British-held forts destroyed and hundreds of settlers killed or captured. Uprisings erupted spontaneously as word of Pontiac's actions spread through the ranks of alienated Natives elsewhere in the northwest. Indigenous military tactics added to the sense of British outrage. On the morning of June 2, at Fort Michilimackinac, Ojibwe warriors staged a game of lacrosse outside the walls of the fort. British soldiers stood by watching the competition and allowed the players behind the walls of the palisade to retrieve an errant ball. Once inside, the Indigenous warriors sprung the trap, and with weapons concealed beneath their garments, took

---

1 Gregory Evans Dowd, *War Under Heaven: Pontiac, the Indian Nations, and the British Empire* (Baltimore: Johns Hopkins University Press, 2002), 71.

2 Alexander Henry, *Travels and Adventures in Canada and the Indian Territories Between the Years 1760 and 1766* (New York: I. Riley, 1809), 44.

3 Anthony F.C. Wallace, *The Death and Rebirth of the Seneca* (New York: Alfred A. Knopf, 1970), 118.

4 J.R. Miller, *Skyscrapers Hide the Heavens: A History of Indian-White Relations in Canada* (Toronto: University of Toronto Press, 1989), 74.

possession of the fort. Twenty-two British soldiers and traders were killed, and a number were taken prisoner. Significantly, some French-Canadian traders within the fort were left unharmed.

The conflict dragged on throughout the summer, at great cost to both sides. At Fort Pitt in the Ohio country, beleaguered British officers grew desperate enough to resort to biological warfare, infecting blankets with smallpox and distributing them in medicine boxes during a parlay with an Indigenous delegation. Historians are divided over the effectiveness of this desperate action. According to Francis Jennings, the British attempt at germ warfare was "unquestionably effective" and greatly weakened the Indigenous cause. Others have argued that smallpox was already widespread throughout the region, and that the outbreak in 1763 cannot be definitively traced to contaminated British blankets.[5] By the fall of 1763, there were signs that support for the uprisings was beginning to wane. At Detroit, nearby French-Canadian settlers failed to join the siege, and some of Pontiac's own warriors began to abandon the field to return to their hunting grounds. Elsewhere, the shortage of powder and guns, or the arrival of British reinforcements, forced a retreat. Furthermore, Pontiac's confederacy suffered from an inherent weakness—traditional rivalries resurfaced and eroded what was essentially an artificial unity.

The uprisings of 1763 failed to force a British withdrawal from Indigenous territory, or to produce a lasting First Nations confederacy. Indigenous resistance did, however, compel British authorities to recognize "the great dissatisfaction" among the Indigenous nations resulting from "great frauds and abuses" perpetuated against them by unscrupulous land speculators, settlers, and traders. Conceding that frontier stability could only be achieved through negotiation and accommodation, the Crown issued a Royal Proclamation on October 7, 1763, that drew a boundary line along the crest of the Appalachians. Lands to the west of the line were declared "Indian Territory," not to be settled or purchased unless acquired by treaty between the Crown and the Indigenous nation affected. Taking a page from French policy, the British attempted to restore good diplomatic relations by resuming the practice of annual gift giving to Indigenous nations.[6] Although these changes in British policy succeeded in restoring a greater peace and security among Indigenous peoples,

---

5 Francis Jennings, *Empire of Fortune: Crowns, Colonies and Tribes in the Seven Years War in America* (New York: W.W. Norton, 1988), 447–48; David Dixon, *Never Come to Peace Again: Pontiac's Uprising and the Fate of the British Empire in British North America, 1754–1766* (Norman: University of Oklahoma Press, 2005), 154; Michael N. McConnell, *A Country Between: The Upper Ohio and Its Peoples, 1724–1774* (Lincoln: University of Nebraska Press, 1992), 195.

6 John Borrows, "Wampum at Niagara: The Royal Proclamation, Canadian Legal History, and Self-Government" in *Aboriginal and Treaty Rights in Canada: Essays on Law, Equality, and Respect for Difference* (Vancouver: University of British Columbia Press, 1997). 155–72.

at least temporarily, they resulted in considerable indignation in other quarters. American colonists were determined to avenge their losses, and land-hungry specu-lators coveted the interior for themselves. In time, the Proclamation line proved ineffective against the tide of American settlers that spilled over the Appalachians.

THE WEST AND THE FUR TRADE

After the conquest of New France by the British, newcomers from England, Scotland, and the American colonies to the south began to form a small but vigorous merchant class in Quebec. These new arrivals established a number of small fur-trading enter-prises that challenged the Hudson's Bay Company's monopoly as they extended the trade further west. Indigenous traders, who had once brought furs to York Factory, were now being intercepted by enterprising "pedlars" based out of Montreal. One of these "pedlars" was an ambitious and ill-tempered Connecticut veteran of the Seven Years' War, Peter Pond. Pond led the way, mapping and trading in the territories that lay beyond the reach of Hudson's Bay Company. A ruthless competitor, he intimidated rivals and was suspected of murdering two of his fellow traders. The success of independent traders such as Pond forced the Hudson's Bay Company to seek alterna-tive sources of revenue.

In December 1770, Samuel Hearne, a veteran of the Royal Navy who entered the fur trade after serving in the Seven Years' War, undertook a trip on behalf of the HBC in search of mineral deposits. He set out from Fort Prince of Wales to follow up on reports of abundant copper to the north. Accompanied by a Chipewyan guide, Matonabbee, Hearne journeyed more than 2,700 kilometres across the tundra, travel-ling north to the mouth of the Coppermine River on the Arctic coast. After enduring intense hunger and cold on the gruelling journey, a disappointed Hearne returned with only a two-kilogram lump of copper. Convinced that the far north offered few prospects, the HBC decided to meet the challenge posed by the independent traders head-on. In 1774, Hearne founded the HBC's first inland fur-trading post, Cumberland House, at a strategic location where the rivers connecting to Hudson Bay and the Arctic met with those of the plains. Finding it increasingly difficult to finance and supply their far-flung operations and determined to strengthen their hand against the HBC, a group of independent Montreal traders—Simon McTavish, Isaac Todd, James McGill, Peter Pond, and Benjamin and Joseph Frobisher among them—decided to consolidate their operations and formed the North West Company in 1779—setting in motion a period of epic competition between the rival companies.

QUEBEC UNDER BRITISH RULE

The Royal Proclamation of 1763 had significant consequences for French Canada, prescribing boundaries, government, and law for the new British colony of Quebec. Deprived of "Indian Territory," Quebec was now confined to the old seigneurial heartland that lay on either side of the St. Lawrence. Anticipating that Quebec's French Catholic population would soon be overwhelmed by an influx of English-speaking and Protestant settlers from the American colonies and would be quickly assimilated, the Royal Proclamation imposed English law and directed the governor to call a general assembly "in such Manner and Form as is used and directed in those Colonies and Provinces in America which are under our immediate Government."[7]

Responsibility for implementing the terms of the Royal Proclamation fell to James Murray, a veteran of the Seven Years' War who had served as Quebec's military governor since the capitulation. In the absence of a large English-speaking population, James Murray proceeded slowly, introducing English criminal law and appointing justices of the peace and bailiffs, but maintaining French property and civil law. Murray's procrastination displeased the small British merchant community that demanded the full and immediate introduction of English law and the establishment of a legislative assembly to protect their rights. Francis Maseres, Murray's attorney general, warned that any assembly would be "representative of only the 600 new English settlers, and an instrument in their hands of domineering over the 90,000 French." "Can such an assembly," Maseres asked rhetorically, "be thought to be just or expedient, or likely to produce harmony and friendship between the two nations?"[8] The answer was obvious to Murray. While an assembly might please the English minority, it was sure to offend the French-Canadian majority who, as Roman Catholics, would be ineligible to participate under English law. An aristocratic soldier, Murray had little patience for the noisy demands of merchants interested only in profits and refused to call an assembly.

British authorities instructed Murray not to re-establish "the Popish hierarchy" and to take measures to induce Canadians "to embrace the Protestant religion and to raise their children in it." Although Murray, like many English Protestants, was suspicious of Roman Catholics, he recognized that, with few Protestants in the colony, there was little hope of converting the French-Canadian majority. Consequently, he adopted a pragmatic approach to the Roman Catholic Church. Although this was counter to

---

7   "Royal Proclamation of 1763" in A. Shortt and A.G. Doughty, *Documents Relating to the Constitutional History of Canada* (Ottawa: S.E. Dawson, 1907), 49.

8   Frances Maseres, "Report," in J.H. Stewart Reid, Kenneth McNaught, and Harry S. Crowe (eds.), *A Source-book of Canadian History: Selected Documents and Personal Papers* (Toronto: Longmans, Green and Company, 1959), 52.

his instructions, Murray advised London that the appointment of "a superintendent of the Romish religion" would provide his administration with a valuable ally capable of keeping French Canadians loyal to their new government. Murray regularly used the new bishop, Jean-Olivier Briand, to circulate pastoral messages in support of the state, and in return for his cooperation and "good behaviour" rewarded Briand with an annuity.[9] For his part, Briand adopted a pragmatic "render unto Caesar" attitude and directed that prayers should be offered to the British royal family at mass: "They are our masters, and we owe them what we owed the French when they were our masters. Does the Church now forbid his subjects to pray for their prince?"[10]

The aristocratic Murray favoured a hierarchical social order and thus looked to seigneurs and the seigneurial system to maintain peace, order, and loyalty among the *habitants*. During the French regime, there was often little economic distance between seigneur and *habitant*, and the latter were far from being submissive peasants who always deferred to their social superiors. Murray's support for the seigneurs thus antagonized many French-Canadian *habitants* as well as the English merchant community, who accused the governor of acting like a despot. "The Governor," the merchants complained in a petition to the King, "instead of acting agreeable to that confidence reposed in him by your Majesty, in giving a favourable reception to those of your Majesty's subjects…doth frequently treat them with rage and rudeness of language, as dishonourable to the trust he holds of your Majesty as painful to those who suffer from it." Murray dismissed the petitioners as "licentious fanatics" who would be content with nothing less than the expulsion of the French Canadians, "perhaps the bravest and best race upon the globe." He urged the extension to Canadian Roman Catholics of privileges that "the laws of England deny" to them at home, confident that this would make them faithful and useful subjects.[11] However, amid angry petitions from the Anglophone merchant class of Quebec, Murray was recalled to London in 1766.

Sir Guy Carleton, one of Murray's lieutenants, replaced him as military governor. An ambitious career soldier with a fiery temper, Carleton was convinced that Murray's "favouritism" toward the Canadians had been a mistake. He cultivated good relations with the British merchants and promised to abolish French civil law and call an assembly. But Carleton, like Murray before him, soon came to distrust the clamouring of the Anglophone commercial class, which he likened to the increasing restlessness within the 13 older British colonies to the south. Carleton also grew to admire the

9   "Instructions to Governor James Murray" in Reid, McNaught, and Crowe, *Source-book of Canadian History*, 50.

10 André Vachon, "Jean-Olivier Briand," *Dictionary of Canadian Biography* (DCB), http://www.biographi.ca.

11 "Merchant's Petition and Murray's Response" in Reid, McNaught, and Crowe, *Source-book of Canadian History*, 51–52.

national spirit of the Canadians and recognized the utility of both the seigneurial system and the Roman Catholic Church. As a result, he began to reconsider British policy in Quebec.

Given the lack of English-speaking immigrants and the high birth rate of the Canadians, Carleton concluded that "barring catastrophe shocking to think of, this country must, to the end of time, be peopled by the Canadian race, who already have taken such firm root, and got to so great a height, that any new stock transplanted will be totally hid."[12] Quebec, Carleton advised British authorities, was a province unlike any other, and its distinctive circumstances needed to be acknowledged, including the French civil law and seigneurial system of landholding. As well, he contended, the rights and privileges of the Catholic Church should be confirmed. Quebec's boundaries should be redrawn to include its natural hinterland around the Great Lakes. Because the Canadians lacked a tradition of representative government, Carleton felt there was no need for an elected assembly. French Catholics should, however, be permitted to serve in an appointed legislative council and other official posts. If such concessions were granted, Carleton concluded, the Canadians would become loyal British subjects and Quebec would remain a bastion of imperial strength.

Carleton returned to London in 1770 and spent the next four years trying to persuade British officials to abandon the assimilationist agenda of the Royal Proclamation of 1763 and to restructure Quebec's laws and institutions to better reflect the French reality of the province. Carleton was joined in London in 1773 by François Baby, a prominent Francophone Montreal merchant. Baby carried with him a petition, signed by most of Quebec's prominent French-Canadian families, appealing for Catholic civil rights and the restoration of French law. "Then our fears will be removed," Baby promised, "and we shall pass our lives in tranquility and happiness, and shall be always ready to sacrifice them for the glory of our prince and the good of our country."[13]

As tensions increased in the American colonies, such professions of loyalty began to sway opinion in England toward Carleton's position. Still, many objected in Parliament to any change in policy toward Quebec and the Canadians. Edmund Burke complained that the establishment of French law would make the monarchy despotic. Lord Chatham warned against the establishment of "popery" and arbitrary power. Lord Cavendish cautioned that the recognition of Quebec's customary laws would forever make them a distinct people. Conversely, Alexander Wedderburn insisted that "experience demonstrates that the public safety has been often endangered by restraints [on religious freedoms], and there is no instance of any state that has been overturned

---

12 "Sir Guy Carleton" in Reid, McNaught, and Crowe, *Source-Book of Canadian History*, 54.
13 Michael P. Gabriel (ed.), *Quebec during the American Revolution: The Journals of François Baby, Gabriel Taschereau and Jenkin Williams* (Ann Arbor: Michigan State University Press, 2005).

by toleration."[14] Carleton's recommendations were eventually incorporated into the *Quebec Act* of 1774.

The *Quebec Act* extended the colony's boundaries to include the Great Lakes and the Ohio country to better enforce the Proclamation line of 1763 and contain the migration of colonial Americans. "For the more perfect security and ease of the minds of the inhabitants" of the province, the Act protected the practice of the Roman Catholic faith, providing a revised oath of allegiance that would not require pledging one's faith to the Church of England. While English criminal law would continue to prevail, as it had since the conquest, for property and civil matters the French Civil Code would be in force, ensuring the continuation of the seigneurial system. One of the most striking aspects of the Act was its retreat from the 1763 plan to establish representative government. The Act declared that it was "at present inexpedient to call an Assembly"— undoubtedly because it would have been dominated by the tiny Anglophone minority.[15] Instead, the governor was to appoint a legislative council to make laws. While the Act made no specific mention of the French language, it did contain, in essence, statutory recognition of the distinctiveness of the Canadians as a people.

On the surface, the *Quebec Act* signalled an abandonment of the assimilationist agenda of earlier British policy. Accompanying the *Act*, however, was a set of secret instructions directing Carleton to introduce English common law gradually, to subject the Roman Catholic Church to state supervision, and to discourage the growth of religious orders, especially the Jesuits. These instructions suggest that British authorities viewed the concessions of the *Quebec Act* as temporary responses to the immediate challenges posed by the growing unrest in its other North American colonies. Carleton, for the most part, ignored the instructions, not wanting to undermine the relationship he had cultivated with church authorities and the seigneurs.

Reaction to the *Quebec Act* was mixed. Although Roman Catholic Church leaders and French-Canadian seigneurs embraced its terms, ordinary French-Canadian *habitants* were far less enthusiastic about the reintroduction of tithes and the legal recognition given to seigneurial dues. Montreal's Anglophone merchants welcomed the incorporation of the old fur-trade heartland back into the province, but complained bitterly about the concessions to the French majority and the absence of any provision for an assembly. The strongest reaction to the *Quebec Act*, however, came from the American colonies.

---

14 Philip Lawson, "'Sapped by Corruption': British Governance of Quebec and the Breakdown of Anglo-American Relations on the Eve of the Revolution," *Canadian Review of American Studies* 22, no. 3 (Winter 1991): 301–24.

15 W.P.M. Kennedy, *Documents of the Canadian Constitution, 1759–1915* (Toronto: Oxford University Press, 1918), 57.

QUEBEC AND THE AMERICAN REVOLUTION

To American colonists, the *Quebec Act* was a betrayal, and the latest in a series of provocations passed by the British Parliament. Discontent had been building in the colonies since the end of the Seven Years' War. The war itself had taken a heavy toll: rising prices, disruption of trade, and high levels of colonial debt caused serious economic hardship in the colonies for many years to come. The cost of empire also weighed heavily upon the debt-laden British government, which was determined to restore its finances by shifting some of the cost of empire to the colonists through taxation and a more tightly regulated colonial trade.

Such actions contributed to growing disillusionment among many American colonists, who began to question British policy and Parliament's authority to tax the colonies. Spokespersons for the discontented began to give voice to a coherent set of political ideas that were rooted in the Whig ideology that had emerged during Britain's Glorious Revolution of 1688. This politics of protest sought to limit the powers of the Crown over Parliament. Whigs believed that humanity was driven by a lust for power and that power was a corrupting force that could only be attained by depriving others of their liberty. To protect liberty, all elements of the body politic needed to be balanced against each other in order to prevent any one part from gaining dominance over the others. American Whigs argued that the power of the Crown over the colonies needed to be restrained and the freedom of colonial assemblies strengthened. Throughout the colonies, popular discontent increasingly found expression in petitions to the King, the burning of effigies, the erection of liberty poles, the boycotting of British goods, the wearing of homespun, and even occasional rioting.

To many American colonists, the *Quebec Act* signalled a dangerous new threat to their freedom and future aspirations. Whigs criticized the Act's unrepresentative government and entrenchment of "despotism." Expansionists attacked the extension of Quebec's borders and interference with the American colonies' natural frontiers. New England Protestants resented the *Quebec Act*'s concessions to "popery." Everywhere colonists questioned why Parliament would choose to reward a traditional but recently defeated enemy and asked if the *Quebec Act* was simply a prelude to extinguishing liberty throughout British North America. In September 1774, representatives from 12 of the 13 American colonies met in the First Continental Congress. Although far from united, delegates issued a Declaration of Rights and Freedoms that outlined colonial grievances, demanded that Parliament repeal "the intolerable acts" and justified colonial defiance of unjust British policies by appealing to the "immutable laws of nature and the principles of the English constitution." The First Continental Congress also issued an appeal to "friends and fellow subjects" in the province of Quebec to "unite with us" to "obtain redress of our afflicting grievances" and to "take a noble chance for emerging from a humiliating subjection under Governors, Intendants, and Military Tyrants." "You are a small people, compared to those who with open arms invite you into a fellowship," the manifesto warned, and "a moment's reflection should convince you which will be most for your interest and happiness, to have all the rest of North America your unalterable friends, or your inveterate enemies."[16]

Most Canadians were unmoved by the manifesto's combination of enticement and intimidation and remained on the sidelines as the American colonies moved toward rebellion. When Britain refused to alter its colonial policies and sent more troops to the colonies, a Second Continental Congress was held in the spring of 1775: it voted to raise an army to defend American liberty. In July, the Second Continental Congress authorized an invasion of Quebec, in the hope of rallying support from French Canadians and preventing the British from using Quebec as a base from which to suppress the rebellious colonies. In the summer of 1775, two American armies marched north to take Canada. One force, under Richard Montgomery, advanced by way of Lake Champlain toward Montreal; another, under Benedict Arnold, struggled through the dense wilderness of Maine to strike directly at Quebec. The Americans were confident that French Canadians would welcome the American invaders and join the revolt against Britain.

Carleton was equally confident that the Canadians, grateful for the concessions of the *Quebec Act*, would rally to the defence of the province. Both sides were disappointed. When Carleton called up the militia few answered the call, despite the admonitions of seigneurs "to defend your country and your king with all your power" and the threat of church leaders to excommunicate anyone who aided the Americans. As Montgomery's army entered Quebec, he was surprised to discover that few Canadians came forward to welcome and support their American "liberators." Thomas Walker, a merchant who had moved to Montreal from Boston in 1763, had assured the Americans that "the bulk of the people both English and Canadian wish well to your cause...which alone will free us from those fears and apprehensions that rob us of our peace."[17] Walker, who was among the most vocal critics of British policy in Quebec, worked tirelessly to recruit French Canadians, promising money and arms to anyone who joined the American cause. Most Canadians, however, had little interest in supporting either their new British overlords or their traditional American rivals and opted to remain neutral. With a few notable exceptions such as Walker,

---

16 "Continental Congress to the Inhabitants of the Province of Quebec, 26 Oct. 1774," in Worthington C. Ford et al. (eds.), *Journals of the Continental Congress, 1774–1789*, vol. 1 (Washington, DC: Government Printing Office, 1904), 105–13.

17 G.F.G. Stanley, *Canada Invaded, 1775–1776* (Toronto: Hackert, 1973).

The Mitred Minuet.

Figure 5.1 The Mitred Minuet. This cartoon captures how American critics viewed the *Quebec Act*.

even the number of American sympathizers among the English-speaking merchant community remained small. Most recognized that their economic stake in the imperial system outweighed their political dissatisfaction with the *Quebec Act*.

In September, Montgomery's army of 1,500 volunteer militiamen reached Fort St. Jean on the outskirts of Montreal. A small of force of 200 British regulars and a handful of Canadian militia held off the Americans for eight weeks. With supplies running short, casualties mounting, and winter approaching, British Major Charles Preston finally surrendered on November 3, 1775. When he received news that Fort St. Jean had fallen, Carleton retreated to Quebec, and Montgomery marched into Montreal unopposed. Five days later, Arnold's army reached Quebec, having endured a gruelling overland journey that claimed nearly half of its 1,200 men. On November 15, Arnold marched to the citadel gates and demanded the immediate surrender of the town. Carleton ignored Arnold's ultimatum, although he was unsure of the loyalty of the town's residents. Even when Montgomery and 300 reinforcements joined Arnold, Carleton continued to stand fast. The siege of Quebec lasted through December, but the Americans were unable to breach the defences. As winter set in, smallpox ravaged American ranks, and morale deteriorated. With nearly half of the American troops due to be discharged at the end of the year, Montgomery and Arnold launched a desperate and unsuccessful attack on Quebec's lower town during a blinding snowstorm on New Year's Eve. Montgomery was killed in the struggle, Arnold wounded, and nearly 400 Americans taken prisoner.

In Montreal, the conduct of the American invaders had squandered whatever support existed among the local population. Betraying an intense anti-Catholic prejudice, the American commander left in charge of the city, Brigadier-General David Wooster, prohibited the celebration of Christmas mass and permitted his troops to use churches as stables for their horses. When supplies began to run short, the American occupiers further alienated the local population by paying for goods with worthless Congressionalist paper money, and by seizing crops from *habitant* farms. In April 1776, the Second Continental Congress sent a commission to Montreal to "convince" the Canadians "of the Uprightness of our Intentions towards them."[18] But Wooster's heavy-handedness and the behaviour of his troops spoke louder than the soothing reassurances offered by Benjamin Franklin and the other commissioners. The commissioners found the Canadians openly hostile and their own troops diseased and dispirited. When a British fleet with 10,000 soldiers arrived at Quebec on May 5, 1776, what remained of Arnold's exhausted army immediately fled. Hoping that the rebels might yet be reconciled to the empire, Carleton did not unleash British forces upon the retreating Americans and ordered them to proceed toward Montreal slowly. On June 15, 1776, the Americans withdrew from Montreal, and the invasion of Canada was over.

NEUTRAL NOVA SCOTIA?

On July 4, 1776, the Second Continental Congress issued its Declaration of Independence. Any hope that the differences between Britain and the American colonies might be settled peacefully through negotiation and compromise was now past. The Declaration of Independence attracted the attention of Nova Scotians, many of whom were disaffected with Britain's colonial policies and the administration of the governing elite in Halifax. Much of this discontent focused on the governor, Francis Legge. A career soldier, Legge owed his position to the patronage of the secretary of state for the American Colonies, the Earl of Dartmouth, a distant relative. Shortly after his arrival in 1773, Legge found himself caught in a struggle between the Assembly, established in 1758, and the Executive Council for control of the government's finances.

18 "Instruction and Commission from Congress to Benjamin Franklin, Charles Carroll and Samuel Chase for the Canadian Mission, Congress, 20 March 1776," *Journals of the American Congress from 1774–1778*, vol. 1 (Washington: Way and Gideon, 1823), 290.

The dispute centred on Jonathan Binney, a Boston merchant who moved to Halifax in 1753. Binney became a close associate of the Halifax merchant elite that dominated the Executive Council. Through his connections, Binney secured an appointment as the magistrate and collector of provincial duties at Canso. Many within the Assembly were critical of such absentee patronage appointments and refused to vote Binney an allowance. The Council routinely overrode the Assembly's wishes and its members appealed to the new governor. Finding Binney a "serviceable and necessary officeholder," Legge cavalierly dismissed the Assembly's protest and turned his attention to Nova Scotia's large debt. Determined to restore the public finances, Legge ordered an audit of the province's books in 1774. During the audit it was discovered that Binney routinely drew upon the fines and duties he collected. Legge issued a warrant for his arrest, and Binney was tried and convicted before the governor by a packed jury. When Binney protested the proceedings and refused to pay back the funds for which he was found liable, Legge ordered that he be imprisoned along with his wife and children. Legge's conduct not only outraged Binney's supporters within the Executive Council and Halifax's merchant elite, but his critics within the Assembly as well. Fed up with Legge's authoritarian behaviour, the Assembly petitioned the British government "on the subject of the Grievances the People of this Province labour under" and demanded Legge's immediate recall.

To many Nova Scotians, Binney was a victim of British persecution. Such sentiments were especially strong among the large community of New England planters who had settled the fertile lands vacated by the Acadians. One of these planters, Jonathan Eddy, represented Chignecto (an isthmus connecting Nova Scotia with New Brunswick) in the Assembly during the Binney affair. Disgusted by the proceedings, Eddy appealed to George Washington and the Continental Congress to send "an army of liberation" to Nova Scotia, but the failure of the Canadian campaign, the powerful British garrison at Halifax, and the lack of an American navy dissuaded Congress from committing any resources. Undeterred, Eddy approached the government of Massachusetts, which promised to arm and supply any volunteers he might enlist to free Nova Scotia. Through a combination of persuasion, deception, and intimidation, Eddy eventually gathered a force of 180 planters and Natives. He promised that a large American army was on its way to assist their cause, and, for good measure, threatened to attack the property of any who would not join them. On November 12, 1776, Eddy's army attacked Fort Cumberland on the Chignecto isthmus. The small British garrison easily held the rebel force at bay, and the rebels fled as soon as reinforcements arrived. Another American sympathizer, John Allan, attempted an assault on the small garrison at the mouth of the Saint John River in June 1777. Allan was the son of Scottish immigrants, had held a number of public positions, and served in the Assembly as the representative for Cumberland. Although not of New England stock, Allan shared American aspirations and attempted to rally Natives and Acadians disaffected with British rule to his cause. Few responded and before he could even launch an attack, a British naval squadron arrived, forcing Allan's small army to disperse.

Although Eddy's and Allan's plans failed to amount to much, many Nova Scotians did identify with American grievances. Why then did Nova Scotia not join with the other American colonies in their revolt against British rule? Certainly, the presence of a large British garrison at the naval base at Halifax allowed the British to respond quickly and forcefully to any attempt to invade the province or incite the locals. Despite their disillusionment with the colonial administration, the close commercial ties with England and dependence upon government contracts kept Halifax's merchant elite from joining with their Boston counterparts and declaring independence. Geography and the make-up of the population also played a role. The distribution of settlements along Nova Scotia's long and rugged coastline impeded communication and the organization of a coordinated resistance to British rule. Although nearly half of Nova Scotia's 19,000 residents were New England planters, significant numbers of Ulster Irish Protestants, Yorkshiremen, Scots, and returning Acadians had arrived in the province in the early 1770s. The cultural diversity and recent arrival of so many settlers precluded the development of a unified political identity and collective sense of grievance. Whatever sympathy existed for the rebels was undermined by the activities of American privateers, who routinely pillaged Nova Scotia's coastal settlements in the name of liberty. The unwillingness of Nova Scotians to support the rebellion owed a great deal as well to a religious awakening that swept through rural planter communities in the 1770s and 1780s.

The "New Light stir," as it was called, was led by a charismatic itinerant preacher, Henry Alline. Alline's family moved to Nova Scotia from Rhode Island in 1760 when he was 12 and settled in the remote farming community of Falmouth on the Minas Basin. Even before the family arrived in Nova Scotia, Alline felt he had been "moved upon by the spirit of God." There was no church in Falmouth, so he studied the Bible on his own, read popular devotional works, and discussed religious matters with his parents. As he grew older, Alline feared that his salvation was endangered by "frolicking and carnal mirth." He wrestled constantly with his soul, "groaning under a load of guilt and darkness, praying and crying continually for mercy." After an intense conversion experience, Alline resolved to "labour in the ministry and...preach the gospel."[19]

In 1776, Alline began an itinerant ministry and launched his New Light movement. His emotional, extemporaneous preaching and effective use of music drew large crowds and resulted in spiritual awakening wherever he went. Alline attracted a large following

19 Henry Alline, *Life and Journal* (Boston: 1906). 34.

in the poor and isolated communities of rural Nova Scotia. Economically deprived and cut off from the centres of power, these farmers and fishers found empowerment in his message that true worth rested on personal intimacy with God rather than status, wealth, or influence. Alline had little interest in the external trappings of religion—creeds, hierarchy, doctrine, and liturgy—and called upon individuals to break free of tradition and become "new and spiritual men."[20] In the midst of the political turmoil sweeping the American colonies, Alline offered Nova Scotians a spiritual assurance that rejected and transcended the tribulations of the secular world; he insisted that God, not the rebels or the British, commanded the allegiance of Nova Scotians. Until his death in 1784, Alline preached throughout the area and caused a revival of faith that eventually laid the foundation of the Baptist movement in the Maritimes.

AMERICA'S FIRST "CIVIL" WAR

The American Revolution divided families, communities, and regions and is rightly considered America's first "civil" war. It is estimated that about one-third of Americans actively supported independence; another third remained loyal to Britain and the empire; and the remaining third preferred neutrality. Many Loyalists tended to be recent arrivals to the colonies and members of ethnic and religious minorities who had not yet fully assimilated to American ways, and who believed their rights and interests would be better protected within the empire. Backcountry farmers who feared the domination of the powerful mercantile elites who resided in the towns and cities along the Atlantic seaboard also figured prominently in Loyalist ranks. Loyalist leaders, disparagingly referred to as "tories" by the American rebels, were typically drawn from those classes whose position and livelihood depended on maintaining the British connection.

It has been argued that Loyalist leaders possessed an ideology distinct from the republican ideology of the American rebels, or "patriots," as they called themselves. From the Loyalist perspective, the movement toward independence was driven by factions of self-interested power seekers, demagogues who sought to direct public anxiety against civic authorities and institutions for their own gain. This diagnosis was rooted in a worldview that emphasized humanity's tendency to act on the basis of passion and self-interest rather than reason and the common good. To Loyalists, the state was a necessary and positive force that controlled the passions, thereby ensuring everyone the quiet enjoyment of their rights and liberty. Loyalists warned that the self-interested actions of the rebels only served to undermine authority and order, and thus posed a far greater threat to liberty than the actions of a government 5,000 kilometres

---

20 Alline, *Life and Journal*, 35.

away. Loyalist and patriot did not differ in their love of liberty, but rather in their perceptions of where the threat to liberty originated, and in their prescriptions for its safekeeping. Loyalist leaders acknowledged problems in the imperial relationship but insisted that the empire could be reformed in ways that both protected colonial rights and strengthened the Anglo-American community. Independence, Loyalists predicted, would expose divisions between and within the colonies and lead to a state of economic and political chaos.

With the outbreak of hostilities in 1775, Loyalists were condemned as enemies of American liberty and subjected to various forms of persecution. Loyalist newspapers were shut down and presses destroyed; Loyalist property was confiscated and sold without compensation; and individual Loyalists were tarred and feathered, beaten, lynched, and imprisoned. The burden of loyalty was especially heavy for Loyalist women. War compelled many Loyalist women to assume roles beyond their normal experience. Many took charge of the family farm or business while their husbands and sons enlisted in Loyalist regiments. A significant number of women played an important role in the war by passing on useful information to the British and providing safe houses for Loyalist fugitives. It was often Loyalist women who were brought before Patriot Committees to plead for their families' safety and the security of their property. As the war ran its course, growing numbers of Loyalist women and children were forced to flee their homes and seek refuge behind British lines. Displaced from their homes and support networks, refugee women found life in the makeshift refugee camps established in New York and Quebec physically, emotionally, and psychologically challenging. Far from appreciating their service and sacrifice, British authorities often viewed these women and their children as unwelcome burdens.

The experience of the Bowman family was typical of many. Jacob Bowman was the son of German immigrants. He joined the British army during the Seven Years' War and was awarded 600 hectares of land on the Susquehanna River in New York for his services. Suspected of being a Loyalist, Bowman was apprehended by patriots in November 1775. "He was surprised at night while his wife was sick by a party of rebels," his granddaughter Elizabeth later recalled, "and with his eldest son, a lad of sixteen years of age, was taken prisoner; his house was pillaged of every article except the bed on which his sick wife lay and that they stripped of all but one blanket. Half an hour after my grandfather was marched off, his youngest child was born." With their cattle and grain all taken away by the rebels, the family only survived with the assistance of "some friendly Indians."[21] The family struggled to get by for a year before joining other

---

21 "Elizabeth Bowman Spohn to Egerton Ryerson, 23 July 1861" in J.J. Talman (ed.), *Loyalist Narratives from Upper Canada* (Toronto: Champlain Society, 1946), 316–17.

Loyalist women and children in an overcrowded refugee camp at Machiche near Trois-Rivières. When he was 13, Elizabeth Bowman's father, Peter, joined Butler's Rangers, one of several companies of Loyalist refugees organized during the American Revolution. The company, formed by John Butler, a wealthy landowner from New York's Mohawk Valley and a veteran of the frontier warfare of the 1750s, wreaked revenge throughout the Susquehanna, Wyoming, and Schoharie valleys. These raids proved effective in spreading terror and keeping the patriots on the defensive. The success of the campaign owed much to the Iroquois warriors who fought alongside Butler's Rangers.

With the exception of the Tuscaroras and some Oneida, most of the Six Nations Iroquois supported the British during the American Revolution. Three people—Sir William Johnson and Joseph and Molly Brant—worked to maintain the Iroquois alliance with the British. Johnson settled near Schenectady, New York, in 1738 where he traded with the local Natives, mastered the Mohawk language, and became thoroughly familiar with Iroquois customs and beliefs. Having earned their confidence and respect, Johnson was adopted into the Mohawk nation and named a *sachem* (chief). From 1744 until his death in 1774, Johnson was superintendent of Indian affairs for New York. He was greatly assisted in his business and diplomatic dealings with the Iroquois by Molly Brant, with whom he established a relationship in 1759. Molly Brant came from a distinguished Mohawk family and exercised great influence among her people. She managed Johnson's household, and together they raised seven children. Although Johnson did not always enjoy the support of his superiors, he pursued a policy of diplomacy and consultation that accommodated Iroquois needs and aspirations and respected Native ownership of the land. Johnson strove to uphold the terms of the Royal Proclamation of 1763, which restricted settlement west of the Appalachians until treaties had been negotiated and Indigenous lands purchased. William Johnson's son Guy strove to maintain good relations with the Iroquois after his father's death in 1774. When hostilities broke out in 1775, Guy Johnson sought an Iroquois pledge of support against the rebels. The Iroquois agreed to protect British supply routes in the interior should they be attacked, but refused to participate in an active campaign to put down the rebellion.

The Iroquois decision to enter the conflict came only after Molly Brant's brother, Joseph (or Thayendanegea), travelled to England as an emissary for the Six Nations to meet with British authorities in 1776. During the Seven Years' War, a young Joseph Brant had been among the warriors who accompanied Sir William Johnson in the attack on Fort Niagara. Impressed by Brant's abilities, Johnson arranged for him to be educated at the school for Indigenous boys run by the Reverend Eleazar Wheelock. Brant excelled in his studies and embraced Christianity. Following his education, he served alongside British forces in maintaining order among the western tribes and lived for a time with the Anglican missionary John Stuart, with whom he prepared a Mohawk translation of the Gospel of Mark and the Book of Common Prayer. While in England, Brant met with the secretary of state for the colonies, Lord George Germain, and expressed Iroquois frustration with the intrusion upon their land by settlers breaching the Royal Proclamation line: "We are tired out in making complaints and getting no redress." Germain assured Brant "of every support England could render them" in addressing their grievances once the rebellion in the colonies had been suppressed. Brant returned to North America convinced that the future of the Iroquois would be better protected by standing with Britain against the colonial rebels, who he feared would finally "ruin us" if their cause succeeded.[22]

Joseph and Molly Brant rallied most of the Iroquois to Britain's side. Molly fed and sheltered Loyalist families driven from their homes, and Joseph led an effective campaign, winning decisive victories at Oriskany in August 1777 and Cherry Valley in November 1778. Determined to put a stop to the Iroquois' activities, George Washington ordered Major General John Sullivan to crush them. With an army of 3,500 soldiers, Sullivan stormed through Iroquois country in September 1779, destroying villages, burning crops, and taking many prison-

Figure 5.2 Joseph Brant. Joseph and Molly Brant played an important role in rallying many of the Iroquois to the British side during the American Revolution.

ers. In the wake of the devastation, some 2,600 Iroquois took refuge at Fort Niagara, straining British resources. Far from neutralizing the Iroquois, Sullivan's campaign stiffened their resolve. For the remainder of the war, Iroquois warriors and Loyalist rangers attacked American frontier settlements as far away as Kentucky. The Iroquois who sided with the British did so as allies and not as subjects of the Crown, and fought to preserve the integrity of their tribal lands against the rising tide of American settlers.

The guerrilla war fought by the companies of Loyalists and Iroquois on the frontier succeeded in keeping the Americans from attempting another invasion of Canada. The efforts of Britain's regular forces to use Canada as a base from which to regain control of the rebellious colonies proved less successful. In the spring of 1777, General John Burgoyne launched an invasion of New York from Quebec via the Lake Champlain corridor. At first, Burgoyne's army of 7,500 British regulars succeeded in forcing the Americans to retreat. Delays at Ticonderoga, however, enabled the American General Horatio Gates to gather reinforcements to the south. On September 17, 1777,

22 Barbara Graymont, "Thayendanegea (Joseph Brant)," *DCB*, http://www.biographi.ca.

the two armies confronted each other at Freeman's Farm near Saratoga on the Hudson River. Burgoyne dug in, but his expected reinforcements never arrived. By October, Gates had virtually surrounded Burgoyne, and on October 12, the British were forced to surrender, giving the Americans their first major victory in the war.

With the British defeat at Saratoga, France saw an opportunity to avenge its losses in the Seven Years' War and to reassert its position on the world stage. France had covertly encouraged and assisted the American rebels almost from the beginning of the conflict. Now that the Americans had demonstrated that they could best the British, the French recognized American independence and entered into a formal alliance with the United States. Having modernized its army and rebuilt its navy, France's entry into the war constituted a serious threat to Britain's efforts to keep its American empire. To prevent the French from establishing a naval base in the Gulf of St. Lawrence, the British launched an expedition against the small French islands of St. Pierre and Miquelon and reinforced the garrison in Newfoundland. Quebec's governor, Sir Frederick Haldimand, worried about the effect of France's participation in the war on the Canadians. French agents were known to be circulating a proclamation from Louis XVI in the province urging Canadians to remember their heritage. "I see myself surrounded by enemies," Haldimand fretted, "since France has allied herself with the rebels."[23]

Haldimand's fears proved unfounded. Although the French and the Americans drafted invasion plans for Canada, nothing came of them. Determined to first free American soil of British forces, George Washington had little interest in invading Canada again. In its treaty with the United States, France had forsaken any ambitions to regain Canada. With the exception of a daring naval raid against Fort Prince of Wales on Hudson Bay, French forces did not attack Canada. France's real contribution to the American War of Independence took place in 1781, when the French navy inflicted heavy casualties upon the British fleet on Chesapeake Bay, Virginia, on September 5, and 8,000 French troops joined with an equal number of Americans to defeat the British at Yorktown that same autumn.

EXILE AND NEW BEGINNINGS

With their defeat at Yorktown, British hopes for victory in America evaporated. On February 27, 1782, the House of Commons voted against continuing the war and on March 5 passed a bill directing the Crown to negotiate peace with the Americans. The negotiations concluded on September 3, 1783, with the signing of the Treaty of Paris. According

---

23 Stuart R.J. Sutherland, Pierre Tousignant and Madeleine Dionne-Tousignant, "Sir Frederick Haldimand," *DCB*, http://www.biographi.ca.

to the terms of the treaty, Britain recognized American independence, accepted a new northern boundary between the United States and what remained of British North America, and granted the Americans access to the important Newfoundland fishery. The Treaty of Paris also urged Congress to "earnestly recommend" to the states the return of all property confiscated from the Loyalists. Congress had little power to enforce this term, and state legislatures were not interested in compensating anyone who had opposed independence. Not only were the Loyalists' claims ignored, victorious patriots continued to persecute their Loyalist neighbours and to seize their property. Under such conditions, some 80,000 "loyal Americans" decided to flee the new republic and seek refuge under the Crown in Nova Scotia, Quebec, and the British colonies of the West Indies.

Beginning in 1783, shiploads of Loyalists left New York City, the last bastion of British strength in the former American colonies, bound for Nova Scotia. Tent communities arose at Shelburne on Nova Scotia's southeastern tip, and at Parr Town and Carleton at the mouth of the Saint John River on the Bay of Fundy. By 1784, more than 35,000 Loyalists had arrived in Nova Scotia, more than doubling the province's population and stretching its resources to the limit. Responsibility for the deluge of refugees fell to Nova Scotia's new governor, John Parr. After a long and distinguished military career, Parr came to Nova Scotia expecting to enjoy a quiet retirement. With the influx of Loyalists, he was confronted with the difficult task of feeding and housing thousands of destitute refugees. As soon as the immediate crisis passed, Parr faced the even greater challenge of distributing land grants, provisions, and farm implements. Delays in surveys, disputes over the size of grants, and shortages of supplies caused Parr to be flooded with complaints and petitions from Loyalists frustrated with their new circumstances and convinced that they deserved to be rewarded for their service and sacrifice.

Some prominent Loyalist leaders, determined to recover the social position they had lost, and convinced that only a landed aristocracy could maintain the Crown's authority, demanded that more than 100,000 hectares of land be set aside for themselves. Such extravagant claims offended the Loyalist rank and file, who insisted that "an enquiry into their respective losses, services, situations and sufferings" would demonstrate that all "shall be found equally entitled to the favour and protection of the Government."[24] Parr was not swayed by those claiming social privilege and strictly adhered to the instructions he received from London. All heads of households received 40 hectares of land and an additional 20 hectares for each family member; only discharged officers who had served during the War of Independence received larger land grants according to their rank.

24 "Vindication of Governor Parr and his Council against the Complaints of certain Persons who sought to Engross 276,000 acres of Land in Nova Scotia, at the Expense of the Government, and to the great Prejudice of the Province and the Loyalists in General," in L.F.S. Upton, *The United Empire Loyalists: Men and Myths* (Toronto: Copp Clark, 1967), 69.

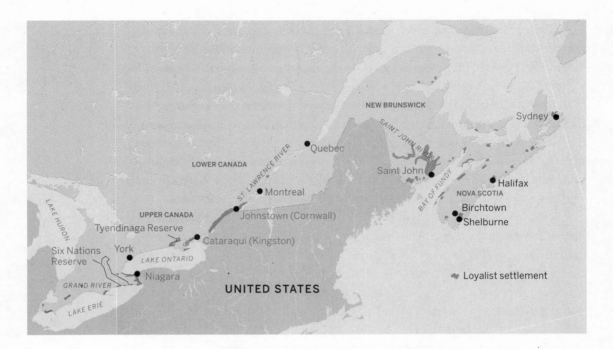

Map 5.2 Loyalist settlement. Some 80,000 Americans loyal to Britain settled in what remained of British North America at the end of the American Revolution.

Many Loyalists soon became disillusioned with "Nova Scarcity," as they bitterly referred to their new home. "All our golden promises have vanished," one Loyalist lamented. "We were taught to believe this place was not barren and foggy, as had been represented, but we find it ten times worse....It is the most inhospitable climate that ever mortal set foot on. The winter is of insupportable length and coldness, only a few spots fit to cultivate, and the land is covered with a cold, spongy moss instead of grass, and the entire country is wrapt in the gloom of perpetual fog."[25] The plight of the Shelburne Loyalists was especially miserable. Governor Parr had confidently predicted that Shelburne would soon surpass Halifax in importance. Although Shelburne boasted an excellent harbour, the rocky countryside was ill-suited to farming, and within a few years the town was all but abandoned. Many of the Shelburne Loyalists returned to their former homes in the new republic; others sold their land and attempted to start over yet again elsewhere in the colony.

The nearly 15,000 Loyalists who settled along the Saint John River valley and on the north shore of the Bay of Fundy fared better. Here at least the soils were fertile, but

---

25 Neil MacKinnon, *This Unfriendly Soil: The Loyalist Experience in Nova Scotia, 1783–1791* (Montreal and Kingston: McGill-Queen's University Press, 1986), 69.

bitterness and dissension set in nonetheless as Loyalists bickered among themselves over the distribution of land and supplies and jockeyed for political power and social prominence. The one thing that united these Loyalists was a general disaffection with the authorities in Halifax and the desire to create a separate Loyalist province. "Take the general map of this province," Edward Winslow wrote to Ward Chipman in July 1783, and "observe how detached this part is from the rest—how vastly extensive it is.... Consider the numberless inconveniences that must arise from its remoteness from the Metropolis [Halifax] & the difficulty of communication. Think what multitudes have & will come here—and then judge whether it must not from the nature of things immediately become a separate government, and if it does it shall be the most Gentlemanlike one on earth."[26] Anxious to quell Loyalist discontent and to create positions for former office holders displaced by the American Revolution, the British government agreed to the partition of Nova Scotia and created the new colony of New Brunswick on June 18, 1784. To members of the Loyalist elite, such as Edward Winslow and Ward Chipman, New Brunswick was sure to become a model of order and hierarchy and the "envy" of the rebellious American states, proving to all that the Loyalists' sacrifice had not been in vain.

Few concessions were made to the Maliseet and Acadians already living in the area when the Loyalists arrived. Rather than purchase the land or negotiate land cessions through treaty, British authorities simply issued licences of occupation to the Maliseet with respect to sites they inhabited. These licences had little legal weight and failed to stop the Loyalists from occupying the fertile Saint John River valley and forcing the Maliseet off their traditional lands. Nor did the Loyalists recognize the claims of Acadians who had returned from exile and settled along the lower Saint John. The region's Acadians were compelled to relocate far upriver to Madawaska, or joined others along the northeast coast, far removed from the main centres of Loyalist settlement.

Nearly 3,500 African Americans were among the 35,000 Loyalists who settled in Nova Scotia. During the War of Independence, the commander-in-chief of the British forces, Sir Henry Clinton, promised freedom and security to any slaves who deserted their rebel masters and joined with the British. Such a policy, it was hoped, would provide the British with additional soldiers and labourers and upset the rebel cause by disrupting the economy and provoking a slave rebellion. Although a widespread slave uprising never occurred, thousands of slaves did seek refuge behind British lines and fought their own "war of independence" for freedom, justice, and equality as members of black regiments. Military considerations, rather than opposition to slavery, lay

26 University of New Brunswick Archives, "Edward Winslow to Ward Chapman, 7 July 1783," Winslow Family Papers, vol. 2, 104.

behind Clinton's policy, and little thought seems to have been given to what would happen to freed slaves when the war ended. After the British defeat at Yorktown, freed slaves flocked to New York where they joined thousands of other Loyalists seeking refuge and safe passage. During the peace talks, American negotiators insisted that all confiscated property, including slaves, be returned. Responsibility for overseeing the evacuation of British troops and Loyalist refugees from New York fell to Sir Guy Carleton, who succeeded Clinton as British commander-in-chief in North America in 1782. Carleton reasoned that slaves who had abandoned their masters and supported the British could not rightly be considered confiscated property. He insisted that Britain honour its promises and evacuate the slaves as free men to Nova Scotia or Britain's colonies in the Caribbean. This decision outraged George Washington and not a few white Loyalists who had slaves of their own.

The largest contingent of black Loyalists settled at Birchtown, across the harbour from Shelburne. For a time, Birchtown was the largest settlement of free blacks anywhere in North America. Freedom, however, did not mean equality. Black Loyalists received fewer provisions and less land than other Loyalists and became the targets of white hostility. "Great Riot Today," deputy surveyor Benjamin Marston recorded in his diary on July 26, 1784. "The disbanded soldiers have risen against the Free negroes to drive them out of Town, because they labour cheaper than they—the soldiers." Marston's diary for the following day noted: "The soldiers force the free negroes to quit the town—pulled down about 20 of their houses."[27]

After enduring years of deprivation and discrimination, and after repeated petitions to local authorities for fair treatment, the black Loyalist community dispatched Thomas Peters to London in 1790 to present their grievances directly to the British government. Peters had served as a sergeant with the Black Pioneers during the Revolutionary War and oversaw the settlement of 200 fellow veterans near Digby. In his meetings with British officials, Peters let it be known that black Loyalists were dissatisfied with their lives in Nova Scotia and New Brunswick, and that many were "ready and willing to go wherever the Wisdom of Government may think proper to provide them as free Subjects of the British empire."[28]

Secretary of State Henry Dundas sent instructions to Governor Parr to investigate the black Loyalists' complaints, but he also arranged for Peters to meet with directors of the Sierra Leone Company, an organization founded by British abolitionists to establish a colony of free blacks in Africa. Upon his return to Nova Scotia, Peters began to promote the Sierra Leone Company's colonization plan. In January 1792, 1,196 black Loyalists

27 James W. St. G. Walker, *The Black Loyalists: The Search for a Promised Land in Nova Scotia and Sierra Leone, 1783–1870* (Toronto: University of Toronto Press, 1992), 48.
28 James W. St. G. Walker, "Thomas Peters," DCB, http://www.biographi.ca.

sailed from Halifax to begin their lives anew in Sierra Leone. Many of those who left were community leaders—ministers, teachers, craftsmen—leaving the remaining black population without the guidance and leadership needed to challenge injustice and inequality.

Another group of nearly 12,000 Loyalists came to Quebec, significantly increasing that colony's English-speaking population. As in Nova Scotia, discontent, disappointment, and division characterized the settlement process. Loyalists encamped in Quebec during the winter of 1783 constantly complained about their primitive accommodations and besieged government officials with petitions for supplies and assistance. Exasperated by their "extravagant" demands, the governor of Quebec, Frederick Haldimand, curtly advised the Loyalist refugees that he would find passage for them at the earliest date for Nova Scotia. Disenchanted with conditions, many left the camps, not for Nova Scotia, but to return to their former homes in the new republic to salvage what they could.

Haldimand faced the difficult decision of where to settle those who remained. Fearing undue influence from Americans nearby, Haldimand rejected the area that stretched south of Montreal to the new international boundary. This decision irked the many Loyalists who had travelled over land from New England and upstate New York and were already encamped in the area around Sorel. Sensitive to relations with French Canadians, Haldimand also rejected the largely unsettled seigneuries that stretched immediately west of Montreal along the St. Lawrence. Having eliminated these two areas as options, Haldimand was forced to look further afield to more remote parts of the province. A few Loyalists were directed to the Gaspé, but most were settled in new townships laid out in the wilderness along the upper St. Lawrence, around the Bay of Quinte on Lake Ontario, and along the Niagara River.

Before settlement could begin, however, title to the land had to be acquired from the Native population, in keeping with the terms of the Royal Proclamation of 1763. In 1784, the Mississauga ceded 1.2 million hectares of land along the Niagara Peninsula for less than £1200 worth of gifts. Similar agreements followed, extinguishing Native title to most of what is now southern Ontario. In many cases, the exact terms of the agreements were vague and subject to different interpretations—British notions of private property were foreign to Natives, who held land communally. While Natives were willing to share their land with the newcomers, they evidently did not intend to give it away forever, nor did they expect the massive influx of settlers that followed.

Relocating thousands of Loyalists to new homes in the wilderness proved difficult. Incomplete surveys, inadequate supplies, and disputes over location tickets produced widespread bitterness and resentment. Civilian settlers charged that regimental Loyalists received favourable treatment and were allotted the best land. A deliberate policy of settling officers and soldiers of the same regiment together, in order to carry

Figure 5.3 Encampment of Loyalists at Johnstown on the banks of St. Lawrence, June 6, 1784. The resettlement process was often fraught with difficulty and discontent.

over into civilian life the cohesion and organizational discipline of the military, produced considerable resentment among the ranks of discharged soldiers. Such were the divisions among the Loyalists that, in the Royal Townships laid out along the St. Lawrence, settlers were divided, at their own request, according to their ethnicity and religion. Many Loyalists arrived on their lots too late in the season to put in crops and remained dependent on government assistance. Desperate for provisions, some Loyalists sold their location tickets to speculators, ensuring that large tracts of land remained undeveloped for many years to come.

The Loyalists who settled in Quebec included some 2,000 Six Nations Iroquois. Despite their vital service to the British cause, Iroquois interests were completely ignored during the peace negotiations. The Treaty of Paris did not recognize Iroquois property rights or provide any protection for Britain's Native allies. Joseph Brant felt betrayed. The British had "sold the Indians to Congress," he exclaimed.[29] "We could not believe it possible," Brant complained to the British Home Office, "[that] such firm friends and allies could be so neglected by a nation remarkable for its honor and glory whom we had served with so much zeal and fidelity."[30] Concerned that they might rise up to avenge their poor treatment, Haldimand appealed to the British government to secure a land grant to compensate the Iroquois for their losses. In 1784, Joseph Brant and his followers received a tract of 273,000 hectares along the Grand River purchased from the Mississauga nation. A smaller group of Mohawks who did not wish to submit themselves to Brant's leadership settled on another tract on the Bay of Quinte.

29 Graymont, "Thayendanegea (Joseph Brant)."
30 William L. Stone, *Life of Joseph Brant-Thayendanegea* (New York: A.V. Blake, 1838), 253–54.

Not content simply to start over on the Grand River, Brant attempted to organize an alliance between the Iroquois and the western tribes to oppose American expansion. Following the War of Independence, the British continued to occupy western forts on what was now American soil from Oswego to Michilimackinac on the pretext that the Americans had not adhered to the terms of the Treaty of Paris and compensated the Loyalists for their losses. More important, the western posts allowed the British to defend Quebec's frontiers, to restore relations with the Indigenous peoples, and to exercise control over the fur trade. For these reasons, the British encouraged Brant's efforts. Brant had his own reasons: such an alliance, he believed, would strengthen the Iroquois' ability to limit American encroachment on their traditional lands and increase Iroquois influence with the British.

Brant persisted with his unity plans for a number of years, but the Americans exploited divisions within the confederacy to negotiate treaties with some Indigenous nations and used force to intimidate others into submission. He also experienced difficulties with British authorities. Determined to exercise Iroquois sovereignty and profit from incoming settlers, Brant maintained that the Six Nations could sell or lease their lands to whomever they chose. British officials insisted that the Six Nations were subjects of the Crown and that the government must approve all transactions involving the Grand River lands. Although he was thoroughly committed to maintaining Iroquois independence, Brant was convinced that his people must adapt to British ways if they were to survive. He encouraged the Grand River Iroquois to embrace Christianity, to seek an education, and to become farmers. Brant himself lived a genteel lifestyle in a grand manor and owned several slaves.

LOYALIST MYTH AND REALITY

Beginning in the middle of the nineteenth century, promoters of a nascent English-Canadian nationalism portrayed the Loyalists as a highly principled and well-educated elite, who chose to sacrifice comfortable lives and endure the hardships of a northern wilderness rather than submit to the tyranny of democratic republicanism. United by their ideology and suffering, it was claimed that the Loyalists formed a close-knit community characterized by an unwavering fidelity to the British Empire and an intense hatred of all things American. The traditional portrait of the Loyalists as aristocratic imperialists and anti-American anglophiles bears little relationship to the historical reality. The Loyalists were not members of a noble class representing gentle birth, wealth, and learning. Some Loyalists did come from urban centres such as New York, Boston, and Charleston, where they were part of the governing Anglican establishment, but many more were farmers, artisans, labourers, and merchants of modest means. In a report to the Loyalist Claims Commission in 1786, the administrator of Quebec, Henry Hope, observed that the Loyalists were "chiefly landholders, farmers and others from the inland part of the continent" and that there were few "persons of great property or consequence" among them.[31]

While some Loyalists were undoubtedly motivated by a sincere commitment to the idea of the Empire and the principles of the British constitution, the motives of many were decidedly mixed. Loyalty was often a product of patronage and commercial ties; many Loyalists were office holders, employees, or suppliers of the British military or the Indian Department. Others were merely opportunists who pledged allegiance to whichever side happened to be in ascendance locally. Still others were reluctant Loyalists who only took sides when forced out of a preferred state of neutrality by rebel harassment or Tory intimidation. Ethnically and religiously diverse, the Loyalists were far from united. Nor is it true that the Loyalists venerated all things British and detested all things American. A rather cantankerous lot, the Loyalists were quick to criticize the policies of the British government and demanded the creation of the same type of public institutions they had experienced in the American colonies. As for the Loyalists' supposed anti-Americanism, contemporary observers noted that hostility quickly subsided as personal ties were renewed and new commercial relationships forged.

---

31 A.L. Burt, *The Old Province of Quebec*, vol. 2 (Toronto: McClelland & Stewart, 1968), 79.

6 A CONTEST OF IDENTITIES: BRITISH NORTH AMERICA, 1784–1815

I n 1784, British North America consisted of six colonies: Newfoundland, Nova Scotia, New Brunswick, Prince Edward Island, Cape Breton, Quebec, and a vast western domain under the control of the Hudson's Bay Company. In each of the colonies, different cultures and races, languages and lifestyles coexisted, resulting in remarkably complex societies. The colonies shared little in common beyond their ties to Britain, manifest locally through the authority of Crown-appointed governors. In the absence of any central body to encourage unity, each of the colonies developed more or less independently of the others. Economically, British North America developed within a mercantilist framework that valued colonies as markets for the manufactured goods of the mother country and suppliers of needed raw materials. The result was the emergence of societies of primary producers subject to a high degree of external ownership and control and extremely vulnerable to vagaries of the market. While the American Revolution had bonded disparate colonies into one nation, British North America developed as a collection of distinct societies that, for the most part, remained politically and economically isolated from each other even when confronted by American aggression during the War of 1812.

THE ATLANTIC COLONIES AFTER THE AMERICAN REVOLUTION

During the American Revolution, Newfoundlanders suffered from the suspension of trade with New England and the predations of American privateers upon the offshore fishery. Cut off from New England foodstuffs and supplies, the population declined as residents fled the colony to escape starvation. The hardships that accompanied the war resulted in a significant restructuring of the Newfoundland economy. New England's trade embargo reoriented Newfoundland's trade to the West Indies and contributed to the rise of a local shipbuilding industry and an increase in agricultural production. With the disruption of the migratory fishery by privateers, the resident fishery emerged as the mainstay of Newfoundland's economy, and locals soon outnumbered the seasonal population. In the wake of the American Revolution, British authorities recognized the need to reduce tensions among its diverse population, and in 1784 religious toleration was extended to Roman Catholics and Protestant dissenters from the Church of England. A supreme court for the colony was established in 1791 and civilians joined naval officers as magistrates. Naval rule, however, did not end until 1825, when British authorities introduced a new constitution and appointed the colony's first civil governor.

Unlike Newfoundland, Nova Scotia and New Brunswick were governed by resident governors advised by appointed councils and elected assemblies that could make laws. Divisions between the leaders of Halifax society, who dominated the appointed councils, and the Loyalist newcomers elected to the Legislative Assembly, defined Nova Scotia politics following the American Revolution. To the Loyalists, the old guard were simply Yankees who continued to enjoy the benefits of the British Empire without having endured any of the hardship or sacrifice that real loyalty demanded. To the Halifax elite, the Loyalists were quarrelsome and ungrateful refugees who held dangerous republican ideas. In the elections of 1785, 13 Loyalists were elected to the 39-person assembly. Although a minority, the Loyalist members tended to vote as a bloc and successfully joined with representatives from outlying areas in securing for the assembly the right to introduce money bills and to impeach corrupt and incompetent judges. Loyalist commitment to the cause of reform subsided when a fellow Loyalist, Sir John Wentworth, became governor in 1792. A former governor of New Hampshire, Wentworth was well practised in the use of patronage and placed Loyalist friends in his Executive Council and other administrative positions. This effectively stifled Loyalist opposition, although tensions between town and country continued to characterize Nova Scotia politics up to the War of 1812.

In New Brunswick, Governor Thomas Carleton and a small group of Loyalist founders reigned over that colony's political affairs. A career military officer and the brother of Lord Dorchester (as Sir Guy Carleton was now known), Carleton shared the vision of Loyalists such as Ward Chipman and Edward Winslow, who sought to create a deferential, well-ordered society governed by a landed gentry that would be free of the faction and democratic excess found in the American states. "It will be best," Carleton insisted, "that the American Spirit of innovation should not be nursed among the Loyal Refugees by the introduction of Acts of Legislature, for purposes for which by the Common Law and the practice of the best regulated colonies, the Crown alone is acknowledged to be competent."[1] The slow development of the colony—and charges that Carleton favoured a small Loyalist clique—contributed to growing discontent, especially among the merchants of Saint John, the growing number of Irish labourers working the colony's lumber camps and fishing grounds, and the pre-Loyalist Acadian population.

A different set of tensions afflicted the small colony of Prince Edward Island. Formerly known as Ile St. Jean, it had been surveyed in 1765 by Samuel Holland and divided into 67 townships of 20,000 acres each. Almost all of the townships were granted as the result of a lottery held in 1767 to military officers and others to whom the British government owed favours. Although these proprietors were required to settle their lands to fulfill the terms of their grants, few made an effort to do so. The costs of the administration of the island were to be borne by a tax paid by the proprietors on the land they held. This was often impossible to collect, and efforts made by the local government to enforce the terms of the grants were usually overruled by the British government under the influence of the landowners, most of whom never set foot in the colony. The proprietors who did bring in settlers charged their tenants steep rents or purchase fees, creating political tensions and demands for land reform that lasted well into the nineteenth century.

The politics of personality and paucity plagued Cape Breton. In 1784, Abraham Cuyler, the Inspector of Loyalists in Quebec and former mayor of Albany, New York, hatched a scheme to relocate some 3,000 refugees from Quebec to the largely undeveloped island. After successfully lobbying the British government to separate Cape Breton from Nova Scotia, Cuyler secured the appointments of secretary and registrar of the new colony for himself. Unfortunately for Cuyler, only a small number of Loyalists chose to settle in Cape Breton. Joseph Frederick Wallet DesBarres was appointed Lieutenant Governor and settled a small group of English immigrants at Sydney. DesBarres and Cuyler soon clashed over their plans for the island. DesBarres, an experienced military officer who was accustomed to being obeyed, had little time

---

1 W.G. Godfrey, "Thomas Carleton," *Dictionary of Canadian Biography* (DCB), http://www.biographi.ca.

for the ambitious Cuyler, who was determined to play a major role in the development of the colony and to recoup his financial losses from his failed settlement plan. The constant shortage of supplies during the colony's early years pitted the two men against each other. Although the supplies furnished by the British government were only to be distributed to troops and Loyalists, DesBarres attempted to appropriate them for the English settlers he had brought to Sydney. The commander of the garrison, Lieutenant-Colonel John Yorke, who was aligned with Cuyler, opposed DesBarres's efforts to supply his supporters. In 1786, Cuyler secured DesBarres's recall, but relations with his successor, William Macarmick, proved equally factious.

After the American Revolution, British authorities sought to maintain a loyal and stable population throughout the Maritime colonies by strengthening the position of the Church of England. In 1787, Charles Inglis, the Loyalist rector of Trinity Church, New York, was appointed bishop of Nova Scotia. Inglis lamented the "times of democratic rage and delusion" and believed that the established church had a role in subduing "restlessness and discontent." "Order," Inglis asserted, "is essential to the well-being of every society." According to Inglis, the peace and order of society were threatened by "ambitious and self-interested" individuals who were not "content with their proper rank in the scale of beings."[2] Inglis's vision of a loyal and deferential society shaped by Anglicanism proved difficult to realize among a religiously and ethnically diverse population where Baptists, Methodists, and Roman Catholics were more plentiful than Anglicans and Acadians, and Yankee planters, Loyal Americans, and recent immigrants from Scotland and Ireland outnumbered the English.

Between 1783 and 1812 some 17,000 Highland Scots settled in Cape Breton and the Pictou area of Nova Scotia. Most of these new arrivals had been displaced by the enclosure of what had previously been common lands or cleared by landlords converting tenant farms to sheep pasture. Thomas Douglas, the Earl of Selkirk, settled 800 Highlanders from his Scottish estates on Prince Edward Island in 1803, nearly doubling its population. Highland Scots also added to the Loyalist and Acadian population of New Brunswick, where they were recruited as labourers in the Miramichi by Scottish entrepreneurs, who recognized the value of the region's timber and its potential for shipbuilding. Mostly Gaelic-speaking and Roman Catholic, the Highland Scots added to the cultural diversity of the Atlantic colonies. So, too, did a growing number of Irish immigrants. Unlike the later famine migrants, this first wave of Irish settlers consisted mostly of individuals of at least modest means who arrived in the maritime colonies with resources and ambitions intact. Protestant Irish from Ulster frequently became

2 Charles Inglis in Thomas R. Millman and A.R. Kelly, *Atlantic Canada to 1900: A History of the Anglican Church* (Toronto: Anglican Book Centre, 1983), 52.

farmers or fishers and quickly integrated into the larger population. Irish Catholics tended to congregate in the larger ports and towns, where they formed the basis of a nascent working class. Differentiated by their religion and heritage from the Protestant majority, Irish Catholics often became the objects of disdain, and understandably tended to stand apart. The arrival of hundreds of Yorkshiremen and Presbyterian Lowland Scots further contributed to the cultural diversity of the Atlantic colonies.

DIVISION AND DUALITY: THE CREATION OF UPPER AND LOWER CANADA

Having fought and suffered to uphold the British constitution and to preserve the British Empire, the Loyalists who settled in Quebec were unwilling to subject themselves to French civil law and the seigneurial system. Insisting that they were entitled to live under British institutions, the Loyalists petitioned the British Parliament in 1785 to demand the establishment of English law and a representative assembly. "The inhabitants of this territory," the petitioners protested, "were born British subjects, and have ever been accustomed to the government and laws of England. It was to restore that government, and to be restored to those laws, for which from husbandmen they became soldiers, animated with the hope…that should they fail in their attempts to recover their former habitations by a restoration of Your Majesty's government, they would still find a resource in some parts of the British dominions, where they might enjoy the blessings of British laws and of British government."[3] Convinced that the Loyalists would never amount to a large part of the population, Frederick Haldimand opposed the repeal of the *Quebec Act* and the establishment of an elected assembly. These views were shared by Lord Dorchester, who returned to Quebec in 1786 to take up the office of governor once more.

Dorchester found himself caught between Loyalist demands for change and the commitments made to the French-Canadian majority in the *Quebec Act*. Suspicious of representative government, Dorchester advised British authorities against establishing an elected assembly. He did recommend, however, the creation of four administrative districts, each with its own courts, in the western part of the province, which was beginning to attract many settlers from the United States. Drawn more by land than by any attachment to the empire, these "late Loyalists" greatly increased the population of the western districts. Soon, these newcomers began petitioning for the division

---

3 "Petition to Sir John Johnson, Bart. and other in Behalf of the Loyalists settled in Canada, 11 April 1785," in A. Shortt and A.G. Doughty (eds.), *Documents Relating to the Constitutional History of Canada, 1759–1791*, vol. 2 (Ottawa: J. de L Tache, 1918), 775.

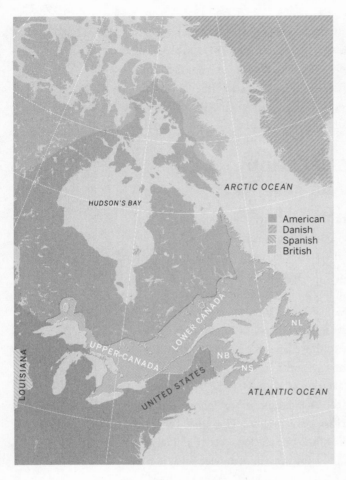

Map 6.1 British North America, 1791.

of Quebec into two provinces, each with its own assembly. Nova Scotia, Quebec Loyalists pointed out, had already been divided. Dorchester remained resolute and counselled London that partition was not advisable. However, William Grenville, Britain's new Colonial Secretary, recognized that the demands of the Loyalists could not be ignored. Overriding Dorchester's opposition, he arranged for an order in council in 1791 that divided Quebec at the boundary of the Ottawa River into two colonies, known as Upper and Lower Canada.

The *Constitutional Act* of 1791 set out a plan of governance for the two new colonies that attempted to satisfy the competing claims of Canadians and Loyalists. Under the terms of the *Constitutional Act*, each colony was provided with a separate government. The older and more populous Lower Canada would continue to be presided over by a governor general; in Upper Canada a lieutenant governor would represent the Crown. Executive councils were appointed to advise the governors;

these were invariably drawn from the wealthy and socially prominent of the colony. In addition, each colony would have an appointed upper house, or legislative council, with veto power over measures passed in the elected legislative assembly. Despite these restrictions on its power, the concurrence of the legislative assembly was required to levy taxes and to vote supply—the funds needed to pay government salaries. Members of the elected assemblies were not paid and, as a result, most elected representatives were persons of means. To be eligible to vote, an individual had to own property or other assets of a specified value. Land was plentiful, however, ensuring a broad elector-ate. Women who held sufficient property were legally entitled to vote, although custom and social disapproval ensured that few exercised their franchise. The creation of two colonies out of the old colony of Quebec ensured that duality became an entrenched

Canadian reality. French civil law, the seigneurial system, and the rights of the Roman Catholic Church were preserved in Lower Canada. English law and freehold land tenure were established in Upper Canada, and one-seventh of all Crown lands were set aside "for the support and maintenance of a Protestant clergy."[4]

Upper Canada's first Lieutenant Governor, John Graves Simcoe, had served with distinction during the American Revolution as an able field commander of the Queen's Rangers. He had high hopes for Upper Canada and predicted that the new colony would prove to be "the most valuable possession out of the British Isles in population, commerce, and principles of the British Empire" and would demonstrate to Americans the folly of the Revolution and its republican ideals. Simcoe enthusiastically set out to transplant the "image and transcript of the British constitution" in Upper Canada.[5] Both Loyalists and late Loyalists criticized Simcoe's attempt to create a "little Britain" in the Upper Canadian wilderness. During the first session of the Upper Canadian Legislative Assembly in 1793, Loyalist Richard Cartwright complained that the lieutenant governor "thinks every existing regulation in England would be proper here," and "seems bent on copying all the subordinate establishments without considering the great disparity of the two countries in every respect." Cartwright advised Simcoe that "a government should be formed for a Country and not a country strained and distorted for the Accommodation of a preconceived and speculative scheme of Government."[6] Such criticism had little impact. Convinced that social and political stability demanded the reproduction of Britain's graduated social order, Simcoe persisted with his efforts to engineer Upper Canadian society along British lines.

At the top of society, Simcoe envisioned a respectable aristocracy that was the natural governing class. To create such a class, Simcoe granted large tracts of land to persons he deemed suitable, especially former military officers whose loyalty had been proven by service to the Crown. Although he was suspicious of merchants, Simcoe recognized the need and importance of a commercial class in a developing society and appointed individuals from this class who he believed had demonstrated merit, integrity, and ability to the Legislative and Executive Councils. At the base of Simcoe's social order was "a happy yeomanry" of farmers and agricultural workers who knew their place and deferred to the judgment of their social superiors. Eager to attract settlers and convinced that many in the United States were dissatisfied with independence and republican institutions, he

---

4   "The Constitutional Act of 1791," in J.H. Stewart, Kenneth McNaught, and Harry S. Crowe (eds.), *A Source-book of Canadian History: Selected Documents and Personal Papers* (Toronto: Longmans, Green and Company, 1959), 64–65.

5   E.A. Cruikshank (ed.), *The Correspondence of Lieut. Governor John Graves Simcoe*, vol. 1 (Toronto: 1923).

6   Jane Errington, *The Lion, the Eagle and Upper Canada: A Developing Colonial Ideology* (Montreal and Kingston: McGill-Queen's University Press), 32, 30.

promised free land to Americans willing to start over in Upper Canada. Simcoe's vision of an ordered society never became a reality in Upper Canada. Land was too plentiful and the distance between social ranks too small to sustain a rigid social hierarchy. Most American settlers, moreover, carried with them liberal ideals of independence and social mobility that chafed at Simcoe's notions of deference and distinction.

Despite his social conservatism, Simcoe abhorred slavery. Loyalists had brought several hundred slaves to Upper Canada following the American Revolution. Most were employed as field hands who helped clear the land or as domestic servants for wealthier families. Convinced that "the principles of the British Constitution do not admit of that slavery which Christianity condemns," Simcoe promised that "the moment I assume the Government of Upper Canada under no modification will I assent to a law that discriminates by dishonest policy between natives of Africa, America or Europe."[7] Simcoe was outraged when Chloe Cooley, an enslaved girl from Queenston, was beaten and bound by her owner and sold to an American in March 1793. Despite his personal opposition to slavery, Simcoe was forced to agree to compromise legislation by slaveholders in the Legislative Assembly and on the Legislative and Executive Councils who were determined to protect their property rights. In November 1793, Simcoe signed an *Act to Prevent the Further Introduction of Slaves*. The Act, which was the first of its kind in the British Empire, permitted slave owners to keep their slaves until death but prohibited new slaves from entering the province and freed children born to slaves at age 25. Simcoe's progressive views on slavery did not mean that he welcomed persons of African descent. In 1794, Simcoe rejected a petition from 19 free blacks who had fought with the British during the American Revolution for a grant of land to establish an all-black settlement on the Niagara peninsula.

Although Simcoe was confident that Upper Canada's "superior, happier and more polished form of government" would convince Americans that independence had been a mistake, he recognized that the province's proximity to the United States made it vulnerable to American aggression.[8] To safeguard Upper Canada, Simcoe promoted the creation of an Indian buffer state south of the Great Lakes. Such a state, Simcoe believed, would divert the westward thrust of American migration and protect the frontiers of Upper Canada. As a demonstration of solidarity with the Indigenous peoples of the region, Simcoe took the audacious step of directing the construction of a new fort on American territory, Fort Miami, in 1794. The Americans responded by sending a hero of the revolutionary war, Major General Anthony Wayne, to demonstrate American control over the region's Indigenous nations and expel the British. On

7 Cruikshank, *Correspondence of Simcoe*, vol. 1.

8 Ibid.

August 20, 1794, Wayne came upon—and quickly routed—a large party of warriors at Fallen Timbers. The survivors retreated and sought refuge at nearby Fort Miami, only to find the gates of the fort closed against them. Not wanting to risk a war with the Americans, the young British commander, Major William Campbell, refused to give shelter to the fleeing Natives. With the defeat at Fallen Timbers and Campbell's refusal to provide assistance, Simcoe's dream of creating an Indian buffer state collapsed. At war with the revolutionary powers in France, Britain was anxious to avoid war in North America and to keep the United States from falling into the French orbit. In November 1794, Britain signed Jay's Treaty and surrendered all its forts in the American northwest. After serving less than five years as Upper Canada's Lieutenant Governor, John Graves Simcoe was transferred to the West Indies in 1796, his strident anti-Americanism having become an embarrassment to British officials.

Simcoe's successor, Peter Hunter, was a military officer, drawn from the landed gentry, with little experience in colonial administration. Hunter set out to develop the province with the determination of a military campaign. His first priority was to implement a systematic reform of the province's land policies. To encourage more orderly settlement and to limit land speculation, Hunter discouraged the opening up of new townships until existing townships were filled. To facilitate the efficient processing of land grants, Hunter regularized procedures, hired additional clerks, and increased fees. The lieutenant governor alienated Loyalists when he ordered a review of Loyalist claims and purged nearly 900 names from the UE (United Empire) List, the roll of all those who had served and sacrificed for the British Empire during the American Revolution. The storm of protest that followed Hunter's changes to Loyalist "rights" was exploited by William Weekes and Joseph Willcocks, two recent arrivals to Upper Canada from Ireland. Elected to the Legislative Assembly by disaffected Loyalists, Weekes and Willcocks formed the basis of a political opposition to the colonial administration. Weekes died in 1806 after he described the lieutenant governor as a "gothic barbarian" and was mortally wounded in a duel.

Despite the opposition to his policies, Hunter moved ahead with his plans to settle the province. Large land grants were given to certain individuals on the condition that they attract settlers. An Anglo-Irish aristocrat, Thomas Talbot, received 5,000 acres on the north shore of Lake Erie in 1803. His domain eventually grew to more than 65,000 acres. Determined to replicate the social order of his family's Irish estates, Talbot sought to surround himself with "a comfortable and respectable tenantry."[9] He personally interviewed all potential settlers and penciled in the names of those who met with his approval on one of his survey maps; he simply erased the names of those who did

---

9 Allan G. Brunger, "Thomas Talbot," *DCB*, http://www.biographi.ca.

Figure 6.1 Clearing the land in Upper Canada.

anything to annoy or offend him. Settlers had three years to build a dwelling, bring the land under cultivation, and clear the road allowance before they received a deed. Even after they had received title to the land, settlers remained bound to Talbot, who managed his domain with a dexterous system of handouts, liquour, and preferment. Such behaviour was a classic example of the system of patronage and clientelism that emerged in Upper Canada. Patrons such as Talbot were able to bestow upon clients tangible rewards, such as access to land, credit, or employment. In return, a client was expected to offer loyalty, service, and personal support.

Clearing the land was the foremost preoccupation of settlers to Upper Canada. The typical family could clear four or five acres of land a year. As a result, most families really operated a farm in the making for a decade or more. Pioneer life was characterized by years of back-breaking labour, monotony, and isolation. Survival on the Upper Canadian frontier required the astute marshalling of the resources of one's immediate family. Wives attended to the domestic household business: raising children, cooking, cleaning, gardening, putting up preserves, and home manufacturing of essentials such as soap, candles, and clothing. Children entered the world of work at an early age, girls helping their mothers with domestic chores and caring for younger siblings and boys assisting their fathers clearing stumps or tending livestock and crops. The income generated by women and children, raising poultry and selling eggs, taking in boarders, or doing laundry, often made the difference between getting ahead and a mere subsistence existence. Wives were frequently left to manage the farm on their own when their husbands took produce to market or sought employment in the winter months to earn cash. Labour was in short supply and cooperation was essential to survival on the frontier. Neighbours often came together to assist each other in barn-raising and land-clearing bees.

It was many years before pioneer farms produced a surplus crop, and those that did faced the problems of a small domestic market, poor transportation system, and competition from cheaper American produce. As a result, most pioneer families were heavily dependent on credit from merchants to purchase supplies, seeds, and implements. This reliance on credit contributed to the rise of a "shopkeeper aristocracy" in Upper Canada.[10] Merchants such as Robert Hamilton of Niagara and Richard Cartwright of Kingston acquired large fortunes supplying settlers, transporting goods, investing in local industries, and securing government contracts and appointments. Both men invested their profits acquiring land as much for the social status it carried as its speculative value and came to exercise considerable influence in both local and provincial politics. Despite the trials of pioneering, the population of Upper Canada climbed from just 10,000 in 1791 to about 60,000 in 1811.

When the Legislative Assembly for Lower Canada first met in 1791, French Canadians held 34 of the 50 seats, but Anglophones held a narrow majority of the seats in the Legislative and Executive Councils. Canadian domination of the Assembly and Anglophone control of the Councils institutionalized the divisions between French and English aspirations and priorities for Lower Canada. The merchant community in Lower Canada, which was dominated by recent arrivals from Scotland and the United States, sought support from the government for improvements to roads and canals to foster economic development. The government proposed that these improvements be funded through the introduction of a land tax, a tax that would fall primarily upon farmers who were mostly Canadians. The French majority in the Assembly rejected such proposals, much to the annoyance of the English-speaking majority on the Councils. The debate over improvements also unmasked divisions among French Canadians. Most of those appointed to the Councils represented the old seigneurial aristocracy, while many of those elected to the Assembly were drawn from a new class of professionals made up of lawyers, physicians, and journalists. Convinced that they constituted the traditional backbone of French-Canadian society, seigneurs looked down upon the upstart professionals and more readily identified with the Anglophones on the Councils with whom they shared a conservative social vision.

With the outbreak of the French Revolution, British administrators feared that the uprising might soon spread to Canada. Although most French Canadians felt little, if any, identification with old France let alone revolutionary France, many British parliamentarians argued that steps should be taken immediately to ensure English

10 Bruce G. Wilson, *The Enterprises of Robert Hamilton: A Study of Wealth and Influence in Early Upper Canada, 1776–1812* (Ottawa: Carleton University Press, 1983), 2.

dominance in Lower Canada. Such views pleased Lower Canada's Anglophone leaders, who wished to assimilate the Canadians through immigration and the abrogation of the constitutional protection provided to their religion, language, and legal system. This agenda was shared by the Lieutenant Governor of Lower Canada, Sir Robert Shore Milnes. Certain that political stability required the creation of an English-speaking landed aristocracy and a Protestant population, Milnes granted large tracts of land to prominent Anglophone merchants and office holders and supported education policies aimed at the conversion and assimilation of French-speaking Catholics. Such actions were widely perceived by Canadians in the Assembly as part of a general attack upon their culture and church. French-Canadian fears seemed to be confirmed by the appearance of the *Quebec Mercury* in 1804, an unabashedly anglophile newspaper that voiced the aspirations of the English party and sought to "defrenchify" the province. The French-Canadian party responded to the launch of the *Mercury* with a newspaper of its own, *Le Canadien*, to defend the interests of French Canada and the elected Assembly against the ambitions of the English merchants and the privileges enjoyed by the "placemen" that filled the Councils.

Relations between French and English continued to deteriorate when a new governor, James Craig, arrived in Lower Canada in 1807. Craig's temperament and outlook were shaped by his previous experience as a veteran of the Napoleonic Wars and colonial administrator in South Africa. As an officer, Craig inherited the reactionary conservatism that marked the British aristocracy following the French Revolution. Although he became aware of the challenges presented by an alien culture during his time in South Africa, he also became accustomed to an autocratic style of administration. Neither set of experiences served him well in Lower Canada. He distrusted the French-Canadian party in the Legislative Assembly and concluded that its attempts to preserve the impartiality of the judiciary and to make the executive more accountable proved that French Canadians favoured a Napoleonic victory. He even suspected that they were prepared to support an American invasion of Lower Canada as a first step toward the creation of an independent republic.

Such fears were ill founded, but Craig became increasingly suspicious of the French-Canadian majority in the Assembly. The leader of their party, Pierre Bédard, argued that the governor's advisors in the Councils should be selected from among the majority party in the elected Assembly. Bédard's concept of ministerial responsibility threatened to place control of all levels of administration into French-Canadian hands—something that was unacceptable to Craig and Lower Canada's Anglophone minority. Convinced that the powers of the executive and English interests needed to be protected, Craig prorogued the Assembly in 1809. In the elections that followed, the French-Canadian party increased its majority. When members of the Assembly and

Le Canadien denounced Craig's "reign of terror," the governor dissolved the legislature and ordered the newspaper's presses seized and its publishers arrested. Although Craig insisted his actions were necessary to counter the spread of disloyalty, dissension, and the spirit of democracy, British authorities became increasingly alarmed by his heavy-handed tactics and recalled him to Britain in 1811.

The growing tension and factionalism that characterized Lower Canadian politics prior to the War of 1812 were rooted in the province's social and economic evolution. Between 1791 and 1815, Lower Canada was transformed from a sparsely populated colony dependent on the fur trade and subsistence agriculture into an increasingly complex commercial society. In 1791, Lower Canada had a population of 165,000 that was predominantly French and overwhelmingly rural. By 1815, the population had more than doubled. Most of this increase was due to a high birth rate among French Canadians. The English-speaking population was bolstered by the arrival of some 9,000 settlers from New England, who were part of the great flood of pioneers leaving the crowded states of the eastern seaboard in search of land and opportunity. Most of these new arrivals settled in the eastern townships, which were open to freehold tenure.

The passage of the Corn Law by the British Parliament in 1791 provided preferential access for colonial grain to the British market, resulting in the gradual commercialization of agriculture in Lower Canada as prices rose and exports increased. The closing of the Baltic, Britain's main source of timber, by Napoleon in 1807, gave rise to an important new export, lumber, and helped to spawn new industries such as shipbuilding. Enterprising immigrants such as Philemon Wright from Massachusetts and William Prince from England established highly profitable timber operations along the Ottawa and Saguenay rivers, employing hundreds of French-Canadian labourers.

Population growth, the commercialization of agriculture, the emergence of new industries, and the growth of exports contributed to the rise of new social groups. Among French Canadians, rising incomes and prices supported the growing middle class of professionals and shopkeepers who increasingly dominated the Legislative Assembly and embraced democratic nationalism. At the same time, the opening of imperial markets and the arrival of new settlers added to the wealth and power of English-speaking merchants, office holders, and land speculators such as John Molson, who operated a successful brewery in Montreal and invested in the first steamship to operate between Montreal and Quebec. While the emergent Canadian middle class was primarily concerned with economic policies that centred on Lower Canada and preserved its influence and way of life, English interests favoured development that facilitated integration into the imperial system and benefited their own privileged position. Although the social and economic basis of Lower Canada's political tensions was deep, Lower Canada's new Governor, Sir George Prevost, did much to heal the wounds left by Craig. An experienced, fluently bilingual diplomat of Swiss origin, Prevost was well suited to the task of reconciling French Canadians and the British administration. As a result, Canadians did not rise up when war broke out between Britain and the United States in 1812.

FUR TRADE RIVALRY IN THE WEST

While French and English struggled for dominance in Lower Canada, and Upper Canadians debated the merits of re-creating British society in the British North American wilderness, rival fur-trade companies competed for control of the western interior. Between 1784 and 1815, the Hudson's Bay Company (HBC) and the North West Company (NWC) established new trading posts throughout the northwest, undercut each other's prices, and bribed, intimidated, and even murdered rival traders. The intense competition took a heavy toll on both companies. An old HBC trader, R.M. Ballantyne, remembered that the brutal rivalry for furs plunged the country into "a state of constant turmoil and excitement," involving "fist fights" and "more deadly weapons. Spirits were distributed among the wretched natives to a dreadful extent, and the scenes that sometimes ensued were disgusting in the extreme."[11]

Distinct social and labour structures evolved in the two fur-trading companies. The Hudson's Bay Company was structured as a joint-stock company with a highly centralized bureaucracy located in London. The Annual General Court, or meeting of the stockholders, elected a governor to oversee the company's operations and policies. Organized along military lines, each HBC post was commanded by a chief factor and his council of officers. Most of the workforce was comprised of men recruited from the Orkney Islands of Scotland. The Orkneys were the last stop for company vessels leaving England bound for Hudson Bay, and both workers and supplies could be taken aboard there. Scotland's superior educational system made these workers attractive: in contrast to many English labourers, they were generally literate and able to do arithmetic calculations. Company servants received an annual minimum wage of six pounds plus room, board, and clothing. With few opportunities to rise in company ranks, many men saved their income to purchase farms back home. Among those who saw work in the fur trade as a means to a better life was an adventurous woman, Isobel Gunn, who presented herself to the HBC as "John Fubbister" in 1806, and took a ship from the Orkney Islands to Fort Albany on James Bay. The sturdily built Gunn worked alongside the men for two years, even undertaking a 2,900-kilometre canoe

---

11 R.M. Ballantyne, *Hudson's Bay, or Everyday Life in the Wilds of North America: During Six Years' Residence in the Territory of the Honourable Hudson's Bay Company* (Edinburgh: W. Blackwood, 1848), 94–95.

journey to Pembina (in present-day North Dakota). It was there that her ruse was discovered. When another company servant learned her true identity, and forced himself upon her, she became pregnant. After giving birth, Gunn was not permitted to return to her former employment and worked for a time as a washerwoman for the HBC before returning to the Orkney Islands in the autumn of 1809.

The HBC had a strict policy against cohabitation with the Natives. A significant number of officers and some labourers, however, established marriage alliances with the daughters of prominent Indigenous leaders. Married "according to the custom of country" rather than the dictates of British law or the church, these relationships helped to cement trade ties. "Country wives" acted as interpreters and intermediaries in trade negotiations and brought to the relationship a host of essential skills, including the ability to make moccasins and snowshoes, preserve food, dress furs, and sew canoe seams. To Indigenous peoples such marriage alliances brought promises of credit and assistance as well as access to arms. For Indigenous women, country marriages offered an elevated status, access to labour-saving tools, a lighter workload, and a more secure food supply. The relative ease of divorce in Indigenous society allowed wives and traders to terminate the alliance if they so desired, and Indigenous women easily returned to their own people. The children of such alliances normally rejoined their mother's family and formed the basis of the "homeguard" who lived around the posts and served as provisioners and casual labourers. After 1800, company men increasingly tended to find their mates among the mixed-blood daughters of their senior colleagues and to regard them as wives in the traditional European sense. Wives were expected to adopt European culture and to raise their children at the fort. Schools were established at some posts to provide these children with a basic education and skills, and officers sometimes sent their sons to England for an education.

Unlike the Hudson's Bay Company, the North West Company consisted of a series of Anglo–Scots partnerships based on close personal and family associations. In 1785, the leading partners of the NWC founded the exclusive Beaver Club in Montreal. The club met at hotels and taverns every two weeks during the winter to dine on venison, quail, and partridge; drink prodigiously; share speeches; imitate Native rituals; and relive adventures in the west. Club members celebrated the exploits of the voyageurs through traditional songs and re-enactments of their exploits, shooting the rapids by riding wine kegs from the table to the floor and sitting on the carpet armed with fire pokers or walking sticks to simulate paddling a canoe. Despite such posturing, a clear line separated the senior partners from the French-Canadian voyageurs who manned the brigades of canoes that transported furs and supplies to and from Montreal. Barred from joining the Beaver Club, the voyageurs occupied a distinctive cultural world that blended elements of French-Canadian and Indigenous cultures.

An American observer, Washington Irving, observed that "natural good will" and a "community of adventure and hardship" existed among the voyageurs, who displayed a fondness for singing, dancing, and telling stories.[12] Historian Carolyn Podruchny notes that such activities were a part of the rhythm of life on fur-trading brigades, setting the pace of work, filling leisure time, providing an outlet for creativity, and keeping hunger and fatigue at bay.[13]

Marriage alliances between Indigenous women and the voyageurs resulted in the creation of a large mixed-blood population, the Métis. Unlike the employees of the HBC, many traders with the NWC left their employers to settle with their Native families. This loss of personnel proved costly, and the NWC outlawed the formation of such relationships. Despite such prohibitions, the Métis grew in numbers and developed a distinct culture and identity that combined both French and Native customs and traditions. In time, the Métis came to dominate the middle rungs of the fur-trade economy, acting as traders, brokers, guides, interpreters, provisioners, and labourers.

The impact of the fur trade upon the Indigenous peoples of the northwest has been a topic of considerable debate among historians. Some historians have emphasized a growing dependence upon European goods and the erosion of Indigenous culture and know-how. North West Company trader Daniel Harmon observed in 1801 that "The Indians in this quarter have been so long accustomed to use European goods, that it would be with difficulty that they could now obtain a livelihood without them."[14] Not everyone, however, was as dependent as the band described by Harmon. Historian Arthur Ray maintains that demand for trade goods remained constant year after year and that many Indigenous peoples retained much of their culture and fitted trade within traditional patterns of seasonal migration. The fur trade was more than an exchange of goods. In trading with the Hudson's Bay and North West companies, Indigenous peoples sought to create and to preserve an intricate system of alliances. Before trade began, Indigenous leaders exchanged gifts with the Chief Factor, made speeches, and smoked peace pipes. Only after these ceremonies were completed, which could extend over several days, did trade begin.

Trade was conducted through a window in the trade room at one of the posts. An Indigenous leader was allowed behind the trade window to ensure fair measure.

---

12 Washington Irving, "Astoria," in Jan Noel (ed.), *Race and Gender in the Northern Colonies* (Toronto: Canadian Scholars Press, 2000), 83–84.

13 Carolyn Podruchny, *Making the Voyageur World: Travellers and Traders in the North American Fur Trade* (Toronto: University of Toronto Press, 2006), 86–89.

14 Daniel Williams Harmon, *A Journal of the Voyages and Travels in the Interior of North America* (Andover: Flagg and Gould, 1820), 101.

Traders for both the Hudson's Bay and North West companies did cheat, short-weighing and short-measuring goods and marking up the price of most trade goods above the official company standard. Indigenous traders, however, were well aware of such practices and frequently exhorted traders to "give us good measure."[15] Official standards of trade served only as points of reference that enabled Indigenous and company traders to come to terms quickly. Indigenous peoples proved to be sophisticated and demanding traders with a sharp eye for quality and a well-defined shopping list. One Hudson's Bay Company trader warned that "these Natives…are cunning and sly to the last degree, the more you give the more they crave. The generality of them are loathe to part with anything they have; if at any time they give, they expect double satisfaction."[16] As competition between the Hudson's Bay and North West companies intensified, the margin of markup diminished as Indigenous traders took advantage of the competitive conditions.

EXPLORATIONS IN THE PACIFIC NORTHWEST

While the North West and Hudson's Bay companies competed to access new sources of furs, Russian, Spanish, and English explorers jockeyed for position on the northern Pacific coast. As early as 1774, news that Russian traders had crossed the Aleutian Islands and landed on the North American mainland prompted Spanish authorities in Mexico to dispatch Juan Josef Pérez Hernández to travel north along the uncharted Pacific coast to search for signs of Russian activity and to protect Spanish claims to the territory. Four years later, British explorer James Cook sailed east across the Pacific and ventured into Nootka Sound, seeking a western approach that would lead to a northwest passage. Anxious to keep the British and the Russians at bay and to preserve their own claim to the Pacific Northwest, the Spanish directed a junior naval officer, Esteban José Martínez, to establish a trading post and naval base on Nootka Sound in 1789. When he arrived, Martínez was surprised to discover British vessels trading with the local Natives for lustrous sea otter pelts and rashly decided to seize the ships and imprison their captains and crews. To avoid war, the Spanish were compelled to sign the Nootka Convention of 1790. According to the terms of the agreement, Spain returned all seized property to Britain and recognized the right of any nation to explore, trade, and settle in the Pacific Northwest.

---

15 Arthur Ray, *Indians in the Fur Trade: Their Role as Trappers, Hunters, and Middlemen in the Lands Southwest of Hudson Bay, 1660–1870* (Toronto: University of Toronto Press, 1998), 62–64.

16 James Isham, "Observations on Hudson's Bay," in Germaine Warkentin (ed.), *Canadian Exploration Literature* (Toronto: Oxford University Press, 1993), 58.

Figure 6.2 Captain James Cook's ship "Discovery" in Nootka Sound (Library and Archives Canada/C-11201).

In 1789, the North West Company commissioned one of its young and ambitious traders, Alexander Mackenzie, to find a new trade route to the Pacific. Mackenzie set out from Fort Chipewyan and travelled 2,500 kilometres by canoe along the length of the river that now bears his name, only to find that it emptied into the Arctic Ocean and not the Pacific. Before his next trip, Mackenzie studied surveying and map-making in England. Armed with a compass, sextant, and telescope, Mackenzie set out from Montreal on May 8, 1792, determined to reach the Pacific. He reached Peace River Landing in October where he spent the winter. The following May, he set out again with six voyageurs and two guides from the Beaver Nation, managed to cross the Rockies, and reached the Fraser River in June. Persuaded by the local people that the Fraser was too hazardous to navigate, Mackenzie set out along the overland route Indigenous peoples used to carry their own trade goods to the coast. Nuxälk-Carrier guides led the party to the headwaters of the Dean Channel. At last, Mackenzie stood at the Pacific Ocean, the first European to reach it by an overland route.

In contrast to the assistance he had received from Natives throughout his journey, Mackenzie was surprised by the hostile reception he received from the local Bella Coola people and felt compelled to retreat before he had an opportunity to survey the coastline. The Bella Coola had formed a poor opinion of Europeans from an encounter with the haughty British naval officer and explorer George Vancouver who had ventured into Dean Channel only a few weeks earlier. Mackenzie's achievement was of little immediate value to the North West Company, the overland route being too hazardous and the coastal Natives inhospitable to trade overtures.

The Americans, too, had developed a keen interest in the Pacific Northwest. In May of 1804, two United States Army officers, Meriwether Lewis and William Clark, set out from St. Louis, Missouri, on an epic 12,800-kilometre journey to the Pacific coast and the mouth of the Columbia River. American ambitions in the Oregon Territory added urgency to the efforts of the North West Company to establish a presence in the region and find a viable trade route through the mountains to the Pacific. A young partner in the firm, Simon Fraser, established a string of posts in New Caledonia (present-day British Columbia) between 1805 and 1807. In late May 1808, he set out on a treacherous journey to explore the Fraser River. The expedition would not have succeeded without the skill of his Indigenous guides, who alerted the different peoples encountered along the way of Fraser's approach and peaceful intentions. All went well until early July, when Fraser reached the mouth of the river and was prevented from proceeding into the Strait of Georgia by hostile Cowichan who had already dealt with European interlopers. Although Fraser reached the Pacific, the mission was in many respects a disappointment: the river was not the Columbia, as Fraser had hoped, and the difficulties of the passage had killed any hopes of using the route for commercial purposes.

The NWC's subsequent bid to be the first to establish a presence on the Columbia River came too late. David Thompson travelled through the mountains to the mouth of the Columbia in 1811. Originally an HBC employee, he shifted allegiances to the NWC in 1797 and charted several routes through the Rockies. In 1799, he took a country wife, Charlotte Small, the 13-year-old daughter of a North West Company partner and a Cree mother. Together they had 13 children. Small, often pregnant, traversed some 25,000 kilometres with her husband over the years, and her knowledge of Cree proved valuable on these journeys. When Thompson arrived at the mouth of the Columbia in July, he discovered that John Jacob Astor's Pacific Fur Company had already constructed a post and had begun to trade with the Indigenous people of the region. Although the Americans established operations on the Pacific first, Fraser's and Thompson's efforts ensured that the British would later have grounds to claim an interest in British Columbia.

TROUBLES AT RED RIVER

The intense competition in the fur trade took a heavy toll on both the Hudson's Bay and North West companies. In 1809, a Scottish aristocrat, Thomas Douglas, Lord Selkirk, took control of the floundering HBC with two of his wife's relatives. By introducing a profit-sharing system similar to that of the NWC, Selkirk succeeded in reversing the company's fortunes. At the same time, Selkirk was concerned about the plight of the farmers on his Scottish estates displaced by the enclosure movement and changes in agricultural production. Convinced that emigration was the best hope for these unfortunate folk, Selkirk had already sponsored the creation of a number

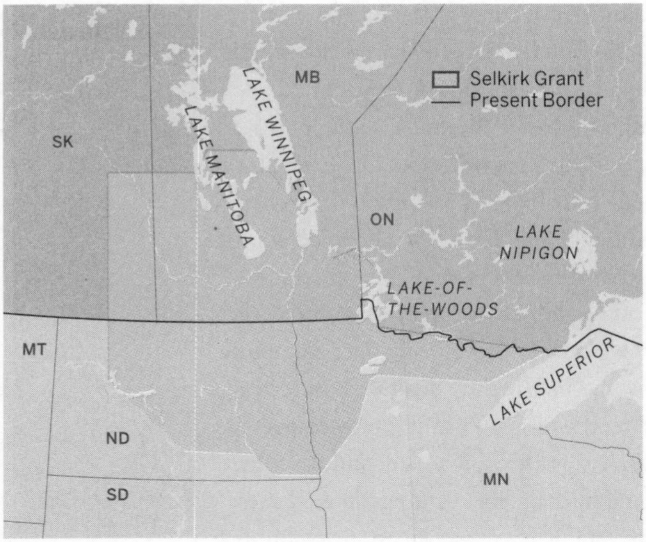

Map 6.2 Lord Selkirk's grant. The creation of Assiniboia and the arrival of settlers created tensions between the Hudson's Bay and North West companies.

of settlements in British North America. Shortly after acquiring HBC stock, Selkirk fixed upon the forks of the Red and the Assiniboine rivers as an ideal location to settle Scottish immigrants. The establishment of such a colony had the further advantage of supplying the company with fresh meat and produce, providing a home for retired servants, and satisfying the need for new recruits.

The Hudson's Bay Company granted Selkirk 300,000 square kilometres of land stretching along the Red River south of Lake Winnipeg—an area already occupied by a growing Métis population and used by the North West Company to transport furs and supplies. In return for the grant, Selkirk agreed to bring 200 settlers to the colony each year. The first party of 105 settlers arrived in late September 1811 and spent a miserable winter on Hudson Bay before setting out for Red River in the spring of 1812. The settlers arrived after an exhausting journey in July, too late to put in a crop. To make matters worse, a second group of settlers arrived in October, placing additional demands upon the settlement's scarce supplies. The first crops were not sown until the spring of 1814. The harvest was poor, however, ensuring another winter of scarcity in the ill-fated colony. During the desperate winter of 1814, the governor of Red River, Miles Macdonell, issued an embargo against the export of any food produced in the colony and ordered a limit to the buffalo hunt. Macdonell's "Pemmican Proclamation" threatened the livelihood and identity of the local Métis and alarmed the partners of the NWC, who had suspected all along that the colony's strategic location across their trade and supply routes was simply part of an HBC ploy to disrupt their activities and to gain control of the fur trade. Determined to eliminate the threat posed by the Red River colony, the NWC offered to relocate the settlers to Upper Canada. Having suffered enough deprivation and adversity, most of the colonists jumped at the opportunity, but 60 remained behind. With encouragement from the NWC, the local Métis, led by Cuthbert Grant, began to harass the remaining Red River settlers, destroying their crops, stealing their livestock, and setting fire to their buildings. Fearing for their lives, the settlers abandoned the colony and fled in their boats up Lake Winnipeg.

Intercepted by HBC officials at the top of the lake, the settlers agreed to return to Red River only if the company promised to protect them from the marauding Métis. When news of the troubles reached London, Selkirk resolved to take charge of the situation himself; recruiting an army of Swiss and German mercenaries, he set out for Canada in the fall of 1815.

THE WAR OF 1812 AND THE CONTEST FOR BRITISH NORTH AMERICA

As tensions intensified in the west, relations between Britain and the United States deteriorated. When war broke out between Britain and Napoleonic France in 1803, Britain blockaded European ports, preventing American vessels from delivering their cargoes to the continent. The British began to intercept American merchant ships at sea to search for deserters from the Royal Navy. The United States regarded the blockade and the interception of ships as illegal affronts to American liberty. In the summer of 1807, the British warship *Leopard* fired upon the American naval frigate *Chesapeake*, killing three American sailors and wounding 18 others. The British then boarded the ship and removed five men suspected of desertion. The *Chesapeake* incident inflamed American opinion. Rather than declare war, however, President Thomas Jefferson chose to pursue a policy of "peaceful coercion," punishing the British by imposing an embargo on trade. To circumvent the embargo, the British declared Halifax, Shelburne, Saint John, and St. Andrews free ports. New England ships regularly came to call at these free ports to unload American cargo and take on British manufactured goods, thereby evading the embargo and contributing to an already expanding commercial economy in the Maritime colonies.

American suspicions that the British were encouraging Native unrest in the interior added to the rising tensions between the two nations. While the British had in fact cultivated the friendship of Indigenous nations, and sought to maintain them in a state of readiness to join in war against the Americans should it come, they discouraged the Natives from initiating hostilities against the United States. Impatient with British diffidence and alarmed by the growing flood of settlers and land speculators into their lands, the Indigenous nations of the interior grew increasingly restless and turned to a Shawnee warrior, Tecumseh, for leadership. Tecumseh was convinced that unity was essential to Indigenous survival and set out to establish a new confederacy. A religious basis for Indigenous unity was provided by Tecumseh's brother, Tenskwatawa. Known as the Prophet, Tenskwatawa preached a powerful message delivered to him by the Great Spirit in a series of visions. He insisted that the land was a gift from the Great Spirit and could not be sold or ceded, and that Natives must reject the white man's religion and return to a simple life. Recognizing the danger posed by the combination of Tecumseh's political movement and Tenskwatawa's religious revival, the American governor of the Indiana territory, William Henry Harrison, attacked Tecumseh's capital at Tippecanoe on November 7, 1811. Although Harrison's troops suffered heavy casualties, Tippecanoe was destroyed during the battle. Many of Tecumseh's followers sought refuge in Upper Canada, confirming American apprehensions of British complicity in stirring up Indigenous unrest.

Within the United States Congress, an increasingly vocal group of "war hawks" demanded that the United States invade Canada. This bold move, they reasoned, would restore America's national honour, avenge British harassment on the high seas and intrigue in the northwest, help eliminate the Indigenous threat, provide new territory for expansion, and spread the blessings of American liberty across the continent. On June 18, 1812, President James Madison declared war on Britain. Although Madison's predecessor, Thomas Jefferson, predicted that the conquest of Canada would be "a mere matter of marching," the United States was not well prepared for war. The American army had only 6,500 poorly trained and ill-equipped men and was commanded, for the most part, by aging veterans of the Revolutionary War. While support for the war was widespread in frontier states and in the south, there was strong opposition in the northeast. Flags even flew at half-mast in Boston when it was learned that war had been declared. The situation was not much better in British North America, which was defended by only 10,000 widely scattered regular British troops. The commander of British forces in Upper Canada, Sir Isaac Brock, questioned the loyalty of the general population and the reliability of the provincial militia. "My situation is most critical," Brock confided to Governor Prevost, "not from anything the enemy can do but from the disposition of the people. Most of the people have lost all confidence—I however speak loud and look big."[17]

The Americans developed a plan for a three-pronged attack to quickly take the British North American heartland. General Henry Dearborn would strike at Montreal via the Lake Champlain corridor, General Stephen Van Rensselaer would attack across the Niagara frontier, and General William Hull would drive northward from Detroit. The American strategy depended on timing and effective coordination of each of the assaults, but long distances and rough terrain made communications difficult. On August 16, 1812, the American commander at Fort Detroit, William Hull, surrendered to Isaac Brock. Knowing that Hull possessed a much larger army, Brock resorted to psychological warfare and exploited the Americans' fear of Indigenous peoples. He directed his Indigenous allies to light a large number of campfires and

---

17 J. Mackay Hitsman, *The Incredible War of 1812: A Military History* (Toronto: Robin Brass Studio, 1999), 67.

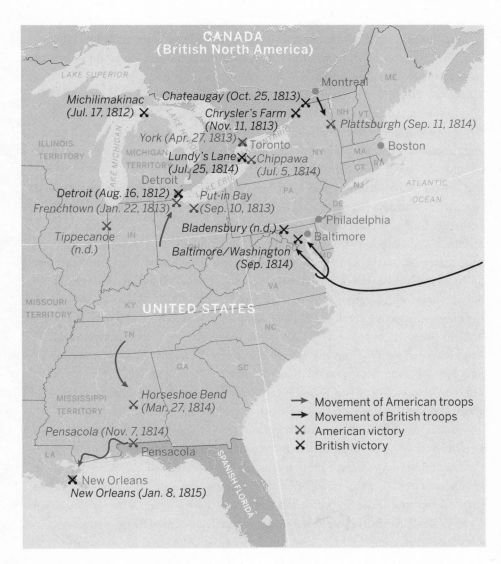

Map 6.3 Major Battles of the War of 1812.

to engage in loud war dances all through the night. In the morning Brock sent Hull a note, warning him that he was not sure how long he could control the Indigenous warriors and demanding Hull's immediate surrender. The tactic worked, and Hull surrendered Detroit without a shot being fired. Brock then hurried back to Fort George on the Niagara frontier where rumours abounded that an American invasion was imminent. On the night of October 12, 1812, the Americans began to cross the Niagara River near Queenston. Brock was killed by a sharpshooter early in the battle. Demoralized by the loss of their leader, the British troops and Upper Canadian militia fell back, but the arrival of reinforcements under Brock's second-in-command, Major

General Roger Sheaffe, and a determined stand by Mohawk warriors led by John Norton (Teyoninhokovrawen), turned the tide of the battle and forced the Americans to retreat back across the Niagara. With news of the American losses at Detroit and Queenston Heights, Dearborn called off the planned offensive against Montreal.

The spring of 1813 brought a re-evaluation of American strategy. Control of the Great Lakes, American commanders reasoned, might be the key to taking Canada. The Americans struck quickly. On April 26, 1813, an American squadron of ships commanded by Commodore Isaac Chauncey landed a force of 1,600, commanded by General Henry Dearborn and Brigadier Zebulon Pike, near York. With only four companies of British regulars defending the capital of Upper Canada, the commander of the British forces and civil administrator of the province, Major General Roger Sheaffe, decided upon a strategic withdrawal and retreated to Kingston. As the American troops advanced upon York, Chauncey's ships began to bombard the town's defences. Feeling abandoned by Sheaffe, a civilian delegation led by the Reverend John Strachan met with Dearborn to negotiate York's surrender. During the negotiations, the powder magazine at the fort exploded, killing Pike and inflicting heavy casualties on both sides. Angry at the losses, American troops set fire to the legislative buildings and proceeded to pillage the town. Emboldened by the fall of York, the Americans next struck at Fort George on the Niagara frontier. On May 25, 1813, the Americans began to bombard the British with hot shot (heated cannon balls) from their positions across the Niagara River, destroying much of the interior of Fort George.

Having learned the lessons of the previous year's defeat at Queenston, the Americans used their naval superiority to land 2,000 troops on the shores of Lake Ontario, rather than attempt another crossing of the Niagara River. With Fort George in ruins, American officers were billeted in the homes of nearby residents, including that of James and Laura Secord. When Laura Secord overheard the Americans discuss plans to attack the British outposts, she set out early on the morning of June 23 to alert the British commander, Lieutenant James Fitzgibbon. The risk was considerable: captured enemy spies could face summary execution. She succeeded in reaching Beaver Dams, a small outpost established by the British to harass the Americans, but Fitzgibbon had already been warned of American movements by Mohawk allies. Secord's heroic journey later became the subject of myth and legend, although little notice was taken in the immediate aftermath. The Mohawks, led by John Brant (Ahyouwaighs), the son of Joseph Brant, ambushed an American raiding party the following day. Warned by Fitzgibbon that the Mohawk warriors could not be restrained, the Americans surrendered.

The occupation of Fort George had permitted the Americans to transport additional ships to Lake Erie, where Commodore Oliver Perry had already assembled an impressive fleet. On September 10, Perry defeated a squadron of British ships at Put-in-Bay, giving the Americans control of Lake Erie and making British control of Detroit and the surrounding frontier untenable. The young and inexperienced British commander at Detroit, Major General Henry Procter, staged a strategic withdrawal, much to the annoyance of Tecumseh and his Indigenous allies. Tecumseh compared Proctor's decision to that "of a fat animal that carries its tail upon its back but when affrighted, it drops it between its legs and runs off."[18] Determined to remain and fight, Tecumseh pleaded with Proctor to leave his arms and ammunition behind. Unmoved by Tecumseh's appeals, Proctor's tired and hungry forces bid a disorganized retreat up the Thames Valley, pursued by Tecumseh's old nemesis, William Henry Harrison, and an American army of more than 3,000 troops. Tecumseh's warriors covered the rear, but the Americans caught up with Proctor's retreating forces at Moraviantown. Exhausted and demoralized, the British fled in disarray, leaving Tecumseh's warriors to battle the Americans. Tecumseh died in the hand-to-hand combat that followed and with his death the dream of a pan-Indian nation received a mortal blow as well.

With their victory at Moraviantown, the Americans were well positioned to conquer Upper Canada. British commanders knew that they could not count on the militia or the civilian population to repel the Americans. Long periods of separation from family and livelihood; inadequate food, shelter, and supplies; and the threat of disease contributed to high rates of desertion and avoidance of service among the militia. One member of the militia warned his commanding officer of the "certain calamity that must befall us if the Militia are thus continued to be called from their families." Another wrote to his brother that "desertion has come to such height that 8 or 10 men go off daily."[19] Relations between the military and the civilian population deteriorated as the war dragged on. Soldiers often complained that civilians charged exorbitant prices for food and supplies and participated in an illegal black market. Civilians resented the damage to their properties caused by soldiers, who used fence rails for firewood and plundered their produce and livestock when supply systems broke down. Populated largely by Simcoe's "late Loyalists," many residents of southwestern Upper Canada quietly sympathized with the Americans and a few actively supported the American cause. Convinced that Upper Canada was about to fall to the Americans, Joseph Willcocks, a member of the Legislative Assembly and one of the government's most vocal critics, began passing military intelligence to the enemy, accepted a commission in the American army, and recruited a Canadian volunteer force to fight alongside the enemy. Despite signs of

18 John Sudgen, *Tecumseh's Last Stand* (Norman: University of Oklahoma Press, 1985), 55.
19 Archives of Ontario, "Colonel Joel Stone to Colonel Lethbridge, 25 October 1812," F356, MU 2892; "Thomas G. Ridout to George Ridout, 16 September 1813," Thomas Ridout Family Papers, F43, MU 2390.

support among the local population, Harrison decided it was prudent to return to Detroit before the onset of winter rather than further his advance.

The American Secretary of War, John Armstrong, turned his attention to the east and devised a plan for the capture of Montreal. Armstrong planned a two-pronged attack: one force would follow the traditional invasion route north from Lake Champlain, and another would proceed from Sackets Harbor, cross the St. Lawrence frontier, and move down the river to join up with the invading forces from Lake Champlain before falling upon Montreal. The Americans expected that few French Canadians would support the British. With rumours of an American invasion rampant, the commander of British outposts south of Montreal, Lieutenant Colonel Charles Michel de Salaberry, fortified a strategic position on the Châteauguay River to confront the attackers. With a force of just 500 Canadian volunteers, the Voltigeurs, and two dozen Mohawk warriors, de Salaberry anxiously waited for the arrival of the American invasion force. On October 26, 1813, the confident Americans, 4,000 strong, opened fire on de Salaberry's small army. Protected by their well-placed defences, the Voltigeurs and the Mohawks stood their ground. Unable to breach de Salaberry's barricades and vulnerable to enemy fire, the Americans withdrew. Despite the American withdrawal at Châteauguay, the second prong of the American attack proceeded as planned. Successfully evading the British post at Prescott, an American force crossed the St. Lawrence on November 9, 1813. Two days later, at John Crysler's farm, British regulars and Upper Canadian militia successfully repelled a much larger American force. With the approach of winter, the Americans ended their ill-fated St. Lawrence campaign. Undeterred, Joseph Willcocks and his band of Upper Canadian traitors burned Newark on December 10 and began to wreak havoc along the Niagara frontier.

With Napoleon's defeat in Europe in the spring of 1814, experienced British troops began to arrive in North America in large numbers. These reinforcements strengthened British resolve to root out disloyalty and dislodge the Americans from Upper Canada. In May, 15 Upper Canadians were tried for high treason at Ancaster. During the "Bloody Assize," eight were condemned to death and publicly executed on July 20 as a warning to anyone who might consider helping the American enemies; the remainder were sentenced to exile. A few days later, British troops began to advance on Fort Erie, which had fallen to the Americans on July 3. British and American forces confronted each other on July 25 in a cemetery at Lundy's Lane in what proved to be the bloodiest battle of the war. By the battle's end, 860 Americans and 878 British regulars and Upper Canadian militia lay dead or wounded among the tombstones. Around midnight, the renegade Joseph Willcocks fled the battle scene, fearing the Americans had lost the battle and that he would be hanged if captured. He was later killed during the protracted British siege of Fort Erie.

While the war had ground to a stalemate in Upper Canada, the British expanded the field of battle, launching a series of naval attacks around Chesapeake Bay in August. On August 24, 1814, the British marched on Washington, burning the White House and other public buildings in retaliation for the destruction of York. By the autumn of 1814, the costs of the war pressed heavily on both sides, and the peace negotiations begun the previous year assumed a renewed urgency. On December 24, 1814, the Treaty of Ghent officially ended the conflict. It took several weeks for the news to reach North America, however, and the British and Americans still fought on in New Orleans from December 23 to January 8, 1815, unaware that the war had ended. The Treaty of Ghent essentially restored matters to the status quo before the war, allowing the Americans, British, and Canadians to claim a measure of victory. One group, however, could not claim victory: the Indigenous peoples. Despite their vital contribution to the war effort, they were not represented at the peace talks, nor did the British stand by their pledge to secure them an Indian territory.

The years between the end of the American Revolution and the restoration of peace in 1815 were transformative ones in British North America. The difficult task of state formation in the Atlantic colonies and the new settlement of Upper Canada raised controversies over civil administration and religious privileges. The ambitions and anxieties of Indigenous nations intersected, and at times conflicted with, Britain's imperial goals. New economic activity, often fuelled by protective tariffs in the mother country, transformed the colonies. The continuation of the old staple trade in furs brought growing conflict to the western interior and a race to the Pacific Northwest. A growing assertiveness on the part of the United States, coupled with provocative British policies, embroiled the colonies in a war not of their choosing. Although the war did little to bind British North Americans together and left a bitter legacy among many veterans, widows, orphans, and property owners directly impacted by the conflict, the mere fact that the colonies had survived ensured their continued development as distinct communities in the decades to come.

7 A DEVELOPING COLONIAL ECONOMY, 1815–1836

The years after the War of 1812 proved to be formative ones in the history of British North America. The peace brought a new era of security: the Rush-Bagot Agreement of 1817 between Britain and the United States limited naval forces on the Great Lakes and Lake Champlain. The following year, the Convention of 1818 resolved fisheries disputes and set the border between the United States and British North America at the forty-ninth parallel from Lake of the Woods to the summit of the Rocky Mountains. For a time at least, the ever-present risk of American annexation of the British North American colonies receded.

The disparate British North American colonies each faced special challenges and new economic opportunities in this era. In Rupert's Land in the western interior, rivalry intensified between the fur-trading empire of the Hudson's Bay Company and the Montreal-based North West Company. Newer economic staples grew in significance in other parts of the continent: the timber trade in the Maritimes and the Canadas, and wheat production in Upper Canada. There was also a flurry of canal building in Upper and Lower Canada. Perhaps the most transformative development for the future was the arrival into the colonies in the era after 1815 of a flood of immigrant newcomers from the British Isles.

HUDSON'S BAY COMPANY AND NORTH WEST COMPANY RIVALRY AND THE BATTLE OF SEVEN OAKS

In the early nineteenth century, chronic conflict in the western interior fur trade erupted into violence. The Hudson's Bay Company and their Montreal-based competitors, the North West Company, were each active in Rupert's Land, and an attempt by HBC director Lord Selkirk to establish a settlement colony at Red River added new complications. Selkirk's small agricultural colony of Scottish and Irish farmers at the junction of the Red and Assiniboine rivers had struggled to survive amid harsh weather, scarce provisions, and harassment from Métis buffalo hunters whose livelihood depended on using the area of "the forks"—the junction of the two rivers—as a base to provision the rival North West Company with pemmican. Unwitting settlers who arrived expecting a bucolic farming community found something more akin to a war zone, and had only returned to the colony in the fall of 1815 upon the HBC's promise to protect them from the Métis.

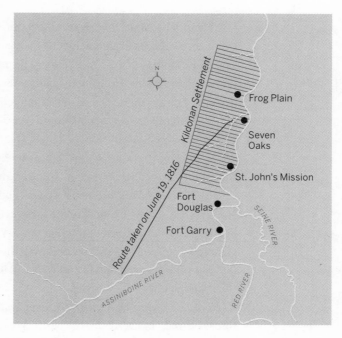

Map 7.1 The Red River settlement.

Around that same time, Lord Selkirk himself arrived in Canada to take matters directly in hand. Negotiations with the NWC in Montreal proved fruitless, but encouraging news reached Selkirk in the spring. Jean-Baptiste Lagimodière, a Métis HBC trapper, arrived in Montreal after a five-month snowshoe journey over 2,900 kilometres with the message that the colony had been re-established. Selkirk was determined to hold onto it and, with promises of land grants, recruited a few dozen soldiers from two Swiss infantry regiments in Canada, the De Meurons and De Watteville, which had been disbanded after the War of 1812. Selkirk and the new reinforcements to the colony had not yet arrived, however, when events took a dramatic turn.

On June 19, 1816, at Seven Oaks in Red River colony, Governor Robert Semple and a small band of settlers confronted a party of Métis who were transporting a cargo of pemmican to NWC traders in violation of the 1814 "Pemmican Proclamation." The Métis were led by 23-year-old Cuthbert Grant, an NWC employee born in the west whom the NWC had recently named "Captain-General of all the Half-Breeds." A tense verbal exchange quickly flared into violence, with the Métis opening fire on Semple and his men. Semple and 20 others in his party were killed, along with one Métis. Grant's men capped their victory by stripping and mutilating the bodies of the dead.

Historian Gerald Friesen sees the Battle of Seven Oaks as a pivotal moment in the emergence of Métis historical identity. Songs and stories commemorated the victory, and in the aftermath the community grew more assertive in maintaining its right to hunt buffalo and live freely on the plains. "Seven Oaks was their ordeal by fire," Friesen explains. "It gave them a sense of nationhood that was to be reinforced by Riel and Dumont later in the century."[1] George Woodcock sees things differently, asserting that Grant "allowed himself to be used by the Nor'Westers" in a bid to advance his career. "There is nothing to suggest that before 1814 he saw the Métis as a nation, or gave any thought to their cause, or even identified himself with them," Woodcock argues.[2]

In the immediate aftermath, the surviving settlers fled Red River settlement, and Nor'Westers seized the local HBC headquarters at Fort Douglas. Chief Peguis of the Saulteaux Nation offered protection to the vulnerable colonists, including Marie-Anne Gaboury Lagimodière and her children, the family of Jean-Baptiste Lagimodière, who had not yet returned from his journey to Montreal. The Lagimodières would later be the grandparents of Louis Riel.

Lord Selkirk, en route to Red River, learned of the Seven Oaks killings as his forces neared Fort William, the North West Company's headquarters at the head of Lake Superior. He seized the fort before continuing the journey on to Red River in the spring of 1817. Peguis sent warning to Selkirk's expedition that the NWC planned to waylay them and kept a force of his own warriors at Sturgeon Creek to ensure that they arrived safely.

The 1816 violence at Red River convinced British and colonial authorities that something must be done to check the bitter rivalry in the fur trade. William Bacheler Coltman, a Lower Canadian businessman and member of Canada's Executive Council, was sent to Red River to investigate, bringing with him a small contingent of troops. Coltman was instructed to re-establish peace and order, restore seized property, and arrest Selkirk. To Selkirk's dismay, Britain's Secretary of State for the Colonies, Lord Bathurst, who had sent instructions on what was to be done, had been getting his information from British member of Parliament Edward Ellice, a prominent North West Company partner.

Even while he faced personal prosecution, before leaving the settlement, Selkirk seized the opportunity provided by Coltman's presence to conclude a land treaty with the local Cree and Ojibwe tribes. He hoped that the evidence of friendship and fair dealing would put to rest NWC claims that the Natives opposed an agricultural settlement. Selkirk had the authority of the Crown to conclude the treaties, and Coltman

1   Gerald Friesen, *The Canadian Prairies: A History* (Toronto: University of Toronto Press, 1984), 76–80.
2   George Woodcock, "Cuthbert Grant," *Dictionary of Canadian Biography* (*DCB*), http://www.biographi.ca/en/bio/grant_cuthbert_1854_8E.html.

acted as witness. On July 18, 1817, Chief Peguis and four other local chiefs, representing some Cree and Ojibwe tribes, gave their consent to a treaty that secured the colonists' right to settle two miles adjacent to the Red and Assiniboine rivers in exchange for annual payments to each tribe of 100 pounds of tobacco or the equivalent. The terms of this treaty would be renegotiated in 1871 as "Treaty 1," the first of a series of so-called Numbered Treaties made in Canada's interior in the post-Confederation era.[3]

Coltman produced a fair and balanced report on May 4, 1818. It questioned the legality of the Red River colony and condemned Selkirk's actions at Fort William. Although Coltman sympathized about the disruption posed by Red River settlement to the interests of the North West Company and the Métis way of life, he denounced their use of "intimidation and violence." Coltman's report did little to ease the tensions in the northwest, however; competition for furs simply shifted west to the Athabasca district, where both the Hudson's Bay and North West companies established rival posts in close proximity to one another. The kidnappings, assaults, thefts, and court cases that followed exacted a heavy price from both companies.

At last, in 1821, British authorities pressed the trade rivals into an agreement. Selkirk had died the year before, after enduring years of legal wrangling over his actions and the fate of the Red River colony, a process that took a heavy toll on his health and reputation. The two companies merged all operations and personnel under the name Hudson's Bay Company. The new Hudson's Bay Company combined the financial and administrative stability of the old HBC with the field experience and adaptability of the NWC. The Red River settlement was able to grow in peace, and the west stood on the verge of a new era in its development, an era that would seriously challenge the continued way of life of the Native peoples and the Métis.

RUPERT'S LAND GOVERNOR GEORGE SIMPSON AND THE HBC

Something of the culture of the HBC in the era after the 1821 merger may be gleaned from the story of George Simpson, the governor of Rupert's Land. Bumptious and autocratic, Simpson rose from humble circumstances to preside over this vast commercial empire: he was born out of wedlock in Scotland and went to work for an uncle, a London sugar merchant, at the age of 13, using personal connections and his own business acumen to secure appointment to the HBC by his early thirties. The "Little Emperor" kept a

---

3   More information on the 1817 Selkirk Treaty may be obtained in Arthur J. Ray, Jim Miller, and Frank Tough, *Bounty and Benevolence: A History of Saskatchewan Treaties* (Montreal and Kingston: McGill-Queen's University Press, 2000), chapter 2, "The Selkirk Treaty, 1817." The treaty itself is available online through the Manitoba Historical Society at http://www.mhs.mb.ca/docs/pageant/21/lordselkirktreaty.shtml.

Figure 7.1 HBC Governor George Simpson (c. 1786–1860).

confidential "Character Book" where he noted his impressions of Hudson's Bay Company employees, including details of their personal faults. In the spring of 1830, his 18-year-old bride and cousin, Frances Simpson, recorded her impressions as she travelled thousands of miles by canoe with her 43-year-old husband into the heart of the continent. Frances Simpson journeyed from her home in England, arriving at York Factory that summer. The new Mrs. Simpson was graciously received by traders and factors at posts along the way and praised for her gentility, civilizing influence, and skill on the pianoforte. Fort Frances on Rainy Lake was named in her honour. However, she was unaware that her arrival in the west had caused some consternation.

George Simpson had maintained a succession of "country wives" and consorts in the west and arrived at Red River with his new young English wife, callously leaving an employee with the task of bundling Simpson's last wife and two children out of the way. Margaret Taylor was hastily married off to stonemason Amable Hogue, who had been one of Simpson's elite crew of voyageurs. While Hogue worked on the new headquarters being constructed at Lower Fort Garry, Margaret Taylor, living in the Métis labourers' camp, would have been able to see the governor and his bride set up residence in their magnificent new home. Unfortunately, Simpson's poor example was copied by subordinates: Chief Factor John George McTavish accompanied Simpson to Red River in 1830 with *his* new bride, Catherine, heedless of the effect on his wife of 17 years and their seven children, who had been eagerly watching the river for signs of their father's return.[4]

George Simpson prided himself on the prodigious distances he could travel by canoe under the most rugged conditions, seeking to set new speed records as he inspected operations in the HBC's interior posts. He would rouse the voyageurs from sleep to commence the day's journey while it was yet dark; he would often then sleep while they paddled. Simpson swam daily in the coldest weather and readily adapted to feast or famine, going without food for days or gorging himself on ducks and geese when they were plentiful.[5] On her journey west, Frances Simpson described the 35-foot-long canoes in which they travelled as "elegant beyond description," and she especially enjoyed the lively voyageur songs—neither cold nor fatigue dampened the spirits of the men who paddled, sung, laughed, and joked, as if on an excursion

---

4   Sylvia Van Kirk, *"Many Tender Ties": Women in Fur-Trade Society in Western Canada, 1670–1870* (Winnipeg: Watson & Dwyer Publishing, 1980), 188.

5   James Morris, *Heaven's Command: An Imperial Progress* (Markham, ON: Penguin, 1982), 120.

of pleasure. However, nerves could be frayed on the long journey and when fisticuffs broke out, the suddenly awakened Governor Simpson would seize a paddle to beat the combatants in the canoe. While liquor was carefully doled out along the way, Simpson fortified his crew for the last push toward the Red River settlement by allowing them to consume all that was left. Infused with new strength, the voyageurs completed a gruelling 24-hour shift. On the last portage, the crew shaved, freshened up, and decorated the canoe. They then made a grand entrance at the fort, with the company flag fluttering and a bugle blast heralding the governor's arrival.[6]

ATLANTIC COLONIAL ECONOMIES

Newfoundland

Far to the east, other challenges were confronting Britain's Atlantic colonies in North America in the years immediately following the Napoleonic Wars. Newfoundland had long been regarded by British policy makers as little more than a seasonal fishing station with proximity to the Grand Banks. By 1817, its population had grown to more than 40,000 inhabitants, and frequent clashes between Irish Roman Catholics and English residents suggested the need for more systematic administration. Naval officer Francis Pickmore arrived that year as the colony's first permanently posted governor. He was disheartened to see that his official residence in Fort Townshend had not been adapted for year-round occupation and that snow drifted into the bedrooms. Worse, fire tore through St. John's in November, destroying 400 houses and leaving 2,000 homeless. Provisions stored in warehouses had also been destroyed, and the winter of 1817–18

Figure 7.2 Government House, Newfoundland, completed 1831.

became a nightmare of hunger, with the population torn by violence, vandalism, and looting. Pickmore struggled to keep order but, wracked by bronchitis, died in February 1818.[7]

---

6 Frances Simpson, excerpt from "Journal of a Voyage from Montreal thro' the Interior of Canada, to York Factory on the Shores of Hudson's Bay, 1830," in Germaine Warkentin (ed.), *Canadian Exploration Literature* (Toronto: Oxford University Press, 1993), 384–95.

7 Frederic F. Thompson, "Francis Pickmore," DCB. http://www.biographi.ca/en/bio/pickmore_francis_5E. html.

The appointment of Sir Thomas Cochrane as governor (1825–34) ushered in a new era for Newfoundland. Cochrane, also a naval officer, immediately commissioned a grand governor's residence. The ornate new Government House, originally budgeted at £8,778, ultimately cost an embarrassing £36,000, but provided employment for many, as did Cochrane's schemes for road building on the Avalon Peninsula. In the early years, Cochrane governed solely with an appointed four-man council; Newfoundland did not have an elected assembly until 1832.

Shipping in Nova Scotia and New Brunswick

In the Maritime colonies, the peace in 1815 threatened the prosperity that the war had created. Nova Scotia had especially profited from privateering, government-sanctioned piracy: privateers captured enemy vessels, with the captains and crews sharing the bounty with the Crown. Nova Scotia's privateers took more than 100 American vessels as prizes of war in 1813 alone. That said, the Maritime shipping industry also suffered throughout the War of 1812 from the depredations of American privateers.

During the war, when Americans were denied the privilege of sending their merchant ships to trade with Britain's Caribbean colonies, Nova Scotia and New Brunswick filled the void, carrying American food products to supply the slave populations of West Indian sugar plantations, and Caribbean molasses to American rum distilleries. Soon after the war's end, American policy makers sought to recapture this valuable carrying trade: in 1818 Congress closed American ports to British ships coming from any colonies not permitting American trade. Britain responded by relaxing the laws of mercantilism to allow Halifax, Nova Scotia, and Saint John, New Brunswick, to operate as free ports, open to American trade. The Americans countered with an 1820 *Navigation Act* that prohibited the importation into the United States of West Indian goods by way of Halifax or Saint John. Britain was compelled to relent, and permitted American vessels trade privileges in their Caribbean ports. Caribbean plantation owners were a powerful lobby group who brought pressure to bear on Britain's parliamentarians—opening these Caribbean ports would keep prices low for essential foodstuffs to feed the slave populations. Yet those same slave-owning sugar producers, had they been sufficiently prescient, might have foreseen that two decades later a shift to free trade would undercut the very basis of their own wealth.

Britain was not ready to abandon protectionism in the 1820s, but in 1825 reduced tariffs on a wide range of products including wool, silk, cotton, linen, and sugar. For Nova Scotia especially, the opening of Caribbean ports to American vessels threatened to undercut a vital sector of their economy. But Britain negotiated reciprocal privileges with the Americans, and Britain's North American colonies were now permitted to carry

American cargos to anywhere in the world. By the mid-nineteenth century, Nova Scotia's merchant shipping fleet was the world's fourth largest. In this era, Nova Scotia's economy was built upon world trade; without inter-colonial transportation links, there was little trade or commerce between Nova Scotia and the other British North American colonies.

The New Brunswick Timber Industry

New Brunswick's timber industry had developed in the wake of Loyalist settlement at the end of the eighteenth century, but the introduction of protective British tariffs during the Napoleonic Wars brought a great surge of growth to the industry. Even after the war's end, high British tariffs on foreign wood were retained, benefiting colonial producers in that substantial market. Saint John grew as an important commercial centre, and related industries flourished, such as shipbuilding.

As the exploitation of timber resources on Crown land in New Brunswick became more competitive, licences were introduced to regulate the activities of lumbermen. After 1819, a tonne of timber could be taken for a fee of one shilling (one twentieth of a pound). Many Irish migrants bound for the popular destination of Boston took advantage of the burgeoning New Brunswick timber industry, working for wages that would help them to establish themselves in the United States.

A nineteenth-century visitor to New Brunswick described the lumbermen he met near Grand Falls. On a "spree" at a nearby inn, the raucous woodcutters drank, sang, and tried their strength in competitive games of stone tossing. They wore red flannel shirts, homespun trousers, loose grey or green jackets that tied around the waists, straw or coarse felt hats, and brown moccasins or boots, the "moccasin or boot furnishing a ready napkin after a meal of salt pork and biscuit." He marvelled at the daring they showed in their work, using creeping irons—L-shaped metal devices that tied to their legs, with a sharp spike at the bottom "like the claw of a wild beast"—to ascend the trees.[8]

While the supply of timber must have seemed inexhaustible to colonial newcomers, devastating fires could claim huge swathes of woodland in a day. The Miramichi Fire of 1825, coming on the heels of a prolonged summer drought, devoured an estimated 4,000 to 8,000 square miles of timber in New Brunswick, including giants of the forest that had stood for centuries. Government House at Fredericton burned to the ground. The fire claimed the lives of up to 300; settlers in remote areas had been unaware of the fire until a terrifying roar was heard from the forest. Some fled to the Miramichi

---

8   James Edward Alexander, *L'Acadie, or Seven Years' Explorations in British America* (London: H. Colburn, 1849), 74–76.

Figure 7.3 Hewing squared timber.

River, hoping to outrun the flames, but many were caught up in a hurricane of flame. Even those aboard ship in the Gulf of St. Lawrence felt the impact of the conflagration, the seas boiling and hissing, and the air thick with smoke and ash.

LOGGING IN THE CANADAS

For Lower Canada, timber provided an economic boost that softened the effect of the declining fur trade and diminishing yields in agriculture. In the early nineteenth century, wheat production in Lower Canada was in decline, with yields not meeting the local demand, much less producing any surplus for export. Soil exhaustion was a factor in long-established agricultural areas, and newer, more northerly areas of settlement tended to be marginal land, with soil and climate unsuited to wheat production. Farming families in Lower Canada turned to subsistence agriculture, producing potatoes, barley, oats, and peas for their own consumption. In this environment, timber production was Lower Canada's "salvation," as historian Fernand Ouellet put it. The colony produced squared timber, essential for naval building, as well as processed lumber and barrel staves, and new sawmills sprang up, both in the Ottawa Valley and around Quebec. By 1831, these numbered 727. Activity in the ports of Lower Canada rose sharply: in 1812, 362 vessels cleared the port of Quebec; by 1834 the number had risen to 1,213. While logging and its related industries offered work to Lower Canadians, most enterprises were British-owned.[9]

Historical focus has traditionally been on timber production for export, but much of the wood that was cut was consumed locally for fuel. A prodigious supply of wood was needed for heating homes, for cooking, to power industry, and for producing the charcoal used for smelting. J. David Wood estimates that in the decade before 1851, household use would have consumed 1 million acres of Upper Canadian forest in that colony alone.[10]

---

9 Fernand Ouellet, *Lower Canada, 1791–1840: Social Change and Nationalism* (Toronto: McClelland & Stewart, 1980), 56–58, 127–29; John McCallum, *Unequal Beginnings: Agriculture and Economic Development in Quebec and Ontario until 1870* (Toronto: University of Toronto Press, 1983), 4–5.

10 J. David Wood, *Making Ontario: Agricultural Colonization and Landscape Re-creation before the Railway* (Montreal and Kingston: McGill-Queen's University Press, 2000), 14.

Unlike other seasonal occupations, logging offered winter work. Cold weather stilled the running sap, making trees easier to fell. With the first snowfall, logs could be moved, or "skidded," more easily, pulled by draft horses or oxen along snow roads. By 1850, an estimated 10,000 loggers were at work in the Ottawa Valley, living in hastily constructed shantytowns. When the spring thaw came to the tributaries of the Ottawa, the loggers would release the logs that had been stored in landings by the sides of the rivers to begin the drive downriver. Daring drivers broke up frequent jams by leaping from floating log to log in the swollen rivers. When the logs reached the Ottawa River from the tributaries, they were trapped by booms and then lashed together into cribs and rafts. Steered by raftsmen, these rafts could consist of 2,000 to 2,500 tonnes of timber and were fitted out with small cabins for accommodating the crew and cooking fires. Enterprising logging companies, frustrated at frequent losses, constructed timber slides to bypass the roughest waters—large wooden chutes that could accommodate a crib built of 20 logs. The first of these, built at Chaudière Falls in 1829, became a popular draw for tourists.[11] The Prince of Wales, the future Edward VII, rode the Chaudière slide during an 1860 visit to Canada. Economic historian A.R.M. Lower noted that the Iroquois were considered the best rapids-men, closely rivalled by French Canadians. A journey through the rapids on a heavy mass of timber was, Lower enthused, "the most exhilarating of experiences, with the surge and roll of the waves, the grinding and bumping of the timbers, the perfect skill of the crew, the rocks missed by a hair's breadth, the terrific speed, and everywhere the consciousness of being in the grip of elemental forces."[12]

UPPER CANADA: LAND CONTROVERSIES AND THE "ALIEN QUESTION"

In the colony of Upper Canada, created in 1791, land policy emerged as one of the most contentious issues. The question was taken up with vigour by Robert Gourlay, a Scottish-born writer, farmer, and cantankerous political agitator. He arrived in Upper Canada in 1817, after his wife inherited 866 acres there. Gourlay was dismayed, though, to discover that this wild and forested land was not likely to attract purchasers and yield profit. Most recent immigrants to Upper Canada were American, and these "aliens" were denied the right to buy land.

This had not always been the case. In the earliest days of Upper Canada, Lieutenant Governor John Graves Simcoe had issued a proclamation offering land

---

11 Graeme Wynn, *Timber Colony: A Historical Geography of Early Nineteenth Century New Brunswick* (Toronto: University of Toronto Press, 1981), 67.

12 A.R.M. Lower, "The Trade in Square Timber," *Contributions to Canadian Economics* 6 (1933): 56.

grants to those willing to take an oath of allegiance, and many Americans took up the offer. After the acrimony of the War of 1812, however, new regulations required residency of seven years before land could be acquired in Upper Canada.

Gourlay was not alone in wishing to see land rights extended to new American immigrants. Many land speculators had acquired large tracts in Upper Canada with the idea of selling land to immigrants. However, the legal status of American immigrants was uncertain: when the United States was formed in 1783, no British law collectively stripped American residents of their status as British subjects. More than land ownership was at stake, for land ownership conferred political rights. To be eligible to vote or stand for election to the assembly, one had to meet a property qualification.

Gourlay set to work preparing a statistical survey of Upper Canada in a bid to generate interest in the colony, but the survey quickly devolved into a collection of colonial grievances. He cited immigrant complaints about a lack of amenities and land policies that left desirable tracts of land isolated, with vacant Crown and clergy reserves scattered through each township. Settlers were "cut off from each other," Gourlay reported, "left imprisoned in the woods. They cannot dispose of their farms: they cannot afford to abandon them; and so they pine on."[13] But the truculent Gourlay moved beyond these complaints to attack the elite of Upper Canada, labelling them vile and loathsome vermin. He called for the removal of the governor and for annexation of the colony to the United States. By 1819, Gourlay was convicted of seditious libel and exiled from the province. He would later end up in an English asylum for striking a British parliamentarian with a riding crop.

Gourlay's removal did not end the controversy over the "Alien Question." In 1821, the election of an American to Upper Canada's legislative assembly prompted a fresh debate. The new member, Barnabas Bidwell, had left his post as Massachusetts's attorney general in 1811 under allegations of embezzlement. John Beverley Robinson, Upper Canada's attorney general and a leading member of the Tory elite, led the campaign to deny Bidwell a seat in the legislature because of his "alien" status. Bidwell was ousted from the assembly by a single vote, although this did not have clear implications for the political rights of other aliens; his unsuitability on moral grounds was part of the debate. Confusion grew when Bidwell's son, Marshall Spring Bidwell, also American-born, was permitted to stand for election in 1824, after having been twice blocked.

Upper Canada's lieutenant governor, Sir Peregrine Maitland (1818–28), was encouraged by Britain's Colonial Office to find a compromise, especially since any

---

13 As quoted by Wood, *Making Ontario*, 4. See also David Mills, *The Idea of Loyalty in Upper Canada, 1784–1850* (Montreal and Kingston: McGill-Queen's University Press, 1988).

ruling that jeopardized so many land titles would raise a storm in the province. Reformers in the elected assembly pushed for full rights for the American-born, while the appointed legislative council, whom the younger Bidwell derisively labelled the "Family Compact," insisted on the alien status of American newcomers. Only in 1828, after much ill will, was the issue resolved. Those who had arrived before 1820, had received a land grant, or held public office were retroactively naturalized. Later arrivals could become citizens by taking an oath of allegiance after seven years' residence.

The immediate crisis ended in 1828, but the event marked a watershed in Upper Canada's political life. This acrimonious struggle raised the larger question of the meaning of "loyalty" in Upper Canada and brought into focus the tension between the ideal of a British colony and the reality of a demographically American one. With the elected legislative assembly dominated for the first time by reformers, the stage was set for future clashes between that body and the appointed executive and legislative councils. Historian Jane Errington suggests that the "Alien Question" was "only a rehearsal for the vitriolic debates which would rock the colony in the 1830s."[14]

Other land policy issues would continue to be contentious in Upper Canada. By 1824, 8 million acres in the colony had been granted to private individuals, but only 3 million of these were occupied, and a half million cultivated. Substantial grants to the privileged, Crown and clergy reserves, and rampant speculation kept vast tracts of land vacant and property values low. Conviction was growing among British policy makers that free land grants were not conducive to colonial development. Some of this shift in sentiment can be traced to the colonial theories of Edward Gibbon Wakefield, who argued that the sale of land at a "sufficient price" would ensure that it fell into the hands of those who had the resources to develop it. Wakefield's ideas were especially influential in later colonial settlements in New South Wales and New Zealand. In Canada, a new policy in 1826 eliminated free land grants, except for military claimants.

Another strategy allowed private companies to take a leading role in land sales and colonial development. In 1825, the Canada Company, led by the novelist John Galt, was granted a total of 2.5 million acres on generous terms. Galt's son, Alexander Tilloch Galt, was the principal agent of a similar enterprise, the British American Land Company, established in 1832, which took possession of 800,000 acres in the "Eastern Townships" of Lower Canada. In the meantime, the earlier land settlement schemes of Thomas Talbot, who had gained control over half a million acres in Upper Canada, were attracting considerable controversy and alarmed colonial officials.

---

14 Jane Errington, *The Lion, the Eagle, and Upper Canada: A Developing Colonial Ideology* (Montreal and Kingston: McGill-Queen's University Press, 1987), 188.

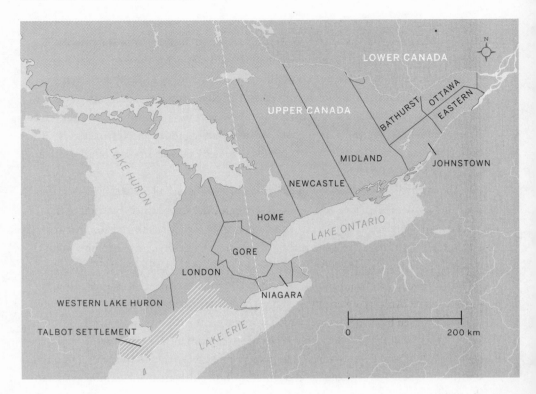

Map 7.2 Upper Canada in the 1830s.

Talbot had become an eccentric and reclusive alcoholic whose record keeping was sloppy. In 1838, he was compelled to turn his settlements over to the control of the province, retaining control only over his personal holdings.

The evident defects of Upper Canada's land policy would continue to be one of the sources of grievance of political reformers. Besides the alleged impediments to compact and efficient settlement, reformers in the colonial assemblies resented the fact that revenues from the companies' land sales flowed directly to the control of the governor and his council. The elected assembly's traditional control of colonial finances was undercut by this independent source of revenue.

A POST-WAR SURGE OF BRITISH IMMIGRATION

Upper Canada's heavily American-born composition would change dramatically after the war's end in 1815. While the impact would be most profound in Upper Canada, all of British North America would be transformed by the arrival of a great wave of immigration from the British Isles—an astonishing 1 million immigrants between 1815 and 1850. Between 1825 and 1842, the population of Upper Canada tripled to 450,000, and it more than doubled again by 1851, reaching close to a million.

Immigrants were lured by the hope of higher wages or independent land ownership, but were also pushed by a wish to escape endemic poverty or to avoid slipping into it. Post-war depression accompanied demobilization, as soldiers swelled the ranks of the unemployed. Even the genteel families of officers felt the pinch and saw emigration as a means to maintain social status on half pay. Britain's Industrial Revolution had itself thrown many out of work, or reduced skilled crafts to machine-assisted unskilled jobs. The 1834 *Poor Law Amendment Act* instituted draconian conditions for poor relief in England and Wales. Parish subsidies for the working poor were no longer permitted. Instead of receiving "outdoor" relief, paupers were compelled to submit to virtual imprisonment in the parish workhouse. Besides heightening the incentive for paupers to choose immigration, the change in legislation made parish-assisted emigration more feasible for the ratepayers who looked for ways to reduce costs.

Most British newcomers to British North America in this era were in fact from Ireland. Donald Akenson notes that from 1815 to the mid-1850s, Irish immigrants to British North America usually exceeded those from England, Wales, and Scotland *combined*. Even before the 1847 Irish potato famine immigration, the Irish made up at least a quarter of Upper Canada's population. And while most of Ireland's population were Roman Catholic, the Irish in Upper Canada were predominantly Protestant: Akenson estimates the ratio of Protestants to Catholics at two to one.[15]

The Scots-Irish and the Orange Order

Among those classified as "Irish" in Upper Canada were the numerous Scots-Irish drawn from Ulster, most of which is Northern Ireland today. Their presence in Northern Ireland dated from sixteenth- and seventeenth-century British schemes to settle communities of Scottish Protestants to subdue Catholic Ireland. This group helped to shape the character of Upper Canada. By 1867, Scots-Irish made up three-eighths of Ontario's population. Historical geographers R. Cole Harris and John Warkentin attributed Confederation-era Ontario's "dourness, attachment to empire, and fierce anti-Catholicism" to the influence of this Scots-Irish population.[16]

The Orange Order, a Protestant fraternal organization founded in Ulster in the 1790s, became, Cecil J. Houston and William J. Smyth argue, "an integral part of what might be called the Canadian colonial identity." The organization followed Loyalist settlement from Nova Scotia up the Saint John River in New Brunswick. Ogle R. Gowan,

---

15 Donald Akenson, "Ontario: Whatever Happened to the Irish?," in Gerald Tulchinsky (ed.), *Immigration in Canada: Historical Perspectives* (Toronto: Copp Clark Longman, 1994), 87, 96, 100.

16 R. Cole Harris and John Warkentin, *Canada Before Confederation: A Study in Historical Geography* (Toronto: Oxford University Press, 1974), 118.

the socially prominent son of a founding member of the Irish Grand Lodge, arrived in Brockville, Upper Canada, in 1829, and the first Grand Lodge of British North America was founded the next year, with a flurry of other lodges following soon after. The lodges afforded an opportunity for male socializing, offered valuable employment contacts and mutual aid, and facilitated political connections.[17] The rituals of membership were no doubt part of the appeal—colourful ceremonies, secret passwords, and an atmosphere of exclusiveness. The climax of the Orange Order's social year, in both the old world and new, was the "Glorious Twelfth," the annual July 12 parade commemorating the Protestant William of Orange's 1690 victory over the Jacobite forces of the Catholic James II at the Battle of the Boyne in Ireland. Orangemen would march behind a rider on a white horse representing "King Billy." The fact that the march was provocative to Roman Catholics was no barrier; in fact, it probably added to the appeal.

Scottish Immigration to British North America

Another leading group of British immigrants after 1815 were the Scots. By 1829, the Scots represented 20 per cent of the arrivals at Quebec—roughly equal to the number of English. By 1867, one-fifth of Ontario's population was Scottish; one-quarter was English. The Scottish element, however, exerted a disproportionate influence. Because of a superior education system in Scotland, Scottish immigrants dominated key positions in business, politics, journalism, the fur trade, banking, railways, and other commercial endeavours.[18] The tendency of well-placed Scottish families to lend assistance to relatives seeking to establish themselves was no doubt a factor as well.

Scottish immigration to British North America began well before 1815. A significant wave of Highland migration began at the end of the Seven Years' War, picking up momentum by the 1770s. An estimated 15,000 Highlanders came to British North America by 1815. The motives appear to have been primarily economic, prompted by rural overpopulation in Scotland and the subdivision of tenant holdings. Tens of thousands of tenant farmers were displaced by "improving" estate managers who converted marginal cultivated land into sheep-grazing areas and deer parks. Nevertheless, most Scottish migrants to British North America opted to leave of their own volition, confident that they could improve their prospects in a new land.

---

17 Cecil J. Houston and William J. Smyth, *The Sash Canada Wore: A Historical Geography of the Orange Order in Canada* (Toronto: University of Toronto Press, 1980), 3, 7. See also Gregory S. Kealey, "The Orange Order in Toronto: Religious Riot and the Working Class," in Gregory S. Kealey and Peter Warrian (ed.), *Essays in Canadian Working Class History* (Toronto: McClelland & Stewart, 1976), 13–34.

18 J.M. Bumsted, *The Scots in Canada*, Canada's Ethnic Groups. Booklet 1 (Ottawa: Canadian Historical Association, 1982), 2–4.

Smaller-Scale Assisted Emigration

Britain's growing population had once been viewed as a positive phenomenon, but attitudes were shifting. Thomas Malthus, in a famous 1798 essay on the "Principle of Population," posited gloomily that populations increased exponentially while food supplies could only grow arithmetically. Emigration was increasingly endorsed as a solution to Britain's problem and a means to reduce poor relief. Britain's Colonial Office supported a scheme promoted by Upper Canadian Peter Robinson in 1823: destitute Irish were encouraged to apply for resettlement in one of two Upper Canadian communities—Scott's Mills, later Peterborough, and Shipman's Mills, later Almonte. Migrants were provided with free passage, provisions, tools, and 70-acre land grants. Of the more than 50,000 impoverished residents of County Cork who applied for the scheme, 2,600 were selected to immigrate in 1823 and 1825. This assisted emigration to Upper Canada was not unique. The Petworth scheme, sponsored by the philanthropist Earl of Egremont, brought 1,800 migrants from the south of England between 1832 and 1837.[19] There were other similar initiatives, notably an exodus of some 3,800 unemployed English labourers from Norfolk and Suffolk in 1835–36. Still, most immigrants made their way without organized assistance. While occasional philanthropic immigration schemes persisted, Britain rejected large-scale assisted emigration as impractical.

Immigrant Impressions

Land companies employed agents to promote immigration in Britain through public lectures, pamphlets, and newspaper advertisements, with agents paid a dividend for every immigrant recruited. Unsurprisingly, colonial life was painted in glowing terms, often with testimonials by successful earlier immigrants. Those arriving later than the 1830s, however, often found the dream of accessible, arable farmland out of reach. The more northerly properties available to them were frequently utterly unsuitable for agriculture: the Canadian Shield, covering 90 per cent of present-day Ontario, descends to within a couple of hundred kilometres of Toronto. This picturesque region of lakes and birch forests—with ground of solid granite—was not an encouraging environment for aspiring farmers.

Even those who acquired arable land had to come to grips with the enormity of the task of land clearing. Trees, to a pioneer farmer, were the enemy. With labour

---

19 See Wendy Cameron and Mary McDougall Maude, *Assisting Emigration to Upper Canada: The Petworth Project* (Montreal and Kingston: McGill-Queen's University Press, 2000). See also Wendy Cameron, Sheila Haines, and Mary McDougall Maude (eds.), *English Immigrant Voices, Labourers' Letters from Upper Canada in the 1830s* (Montreal and Kingston: McGill-Queen's University Press, 2000).

scarce and not all farmers having access to oxen or draft animals, this was a considerable obstacle. Once the trees had been felled, the removal of stumps was another problem. Historical geographer J. David Wood reminds us that "the massive challenge of clearing the woodland…was *the* factor—usually combined with sickness, particularly the malarial 'fever and ague,' and isolation—that broke the settlers who gave up."[20]

Some immigrants suffered more than mere disappointment. The New Brunswick and Nova Scotia Land Company was modelled on the Canada Company and British North American Land Company active in Upper Canada. The company purchased 589,000 acres between the Saint John and Miramichi Rivers and attempted to settle English and Scottish immigrant parties in 1836. Unfortunately, the sites had been poorly prepared for their arrival late in the shipping season, and 41 died that cold winter. The New Brunswick Company also launched one of the earliest experiments in assisted child immigration, a concept that gained ground in the post-Confederation era. Critics of the scheme focused not on the potential for exploitation of vulnerable children, but rather the risk that colonial society would be infected with "moral leprosy." The *New Brunswick Courier* complained that the urchins, "the most depraved and vicious of the human race," were better suited for a convict colony.[21]

Immigration and Disease

One well-founded reason for resentment of immigrants was the fact that disease travelled along the same routes as the migrants, and the general population fell victim as well. After they had endured a nine-week journey, the immigrants' immune systems were weakened by privation and overcrowding, and contagious disease was virtually a certainty. Typhus, spread by the bite of lice or fleas, plagued those crowded into rat-infested dwellings. In 1827, 800 died of typhus in the city of Halifax alone. In the narrow hilly streets below Citadel Hill, scores of people were packed into dirty, ramshackle wooden houses. Authorities reported that one garret housed 47 paupers, with 48 living in the one next door.

Cholera was an especially feared scourge. Spread via a microorganism that enters the body through the mouth, the disease causes massive dehydration as victims vomit and suffer severe watery diarrhea—as much as a litre per hour. With the body drained of vital fluids, the mineral balance is upset, disrupting the normal body processes. Ineffective nineteenth-century treatments included bleeding and turpentine enemas,

---

20 Wood, *Making Ontario*, 85.

21 Bruce Elliott, "The New Brunswick Land Company and the Settlement of Stanley and Harvey," online, http://history.earthsci.carleton.ca/company/history/elliott1.htm.

and death came within days or even hours. Epidemics in Canada in 1832 and 1834 claimed an estimated 20,000, with most victims in the port cities of Quebec and Montreal.

A newly established Board of Health fuelled local panic by attempting at first to deny the epidemic, even amid the daily spectacle of carts bearing away the dead under yellow warning flags. Cannons were discharged and barrels of tar burned to create smoke in futile attempts to purify the air. Early in 1832, a quarantine station was constructed at Grosse Île; immigrant ships bound for Quebec were required to stop for inspection by a health officer and might be required to serve a quarantine of up to 30 days. The quarantine was a permeable one, however, and hence ineffective, with healthy passengers mingling with infected ones and supplies brought to the island from nearby towns.

Immigrant Literature

Emigration literature was a popular genre in nineteenth-century Britain, and this material leaves behind a record of contemporary attitudes about British North America. Of course, those with sufficient education and leisure to write and publish their impressions would hardly have been typical immigrants. Among the most famous of such works today are Susanna Moodie's *Roughing It in the Bush* (1852) and *Life in the Clearings* (1853), personal accounts of a gentlewoman's migration and settlement in Upper Canada. No doubt some readers were discouraged from immigrating by her expressed hope that "these sketches should prove the means of deterring one family from sinking their property, and shipwrecking all their hopes, by going to reside in the backwoods of Canada...." Moodie complained of the pervasive spirit of democracy among the "semi-barbarous Yankee squatters" who surrounded her: "They think they can debase you to their level by disallowing all your claims to distinction," she fumed, while allowing that the "native-born Canadian is exempt." Household servants brought from Britain soon "fancy themselves not only equal to you in rank, but [imagine] that ignorance and vulgarity give them superior claims to notice." They demanded the highest wages and would quit instantly if reprimanded, confident of another position. Moodie wrote that, while she had heard much about the "savages" of Canada, she found considerable more "delicacy of feeling" and "natural courtesy" among Indigenous Canadians. "[T]he Indian," she asserted, "is one of Nature's gentlemen—he never says or does a rude or vulgar thing."[22] A Scottish immigrant, Robert

22 Susanna Moodie, *Roughing It in the Bush, or, Life in Canada* (1852; Toronto: McClelland & Stewart, 1989), 489, 197–201, 29.

MacDougall, made a similar observation in an 1841 publication, *The Emigrant's Guide to North America*. He praised the physical appearance and bravery of the Natives and noted that "I do not ever expect to see men who are more respectful toward others." Their "slow, soft, pleasant, speech" he likened to his own Gaelic.[23]

Susanna Moodie had come to Canada at the urging of her sister, Catharine Parr Traill, also an accomplished author. In contrast to Moodie, Parr Traill positively relished immigrant life, painting landscapes, pressing wildflowers, and writing illustrated children's stories set in the Canadian wilderness. *The Backwoods of Canada* (1836) is Parr Traill's most famous work, and she also authored practical manuals that display an admirable spirit of improvisation and optimism. *The Canadian Emigrant Housekeeper's Guide* (1861) is a comprehensive domestic manual offering advice on topics ranging from how to make vinegar out of maple sap to what wild plants yield substitutes for coffee and tea. Parr Traill's unflagging energy and enthusiasm carried her through difficult times—the deaths of two of her nine children in infancy, the loss of her home in a devastating fire, and her husband's debilitating depression. She lived to age 97.

TRANSPORTATION AND CANAL BUILDING IN THE CANADAS

One of the chief difficulties faced by early British North American pioneers—besides the challenge of land clearing—was travel. In central Canada, the railway age began in a modest way with the 16-mile-long Champlain and St. Lawrence Railroad in Lower Canada in 1836. Even so, by mid-century there were still only a few dozen miles of railway track in all the British North American colonies. Before the advent of the railway age, road building had been similarly slow to progress, the source of perennial complaint by isolated farmers. In Upper Canada, settlers were compelled to clear lands for roads fronting their own properties. In swampy areas, "corduroy" roads were built of logs laid in rows—a solution which made good use of available material but ensured that travellers would endure a jolting, bumpy ride. Smooth plank roads were a comparative luxury, but deteriorated quickly, and horse-drawn traffic was exposed to the perils of accidents, perhaps a hoof crashing through rotted planks. The first fall of winter snow brought relief: travellers bundled in layers of buffalo robes could enjoy swift sleighing through the frosty air, grain could be shipped overland to gristmills, and barrels of goods delivered to waiting merchants. In all other seasons, inland

---

23 Robert MacDougall, in Elizabeth Thompson (ed.), *The Emigrant's Guide to North America* (Toronto: Natural Heritage, 1998), 31, 39.

canals facilitated trade. Commercial navigation of the upper St. Lawrence River was hampered by rapids at Lachine, just up the river from Montreal, but the Lachine Canal, completed by 1825, bypassed the rapids and helped assure the commercial ascendancy of the port of Montreal. The canal also provided a source of hydraulic power, and new industries clustered nearby to take advantage of that resource. The canal project had been launched by a chartered company of merchants, but the government of Lower Canada bought out the canal when the original company foundered.

The Rideau Canal, connecting the Ottawa River to Lake Ontario, was built between 1826 and 1832 for military, rather than commercial, purposes—a way to bypass the vulnerable St. Lawrence route in the event of war with the Americans. Mindful of these defence considerations, the British government provided both the expertise and the capital for the Rideau Canal—at £1 million it was the most expensive defence project the British had ever undertaken in North America. Lieutenant Colonel John By of the Royal Engineers supervised its construction. "Bytown," the camp established at the junction of the Ottawa and Rideau Rivers, was renamed Ottawa in 1855. Two companies of the Royal Sappers and Miners worked on the canal project, but most of the 2,000 "navvies" who toiled barefoot for 14 or even 16 hours a day, six days a week, using picks, chisels, shovels, and wheelbarrows, were Irish immigrants. Illnesses and accidents stalked these overworked men—they might be maimed or killed by gunpowder used for blasting, or fall victim to malaria. While malaria is more commonly associated with tropical climates, hundreds were afflicted in these boggy and pestilential conditions. Colonel By himself fell ill with malaria. Although he recovered sufficiently to complete the project, he returned to England in broken health to face a probe over excessive expenditure and died soon afterward.

Other canal projects, notably the Welland Canal, proved to be of vital importance to Canada's future commerce. Commercial traffic between Lake Ontario and Lake Erie faced the formidable barrier of Niagara Falls. Before the construction of the canal, cargoes on Lake Erie destined for a seaport had to be transported over lengthy portages to bypass that obstacle. By 1825, the Americans completed construction of the Erie Canal, linking Lake Erie to the Hudson River, providing an outlet to the Atlantic port of New York. The Welland Canal, constructed in 1829, was designed to recapture that trade for the St. Lawrence route and to carry a considerable proportion of goods for the internal American market. While construction began under the auspices of a private company, the government of Upper Canada purchased the Welland Canal and made improvements through the 1840s, replacing the obsolete system of wooden locks with stone. Besides the obvious commercial advantages, such public works projects offered a kind of economic safety valve, providing work to those for whom land ownership was a distant prospect.

CONDITIONS OF LABOUR

The prospect of work on the Welland Canal drew many who had worked on the Erie Canal to St. Catharines, Merriton, and Thorold. Other immigrants who lacked the resources to establish themselves on farms found wage labour cutting timber, working on the docks or in shipyards, or at other industries, especially in the main commercial centre of Montreal. Molson's brewery, founded in 1786, as well as warehouses, factories, and foundries, drew job seekers to the city.

The harsh conditions of work, long hours, and low pay made the plight of wage labourers a harsh one, but the onset of winter raised the spectre of genuine want. Not only was there no agricultural work, but winter halted public works projects and stilled commercial traffic on the ice-locked docks. Only the timber industry offered an outlet for those who could withstand the rigours of the work. The glut of workers in wintertime affected wages even for those whose work was not seasonal. The cruel dictates of supply and demand meant that January wages in Lower Canada for labourers were one-quarter to one-half less than they were in August. Further, winter brought the need for firewood for fuel, not readily obtainable in urban areas where the working poor congregated. Staple foods were priced higher in winter; bread prices could rise by 50 per cent.

Poor relief efforts were piecemeal and varied from one colony to another. New Brunswick and Nova Scotia had adopted English-style Poor Laws, with a system of poor rates and poorhouses; Upper Canada, more recently settled, did not have such programs; in Lower Canada, begging was regulated and licensed, and the religious orders oversaw most charitable and social programs. The St. Vincent de Paul Society, an international Roman Catholic association founded in Paris in 1833 and transplanted to Canada in 1846, was among the religious organizations that ministered to the needy. The Society's reports offer a glimpse into the state of life for the poorest. In St. John's, Society members visited fishermen's families and found that many had endured days without food. They found one desperate mother with nine starving children. While suffering the ravages of hunger herself, she continued to breastfeed her 18-month-old twins, as she had no other nourishment to give them.

CONCLUSION

Many sought and found a better life in Britain's North American colonies. Opportunities for independence and prosperity were more plentiful, and, despite misfortune that could appear in many guises, some immigrant newcomers were able to move beyond the limits of old world constraints and rise from very humble circumstances to positions of real influence in a rapidly developing society. British North America's economy was being transformed, with British tariff protection supporting a variety of developing economic activities.

The foundation of Canada's modern identity as a nation of immigrants was laid in its early colonial history. In the years immediately following the Napoleonic Wars, the arrival of a million newcomers from the British Isles transformed British North America. In the colony of Upper Canada, these British—Irish, Scottish, and English—immigrants arrived into a population that previously had been dominated by the American-born. In Lower Canada, this new influx raised the spectre of cultural assimilation to the French Catholic population that had been established since the seventeenth century. The emergence of more populous colonies—and a growing assertiveness in those colonies that government should be responsive to their needs—contributed to a quest for political change. Some sought moderate reform and were fundamentally committed to British constitutional models. But increasing frustration at an inability to effect change by peaceful means led others to take up arms in rebellion. A dangerous crisis lay ahead.

8 REBELLION

Canadians often celebrate the peaceful nature of their history, especially in contrast to the cataclysmic events that shook the United States—the American Revolution in the eighteenth century and the Civil War in the nineteenth. The armed uprisings that swept through Canada in 1837 and 1838 do not fit into the narrative of a Canada formed through peaceful evolution.

In English Canada, the events of 1837–38 are often seen as a necessary step toward Canada's achievement of self-government, the price paid to win concessions from the British Empire. Historical treatments tend to assume a cause-and-effect relationship between the rebellions and the later advent of "responsible government." Within this paradigm, Upper Canadian rebel William Lyon Mackenzie becomes a heroic figure, devoted to rooting out systemic flaws and abuses in Canada's constitution and winning more democratic governance. A commemorative statue of Mackenzie stands outside Ontario's legislature in Toronto.

In Quebec, the events of 1837–38 form a more prominent part of historical memory. When English Canada celebrates Victoria Day in May, Quebec celebrates *la journée nationale des patriotes* to commemorate the *patriotes* who fought against British rule. (Before 2003, the Quebec equivalent to Victoria Day was "Dollard Day," named in honour of a Montreal man killed in a battle with the Iroquois in 1660.) In Quebec, the 1837–38 insurrections are understood in nationalist terms, as part of a revolutionary attempt by French Canada to throw off rule by an alien power. Louis-Joseph Papineau, whose statue stands outside Quebec's National Assembly, is viewed as a defender of French-Canadian nationhood.

These events have been commemorated in other ways throughout Canada's history. During the Spanish Civil War in 1936–39, some Canadian volunteers went to fight with the anti-fascist International Brigades. These 1,500 or so volunteers, many of them communist, socialist, or anarchist, called themselves the "Mackenzie-Papineau Battalion." Even more controversially, the *Front de libération du Québec*, or FLQ, which sought to secure Quebec independence through Marxist revolution and garnered world attention in October 1970 with political kidnappings, named a "cell" of their organization the "Chénier" cell, in commemoration of Dr. Jean-Olivier Chénier, a rebel commander killed at St. Eustache in 1837. The FLQ illustrated their 1970 revolutionary manifesto with an image of an armed 1837 *patriote*.

Generations of Canadians have found meaning in the rebellions of 1837–38, but precisely *what* meaning is contested. Neither observers at the time, nor those viewing events retrospectively, have entirely agreed on their causes, nature, or consequences. Nor is it clear to what extent the uprisings in the two colonies were connected. More than 300 were killed in the much more serious insurrection in Lower Canada, compared to a handful in Upper Canada. In the aftermath of the rebellions, Lord Durham famously described the episode as "a struggle not of principles, but of races."[1] Yet this explanation leaves many questions unanswered, especially with respect to Upper Canada. It does not explain the support for the Lower Canadian rebellions among many non-French Canadians, for example the prominent brothers Wolfred and Robert Nelson. It ignores important economic factors and overlooks political and constitutional grievances. The role of outside influences also complicates our historical understanding of the rebellions—in particular, the inspiration provided by the American Revolution.

Whatever explanation is favoured, there *were* some core political grievances in the Canadian colonies. Despite the outward appearance of a government that copied British models, colonial autonomy was limited. Upper and Lower Canada had each had representative government—that is, an elected assembly—since the 1791 *Constitutional Act*, or *Canada Act*. The governor represented the Crown—the governor-in-chief in Lower Canada, and lieutenant governor in Upper Canada. Each colony also had an upper house, or legislative council, modelled on the British House of Lords. The elected legislative assembly was modelled on Britain's House of Commons. The legislative assembly had some important powers—not least the "power of the purse," the sole authority to tax and authorize spending. However, the executive council appointed by the governor was in no way responsible to the assembly. The governor

---

1   G.M. Craig (ed.), *Lord Durham's Report*, new edition (Montreal and Kingston: McGill-Queen's University Press, 2007), 13.

Figure 8.1 Louis-Joseph Papineau (1786–1871).

simply selected loyal men as his advisors, men whose prominence generally implied deeply conservative views. This council was not a cabinet in the modern sense. Today, if an administration ceases to have the support of the elected House of Commons, it is deemed to be defeated, which would usually signal an election. Despite the structural similarities to British models, the colonies did not have "responsible government."

PAPINEAU AND LOWER CANADA

The aspirations of French Canada went beyond mere political reform. By 1811, Lower Canada's *parti canadien* was becoming a voice for the colony's nationalist hopes. The new leader, Louis-Joseph Papineau, was a complex figure: his political views grew more radical over time, but he was very much a conservative in other respects. He believed in the preservation of what he saw as the core traditions of Lower Canada—the Roman Catholic Church, the French language, the seigneurial system, and a distinct civil law. Papineau's elite family possessed a seigneurie, Petite-Nation, and Papineau had been educated in a Roman Catholic seminary. He then undertook training in law in the Montreal offices of his cousin, Denis-Benjamin Viger, who also became a leading figure in the *parti canadien*. Papineau qualified as a lawyer in 1810, but had already begun a lifetime career in politics by age 22. It was a natural fit for a man remarkable for his eloquence. Indeed, he was only 29 when selected to be speaker of Lower Canada's assembly.[2]

The *parti canadien* dominated Lower Canada's assembly by the early 1820s and used its majority to attempt to force change. It adopted obstructionist tactics, refusing to pass essential financial measures—including provisions to apportion some of each year's customs revenue to Upper Canada. Britain's parliament hoped to outflank the *parti canadien* by forcing a union of Upper and Lower Canada, but Papineau and

2 Fernand Ouellet, *Louis Joseph Papineau: A Divided Soul* (Ottawa: Canadian Historical Association Booklet, 1961).

moderate reformer John Neilson travelled to London to submit a petition of protest, and Britain's 1822 bill for union was abandoned.

The Scottish-born Neilson, a successful publisher, exemplifies the fact that not all Lower Canadians saw the political struggle in ethnic terms. He married a French Canadian and spoke French as comfortably as English. Neilson demonstrated to imperial authorities that Lower Canadian political aspirations were not exclusively based on national identity. In 1828, Neilson was again in London to lay a petition of complaints before a Select Committee of the British House of Commons.[3] The petition bore 87,000 signatures, although 78,000 had only signed with crosses. Papineau worried that this evidence that so many political agitators were not sufficiently literate to sign their own names would undermine the cause.

The petition Neilson bore complained of abuses by Lower Canada's governor, Lord Dalhousie (1820–28). The crusty Dalhousie had been frustrated by the assembly's unwillingness to vote necessary funds, and when things reached an impasse in 1826–27, Dalhousie simply used provincial treasury funds to meet costs without the legislature's consent. Dalhousie called an election in 1827, hoping for a more tractable assembly, but instead an even stronger and more radical reform element was returned. Dalhousie refused to accept the assembly's nomination of Papineau as speaker, and when the assembly refused to reconsider, the thwarted governor abruptly ended the legislative session. In the face of colonial complaints, British authorities relieved Dalhousie of his post.

Dalhousie's dismissal would not be enough to satisfy an increasingly discontented Lower Canada. The *parti canadien* itself was changing, and moderates like John Neilson were being crowded out. In 1826, the party was renamed the *parti patriote*, a name with echoes of the American Revolution. A new newspaper, *La Minerve*, was launched in 1826 as a party organ. Papineau began to look increasingly to the republican United States for political models; he especially admired former US President (1801–09) Thomas Jefferson, the author of the Declaration of Independence. Papineau valued Lower Canada's traditional agricultural character, and Jefferson's ideas about the primacy of a virtuous agrarian class resonated with him.

WILLIAM LYON MACKENZIE AND UPPER CANADA

Agitation for political reform was growing in Upper Canada, too, although there were no "nationalist" goals intertwined with the movement as was the case in Lower

---

3 *Report from the Select Committee on the Civil Government of Canada* [1828] (reprinted, Quebec: House of Assembly of Lower Canada, 1829) http://www.torontopubliclibrary.ca/detail. jsp?Entt=RDMDC-37131055420509D&R=DC-37131055420509D.

Figure 8.2 William Lyon Mackenzie (1795–1861).

Canada. Among the most vocal agitators was William Lyon Mackenzie, a journalist and printer with an untidy red wig and a combustible temper. Mackenzie had emigrated from Scotland in 1820, leaving behind bankruptcy and disgruntled business partners. He settled in York (Toronto) in 1824 and launched a newspaper, *The Colonial Advocate.* The paper's attacks on the Tory elite of Upper Canada were garnering attention, but circulation was modest, and Mackenzie was soon mired in debt. Unable to pay his creditors, Mackenzie fled to New York in May 1826 to avoid arrest.

Mackenzie's salvation came in an unexpected guise. A group of young tories took advantage of his absence to vent their rage at his printed attacks: they smashed his presses, throwing the type into Lake Ontario. Mackenzie turned the episode to advantage, suing the wrongdoers for £625, a sum that exceeded the actual damages and gave him enough financial independence to start a career in politics. Members of the assembly were unpaid, but newly bankrolled, Mackenzie won election in 1828 as Upper Canada's member for York, one of a reform majority elected to the assembly that year.

Like Papineau, Mackenzie found much to admire in the United States. In 1829, he travelled south to meet the new president, Andrew Jackson. Jackson's election seemed to herald a shift to a more democratic polity in the United States. He was not a member of the eastern political elite, and supporters welcomed this triumph over entrenched privilege. Individual states were beginning to move toward universal white male suffrage. Mackenzie was also drawn to Jackson's idea that "to the victor belong the spoils"—that is, that a new administration should have the ability to reward its supporters with patronage. Mackenzie had been frustrated by the power of Upper Canada's elite cadre—the "Family Compact"—who shared opportunities exclusively among themselves. Andrew Jackson's opposition to the power of big banks also struck a chord with Mackenzie, who resented the monopoly of the Bank of Upper Canada.

While Mackenzie was re-elected to the assembly in the autumn of 1830, reformers were now in a minority. He clashed frequently with the Tory majority and levelled bolder-than-ever attacks in *The Colonial Advocate*, deriding Upper Canada's elite as sycophants. In December 1831, the assembly voted to expel him. Mackenzie's constituents swiftly re-elected him in a January 1832 by-election. A victory procession of 134 sleighs bore the triumphant Mackenzie down Yonge Street to the accompaniment of bagpipes. This was only the first of five occasions on which Mackenzie's expulsion from the assembly would be followed by immediate re-election. He was also making his voice heard in imperial corridors of power and met with the Secretary of State for the Colonies, Lord Goderich, on an 1832 visit to London. Goderich was evidently swayed by Mackenzie's entreaties and wrote to Upper Canada's governor, Sir John Colborne, to urge a more conciliatory policy. Tories were outraged.[4]

INFLUENCES ON CANADIAN REFORMERS

Upper and Lower Canadian reformers conferred about common goals and increasingly saw grounds for optimism. The trend toward greater democracy in the United States was encouraging. In France, a July 1830 revolution culminated in a new constitutional monarchy, inspiring revolutionary movements in Belgium and Poland that same year. Events on the continent sent a chill over British policy makers: with revolution the alternative, reform became a matter of urgency. The climate of fear was exacerbated by the Swing riots in rural England in the early 1830s. Agricultural workers, made desperate by falling wages, unemployment, and the introduction of mechanized harvesting, burned barns and houses and destroyed machinery. Britain's 1832 *Great Reform Act* extended the vote to more of the middle classes and reallocated Commons seats more equitably—a necessary concession with the fundamentally conservative goal of preserving the existing system. Lower Canadian *patriotes* may have also been encouraged by the observations of the French political philosopher Alexis de Tocqueville, who visited Lower Canada in 1831. Tocqueville recorded his views in his published travel diary, *Journey to America*. He noted that, while the French showed every sign of being a conquered people, dominated commercially and politically by the English, this would soon change: the French-Canadian nation now "knows its strength." French and English could never merge, he predicted, nor could "an indissoluble union...exist between them."[5]

---

4 Frederick H. Armstrong and Ronald J. Stagg, "William Lyon Mackenzie," *Dictionary of Canadian Biography* (*DCB*), http://www.biographi.ca/en/bio/mackenzie_william_lyon_9E.html.

5 Alexis de Tocqueville, *Journey to America*. https://english.republiquelibre.org/Notes_of_Alexis_de_Tocqueville_in_Lower_Canada.

LOWER CANADIAN ECONOMIC GRIEVANCES

Growing economic woes also fed *patriote* fervour in Lower Canada. The population of Lower Canada exceeded half a million by the 1830s, and land holdings were shrinking as farms were repeatedly subdivided. Outmoded agricultural techniques failed to derive the best yield from the land, and unseasonable frosts, droughts, and wheat fly plagues devastated successive harvests. Lower Canada had no surplus to export and could not even produce enough wheat to meet its needs. Farmers lapsed into chronic debt, and actual starvation was being reported in some parishes. Paternalistic relationships between seigneur and *habitant* were breaking down, with more modern capitalistic attitudes prevailing. Resentment also festered about tax burdens on land that were financing infrastructure improvements of primary benefit to the English commercial class. Amid these troubles, British immigration into the colony continued unabated, and growing numbers of native-born French Canadians were leaving for Upper Canada or to seek industrial work in the New England states.

Still worse, immigrants disembarking at Quebec and Montreal in the spring of 1832 brought cholera with them. Within a few weeks, more than a thousand people died in Montreal alone. *Patriote* anger boiled over, with one Lower Canadian accusing British authorities of "rid[ding] themselves of their beggars" by casting them on Canadian shores—"miserable beings, who after having partaken of the bread of our children," spread pestilence and death.[6]

Yet in a paradoxical way, the cholera epidemic of 1832 may have helped to stave off an immediate political crisis. An especially contentious by-election was underway in Montreal West that spring. Daniel Tracey, an Irish medical doctor and the editor of *The Vindicator*, was the reform candidate. Many of Lower Canada's numerous Irish Roman Catholics endorsed the *patriote* cause, having their own deep-seated resentments of British rule. Tracey, along with Ludger Duvernay, editor of *La Minerve*, had only recently served a jail term for libellous attacks on the legislative council in their respective newspapers.

The poll was held at Place d'Armes from April 28 to May 22. Elections did not take place within a single day, but could last for weeks, and were not done by secret ballot. Men were expected to openly declare their support for a candidate; violence, intimidation, bribery, and liquor-assisted persuasion were frequent. Newspapers printed voters' choices, along with their names, addresses, and occupations. In Montreal West, feelings were running high, occasionally bubbling over into violence, and, as

---

6   *Montreal Gazette*, August 21, 1832, as quoted by J. Verney, *O'Callaghan: The Making and Unmaking of a Rebel* (Montreal and Kingston: McGill-Queen's University Press, 1994), 55.

a precaution, the militia was called out. At the end of the penultimate day of polling, Tracey was ahead of the Conservative Stanley Bagg by three votes, and a crowd of jubilant supporters accompanied him home.

The spectacle of the lately imprisoned Irish radical anticipating victory was too much for Bagg's disappointed partisans. They pelted their opponents with stones, and Tracey's men responded in kind. The militia, caught up in the mob's hail of stones, opened fire. Three of Tracey's supporters fell dead; another 20 were wounded. Outraged reformers hastily summoned mass meetings to fan the flames of indignation. "The Governor sleeps in his château, and they leave us with these murderers," Papineau fumed to Neilson.[7] But as cholera struck the city, all who could fled to the countryside, and public meetings were out of the question. Dr. Tracey, whose victory had been anticlimactically declared the day after the shootings, bravely ministered to the sick. By July 18, he was dead.

REFORMERS' COMPLAINTS TO BRITAIN

In 1834, Lower Canada's *patriote*-dominated assembly petitioned Britain's parliament for redress of their grievances. They produced "Ninety-Two Resolutions," a torrential stream of complaints over dozens of closely spaced pages. The resolutions alleged that the Crown's power was exorbitant and unbalanced, and that the executive council was entirely irresponsible to the elected assembly. American models, it was suggested, were more applicable to Canada than British ones, since the state of society in Great Britain "is altogether different from our own." A substantial portion of revenues of the colony were beyond the control of the elected assembly, the resolutions complained, and official posts were being disproportionately awarded to those of British origin, and especially to members of the same elite families.[8]

Lower Canada's governor, Lord Aylmer, condemned the resolutions as tantamount to a Declaration of Independence. John Neilson, who had now broken entirely with the radical reformers, published an anonymous critique in the Quebec *Mercury* that condemned the bulk of the resolutions, dismissing some as ridiculous, abusive, or seditious.[9] The British cabinet evidently found it difficult to navigate the clumsy prose of the document: "Such is the copiousness and warmth of expression…that in many cases it is difficult to discern what is the subject matter to which the writers refer," one complained.[10]

---

7 As quoted in Joseph Schull, *Rebellion: The Rising in French Canada, 1837* (Toronto: Macmillan, 1971), 19.

8 The 92 Resolutions appear in full in W.P.M. Kennedy (ed.), *Statutes, Treaties and Documents of the Canadian Constitution, 1713–1929* (Toronto: Oxford University Press, 1930), 270–90.

9 As quoted by Alfred D. Decelles, *The 'Patriotes' of '37* (Toronto: Glasgow, Brook & Co., 1916), 39.

10 As quoted in Schull, *Rebellion*, 37.

Upper Canadians were also busy articulating their dissatisfaction. William Lyon Mackenzie chaired an assembly committee in 1835 that produced the Seventh Report on Grievances. The report noted that earlier expectations of constitutional change remained unmet. Chief among the demands was responsible government—"there should be an entire confidence between the Executive and the Commons House of Assembly." The report lamented the "almost unlimited extent of the patronage of the Crown" and the limited power of the assembly over expenditure, "a system that admits its officers to take and apply the funds of the Colonists without any legislative vote whatever." The Canada Company, with vast control over land reserves, as well as banking and canal companies were further sources of dissatisfaction, since public funds were awarded to such companies without proper scrutiny. The appointed legislative council continually refused to assent to bills passed by the assembly, rejecting "many valuable measures earnestly prayed for by the people." The report acknowledged the "great excellence of the English constitution," but complained that the system had not been properly adapted in Canada, leaving the elected assembly "powerless and dependent." "At the root of all the evils" was the appointed legislative council: an elected upper house was a favourite remedy of Mackenzie's. More boldly, the report complained of "a succession of Colonial ministers in England who have never visited the country, and can never possibly become acquainted" with "the affairs of people 4,000 miles off.[11]

BRITAIN'S REACTION TO COLONIAL COMPLAINTS

Mackenzie's complaint about a succession of ill-informed Secretaries of State for the Colonies was rather close to the mark, with 10 different statesmen filling the portfolio between April 1827 and April 1835. In fact, the Colonial Office only became a separate ministry in 1854; prior to this, the same ministry oversaw "War and the Colonies," rather a daunting task given the scope of the British Empire. Cabinet ministers were often compelled to make critical decisions about far-removed places of which they knew little.

One of the easiest ways for Britain's government to demonstrate responsiveness was with a change of personnel. Lower Canada's governor, Lord Aylmer, was recalled in 1835. Aylmer had undertaken his work in 1830 with earnest hopes of reconciliation. He had even offered seats on his executive council to Papineau and John Neilson in 1831. Both had refused on principle, but Aylmer had managed to secure a few Francophone appointees with reform leanings. His early optimism soon gave way to bitter frustration, however, and, after the bloodshed of the 1832 by-elections, relations between governor and reformers seemed beyond redemption. Parliamentary sessions

---

11 "The Seventh Report on Grievances, 1835," *Statutes, Treaties and Documents*, 295–307.

in Lower Canada were stalled in complete paralysis, with members of the assembly unwilling to pass necessary financial measures, the legislative council refusing to pass bills from the lower house, and the governor vetoing other legislation in a vain attempt to exert pressure. Papineau openly denounced British-appointed colonial governors as self-interested aristocrats who took office only to revive their flagging personal fortunes. At least one appointee sought in Canada "the wherewithal to repair his dilapidated old castle," he sneered.[12] As Aylmer departed Lower Canada, he gave a wistful speech on the wharf, acknowledging that his "anxious endeavours" had fallen far short of his hopes. Overcome by emotion at the cheers of a small crowd of supporters, he burst into tears. Aylmer's replacement was Lord Gosford, an Irish peer with a reputation for progressive views about Ireland's Roman Catholics, who was now instructed to investigate discontent in Lower Canada.

Amid this steady deterioration of any spirit of compromise, a growing sense of national consciousness swelled among Lower Canadian *patriotes*. A new organization, the Société Saint-Jean-Baptiste, was formed in 1834. That same year, Ludger Duvernay, publisher of *La Minerve*, resurrected traditional Saint-Jean-Baptiste Day celebrations on June 24, as both an opportunity to celebrate French Canada's cultural identity and to rally support to the *patriote* cause. George-Étienne Cartier's "Ô Canada! Mon pays! Mes amours!" was sung, and villages along the St. Lawrence were illuminated with a chain of bonfires.

At the same time, Montreal Tories joined together to form a "Constitutional Association," along with rifle clubs whose purpose was ominously military. The Constitutional Association declared its goal of using every effort to maintain the imperial connection. John Molson, Junior, of the prominent brewing family, rallied Montreal's business elite, whom he characterized as "an insulted and oppressed people" to "a sense of impending danger."[13]

British authorities also appointed a new lieutenant governor in Upper Canada in 1836. The recalled governor, Sir John Colborne, had angered Upper Canada's numerous Presbyterians and Methodists with his handling of the contentious clergy reserves question: 15,000 acres of land, set aside in the 1791 *Constitutional Act* for the maintenance of the Protestant clergy, was awarded wholly to the Anglican Church, along with another 6,600 acres of Crown land. The British government dismissed Colborne to assuage Canadian anger, but appointed him commander of the forces in Canada instead.

---

12 Papineau, *La Minerve*, February 18, 1834, as quoted by Fernand Ouellet, *Lower Canada, 1791–1840: Social Change and Nationalism* (Toronto: McClelland & Stewart, 1980), 221.

13 John Molson, Jr. "An Address by the Constitutionalists of Montreal to Men of British or Irish Origin, 1834," *Statutes, Treaties and Documents*, 291–94.

Colborne's successor as governor was Sir Francis Bond Head. Bond Head was unconvinced that "demagogues" like William Lyon Mackenzie represented the "real sentiments of the people." He lamented the pernicious influence of American political ideals and resolved to "suppress rebellion, and, above all, to resist the smallest attempt to introduce that odious principle of 'responsible government' which a few republicans in the province had been desirous to force upon them."[14] Although Bond Head appointed some reform-oriented men to his executive council—including Robert Baldwin, a moderate lawyer—he quickly clashed with even such temperate councillors, and his executive council resigned in protest in March 1836.

Bond Head also battled with Upper Canada's assembly: it refused to vote for necessary financial measures, and the governor in turn refused to give his assent to measures already passed. He dissolved the assembly and called an election for June 1836. Bond Head did not follow the usual gubernatorial practice of remaining aloof from partisan politics; instead, he openly supported the Tory side, warning that outside threats, especially from the United States, jeopardized Upper Canada's security. He urged voters to opt for loyalty, law, and order. As added insurance, Orange Order gangs intimidated those suspected of supporting reform candidates. The result was a resounding defeat for the reformers. William Lyon Mackenzie was dismayed to lose his seat and frustrated at the impossibility of achieving his goals through peaceful political means. Within days, he launched a new newspaper, *The Constitution*, inaugurated on July 4, 1836, the sixtieth anniversary of the American Declaration of Independence.

Even as Mackenzie moved toward a more radical position, alienating many former supporters, reform politician Robert Baldwin adhered to a patient and measured approach. That July, he wrote to Lord Glenelg, the Secretary of State for the Colonies, urging a solution to the constitutional impasse that would "strengthen the attachment of the people to the connection with the Mother Country." The solution did not involve a change to the legislative council—eliminating it or making it elective, as urged by others. Instead, Baldwin recognized that the remedy lay in the transformation of the executive council into a true cabinet. A system of ministerial responsibility was "an English principle," he stressed.[15] Yet Baldwin's respectful entreaties proved no more effective than Mackenzie's incendiary and provocative ones. Furthermore, Baldwin's absence from Upper Canada's political scene during his extended stay in Ireland and England meant that reformers were denied the benefit of a voice of moderation and reason.

---

14 Sir Francis Bond Head, *The Emigrant* (London: John Murray, 1846), 154–57.

15 Robert Baldwin to Lord Glenelg, July 13, 1836, Appendix No 5, *Journals of the House of Assembly of Upper Canada from the 8th day of November, 1836 to the 4th day of March, 1837* (Toronto: W.L. Mackenzie, 1837).

CALLS FOR REFORM IN THE MARITIME COLONIES

Robert Baldwin was not alone in believing that constitutional change was entirely consistent with maintaining a strong British connection. In Nova Scotia, Joseph Howe emerged as a spokesman for reform, for a more faithful adherence to British constitutional models. Howe's family had been Loyalists, with a deep reverence for the imperial connection. His newspaper, the *Novascotian*, became a forum to educate colonists about the workings of their government. It published the assembly's debates in detail, as well as offering insights into political changes in the wider world. Howe's reputation in Nova Scotia grew when, in 1835, he successfully defended himself against libel charges; he was elected to the assembly the following year.

Just as in the Canadian colonies, a business and social elite dominated Nova Scotia's politics, using their power to promote their own interests. This ruling oligarchy, known as the "Council of Twelve," monopolized places in the governor's appointed council. In Nova Scotia, unlike other colonies, the executive council and legislative council was one and the same. In Nova Scotia's assembly in February 1837, Howe moved a series of "Twelve Resolutions" to urge reform. The resolutions insisted upon Nova Scotia's reverence for British institutions, but complained that the colony's representatives had "no effectual control." The resolutions called for a separation of the executive and legislative councils, with the latter body to be elected. The Colonial Office was not prepared to concede an elected upper house, but in 1837 introduced one important change for Nova Scotia: dividing the executive and legislative councils into two bodies.[16]

Britain similarly made a modest concession in New Brunswick. New Brunswick's elected assembly sought control over timber leases on Crown lands, which had often been unfairly awarded to those with personal connections to the appointed council. The assembly complained that, with the considerable revenue from timber leases not under its control, its traditional power over colonial finances was moot. In 1837, the Colonial Office gave New Brunswick's assembly the control it sought over timber revenues.

A WORSENING ATMOSPHERE

These modest concessions in New Brunswick and Nova Scotia were not indicative of any sweeping change in Britain's colonial policy. In March 1837, British cabinet minister Lord John Russell produced "Ten Resolutions," which were essentially a complete denial of the reformers' aspirations. Russell's resolutions rejected an elected

---

16 A copy of the Twelve Resolutions may be read at http://nslegislature.ca/index.php/about/joe-howe/ TwelveResolutions.

legislative council, dismissed responsible government as "inadvisable," and undercut one of the key principles of representative government: to address the paralysis in colonial finances, the governor was authorized to spend provincial funds without the consent of the assembly. Even British newspapers condemned this as an act of robbery.

Equally unsettling were the effects of a worldwide economic recession. An era of heady financial expansion and railway and canal construction had ended, and Britain and the United States were in the grip of a severe commercial crisis. President Andrew Jackson's attempts to rein in the power of the Bank of the United States had set off a financial panic, and Canada's banks also suffered. By disastrous coincidence, harsh weather and insect plagues reduced Lower Canada's already inadequate wheat yields, and crop failures now extended to Upper Canada. Grain prices soared and declining trade dried up traffic at the ports, throwing many out of work. Unemployment in the lumber camps and among canal workers fed simmering rivalries between gangs of Irish and French Canadians.

THE ROAD TO REBELLION

In both Lower and Upper Canada, radicals increasingly adopted tactics that echoed those of the American Revolution. Mackenzie urged readers of *The Constitution* to boycott British goods—not to buy, wear, or use British manufactured goods or British West Indian liquors. In Lower Canada, *patriotes* began wearing homespun cloth, straw hats, and crude homemade shoes—subject to no import duties. Mackenzie arranged a printing of Thomas Paine's *Common Sense*, the book whose 1776 appearance in the rebellious Thirteen Colonies has been credited with converting agitation for reform into a drive toward independence. Upper Canadians issued the "Declaration of Toronto" in the summer of 1837, a document that drew heavily on the American Declaration of Independence and insisted on the people's "natural right given them by their Creator" to establish "such institutions as will yield the greatest quantity of happiness to the greatest number."[17] In Lower Canada, the *Société des Fils de la Liberté* (Sons of Liberty) copied the American Revolutionary movement of the same name with a military branch to provide militia training. In Upper Canada, Mackenzie boasted that manpower, as well as ideological inspiration, could be drawn from south of the border. "There are thousands, aye tens of thousands of Englishmen, Scotchmen, and above all, of Irishmen, now in the United States, who only wait till the standard be

---

17 R.A. Mackay, "The Political Ideas of William Lyon Mackenzie," *The Canadian Journal of Economics and Political Science* 3 (February 1937): 17.

planted in Lower Canada, to throw their strength and numbers to the side of democracy," he claimed.[18]

Mackenzie kept up a channel of communication with counterparts in Lower Canada, especially the Montreal medical doctors and brothers Wolfred and Robert Nelson. Despite Loyalist family roots, the Nelsons were among Lower Canada's most vehement *patriotes*. Robert kept a respectable surgical practice but had a secret passageway in his home to accommodate meetings with *patriote* associates.

During the summer of 1837, political meetings throughout the parishes and towns of Lower Canada were drawing ever-larger crowds. By mid-June, Gosford was sufficiently alarmed to forbid meetings "having for their objects the resistance of the lawful authority of the King and Parliament, and the subversion of the laws." Notices carrying the governor's proclamation were torn down, and the decree proved unenforceable. Gosford exerted pressure by dismissing any magistrates or militia officers who were found to have attended the banned meetings. Others voluntarily resigned their posts in protest.

Strong social pressure also prompted some of these resignations. Ardent *patriotes* used the time-honoured tactic of the *charivari* to intimidate those showing any support for the colonial regime. The ritual had traditionally voiced social disapproval for unconventional marriages: a widow who remarried too soon, or perhaps a couple separated by too wide a gap in age or social standing might find themselves the object of an unwelcome nocturnal visit by local rowdies disguised in costumes and banging pots. In the tense atmosphere of 1837, however, the ritual turned political, and authorities were alarmed by the spectacle of nighttime raiders, their faces blackened to ensure anonymity, roaming the countryside unchecked.[19]

Roman Catholic clergy condemned revolution from the pulpit, reminding parishioners of the Pope's message of obedience to political authority. Prayers marking the June 1837 accession to the throne of 18-year-old Queen Victoria were met with sullen silence.

An October 23, 1837, *patriote* rally at Saint-Charles drew a crowd of 5,000. The demonstration had a celebratory air, with hymns, booming volleys of musketry and cannon, and overt revolutionary symbols. There was a "liberty pole" crowned with a red cap and tricolour flags of the French Revolution. Banners bore incendiary messages: "Liberty! We'll Conquer or Die for Her," one read. Another featured the American eagle with a maple leaf in its mouth, and a skull with the slogan "Death

---

18 As quoted in Gerald Craig, *Upper Canada: The Formative Years, 1784–1841* (Toronto: McClelland & Stewart, 1963), 244–45.

19 Allan Greer, "From Folklore to Revolution: Charivaris and the Lower Canadian Rebellion of 1837," *Social History* 15, no. 1 (January 1990): 25–43.

to the Legislative Council." Papineau, however, gave signs of wishing to restrain the revolutionary fervour his activism had helped to unleash. He urged the replacement of the administration with "men worthy of confidence." It was hardly a revolutionary call to arms. Wolfred Nelson jumped to his feet, exclaiming, "I differ from Mr. Papineau!" "The time has come," he roared, "to melt our spoons into bullets." Another *patriote*, Dr. Cyrille Côté, called on the crowd to throw lead at their enemies.[20]

By early November, street fighting in Montreal between Loyalists and the *Fils de la Liberté* sharpened Gosford's anxieties about Lower Canada's defences. Troops were moved from Halifax and Upper Canada and supplemented with volunteer militia. In Upper Canada, Lieutenant Governor Bond Head naïvely waved off warnings that his jurisdiction was under-defended. He assured the acting adjutant-general of militia, James Fitzgibbon, that "nothing can be more satisfactory than the present political state of this province."[21]

But, far from being tranquil, Upper Canada was moving steadily toward open revolt. Mackenzie was busy drafting a new constitution for the colony and issued an "Appeal to the People" under the bold heading "Independence." "Do you love freedom?," he challenged Upper Canadians. "I know you do. Do you hate oppression? Who dare deny it?…Then buckle on your armour, and put down the villains who oppress and enslave our country." He asserted that, in Lower Canada, "the vile hirelings of our unlawful oppressors have already bit the dust in hundreds." The *patriotes*, he claimed, outnumbered their opponents one hundred to one.[22] Clearly, this was wishful thinking.

REBELLION IN LOWER CANADA

Things were actually taking a very different turn in Lower Canada. Gosford issued arrest warrants for 26 of that colony's rebel leaders. Some were scooped up, but Papineau and others joined Wolfred Nelson at Saint-Denis on the Richelieu River. Nelson assumed military leadership of the *patriote* forces there, while Papineau, according to his later explanation, retreated to a safe place in order to be available to oversee negotiations in the event of a defeat.

Nelson secured an excellent tactical position for his forces at Saint-Denis, with *patriote* sharpshooters placed behind stone walls. When, on the morning of November 23, Crown troops under the command of Colonel Charles Gore confronted the *patriotes* after an all-night march in freezing rain, Gore's troops were quickly forced to retreat.

---

20 As quoted in Schull, *Rebellion*, 58.

21 As quoted in S.F. Wise, "Sir Francis Bond Head," *DCB*. Online at www.biographi.ca.

22 As quoted by John Sewell, *Mackenzie: A Political Biography of William Lyon Mackenzie* (Toronto: James Lorimer, 2002), 146–48.

However, Wolfred Nelson's triumph at Saint-Denis was tempered by the discovery that Papineau had left them "in the lurch," as he later put it, and had fled to the United States. Papineau was not the only *patriote* who opted for flight. Nelson was dismayed to discover that many of his supporters had melted away, not wishing to risk further engagement. He set out for the American border himself but was captured by militia forces a few days later. Martial law had just been declared and the penalty for high treason was death.

Two days after the rebel victory at Saint-Denis, a *patriote* force at Saint-Charles prepared for battle under the leadership of Thomas Brown, a bankrupt hardware merchant who had lost an eye

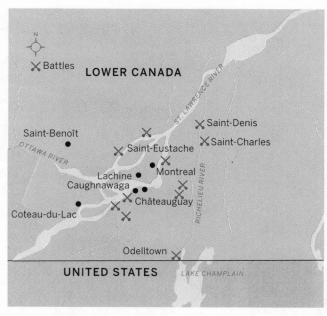

Map 8.1 Selected Lower Canada rebellion sites.

in earlier clashes with Montreal Loyalists. An intercepted message led Brown to believe that the 350 British regulars commanded by Colonel George Wetherall had been ordered back to Montreal. The sudden shattering of the village church with artillery announced to Brown that he had been misinformed. Only a few dozen *patriotes* were at the ready. Wetherall's forces set homes and barns ablaze, targeting buildings from which musket fire had emanated. Some *patriotes* drowned attempting to escape across the Richelieu River, and Brown himself fled. By the evening, the small rebel force was overwhelmed and 56 *patriotes* lay dead in the burning grass. Within the week, Wetherall's force marched into Montreal leading 30 prisoners. A red-capped liberty pole captured from Saint-Charles completed the sorry procession.

Further west, at Saint-Eustache, *patriotes* Jean-Joseph Girouard, an Acadian notary, and Amury Girod, a Swiss-born farmer and author, attempted to impose some order in another rebel camp. The number of supporters fluctuated in strength from day to day, with as few as 200 or as many as 1,500 marshalling to fight. Parish priest Jacques Paquin, arrested by the insurgents, sneeringly dismissed any notion of discipline among the rebels: "These men would recognize no rules and believed themselves masters to do anything they pleased. This is how they conceived of the freedom of patriotism."[23]

23 As quoted in Allan Greer, *The Patriots and the People: The Rebellion of 1837 in Rural Lower Canada* (Toronto: University of Toronto Press, 1993), 319.

Figure 8.3 Historical revisionism? In 2012, Quebec's *Parti Québécois* government commemorated Papineau with a monument at Saint-Denis, the battlefield from which he fled.

On the morning of December 14, 1837, Sir John Colborne led a force of 1,280 British regulars, 220 volunteer militia, and 200 Iroquois warriors from Caughnawaga (Kahnawake) to Saint-Eustache. The Iroquois answer to the call for volunteers had been much welcomed by the Lachine militia, who cheered the sight of their canoes on the St. Lawrence. The 300 *patriotes* at Saint-Eustache had been caught off guard, deceived by a small diversionary force. Girod fled; he would later shoot himself when faced with capture. In his absence, Jean-Olivier Chénier, a medical doctor, assumed command, leading a group of 50 insurgents to the village church. They held Colborne's force back for a time with sniper fire, even amid a continued artillery barrage, but when Crown forces set the building alight, the *patriotes* were forced to abandon the position. Many were killed in the escape, including Chénier himself. By the afternoon, Colborne's forces had prevailed, with 70 of the Saint-Eustache insurgents killed and 118 taken prisoner. Colborne's force advanced to nearby Saint-Benoît the following day, where Girouard encouraged the rebel force under his command to surrender. He fled to Coteau-du-Lac, but soon gave himself up as prisoner.

REBELLION IN UPPER CANADA

In the meantime, plans for rebellion in Upper Canada were beginning to unravel. Mackenzie had planned to stage a *coup d'état* on December 7, 1837, but pinned his hopes on American military intervention to force a political union with the United States and had made little military preparation. Some Upper Canadians were ambivalent about the rebel cause, waiting to see if the uprising was successful before committing themselves. Dr. John Rolph, an English-born lawyer and medical doctor who had served in the legislative assembly, was a case in point. He did not openly support the radicals, yet struck a secret deal with Mackenzie to take a leading role in government once the coup succeeded. Rolph learned that Mackenzie was about to be arrested and urged him to move the date of the rebellion forward. However, when Rolph saw the true state of preparations, he proposed instead that the plan be abandoned.

It was too late. That same day, December 4, rebels were already answering Mackenzie's call, assembling at Montgomery's Tavern just outside Toronto. Governor Bond Head belatedly took alarm and hastily bundled his family aboard a steamer. He sent emissaries to meet with Mackenzie, promising amnesty if the rebels laid down their arms; one was Robert Baldwin, but John Rolph was the other. Rolph carried out his duties as if a neutral arbiter but gave the rebels a secretive wink. Mackenzie refused to surrender. With several hundred rebels carrying out military drills on Toronto's Yonge Street, Lieutenant James Fitzgibbon was forced to improvise a defence of the colony with only 300 poorly trained militia. Fitzgibbon was even more demoralized when Bond Head placed Allan MacNab, an inexperienced, but socially prominent, lawyer and real estate magnate, in overall command. Humiliated, Fitzgibbon protested to Bond Head, who relented and reappointed Fitzgibbon. The government's inadequate preparations were met with even poorer preparation on the rebel side.

On the evening of December 5, Mackenzie's rebel forces were reinforced by the arrival of another 700 supporters, led by a Pennsylvania-born Quaker blacksmith Samuel Lount.[24] Only a minority of the rebel forces were armed. The rest made do with pikes and pitchforks. Toronto Sheriff William Jarvis confronted the rebels with a small defence force of two dozen. They fired a musket volley at the rebels advancing down Yonge Street and then fled in the darkness and smoke. Lount ordered the fire returned, but events descended into farce: when Lount's rear-rank troops saw the front ranks drop to the ground—to allow a volley to be fired over their heads—his inexperienced troops assumed they had fallen dead and took to their heels.

Disorganization in the rebel headquarters prompted widespread defections; more than half those who had gathered at Montgomery's Tavern deserted the cause, leaving a force of approximately 500. Mackenzie himself did not inspire confidence and was preoccupied with personal vendettas. On December 7, Anthony Van Egmond belatedly arrived to command the rebels, not knowing that the date for the uprising had changed. The Dutch-born Van Egmond had adopted his aristocratic surname while a fugitive from the law and invented a dazzling military résumé that impressed his fellow conspirators. Van Egmond attempted to impose some order on the band of insurgents at Montgomery's Tavern but quickly despaired of any success; Mackenzie sharpened Van Egmond's resolve to continue by levelling a pistol at his head. Fitzgibbon likewise was suffering a crisis of confidence. He sank to his knees in prayer,

---

24 Members of the Society of Friends, or Quakers, are typically pacifist in their beliefs. Some sources have cast doubt on Lount's affiliation with the Quakers, but historian Robynne Rogers Healey, an expert on the Upper Canadian Quakers, identifies Lount as Quaker. Robynne Rogers Healey, *From Quaker to Upper Canadian: Faith and Community among Yonge Street Friends, 1801–1850* (Montreal and Kingston: McGill-Queen's University Press, 2006), 145.

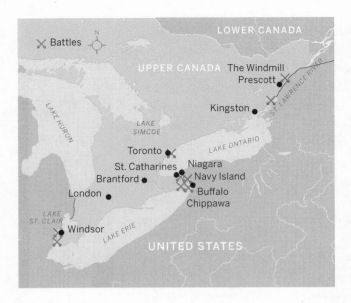

Map 8.2 Selected Upper Canada rebellion sites.

marshalled his courage, and resolved to attack. Fitzgibbon led his troops up Yonge Street to the accompaniment of martial bands and the cheers of Toronto's loyal citizens. A cannon blast through the roof of Montgomery's Tavern sent a stream of rebels rushing from their shelter, and the assault quickly became a rout. It was over within 20 minutes, with one rebel killed and several wounded. Five members of the militia sustained wounds.

As the skirmish collapsed, Van Egmond was captured; cast into a cold, dank Upper Canadian jail in December, he died within a month. Fitzgibbon resigned as adjutant general the day after the successful defence of the colony, deeply embittered by Bond Head's actions. Mackenzie fled to the United States with a price of £1,000 on his head, but boasted that no Upper Canadian betrayed him: "I found them ready to risk life and property to aid me." The hardest part of Mackenzie's journey south—"the most cruel and intense sensation of pain I ever endured"—was a neck-deep crossing of the icy Sixteen Mile Creek on a bitter December night, his clothes held above his head to keep them dry.[25]

In Upper Canada's London district, just west of Brantford, the American-born Dr. Charles Duncombe, a former member of the legislative assembly, commanded another contingent of several hundred rebels. On December 13, 1837, Colonel Allan MacNab, leading a force of militia and Six Nations volunteers, put these would-be revolutionaries to flight.

Unwilling to concede defeat, Mackenzie established a base of operations on Navy Island, in Canadian territory in the Niagara River. He declared a provisional government, soliciting American volunteers to his cause. On Christmas night, MacNab left his palatial home, the 72-room Dundurn Castle, and marshalled a force of 2,500 volunteers—including Six Nations warriors and a company of 50 black Canadians from St. Catharines—to defeat Mackenzie. Mackenzie later insisted that black volunteers had been misguided in their allegiances, regretting that their "unfounded fear of a union with the United States…induced them to oppose reform and free institutions."[26]

25 As quoted in Charles Lindsey, *William Lyon Mackenzie* (Toronto: Morang, 1911), 386.

26 As quoted in Owen A. Thomas, *Niagara's Freedom Trail: A Guide to African-Canadian History on the Niagara Peninsula* (Thorold: Niagara Region Tourist Council, c. 1995), 15.

MacNab's forces watched the rebel encampment on Navy Island from the shore near Chippawa but hesitated to act for fear of provoking the Americans. When a steamer, the *Caroline*, delivered supplies and weapons to the island on the night of December 29, MacNab saw his opportunity and resolved to intercept it. Royal Navy Commander Andrew Drew and a crew of 50 set out in seven rowboats across the fast-running Niagara River, two miles above the falls. They found that the *Caroline* had already left the island, and was tied up at Fort Schlosser, New York. Drew's crew boarded the *Caroline*, shot one of the crew and chased off the rest, set the vessel ablaze, and cut it loose from its moorings. The burning vessel broke apart and was swept over the falls.

The *Caroline* affair outraged Americans: American sovereignty had been violated during peacetime, with an American ship destroyed in United States territory. American newspapers reported the massacre of dozens, inventing details of the anguished cries of passengers trapped aboard the burning vessel as it plunged over the falls. A fresh infusion of American recruits crowded Navy Island in the wake of the incident, eager to avenge the insult. Yet all semblance of military discipline there was breaking down. Rolph visited the island but left within the hour, disgusted by the filth, disorder, and drunken bickering. Soon afterward, Mackenzie was arrested in Buffalo while taking his wife to a doctor; he would ultimately serve a year in prison.

BORDER RAIDS AND RETRIBUTION, 1838

The fizzling end to the rebel base at Navy Island did not bring a return to security for Canada. The year 1838 began with a series of skirmishes along the border, as rebels who had fled south the previous autumn continued their quest for revolution. However, much to the disgust of his compatriots, Papineau abandoned the cause. He disapproved of the plan to overthrow the seigneurial system and break the influence of the Catholic Church. Robert Nelson condemned Papineau as a selfish man, a man of words and not action; Nelson was elected by his co-conspirators as President of the future Republic of Canada.

Britain's cabinet suspended Lower Canada's constitution in early February 1838; the assembly would not meet, and all power would be in the hands of the governor and a non-elected special council. Habeas corpus—a traditional safeguard to individual liberty, requiring that grounds for someone's imprisonment be shown before a court of law—was suspended.[27] Lord Gosford, who had already tendered his resignation as governor, departed the colony on February 27, a day after proclaiming a general thanksgiving to mark the restoration of tranquillity.

27 A.V. Dicey, *An Introduction to the Study of the Law of the Constitution* (London: Macmillan, 1965), 215.

This proved premature: on the night of February 28, Robert Nelson led several hundred *patriotes* across the border into Lower Canada, armed with rifles and cannons, stolen from an arsenal at Elizabethtown, New York. However, their goal of proclaiming Lower Canada's independence was undercut by the sudden evaporation of supporters; the muster of *patriotes* the next morning revealed only 160. Lower Canadian militia smartly drove the invaders back across the border, where American army troops were waiting. Nelson was among those arrested.

Upper Canada's governor, Sir Francis Bond Head, also resigned, his replacement, Sir George Arthur, arriving in March 1838. Arthur was determined to make examples of some of the captured rebels. Samuel Lount and Peter Matthews were swiftly tried, convicted, and, on April 12, 1838, hanged. Sheriff William Jarvis, who had led the small band of militia defenders who defeated Lount's forces on Yonge Street, wept as he prepared the prisoners for execution. They embraced him and assured him that they were prepared to meet their judgment in heaven. They dropped through the trapdoor of gallows reciting the Lord's Prayer.

In Lower Canada, Sir John Colborne, acting as temporary administrator, recognized the volatility of the situation. With more than 500 languishing in the colony's jails and a broad base of support for the *patriote* movement, Colborne moved cautiously. He released all the prisoners except for 161 who were believed guilty of the most serious offences. The newly appointed governor, Lord Durham, who arrived in May 1838, would have the unenviable task of meting out justice amid a tense and still-threatening atmosphere.

John George Lambton, first Earl of Durham, was a major player in British politics, a man of tremendous wealth and prestige. His family coalmines in the north of England employed more than 2,000 men. Durham was handsome and youthful in appearance, dark-haired and dark-eyed, but bore the burden of ill health. His first wife and four children had all died of tuberculosis, the disease that would claim him in 1840. He suffered greatly from nosebleeds, migraine headaches, and the irritability that is symptomatic of tuberculosis. He had been reluctant to accept the appointment to Canada, where he was to both govern and conduct a commission of inquiry. He had just served as ambassador to Russia and feared the further effects of cold climate on his health. Nevertheless, he accepted the post, without salary—even spending an estimated £35,000 of his own money during his time in Canada. He brought with him a vast supply of fine wine, crystal, plate, and other luxuries for vice-regal entertaining and was accompanied by a large retinue of aides-de-camp and advisors, some of whose salaries he paid himself.[28]

---

28 Chester New, *Lord Durham's Mission to Canada* (Toronto: McClelland & Stewart, 1963). See also Leonard Cooper, *Radical Jack: The Life of John George Lambton, First Earl of Durham* (London: Cresset Press, 1959); Ged Martin, *The Durham Report and British Policy: A Critical Essay* (Cambridge: Cambridge University Press, 1972), 15; and Ged Martin, "Attacking the Durham Myth: Seventeen Years On," *Journal of Canadian Studies* 25 (Spring 1990): 50–51.

Durham recognized that he would have to tread carefully in the explosive atmosphere of Lower Canada. South of the border, rebel refugees were busy forming secret societies and planning fresh raids: Colborne believed that the *Frères Chasseurs* numbered in the tens of thousands, although this is almost certainly an exaggeration. Other such organizations planned raids on Upper Canada. From Lockport, New York, the so-called Canadian Refugee Relief Association launched a raid against the Short Hills area of Pelham Township in early June 1838. The raiders had been assured that 25,000 supporters were waiting to join them, but only 26 rallied to the cause. After a brief skirmish with a small troop of British regulars and pursuit by Iroquois warriors, some raiders were captured, including the leader, James Morreau, an American-born tanner. On July 30, 1838, Morreau was hanged for treason.[29] Morreau's co-conspirators faced imprisonment or transportation to penal colonies; 102 were sent to British penal colonies, most to Van Diemen's Land (later Tasmania).[30]

In Lower Canada, Durham found what he believed to be a good expedient for the many who awaited trial. He persuaded some prominent instigators, including Wolfred Nelson, to acknowledge their guilt, promising merciful treatment. Spared the noose, eight were instead transported to Bermuda. Sixteen of the rebels who had fled south of the border, Louis-Joseph Papineau and Cyrille Côté among them, were banished from Canada, subject to execution if they should return.

Durham's conciliatory gesture was rejected in Britain, his ordinances to deal with the rebels disallowed. Pronouncing sentences on fugitives and exiling men who had not had the benefit of a trial violated core British legal principles. On October 9, 1838, Durham indignantly announced his resignation, complaining publicly about "incessant criticism" from the imperial government, which acted under "ignorance and indifference." Since his ordinance for the exile of prisoners had been disavowed, those who had "made the most distinct admission of guilt" were free to return without punishment, he proclaimed. In Britain, *The Times* criticized Durham as "Lord High Seditioner," who demonstrated that he placed his own fragile dignity over the safety of the colony by abandoning his post while rumours of renewed insurrection were rife.[31]

Indeed, two days after Durham's November 1 departure, Robert Nelson, Cyrille Côté, and the *Frères Chasseurs* launched an invasion from the United States at Napierville. Nelson proclaimed himself president and declared Canada's independence before a crowd of more than 3,000.[32] Throughout the vicinity, an estimated 4,000

29 Colin Read, "The Short Hills Raid of June, 1838, and Its Aftermath" *Ontario History* 68 (June 1976): 93–115.
30 See Cassandra Pybus, "Patriot Exiles in Van Diemen's Land," *Canadian State Trials: Rebellion and Invasion in the Canadas, 1837–1839*, vol. 2. (Toronto: Osgoode Law Society, 2002), 188–204. See also Barry Wright, "The Kingston and London Courts Martial," *Canadian State Trials*, II: 130–59.
31 As quoted in Cooper, *Radical Jack*, 268.
32 F. Murray Greenwood and Barry Wright, *Canadian State Trials*, 15.

joined the insurgents, attacking Loyalist homes and seizing arms, ammunition, and other property. Nelson's nominal leadership could not disguise the fact that the *patriotes* embraced a wide variety of dangerous and radical schemes. Some targeted Roman Catholic priests, others called for the confiscation of the Lachine Canal, a forced levy from brewing magnate John Molson, the murder of all bureaucrats, and a raid on bank assets. Another plot called for Montreal's Jews to be strangled and their property confiscated.[33] The nearby village of Châteauguay was seized and sealed off to ensure that its terrified residents could not raise a general alarm. At the neighbouring Indigenous settlement of Caughnawaga, the insurgents tried to convince the Iroquois that they had already taken control of most of Lower Canada; if they surrendered, they would be allowed to keep their land under the new regime. Instead of being taken in by this ruse, the Iroquois captured 64 rebels and brought them by canoe to Lachine, where a grateful militia—who had not been aware of the uprising—took them into captivity.

Commander of the forces Sir John Colborne, also acting as administrator after Durham's departure, declared a renewal of martial law and quickly mustered all the troops at his disposal, including the local Iroquois. Canadian volunteers intercepted an American schooner bringing rebel reinforcements and arms, and American troops prevented the *patriotes* from retrieving the arms and ammunition they had cached south of the border. On November 8, Robert Nelson suddenly abandoned Napierville, announcing that he was preparing the ground for an invasion from the south. But this sudden flight toward the border looked suspiciously like desertion in the face of looming defeat, and fellow *patriotes* stopped him at Odelltown. On the morning of November 9, amid a blinding snowstorm, the rebel forces at Odelltown were resoundingly defeated by militia volunteers, with 50 *patriotes* killed. As the battle raged, both Nelson and Cyrille Côté slipped south to the United States. The following night, British troops, volunteers, and Indian allies burned and looted their enemy's deserted former stronghold of Châteauguay. This was only the beginning of a cruel campaign of destruction and burning as British troops marched through the countryside, crushing the last vestiges of rebellion and leaving a legacy of bitterness among French Canadians.

Upper Canada, too, was subject to renewed attacks in the autumn of 1838. On November 11, a couple hundred insurgents crossed from New York into Prescott, led by a Finnish-born New Yorker, Nils von Schoultz, who claimed to be an officer in the Polish army. He was a romantic figure who had served in the French Foreign Legion and left in Europe a trail of gambling debts, abandoned children, and broken hearts.

---

33 Gerald Tulchinsky, *Taking Root: The Origins of the Canadian Jewish Community* (Lebanon, NH: University Press of New England for Brandeis University Press, 1993). 37.

From a defensive position in a stone windmill, von Schoultz awaited an infusion of sympathetic Upper Canadians eager to support the cause of rebellion. Instead, an attacking force of British regulars and Canadian militia forces descended on Prescott. After several days' bombardment, his forces reduced to firing cannon loaded with scrap metal, von Schoultz was compelled to surrender. The "Battle of the Windmill" ended with an estimated 30 killed in the rebel forces, many more wounded, and 16 Crown troops dead. Von Schoultz was among the band of 131 ragged and rope-bound prisoners who were jeered as they were marched to Fort Henry. A rising young Kingston lawyer, the 23-year-old John A. Macdonald, conducted von Schoultz's court martial defence, but Macdonald's exotic client was one of a dozen condemned to death.

The sentence reflected growing official exasperation with continued alarms along the border. A couple of weeks after the Battle of the Windmill, on December 4, 1838, another band of 150 would-be revolutionaries crossed the Detroit River at Windsor, killing four Upper Canadian militia and setting fire to the barracks. Neighbouring militia forces converged on Windsor, killing 27 invaders and taking another 44 prisoner. Colonel John Prince was outraged to discover a close friend bludgeoned to death with an axe in the mêlée and ordered the summary execution of five rebel prisoners. This flagrant violation of the rules of war shocked Lieutenant Governor Sir George Arthur, but Arthur reflected that Prince's rash act would be applauded in Upper Canada and might deter other adventurers.

Despite Durham's earlier resolve to be merciful, the latest round of insurrections demonstrated the limits of conciliation. Some 850 Lower Canadians were swept up and imprisoned under the provisions of martial law. Of these, 106 would ultimately face trial, with 90 condemned to death. Most did not hang; some 58 were transported to penal colonies instead.

THE DURHAM REPORT (1839) AND AN UNJUST UNION

As these punishments were meted out, Durham prepared a famous report on the crisis in British North America. His precipitous departure from Canada seemed to suggest that he was abandoning any concern for the colonies, but on his return to England he busied himself in making recommendations. The most significant of these were the union of the colonies of Upper and Lower Canada—the measure abandoned by British policy makers in 1822—and responsible government. Responsible government simply meant following the practices and principles of the British constitution. The governor should select as his executive council men who commanded the support of a majority of the legislative assembly and, in internal matters, act upon their advice. This required "no change in the principles of government, no invention of a new constitutional theory," Durham explained. The imperial government could continue to oversee external matters such as foreign relations and the regulation of foreign trade, but in internal matters the colonists had a "greater interest in coming to a right judgment on these points, and will take greater pains to do so than those whose welfare is very remotely and slightly affected."[34]

Durham also weighed in on the contentious question of the clergy reserves. Durham noted that the elite of Upper Canada, who "possessed almost all the highest public offices," had used its domination to ensure that the Anglican Church alone benefited by the substantial land reserves set aside for the Protestant Church in the 1791 *Constitutional Act*. Attempts by Methodists and Presbyterians to redress this had been constantly thwarted by upper councils dominated by the Anglican elite.[35] Durham urged that the reserves be apportioned among the Protestant sects, a solution that was put into effect in 1840.

Lower Canadians found the report deeply objectionable. This was because Durham insisted that the "vain endeavour to preserve a French Canadian national- ity" must be abandoned in favour of assimilation into the "great race" of the British Empire. Indeed, he blamed the rebellions on ethnic tensions: "I expected to find a contest between a government and a people: I found two nations warring in the bosom of a single state: I found a struggle, not of principles, but of races." Durham recognized that assimilation was a "hard measure," especially insofar as "the English are new-comers," but he firmly rejected any claim to group rights or group identity.[36] He believed that responsible government would put English and French Canadians on an equal footing as individuals, with the appointed legislative council and governor acting as the protectors of minorities who might suffer at the hands of the democrati- cally elected dominant group.[37]

Britain's parliament was not yet willing to concede responsible government, as Durham recommended, but in 1840 passed the *Act of Union* to combine Upper and Lower Canada. The Act deviated from Durham's recommendation in a critical way. It created one legislature for the hitherto separate colonies of Lower and Upper Canada, but then divided the representation in half, with an equal number of members for each segment of the province. Equal representation was hardly fair representation: Lower Canada had a population of 650,000, Upper Canada of just 450,000. This short-sighted attempt to systematize political inequality bore the seeds of future trouble.

---

34 *Lord Durham's Report*, 140.

35 Ibid., 74, 89–91.

36 Ibid., 44, 13, 144.

37 Janet Ajzenstat, *The Political Thought of Lord Durham* (Montreal and Kingston: McGill-Queen's University Press, 1988), 4–12.

9 A NEW UNION AND NEW EXPLORATIONS

ACT OF UNION, 1841

L ord Durham's sudden departure in the autumn of 1838 left Canada in a state of uncertainty. When Charles Poulett Thomson arrived in Quebec to take up the governor's post in October 1839, Lower Canada was still under the governance of an appointed special council, with representative government suspended. Historian Allan Greer notes that this authoritarian government did not function as a mere "neutral caretaker" government, but instead "enacted far-reaching programs of political, legal, and institutional reform, with changes...that favoured the interests of the urban business community."[1] Thomson was untroubled by this state of things, opining that "the best thing for Lower Canada would be a despotism for ten years more." Lower Canadians, disgusted by the plan for a forced union of Upper and Lower Canada, derisively played on the governor's name by labelling him *le poulet* (the chicken).[2] When the *Act of Union* was passed in Britain in 1840 to replace Canada's 1791 constitution, Thomson was eager to put the measure into effect; he gave Lower Canada's special council only two days to debate the measure, even though a snowstorm kept all but 14 members from attending the discussion.[3]

---

1 Allan Greer, *The Patriots and the People: The Rebellion of 1837 in Rural Lower Canada* (Toronto: University of Toronto Press, 1993), 356–57.

2 Phillip Buckner, "Charles Edward Poulett Thomson, 1st Baron Sydenham," *Dictionary of Canadian Biography* (*DCB*), www.biographi.ca.

3 Http://www.thecanadianencyclopedia.ca/en/article/special-council-of-lower-canada-18381841/.

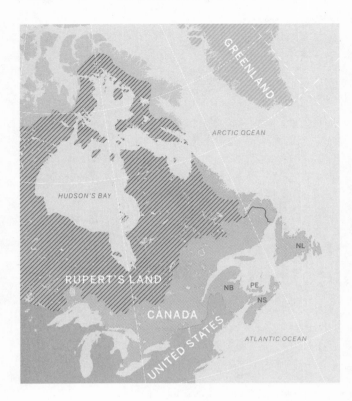

Map 9.1 The *Act of Union* combined Upper and Lower Canada to create the province of Canada.

Having obtained the formal "consent" of Lower Canada, Thomson carried on to Upper Canada, where on November 22, 1839, he took up the office of governor in that province as well. Support for union was lukewarm in Upper Canada, and Thomson's swearing-in was greeted, in the words of one witness, "with an abortion of a cheer which was worse than silence." The promise of an imperial loan guarantee for £1.5 million to finance public works projects and to pay off the accumulated colonial debts helped to sugarcoat the measure. Upper Canada's recent program of canal building and other public works infrastructure had left it with a debt exceeding £1 million.[4] By contrast, Lower Canada had accumulated a surplus. Upper Canada's legislature attempted to insist that the seat of government should be permanently in Upper Canada, that the language of the courts should be exclusively English, and that Upper Canada be allocated more seats in the legislature than Lower Canada, but Thomson managed to resist these "unjust and oppressive" conditions.[5] The now-united colony would have one governor, one executive council, one legislative council, and one elected legislative assembly. Britain rewarded Thomson for his success by elevating him to the peerage in 1840 as Baron Sydenham.

Upper Canada's claim to more seats in the legislature was especially audacious given its lower population—450,000, as compared to 650,000 in Lower Canada. The arrangement actually put into effect—an equal number of seats for each half of the legislature—was still an injustice to the more populous French-dominated half. Yet at

---

4 This was the figure given by Lord Durham in 1839. *Lord Durham's Report*, 100. Sydenham (Thomson) reckoned the debt to be £1,226,000 in early 1841, but did not indicate if any part of that was attributable to Lower Canada. Sydenham to Lord John Russell, February 22, 1841, in Paul Knaplund (ed.), *Letters from Lord Sydenham, Governor General of Canada, 1839–1841 to Lord John Russell* (Clifton, NJ: Augustus M. Kelley, 1973), 112.

5 Buckner, "Charles Edward Poulett Thomson."

the same time, the arrangement hinted at Canada's later federal structure. In a federal constitution, each political unit retains some degree of autonomy even as it submits to a central government. The new united colony was not technically a federation, but the *Act of Union*'s provision of equal seats for each section of the colony—a measure meant to reduce the influence of more populous French Canada—paradoxically set the tone for a long tradition of federalism in Canada. Moreover, even after 1841, each half of the colony retained distinct legal and education systems.

The *Act of Union* made no specific provision for responsible government, stipulating only in vague terms that the governor would act with the advice, or advice and consent, of his executive council and offering no guidelines as to how that executive council should be selected. Responsible government—a key demand of reformers and one of Durham's central recommendations—remained an unrealized goal. But some modest reforms were enacted: the Crown relinquished any control over revenues—for example, the governor's traditional control over the proceeds of land sales—and it was specified that only the elected legislature had the power to initiate money bills, confirming that body's "power of the purse." Duties and other revenues would flow into a single treasury. However, this curtailment of the governor's autonomy was accompanied by a measure that denied the legislative assembly recourse to one of the devices it had used to exert pressure: there would now be a permanent civil list, which meant that the salaries of officials could not be hostage to an obstructionist legislature.

On February 10, 1841, the *Act of Union* was proclaimed in Canada. Three years earlier to the day, Lower Canada's constitution had been suspended amid alarms of invasion and domestic insurrection. The rebellions had been quashed and the project of political reform tainted by treason. The governors who would follow Lord Durham were not ready to concede the hoped-for constitutional reforms, yet a new alliance in the 1840s paved the way for British North America's political maturation. Despite Durham's expressed conviction, reform principles, and not ethnicity, would be the motivating force in this alliance.

THE BALDWIN–LA FONTAINE ALLIANCE

The matchmaker of the new political alliance emerging in the 1840s was Francis Hincks, an Irish-born businessman, newspaper editor, and politician. The *Examiner*, his Toronto-based newspaper, launched in 1838, was dedicated to political reform, and Hincks published weekly articles elucidating the concept of responsible government for his readers. Hincks rented a Toronto warehouse from William Baldwin, an earlier Irish immigrant, and his son Robert, and this business relationship blossomed into a significant friendship. Hincks knew that Durham had hoped union would

Figure 9.1 A statue was erected on Parliament Hill, Ottawa, in 2010 to commemorate Robert Baldwin and Louis-Hippolyte La Fontaine.

eradicate French-Canadian national sentiment, but he himself visualized a future in which French and English could work together to achieve reform. Two reformers—Robert Baldwin in Toronto and Louis-Hippolyte La Fontaine in Montreal—had important goals in common. Hincks wrote to La Fontaine to set out a case for cooperation: "Lord Durham ascribes to you national objects. If he is right, union would be ruin to you," but if Durham was wrong, union would "give you all you desire." Hincks encouraged La Fontaine to lay aside ethnic differences and embrace an alliance with his English-Canadian reform counterpart, Robert Baldwin. Baldwin, Hincks insisted, "is *incorruptible.*"[6]

Most of Baldwin's acquaintances would have agreed. Despite his firm principles, however, Baldwin was not a natural politician. He had a cold and diffident manner and was a poor orator with stooped posture and a saturnine countenance. This outward appearance masked a deeply religious and highly emotional nature, a nature that found expression in poetry and in an all-consuming, but forbidden, love for his first cousin, Eliza. Despite the family's attempt to separate the young couple, they married when Robert was 23 and Eliza 17. Their happiness proved short-lived: the Caesarean birth of their fourth child injured Eliza's health, and she died in 1836 at age 25. Robert never recovered from the blow. He suffered from chronic depression and became an invalid while in his early fifties.[7]

---

6   Quotations are from William G. Ormsby, "Sir Francis Hincks," *DCB*; Michael S. Cross and Robert L. Fraser, "'The Waste That Lies Before Me': The Public and Private Worlds of Robert Baldwin," *Canadian Historical Association Historical Papers* (1983): 166.

7   Cross and Fraser, "'The Waste That Lies Before Me'," 169, 177. See also Robert L. Fraser, "Robert Baldwin," *DCB*.

Baldwin's tormented personal life did not prevent him from playing a pivotal role in Canada's political evolution. Urged by his father William, Robert Baldwin made law his profession and put aside his distaste for public life to work for the achievement of responsible government. His French-Canadian counterpart in the struggle, Louis-Hippolyte La Fontaine, was a lawyer and scion of a prominent Lower Canadian family, who in 1830 had first won election to Lower Canada's assembly when he was 23. La Fontaine was much admired for his intellectual gifts, but was socially withdrawn and uncommunicative, by no means a natural politician. It is fortunate that Hincks seized the initiative to bring these two introverted men together. La Fontaine was also noteworthy for his resemblance to Napoleon Bonaparte, a resemblance he cultivated. His steady black eyes and carefully copied hairstyle echoed Napoleon's, and La Fontaine adopted the imitative habit of thrusting one hand between the buttons of his waistcoat. La Fontaine had at first been active in the *patriote* cause, and had even been wounded in the clash of arms that accompanied the stormy 1832 Montreal by-election of Daniel Tracey. Yet he rejected violence and, rather than taking up arms in the fall of 1837, travelled to England to lay the case for reform before Colonial Office officials. In his absence, his wife Adèle visited imprisoned rebels and helped provide relief to their families; La Fontaine himself visited the exiled Papineau in New York. This evidence of support for the rebel cause made La Fontaine an object of suspicion, and he was briefly imprisoned in 1838.

In common with many Lower Canadians, La Fontaine at first refused to cooperate in any way with the *Act of Union*. When Governor Sydenham offered him the post of solicitor general in 1840, he refused it on principle. However, La Fontaine was swayed by Hincks's proposal of cooperation between French- and English-Canadian reformers. He had already been thinking along the same lines, noting to a correspondent that "it is a great mistake to suppose that there is no means of rapprochement between the two parties…their interests are the same." The very union "unjustly designed to punish" and "destroy my countrymen" could instead be used to save them.[8]

In the summer of 1840, La Fontaine travelled to Toronto to meet with Robert Baldwin and came away with a clear commitment to making "common cause" with reformers in Canada West (Upper Canada). In an August 25, 1840, address to the electors of Terrebonne, Canada East (Lower Canada), La Fontaine urged a "spirit of peace, union, friendship and fraternity."[9] But Governor Sydenham's views did not augur success for the project of achieving responsible government; he privately ridiculed

---

8 As quoted in Jacques Monet, "Louis-Hippolyte La Fontaine," *DCB*.

9 John Ralston Saul, *Reflections of a Siamese Twin: Canada at the End of the Twentieth Century* (Toronto: Penguin, 1997), 177; Quoted passage: Louis-Hippolyte La Fontaine in Jacques Monet, "Louis-Hippolyte La Fontaine," *DCB*.

the "absurdity of claiming to put the council over the head of the governor....Either the governor is the sovereign or the minister."[10] In fact, Britain's Secretary of State for the Colonies, Lord John Russell, had already warned Sydenham that the principles of British cabinet government could not be copied in a colony: "it may happen...that the Governor receives at one and the same time instructions from the Queen, and advice from his executive council, totally at variance with each other."[11]

Deeply suspicious of reformers, Sydenham used a full arsenal of tricks to keep them from winning seats in the first election held under the *Act of Union*—strategically placed polling booths, patronage rewards, and blatant intimidation of voters. La Fontaine felt compelled to withdraw from the election, appalled by the violence and worried about the safety of his supporters. Sydenham, however, waved off La Fontaine's criticism, denouncing him as "a scoundrel." La Fontaine had armed "his people with dirks and bludgeons loaded with lead" but "was scared away by a few Irishmen," he sneered. Sydenham also ridiculed La Fontaine's assertion that the governor had tried to buy his support: "He is a cantankerous fellow without talent & not worth buying or I would have had him when I pleased," he boasted privately.[12]

Robert Baldwin, for his part, agreed to serve on the Tory-dominated executive council and accepted Sydenham's appointment as solicitor general. He immediately clashed with the governor, insisting that Sydenham should follow the principles of responsible government: that the governor should act on the advice of his executive council and that council should be responsible to the assembly. Sydenham had little patience for Baldwin's stubborn idealism: "Was there ever such an ass!" was his exasperated verdict.[13] When the newly elected legislature met at Kingston in June 1841, however, Baldwin found that there was little support for his project of responsible government, and he resigned from the council. The governor crowed to Lord John Russell that he had "gained the most complete victory. I have got rid of Baldwin and finished him as a public man for ever."[14] Moreover, divisions grew between Francis Hincks and Baldwin. Hincks, a pragmatist, did not have Baldwin's deep sense of principle and decided that Sydenham's commitment to the economic progress of the United Canadas was more important than constitutional niceties. Although

10 "Poulett Thomson to a Friend, December 12, 1839," in W.P.M. Kennedy (ed.), *Statutes, Treaties and Documents of the Canadian Constitution, 1713–1929*, 2nd ed. (Toronto: Oxford University Press, 1930), 430.

11 "Lord John Russell to Poulett Thomson, October 14, 1839," in Kennedy, *Statutes, Treaties and Documents of the Canadian Constitution, 1713–1929*, 421.

12 "C. Poulett Thomson to Lord John Russell, private, April 10, 1841," in Knaplund, *Letters from Lord Sydenham*, 130.

13 J.M.S. Careless, *The Union of the Canadas: The Growth of Canadian Institutions, 1841–1857* (Toronto: McClelland & Stewart, 1972), 40.

14 "Sydenham to Russell, private, June 27, 1841," in Knaplund, *Letters from Lord Sydenham*, 145.

Sydenham had not conceded responsible government, "we have *practical* responsibility," Hincks insisted.[15]

Sydenham's triumph over Baldwin and the principle of responsible government did not last. Ill health forced Sydenham to resign the following month and, as he awaited his return to England, he suffered a further mishap. In September 1841 he fell from his horse and broke his leg. The wound became infected and within days Sydenham was dead of lockjaw.

Sydenham's unscrupulous machinations had tempted Baldwin to give up politics altogether. Discouraged, he confided to his father that he feared he was not made for it. Yet Baldwin soon rebounded with a new plan and approached his father with a suggestion. While La Fontaine had had to withdraw from the electoral contest, both Baldwins had been elected in Toronto ridings. Could the elder Baldwin's constituents accept his retirement and consider "returning Mr. La Fontaine, if he will accept the nomination instead of you [?]" Nothing, he predicted, "would have a better effect." His father graciously agreed to stand aside.[16]

On September 23, 1841, the Fourth Riding North York (Toronto) elected La Fontaine in a by-election. Upper Canadian voters had proved that, despite Durham's views, ethnic differences were incidental: they were committed to political reform and happy to select a leading French Canadian to win it for them. La Fontaine was later able to repay the favour: in 1843 he arranged a safe seat for Robert Baldwin in the riding of Rimouski, Canada East.

Sydenham's replacement as governor, Sir Charles Bagot, arrived in January 1842. While there had been a change of government in Britain, the governor's directions remained the same: there was to be no concession of responsible government. Nevertheless, that September Bagot appointed both Baldwin and La Fontaine to his executive council. The only alternative, he explained to his home government, was to appoint men "prepared to act without the sympathy and against an overwhelming majority of the House of Assembly," something he believed would be "disastrous." Realizing the significance of what he had done, Bagot privately admitted that "whether the doctrine of responsible government is openly acknowledged, or is only tacitly acquiesced in, virtually it exists."[17] If these developments seemed to herald a new and hopeful era for Canadian political reformers, such hopes were soon dashed: not only

---

15 As quoted in Careless, *Union of the Canadas*, 53.

16 As quoted in *Canada: A People's History*, episode 7, "Rebellion and Reform," http://history.cbc.ca/history.

17 "Bagot to Stanley, September 26, 1842," in Kennedy, *Statutes, Treaties and Documents*, 478–82; "Bagot to Stanley, October 28, 1842," as quoted in W.P. Morrell, *British Colonial Policy in the Age of Peel and Russell* (London: Frank Cass & Co, 1996), 56.

did Britain's cabinet heartily disapprove, but Bagot's ill health forced his resignation six months later. He died at Kingston in May 1843.

Bagot's successor was determined to turn back the clock on reform. Charles, Baron Metcalfe came to Canada against his own better judgment: "I never undertook anything with so much reluctance, or so little hope of doing good," he confided to a friend. Decades of imperial service in India and Jamaica had hardly equipped Lord Metcalfe for the demands of an assertive representative government, and the recent move in the direction of responsible government raised hopes that he feared must be crushed: "It is now, perhaps, too late to remedy the evil," he wrote sourly to his superior in London.[18]

Metcalfe's fears were quickly realized. In November 1843, the governor clashed with his executive council by refusing his assent to legislation and by making appointments without the council's approval; all but one council member resigned. In the elections of the following year, Metcalfe, like Sydenham, openly promoted conservative candidates and implied that reform equalled disloyalty to the Crown. The tactic succeeded, and conservatives won most seats. Yet by November 1845, Metcalfe too was forced from office by illness. Even his detractors were moved to pity as a painful and disfiguring facial tumour opened a gaping hole in his cheek. Scarcely able to speak or eat, blind in one eye, Metcalfe returned to England to die. He was replaced by Lord Cathcart, the commander of the forces in British North America. By the mid-1840s, relations with the United States were increasingly strained, and British authorities evidently decided that a governor with military credentials might be useful.

UNEASY RELATIONS WITH THE UNITED STATES

Tensions between Britain's North American colonies and the United States were nothing new. Even after the War of 1812, Anglo–American accord could never be taken for granted. Long before Sir Charles Bagot served as governor, he had acted as a special envoy to the United States, negotiating the Rush-Bagot Agreement of 1817 and the Convention of 1818. The Rush-Bagot agreement limited armed vessels on the Great Lakes, while the convention of the following year established rules for fishing rights and set the boundary at the forty-ninth parallel from Lake of the Woods to the Rocky Mountains. Other issues remained unresolved, and the atmosphere was especially strained because of border raids during the rebellions of 1837–38.

18 Metcalfe, as quoted in Jacques Monet, *The Last Cannon Shot: A Study of French-Canadian Nationalism, 1837–1850* (Toronto: University of Toronto Press, 1964), 137; "Metcalfe to Stanley, August 5, 1843," in Kennedy, *Statutes, Treaties and Documents*, 489–493.

By 1839, a conflict over the boundary between the colony of New Brunswick and the state of Maine was reaching a crisis point. The 1783 Treaty of Paris ending the American Revolutionary War defined the border, but the wording was ambiguous. A growing timber industry in New Brunswick and Maine raised the stakes, touching off the so-called Aroostook War of 1839. Americans from Maine tried to encourage residents of New Brunswick to renounce British authority, while timber men from New Brunswick encroached into the Aroostook Valley, which surrounded a tributary of the Saint John River, in their quest for big trees. Attempts to reach an arbitrated agreement failed when the American Senate refused to accept a compromise, and clashes between rival woodsmen even made it necessary for both sides to send troops into the area. At one point, American lumberjacks taunted their New Brunswick rivals across the river by singing:

> Britannia shall not rule the Maine,
> Nor shall she rule the water;
> They've sung that song full long enough,
> Much longer than they oughter.[19]

Despite the name, the "Aroostook War" did not progress beyond a war of words, but the Maine–New Brunswick border conflict was not the only point of strain in Anglo–American relations.

Another outstanding irritant stemmed from the *Caroline* affair: in 1838, British and Canadian authorities destroyed this American vessel, which had been supplying William Lyon Mackenzie's rebel base on Navy Island. Upper Canadian Alexander McLeod, who had drunkenly boasted of his role in the burning of the *Caroline*, was being held in an American jail on murder charges, and Britain insisted that McLeod's execution would be deemed an act of war. Fortunately, McLeod was acquitted after a trial.

Most of the differences between the United States and Britain were patched up by treaty in 1842. The Ashburton-Webster Treaty included an agreement by the Americans to patrol the African coast to stop the illegal slave trade and settled the international boundary from Lake Huron to Lake of the Woods. For British North America, however, the treaty settlement of the Maine–New Brunswick border left lingering resentment. Not only were some New Brunswick Acadians now living under

19 M.E. Chamberlain, "Canadian Boundaries in Anglo-American Relations," in C.C. Eldridge (ed.), *Kith and Kin: Canada, Britain and the United States from the Revolution to the Cold War* (Cardiff: University of Wales Press, 1997), 51; see also W.S. MacNutt, *The Atlantic Provinces: The Emergence of Colonial Society, 1712–1857* (Toronto: McClelland & Stewart, 1965), 216–17.

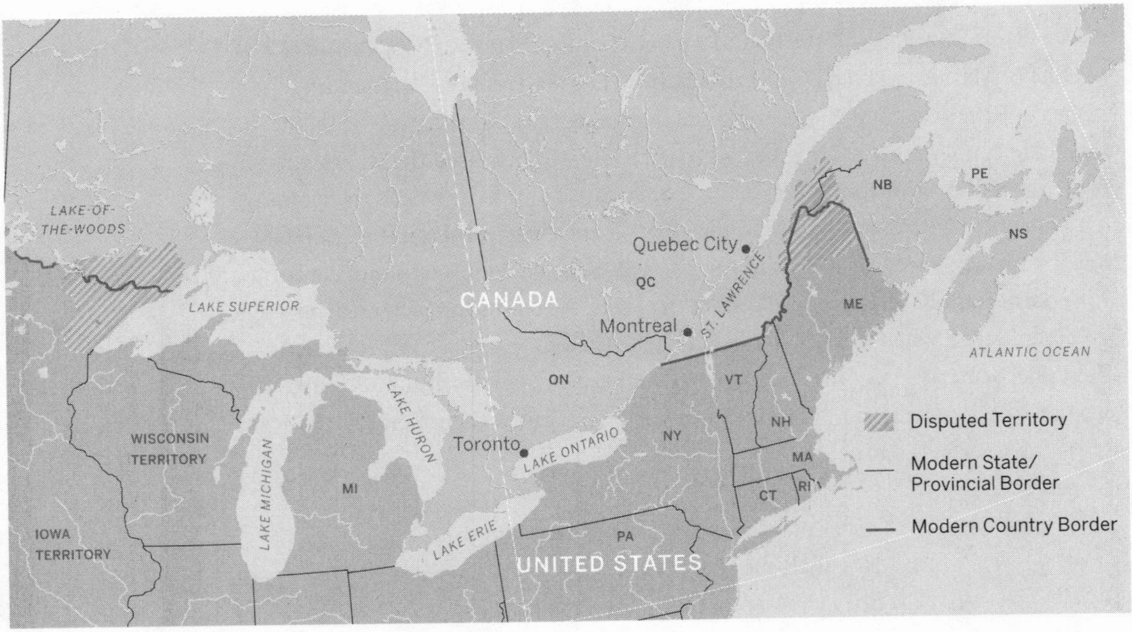

Map 9.2 The 1842 Ashburton-Webster Treaty settled the border between New Brunswick and Maine.

the American flag, but suspicions also abounded that the British Foreign Secretary, Lord Ashburton, in his quest to win the goodwill of the United States, had fallen victim to smart Yankee manipulation and failed to protect colonial interests. Worse, few British parliamentarians even bothered to attend the debate on the treaty in the House of Commons. The final settlement left only a narrow strip of British territory on the south shore of the St. Lawrence. Future rail traffic bound for the Atlantic would have to swing far north to bypass the state of Maine. A later historian complained of Canadian territorial interests being "treated by England as a fund from which she can make payments at her own discretion to purchase the goodwill of the United States."[20] Unfortunately, this same sentiment would be echoed when British and American diplomatic authorities considered the Pacific coast boundary in 1846.

THE PACIFIC COAST

After the 1821 merger of the Hudson's Bay Company and the North West Company, the British government extended the HBC's jurisdiction to the Pacific coast. Up to that point, few newcomers had ventured to the area that would later be British Columbia, but even minimal Native–newcomer contacts had been devastating to western

20 Richard Jebb, *Studies in Colonial Nationalism* (London: Edward Arnold, 1905), 20.

Indigenous nations, with mortality following the same sad pattern of more easterly Natives. Newcomers unwittingly spread diseases to which Native people had no immunity, bringing a scourge of smallpox, measles, tuberculosis, and other ailments. For some nations, direct contact had not even been necessary to spread contagion, with illness coming into their communities via other Native travellers. The occasional elder's pockmarked skin bore witness to earlier smallpox plagues. In 1936, Old Pierre, of the Katzie Nation along the Pitt River in British Columbia's lower mainland, told an anthropologist his great-grandfather's account of a devastating epidemic that swept his home village away. While Native oral traditions do not always allow events to be pinpointed chronologically, these events may well date from the outbreak of smallpox that ravaged British Columbia's Indigenous nations in the 1830s:

> My great-grandfather happened to be roaming the mountains at this period, for his wife had recently given birth to twins, and, according to the custom, both parents had to remain in isolation for several months. The children were just beginning to walk when he returned to his village at the entrance of Pitt Lake, knowing nothing of the calamity that had overtaken its inhabitants. All his kinsmen and relatives lay dead inside their homes; only in one house did there survive a baby boy, who was vainly sucking at its dead mother's breast. They rescued the child, burned all the houses, together with the corpses that lay inside them, and built a new home for themselves several miles away. If you dig today on the site of any of the old villages you will uncover countless bones, the remains of the Indians who perished during this epidemic of smallpox.[21]

The Katzie people were not unique in this respect. The smallpox epidemics through the 1830s killed an estimated one-third of the Tsimshian people and probably even more of the Haida.

Despite the accidental introduction of disease, most traders had little wish to alter Indigenous patterns of life. Because traders required Indigenous cooperation, they were compelled to make adaptations themselves. As in Rupert's Land, trade ties were often cemented with marital alliances, and the establishment of permanent coastal and interior forts led to the growth of mixed-race families.

Hudson's Bay Company operations were overseen by the company's dictatorial governor, George Simpson, who made canoe journeys to the Pacific Northwest in 1824, 1828, and 1841. One chief factor, who dreaded the inspections, grumbled that Simpson's

---

21 As quoted in Cole Harris, "Voices of Disaster: Smallpox Around the Strait of Georgia in 1782," *Ethnohistory* 41 (Fall 1994).

methods combined the despotism of a military tyrant with a miserly scrutiny of accounts. Even the hard-driving governor, however, enjoyed occasional moments of light-heartedness: during one trip, Simpson attempted to impress a group of Carrier Natives by pretending that the sounds emanating from a music box were being made by his dog. On his 1841 journey, Simpson was pleased to see that the Kwakiutl Natives of Port Neil on northern Vancouver Island had been spared any smallpox outbreak and pleaded with the chief to allow the tribe's children to be vaccinated.[22]

Simpson's main goal, of course, was to determine the profit potential west of the Rockies. The area at the mouth of the Columbia River, an arterial waterway that today divides the American states of Washington and Oregon, attracted rival American and British traders in the early nineteenth century. The Americans' overland Lewis and Clark expedition of 1804–06 had spurred growing interest in the area. The Anglo–American Convention of 1818 had allowed for joint British and American occupation of the territory between the Rockies and the Strait of Georgia, and by the 1820s, the Columbia River emerged as the unofficial dividing line between British and American activities. The HBC was not altogether convinced that trade in the Columbia River area was worthwhile—malaria was frequent and vessels were apt to come to grief on sandbars at the river estuary—but the British Foreign Office insisted a presence be maintained on the north shore to strengthen any possible claim. Fort Vancouver, the site of present-day Vancouver, Washington, was established in 1825. Simpson hoped that the Fraser River would prove a viable trade route; the establishment of Fort Langley on the lower Fraser River in 1827 reflected this optimism.

Simpson placed the management of the HBC's Fort Langley operations in the capable hands of Archibald McDonald, who in 1813 had led a group of Selkirk's Scottish settlers to Red River. McDonald virtually founded a personal dynasty in the west, as well. In 1823, near the mouth of the Columbia River, he had married Princess Sunday (Koale Koa), the daughter of a prominent Chinook chief, but she died soon after giving birth to their son, Ranald. Soon afterward, the 35-year-old McDonald married Jane Kyne, the 15-year-old mixed-race daughter of a Hudson's Bay Company postmaster, with whom he had 13 additional children. At Fort Langley, when the energetic Archibald McDonald was not serving as a home schoolmaster to his wife and sons, he launched salmon preserving operations with fish caught by the local Native people. Fraser River salmon was dried or preserved in locally made barrels and found markets as far away as Hawaii and Japan. Hawaii, then known as the Sandwich Islands, supplied both the salt needed for salmon preservation and hundreds of

22 Edward Jenner famously launched experiments in the 1770s in which he injected patients with the cowpox virus in order to protect them against smallpox. This successful experiment led to the development of a smallpox vaccine, which was growing in use by the early nineteenth century.

workers, known as Kanakas, whom the HBC brought to the Pacific Northwest as a more cost-effective alternative to Scottish and Canadian employees. McDonald's spirit of initiative impressed Simpson and lent new purpose to Fort Langley, since Simpson was forced to concede that the Fraser River was not a viable trade route. After a hair-raising journey through the Fraser River canyon, Simpson ruefully described the river as "certain death in nine attempts out of ten. I shall no longer talk of it as a navigable stream."[23]

The Hudson's Bay Company sought to outflank its American rivals by establishing trading posts along the northern Pacific coast: Fort Simpson in 1831 at the mouth of the Nass River, just south of the Alaska panhandle, and Fort McLoughlin in 1833, further south on

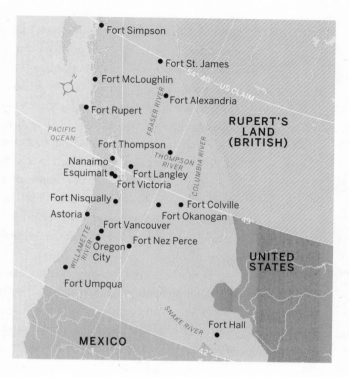

Map 9.3 HBC forts in the Pacific Northwest.

the mainland coast just across from the southern tip of the Queen Charlotte Islands (Haida Gwaii). The launching of the wood-burning steamship ss *Beaver* in 1836 further expanded trade. This paddlewheel steamer was able to enter narrow waterways and won for the HBC the contract to provision Russian posts. In 1839, Simpson successfully negotiated a lease of the Alaska panhandle from the Russians for the HBC.

The HBC's 1840 launch of a subsidiary, the Puget Sound Agricultural Company, posed another potential threat to American interests. More than 75 per cent of the Indigenous population in the area south of the lower Columbia River had been wiped out by a devastating malaria epidemic in 1830–33, and the HBC imported sheep and cattle for grazing on this depopulated land. The HBC appointed as chief factor at Fort Vancouver the formidable John McLoughlin, a six-foot-four-inch Scottish immigrant who had qualified as a physician at the age of 19. McLoughlin possessed what George Simpson called a "violent temper and turbulent disposition," something a young Oxford-educated Anglican minister, Herbert Beaver, sent to Fort Vancouver in 1836,

23 As quoted by Jean Murray Cole (ed.), *This Blessed Wilderness: Archibald McDonald's Letters from the Columbia, 1822–44* (Vancouver: University of British Columbia Press, 2001).

was quick to discover. Reverend Beaver made the mistake of remarking on the "loose character" of McLoughlin's country-born wife, Marguerite Waddens, and McLoughlin treated Beaver to a sound thrashing in the public courtyard.[24] McLoughlin welcomed American pioneer farmers to the Puget Sound, even extending generous credit terms for seed and implements. Despite the HBC's ostensible control over the region, in the end the preponderance of American settlers would strengthen American, rather than British, claims to the Puget Sound. McLoughlin himself would eventually become an American citizen and is celebrated as the "father of Oregon."

George Simpson seemed to recognize that the Columbia River region would ultimately fall into American hands and, in 1843, launched plans for a new HBC fort on the southern tip of Vancouver Island, Fort Camosun, later re-named Fort Victoria. James Douglas, sent to establish the HBC presence there, enthused that the site was a perfect Eden.

Simpson proved prescient. Within a few years, the American idea of "manifest destiny"—the notion that the stars and stripes were destined to fly over the entire North American continent—gave rise to a clamour for control of the Pacific Northwest. Democratic presidential candidate James Polk fought a vigorous election campaign in 1844 on the platform "Fifty-four forty or Fight!" The northern latitude of 54° 40' was the beginning of the Alaska panhandle and the southernmost limit of Russian territory, and a growing chorus of Americans believed they should possess everything south of that latitude.

Fortunately, the Americans chose not to fight. By 1846, they were at war with Mexico, having recently annexed the former Mexican possession of Texas, and the prospect of simultaneous hostilities with Britain was too much even for an expansionist like Polk. By the terms of the 1846 Oregon Treaty the Americans agreed to set the boundary at the forty-ninth parallel.

As in the case of the Ashburton-Webster Treaty of 1842, suspicions abounded that the British had not pursued justice for their colonial possession as vigorously as they might have done, and many complaints were raised about the new boundary. It was not logical geographically: the Columbia River formed the natural boundary and the simplest means of gaining inland access. With that river in American hands, the Coast Mountain range posed a formidable barrier to communication with the colony's interior. This would present a great challenge when, in future years, engineers sought

---

24 W. Kaye Lamb, "John McLoughlin," *DCB*. Online at www.biographi.ca. Stephen Woolworth, "'The School is Under My Direction': The Politics of Education at Fort Vancouver, 1836–1838," *Oregon Historical Quarterly* 104 (Summer 2003), online at http://www.historycooperative.org/journals/ohq/104.2/woolworth.html. It is noteworthy that Marguerite Waddens's father was Jean-Étienne Waddens, one of the men purported to have been killed by early fur trader and western explorer Peter Pond (see Chapter 6). .

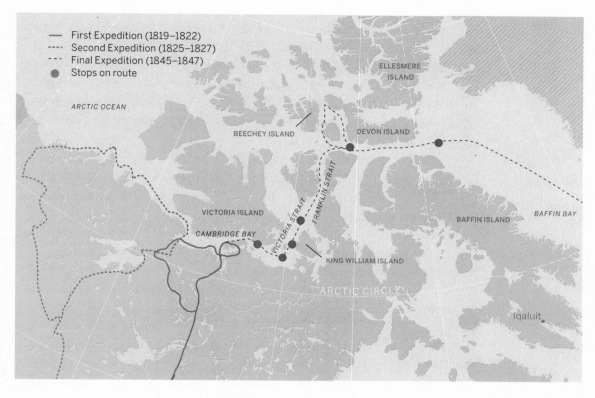

- — First Expedition (1819–1822)
- ---- Second Expedition (1825–1827)
- - - - Final Expedition (1845–1847)
- ● Stops on route

ARCTIC OCEAN

ELLESMERE ISLAND

BEECHEY ISLAND

DEVON ISLAND

FRANKLIN STRAIT

VICTORIA STRAIT

VICTORIA ISLAND

BAFFIN ISLAND

BAFFIN BAY

CAMBRIDGE BAY

KING WILLIAM ISLAND

ARCTIC CIRCLE

Iqaluit

Map 9.4 Nineteenth-century Arctic exploration.

to plan a transcontinental railway. Nor did the treaty put an end to American ambitions for more territory in the Pacific Northwest, as subsequent events would show.

EXPLORATIONS IN THE NORTH

Early-nineteenth-century British activity on North America's Pacific coast revived Britain's long-cherished dream of finding a Northwest Passage from the Atlantic to the Pacific. Such a route would shave months from the journey around Cape Horn or make it possible to avoid a land passage across Central America at the Isthmus of Panama, a route that exposed travellers to tropical diseases. It would also help consolidate Britain's claims to the Pacific coast in the face of growing American interest. Earlier explorations had ended in failure, but at the end of the Napoleonic Wars in 1815, the British Admiralty looked to Arctic exploration as a worthwhile way to employ naval officers left idle by the peace. Two 1818 expeditions, led by Commander John Ross and Commander David Buchan, had been aborted when they encountered impenetrable ice north of Spitsbergen. The following year, William Parry's expedition was able to sail through Lancaster Sound almost as far west as the 114th meridian.

Not only was Parry able to boast that all but one of his crew of 94 remained in robust health, relying entirely on provisions they had brought with them, but the expedition earned a reward of £5,000 offered by the British Crown for any Arctic expedition able to reach further west than 110° longitude. Parry's successful organization became a model for future Arctic expeditions; he had kept up the morale of his crew with musical and theatrical entertainments, classes, hunting parties, scientific observations, and even a weekly newsletter.

As Parry made his 1819 voyage, John Franklin led a concurrent overland expedition. Franklin had been part of Buchan's failed 1818 voyage, and also brought a wealth of experience drawn from service around the globe in the British Royal Navy. The Franklin party was to chart the north coast east of the Coppermine River, travelling from York Factory on Hudson Bay via fur-trade river routes. Only two Europeans had ever explored this territory, Samuel Hearne of the HBC and Alexander Mackenzie of the North West Company, in separate eighteenth-century expeditions. Franklin was forced to rely on the assistance of traders from the two companies, who were then at the height of an acrimonious trade war. Arranging transport for his supplies proved difficult, and the mission was plagued by hunger and poor morale. While most of his party wintered at Cumberland House, Franklin led a small group on snowshoes to Fort Chipewyan to learn more about the area. The two parties met up in the spring and, by August 1820, reached Winter Lake, north of Great Slave Lake. Any goodwill Franklin had with the Natives, voyageurs, and traders steadily eroded as quarrels erupted over short supplies. At last able to secure transport of the supplies left behind at York Factory, the expedition continued down to the mouth of the Coppermine River. The success of the mission depended upon being able to obtain provisions from the Inuit, but the local people took alarm at the party's approach. By late summer 1821, with supplies exhausted, their canoes too damaged to travel in icy seas, and 10 of the party dead—nine of hunger or exposure and one shot for cannibalism—a discouraged Franklin was forced to turn back. He returned to England in the autumn of 1822, having gained some valuable geographic knowledge of the Arctic coast. HBC Governor George Simpson contemptuously blamed the mission's problems on Franklin, sneering that he was the sort of man who insisted on three meals a day washed down with regular cups of tea.

Franklin was made of sterner stuff than Simpson's assessment suggests; he began to plan a fresh expedition within the year. By the time the mission was launched early in 1825, Franklin had married and become the father of a baby girl. News of his wife's death reached him as he landed at New York, but Franklin pressed on. This 1825–27 expedition, much better planned than the first, charted 640 kilometres of the Arctic shore.

Franklin was fêted as a hero upon his return. He published two narratives of his adventures, was knighted, and received an honorary Oxford doctorate and a gold medal from the Société de Géographie de Paris. He also remarried. After another stint of naval service, he arrived in Van Diemen's Land (Tasmania) with Lady Franklin in 1837 to take up a post as governor. By 1845, with renewed British interest in the Northwest Passage, the 58-year-old Franklin persuaded the Admiralty to entrust him with command of a new expedition. Two steam-powered vessels with iron-reinforced hulls, the *Erebus* and the *Terror*, carried a crew of 134, along with every imaginable necessity, including tinned food. This technology, first developed in 1811, was still not entirely practical; each can had to be produced by hand and had to be opened with a hammer and chisel. Nevertheless, Franklin eagerly obtained thousands of cans, enough food to last three years, determined to avoid the misery of his past. Franklin wanted to chart the remaining area of the mainland coast between his earlier explorations and the area mapped by two HBC traders, Peter Warren Dease and Thomas Simpson. Whalers in northern Baffin Bay encountered Franklin's party setting out late in July 1845. They were the last to see the expedition members alive.

The disappearance of Franklin's expedition was one of the great mysteries of the Victorian Age. Between 1847 and 1859, some 30 separate search missions were launched. The British Admiralty offered a reward of £20,000, and Lady Franklin travelled the Empire, desperate to keep the search alive by publicizing the story. From York Factory, Letitia Mactavish Hargrave, wife of the chief factor, observed that HBC traders pretended to offer encouragement for the Admiralty's search but considered it a lost cause.[25] In 1850, Inuit hunters discovered the mutilated bodies of 30 men, some of which bore marks suggesting cannibalism. The discovery in 1859 of more human remains and relics of the expedition, including notebooks, confirmed the worst fears: Franklin's body was not found, but notes made by the crew confirmed that he died aboard his ship in 1847 and that the survivors abandoned the ice-locked vessels.

In the decades that followed, more remains and relics came to light. University of Alberta anthropologists, still fascinated by the Franklin mystery, exhumed some of the bodies in 1984 and 1986, and, besides detecting scurvy, raised the new theory that the lead solder used to seal up the tins of food purchased for the expedition may have been a factor in the explorers' deaths.

Speculation about the macabre details of the death of Franklin and his crew should not, however, deflect attention from the expedition's achievements. Sir John Franklin charted considerable unknown territory, adding greatly to knowledge of

25 Clive Holland, "Sir John Franklin," DCB. http://www.biographi.ca/en/bio/franklin_john_7E.html.

Arctic coastal waters. He did not find the navigable Northwest Passage Britain sought, but fascination with the fate of Franklin's expedition has continued unabated and, in an era when warming temperatures offer more scope for Arctic navigation, Canadians have taken greater interest in our northern history. At last, in 2014, Franklin's ship, the *Erebus*, was found. An exploratory mission led by Parks Canada with the Canadian Hydrographic Service, Canada's Coast Guard, the Government of Nunavut, and other key partners captured sonar images of the vessel, rendering immediate a Victorian mystery that had been frozen in time.

CONCLUSION

The mid-nineteenth century saw some important and far-reaching explorations in the North American Arctic and significant, if still modest, newcomer incursions in the Pacific region. In the province of Canada, the 1840 *Act of Union* inaugurated a new era of unexpected cooperation between political reformers in the English- and French-speaking districts. Robert Baldwin and Louis-Hippolyte La Fontaine struggled to remain optimistic as a string of colonial governors thwarted their quest to obtain responsible government for Canada.

Meanwhile, Britain was about to enter into a new era of empire. The most pressing tensions with the United States had been settled, with border disputes resolved for New Brunswick and the Pacific coast. Lord Cathcart was recalled as governor in chief of British North America, his military credentials no longer being the most important qualification for office. A fresh administrative approach would be needed: Britain's looming shift from mercantilism to free trade would give rise to a new theory of colonial governance. But, for the United Canadas, violence and the flames of destruction would punctuate this critical transition.

10 A TURNING POINT FOR BRITISH NORTH AMERICA, 1846–1849

BRITAIN ABANDONS IMPERIAL PROTECTION

A momentous political and economic change was sweeping Britain in the mid-nineteenth century, and the impact on its North American colonies would be profound. Since the seventeenth century, Britain's overseas colonies had been part of a regulated economic system known as mercantilism. Indeed, the very existence of colonial possessions was largely a product of mercantilist ideas, and Britain was not the only European nation that embraced this theory. Mercantilism was not a single rule but many complex, interrelated laws regulating trade. The idea was that a nation could only prosper at the expense of its rivals, and the goal was to prevent the outflow of currency to other countries. Colonies would benefit the mother country by supplying goods that could not be produced domestically—ensuring that these would not have to be bought from competing nations—and by serving as a market for its manufactured goods. Tariffs—that is, taxes on imports—would be levied against foreign goods entering Britain's market place. These tariffs were often prohibitory—so high that foreign sellers could not hope to compete in that market. The produce of Britain's own colonies enjoyed preferential treatment with significantly lower tariffs. In concert with these protective tariffs, Britain's Navigation Laws restricted the carrying of most cargoes to British or British colonial ships, which also offered the benefit of ensuring that the merchant marine would be a source of potential sailors for the Royal Navy.

In the West Indies, or Caribbean islands, Britain's system of mercantilism achieved almost perfect expression. These sugar-producing islands were a great cash cow for the empire; in the late eighteenth century, an estimated four-fifths of Britain's overseas income originated there. While British preferential tariffs made this commercial activity profitable, it was the cancer of slavery that made it possible. An estimated 2 million enslaved Africans were moved across the Atlantic to British colonies between 1680 and 1786. Nova Scotia merchants cashed in on this lucrative business by provisioning the Caribbean slave population with preserved fish and by exporting timber to the islands, a maritime trade that picked up sharply when the American Revolution cut off the new republic of the United States from the benefits of Britain's closed mercantilist network. These Nova Scotia vessels carried cargoes of molasses on the return journey for processing into sugar or rum.

In 1833, the abolition of slavery dealt a blow to the privileged world of Britain's Caribbean planters. Philanthropists in Britain and elsewhere, especially among the ranks of the Quakers (the Society of Friends) and Methodists, had long fought for the emancipation of the slaves. The slave trade had been abolished in 1807, but that measure had not freed those already in bondage, and in fact had prompted a new evil: outlaw slave traders, subject to a £100 fine per slave found on board their vessels, were known to throw their captives overboard to escape detection. Evangelical Christian William Wilberforce worked for the abolition of slavery in his earlier career in Britain's House of Commons and died in 1833, just as legislation to end slavery was making its way through Parliament.

The long-awaited dawn of freedom in Britain's empire brought economic devastation to the Caribbean colonies that had depended upon it. When emancipated slaves had finished serving the four-year "apprenticeship" dictated by law, they—unsurprisingly—fled the scene of their oppression, disinclined to work for wages for their former masters when squatting on vacant land was an attractive alternative. This blow to the colonial economy was followed by the end of preferential tariffs on British colonial sugar: in 1846, Britain's Conservative government, under Sir Robert Peel, passed a series of measures introducing free trade in a number of commodities. Lowering prices for consumers at home was deemed a higher priority than subsidizing the profits of merchants overseas through artificial protection in the market. The British public, having condemned the evil of slavery, now opted to buy the cheaper sugar produced by Spanish and Portuguese colonies that still permitted slavery.

The West Indian spiral into economic ruin spread a wider contagion. Property values on the islands plummeted: Bog Estate in Jamaica, valued at £80,000 in the 1830s, sold for £500 in 1849; by 1852, 240 estates in Jamaica had been abandoned altogether. Caribbean banks failed, as did dozens of merchant houses in England that depended on the sugar trade. Nova Scotia, which had reaped benefits under the old system, suffered a steep decline in exports and the carrying trade. Between 1832 and 1836, the value of British North American exports to the British Caribbean—mostly fish for slave rations and timber coming from Nova Scotia ports—fell from £268,000 to £25,000.[1]

Besides Britain's removal of protective tariffs on sugar, the shift to free trade extended to other commodities. Tariffs on foreign timber entering Britain were reduced in 1841 and were cut still further in 1846. By 1860, the protective tariffs on timber that had protected colonial suppliers since the Napoleonic Wars would be eliminated altogether. Thomas Chandler Haliburton, a prominent Nova Scotia writer and judge, who became a British member of Parliament in 1859, fought a futile rear-guard action against the shift to free trade: "Those who begot children were bound to protect and support them," he insisted in 1860.[2] However, the economic consequences to Britain's colonial "children" were a secondary consideration, and the abandonment of protectionism was not to be undone.

The increased competition from Baltic timber suppliers in the wake of reduced tariffs undoubtedly hurt British North American timber interests. The effect was lessened by Britain's railway building boom; demand surged for wooden railway ties in the 1840s. Nevertheless, there was a glut of wood in the British market, and timber prices fell.[3] The timber trade had been the mainstay of New Brunswick's economy. Historical geographer Graeme Wynn noted that New Brunswick's early-nineteenth-century growth "from an undeveloped backwater of 25,000 people to a bustling colony of 190,000" flowed from the timber industry.[4] However, the loss of protective tariffs in the 1840s left "scarcely a solvent house from Saint John to Grand Falls," Joseph Howe observed.[5] Some disenchanted residents of New Brunswick proposed that the colony should join the United States, and colonial authorities were alarmed to see Independence Day being celebrated in Miramichi towns in 1849. Others simply emigrated, seeking better fortunes south of the border or in Australia or New Zealand.

1 William A. Green, *British Slave Emancipation* (Oxford: Clarendon Press, 1976), 234–35; Cyril Hamshere, *The British in the Caribbean* (London: Weidenfeld and Nicolson, 1972), 157; Julian Gwyn, *Excessive Expectations: Maritime Commerce and the Economic Development of Nova Scotia, 1740–1870* (Montreal and Kingston: McGill-Queen's University Press, 1998), 54–56.

2 Thomas Chandler Haliburton as quoted by Robert Livingston Schuyler, "Abolition of British Imperial Preference, 1846–1860," *Political Science Quarterly* 33 (March 1918): 91.

3 A.R.M. Lower, "The Trade in Square Timber," *Contributions to Canadian Economics* 6 (1933): 45.

4 Graeme Wynn, *Timber Colony: A Historical Geography of Early Nineteenth Century New Brunswick* (Toronto: University of Toronto Press, 1981), 33.

5 As quoted by W.S. MacNutt, *The Atlantic Provinces: The Emergence of Colonial Society, 1712–1857* (Toronto: McClelland & Stewart, 1965), 236.

The most significant British free trade measure adopted by Robert Peel's government was the 1846 repeal of the Corn Laws. Britain's Parliament, dominated by landowners, had for centuries protected domestic prices with tariffs on wheat. (Despite the misleading label, the Corn Laws regulated other grains, such as wheat, barley, oats, and rye.) The tariffs operated on a sliding scale: when wheat prices dropped below a certain level, tariffs rose to ensure that British farmers would not be undercut by a flood of competing wheat. Tariffs on colonial wheat were always a fraction of those levied against foreign imports, a policy that brought great benefits to the British North American economy. Yet the Corn Laws were intensely unpopular with reformers in England, who insisted that food prices should not be kept artificially high to guarantee the profits of privileged landowners. British industrialists, in the meantime, lobbied for the repeal of the Corn Laws, recognizing that cheaper food would mean that wages could be reduced and British manufacturers made more competitive.

Under the protective shelter of imperial preference, wheat production was booming in Canada West (Upper Canada). Economic historian John McCallum noted that the colony's economy was even more specialized in wheat than that of late twentieth-century Saskatchewan. Before 1860, three-quarters of Canada West's cash income flowed from wheat exports. By contrast, Canada East (Lower Canada), plagued by crop failures, soil exhaustion, and population pressure on agricultural land, had been a net importer of wheat since the 1830s.[6] Nevertheless, the port city of Montreal in Canada East was the main commercial and shipping centre for the United Canadas, while canal improvements on the St. Lawrence and construction of the 1829 Welland Canal in Canada West made it easier for wheat to be shipped through Montreal. Banking, brokerage, and insurance companies established headquarters in Montreal, as did a host of other industries—foundries, brickyards, distilleries, breweries, shoe factories, manufacturers of soap and candles—drawn by the availability of labour and access to water power and transportation.

American wheat producers even found it worth their while to ship their grain to Montreal for export via the Welland Canal. Ground into flour in Montreal mills, this American wheat found its way to the British market as protected colonial grain. In fact, it has been estimated that the lion's share of the "Canadian" wheat exported to Britain in some years actually originated in the United States. In 1841, for example, Canada imported 210,000 quarter tonnes of wheat from the United States and exported a total of 280,000 quarter tonnes.[7] Montreal's warehousing, milling, and transport capacity

---

6   John McCallum, *Unequal Beginnings: Agriculture and Economic Development in Quebec and Ontario until 1870* (Toronto: University of Toronto Press, 1980), 4.

7   D.L. Burn, "Canada and the Repeal of the Corn Laws," *Cambridge Historical Journal* 2 (1928): 253, n.4.

boomed, and the British government encouraged improvements to facilitate trade with an imperial loan guarantee of £1,500,000 for canal building.

The British decision to repeal the Corn Laws in 1846 has often been historically linked with the great Irish famine in the same era. The widespread failure of the staple Irish potato crop in 1845, followed by a total failure the following year, made any policy that taxed food indefensible. When he introduced his measure to sweep away the Corn Laws, British Prime Minister Robert Peel admitted that the famine in Ireland had left him with no alternative. But he denied that the temporary scarcity was the fundamental point. Peel was a committed free trader on simple grounds of social justice and was prepared to watch Britain's Conservative Party torn in two over the issue. Tory landowners in Parliament turned against Peel; his bill to repeal the Corn Laws passed with the support of Liberals, but his government was defeated in another vote that same day. As he acknowledged parliamentary defeat, Peel mused aloud that he hoped he would be "sometimes remembered with expressions of good will in the abodes" of labourers, "when they shall recruit their exhausted strength with abundant and untaxed food, the sweeter because it is no longer leavened by a sense of injustice."[8] The Whig, or Liberal, administration of Lord John Russell that took office in 1846 was equally committed to free trade principles.

THE IRISH POTATO FAMINE AND IMMIGRATION TO BRITISH NORTH AMERICA

Regardless of any impact the Irish famine may have had on British tariff policy, it was undeniable that the failure of the potato crop wrought profound changes. Ireland had come to be deeply dependent on this single staple crop. A small plot planted with potatoes could sustain a large family—one-quarter of the land needed for an equivalent grain crop—and potatoes could easily be cultivated in boggy or hilly ground. Between 1779 and 1841, Ireland's population grew by 172 per cent to reach 8.2 million, and English agriculturalist Arthur Young remarked approvingly of the nutritious diet that produced the "well-formed vigorous bodies" of the Irish, "their cottages swarming with children."[9] Yet Ireland's reliance on this single crop was a dangerous strategy.

8 Extract from Sir Robert Peel's final ministerial speech in the House of Commons, June 29, 1846. http://www.victorianweb.org/history/pms/peel/peelov.html.

9 As quoted by Donald MacKay, *Flight from Famine: The Coming of the Irish to Canada.* (Toronto: McClelland & Stewart, 1990), 217. See also Cecil Woodham-Smith, *The Great Hunger: Ireland, 1845–1849* (New York: Harper & Row, 1962).

BOY AND GIRL AT CAHERA.

Figure 10.1 Scene at Skibbereen [Ireland] during the Great Famine, James Mahony, commissioned by *The Illustrated London News*, 1847.

The potato crop of 1845 at first promised to be especially abundant, but reports circulated of an air-borne fungus that caused the plants to turn black, wither, and die, and which even affected potatoes already harvested. Overnight, a crop of healthy potatoes could be reduced to stinking black liquid putrefaction. One-third to one-half of Ireland's potato crop was destroyed in 1845, yet in an unpredictable patchwork pattern that saw some areas totally affected and others mysteriously spared.[10] Ireland looked ahead with hope to the 1846 harvest, confident in the folk belief that crop failures never struck in successive years. Instead, the crop failure in 1846 was total.

"Black '47"—the year in which people would have relied on the harvest of 1846—brought devastation to Ireland. Protracted hunger had already weakened the population, and the diseases that accompany famine—cholera, typhus, fevers, and bowel disorders—took a further toll. Ireland's population fell by an estimated 2 million during the famine years, with 1 million emigrating and another million lost to death. Indeed, the population of Ireland has never rebounded since its high of over 8 million; it remains under 5 million today. British authorities, who had directly governed Ireland since the union of 1801, struggled to ameliorate the disaster, yet clung to *laissez-faire* convictions that market forces ought not to be hampered. Too much assistance would carry the danger that the Irish might "relax in their exertions to provide for themselves," one statesman worried.[11] "It is possible to have heard the tale of sorrow too often," *The Times* of London callously proclaimed.

10 As quoted by MacKay, *Flight from Famine*, 220, 224–25.

11 Grey to Elgin, dispatch 109, July 19, 1847, *British Parliamentary Papers Relating to Canada*, 1847–48, vol. 17, 202.

The paper condemned Ireland's "indolent preference of relief to labour" and contemptuously explained that the Irish had been taught to repeat the same mistakes and to look to the state for assistance.[12]

As the winter of 1846–47 came on, even scarce supplies of nettles, edible roots, and cabbage leaves upon which people had subsisted were gone. Starving people pawned their bedding and the very rags they wore. Nature's cruelty to suffering Ireland was unremitting as the cold struck early and with unaccustomed severity, bringing snow in November. Ill-clad men left the warmth of a peat fire to labour on government public works projects, breaking rocks and building roads. Many fell down dead of hunger and exposure to cold, rain, and snow.

Authorities touring the devastation brought back alarming reports. A Quaker relief worker operating a soup kitchen in County Leitrim saw children wasted to "skeletons, their features sharpened with hunger," their faces bearing "the anxious look of premature old age."[13] A parish priest visiting a cottage in County Cork found a man, still living, lying in bed with his dead wife and two dead children, while a cat devoured a dead infant nearby. The typhus, or "black fever," that accompanied famine caused gangrene and the frequent loss of fingers, toes, and feet. The odious stench of black fever in a cottage announced itself before visitors even reached the door; one medical officer complained of being forcibly driven back, retching, by the smell. Workhouses that might have offered relief had to close their doors because sufficient tax revenue to run them could not be collected. The British government rejected widespread cries for a systematic government program of assisted emigration to deal with the crisis. "There is no use in sending them from starving at Skibbereen to starving at Montreal," the prime minister explained.[14]

Landlords, unable to collect rents owing, faced cries for clemency toward defaulting tenants, but many had endured habitual arrears and doubted that crops would ever recover sufficiently. The famine was the breaking point, and some felt forced to evict, demolishing cottages so that the homeless would not squat in their former homes. Troops grimly enforced this heartbreaking policy, keeping the anguished tenants at bay while demolition crews pulled down their homes. Some landlords offered assistance to their tenants to emigrate in exchange for the surrender of their leases, but often failed to provide enough aid for a safe passage. Canadian authorities were indignant at arrangements made by the agent for the estate of British parliamentarian Lord Palmerston. Palmerston's agent acknowledged sending some 2,000 tenants

12 *The Times* [of London], August 3, 1846, September 22, 1846, September 2, 1846.

13 As quoted by MacKay, *Flight from Famine*, 237.

14 Lord John Russell to Bessborough, as quoted in W.P. Morrell, *British Colonial Policy in the Age of Peel and Russell* (London: Frank Cass & Co, 1966), 430.

to British North America, destitute people who needed immediate assistance upon arrival. When one vessel, the *Lord Ashburton*, arrived at Quebec very late in the shipping season, emigration agents found that 87 of Palmerston's former tenants aboard were naked, with children huddled together under a coarse canvas sail, shivering in the biting winds of a November Atlantic crossing.

Most immigrants were not assisted, yet the 1847 shipping season saw approximately 90,000 immigrants arrive, almost triple the number of the years immediately preceding. The ports of Quebec and Montreal bore the brunt, and officials there reeled at the enormity of the task that lay ahead of them. The more prosperous Irish tended to make up the bulk of immigration in the pre-famine years, and historian Donald Akenson has demonstrated that, contrary to popular belief, this continued to be the case in the famine years.[15] To officials in Canada, however, the number of indigent arrivals in 1847 was staggering. Ships were crowded with "the decrepit, the maimed, the lame, the subjects of chronic disease, [and] widows with large families of tender age," Canada's executive council complained. Montreal alone had more than a thousand orphaned children.[16] The population opened their homes and their hearts to these unfortunates, who were raised as French Canadians.

Crude hospital facilities at the quarantine station at Partridge Island, near the mouth of the harbour at Saint John, New Brunswick, built long before, had been meant to accommodate 200 at most, and the island was ill-prepared for the almost 15,000 people who would land there in 1847. In that year alone, 1,195 died on Partridge Island. Twenty-three-year-old Dr. James Patrick Collins accepted an offer to serve as physician on Partridge Island. He was an immigrant from County Cork himself, and the salary of £50 per month was very tempting; it was 10 times what he might otherwise earn, and the newly married Dr. Collins had a baby on the way. Sadly, the decision was a costly one; he was dead within weeks.

Middle Island in New Brunswick's Miramichi River had not been intended as a quarantine station, but in June 1847, a vessel carrying 462 mostly Irish immigrants from Liverpool to Quebec, the *Looshtauk*, was struck by typhus. The desperate captain, with 146 already dead on his ship, made for the port of Miramichi and the vessel was quarantined on Middle Island. Two more stricken ships were detained there soon after. A young Miramichi-born doctor, John Vondy, who had trained in London, staggered under the burden of caring for so many dying people. Ninety-six more immigrants

---

15 Donald Akenson, "Ontario: Whatever Happened to the Irish?," in Gerald Tulchinsky (ed.), *Immigration in Canada: Historical Perspectives* (Toronto: Copp Clark Longman, 1994), 108–09.

16 "Extract from a Report of a Committee of the Executive Council," December 7, 1847, *British Parliamentary Papers Relating to Canada*, 1847–48, vol. 17, 384.

Figure 10.2
Famine-era graves on Grosse Île.

died on the island, and within weeks Dr. Vondy himself was seized by typhus. His sister risked death by hurrying to the island to nurse him, but it was too late. He died at age 28, on the same day as Dr. Collins on Partridge Island.

Grosse Île, converted into a quarantine station during the cholera epidemic of 1832, was downriver from Quebec and was the first port of call for vessels bound for ports in Canada East. In the 1847 shipping season, queues of vessels miles long waited to discharge their passengers there. The frantic reports emanating from the island offer some of the most poignant glimpses of the tide of human misery arriving on Canadian shores. The Montreal Emigrant Society described Grosse Île as a "great charnel pit of victimized humanity."[17] During the 1847 shipping season, Dr. George Douglas, the medical superintendent at Grosse Île, reported that more than 10,000 had died either en route to British North America or soon after arrival. A further 30,000 were sick, and 38,000 completely destitute. More than 2,000 dead had to be removed from arriving vessels; ships' crews had to use boat hooks to drag the bodies of the dead out of the berths they shared with the living.[18]

Montreal was gripped by a heat wave in the summer of 1847; in June three people dropped down dead in the streets from the effects. Thousand were infected by typhus; in Montreal alone, it claimed 924 residents before the summer had ended.

17 As quoted by J.M.S. Careless, *The Union of the Canadas, 1841–1857* (Toronto: McClelland & Stewart, 1967), 113.

18 "Extract from Report of G.M. Douglas, Medical Superintendent, Grosse Île," and "Extract from Report of A.C. Buchanan, Chief Emigration Agent, 8 December 1847," *British Parliamentary Papers Relating to Canada*, 1847–48, vol. 17, 385, 201.

Some Canadians showed incredible bravery in ministering to desperate immigrants suffering from disease. Dr. Wolfred Nelson, who had once led Lower Canada's disaffected in rebellion, now risked his life to minister to the sick at Montreal's waterfront. The Roman Catholic Bishop of Toronto, Dr. Michael Power, succumbed to fever after visiting the sick. Dr. George Douglas, the medical superintendent at Grosse Île, recovered from the fever he contracted there, although it permanently damaged his health. Living and working amid constant sorrow marked him in other ways, too. Douglas arranged a monument to his medical colleagues and the many others who died at Grosse Île: "In this secluded spot lie the mortal remains of 5,425 persons who, flying from pestilence and famine in the year 1847, found in North America but a grave." Sometime later, at his home near the site, Douglas committed suicide.[19] Today, this picturesque but inexpressibly sad place is maintained by Parks Canada, a Celtic cross commemorating the many who died there.

BRITAIN CONCEDES COLONIAL SELF-GOVERNMENT

Britain's embrace of free trade in the mid-nineteenth century contributed to a questioning of the very value of colonial possessions. The empire was of course important to British global clout; as Prime Minister Lord John Russell explained, "the loss of any great portion of our Colonies w[oul]d diminish our importance in the world, and the vultures w[oul]d soon gather together to despoil us of other parts of our Empire."[20] But reformers wondered why English taxpayers should be burdened with the cost of defending colonies and questioned why mature colonies with traditions of representative government should be directly governed by Britain in matters that had no bearing on the larger empire.

Russell's government now prepared to take the next dramatic step: granting self-government over domestic matters to those colonies with elected legislatures. Britain's Secretary of State for the Colonies, the third Earl Grey, in November 1846 set out his ideas about how this revolutionary idea would work in a dispatch to the British-appointed governor of Nova Scotia, Sir John Harvey. This dispatch has become a foundational document in the constitutional history of British North America.

Grey explained to Harvey that the government of the colony should be modelled on that of the mother country. The governor should follow the wishes of his executive council as long as they possessed the confidence of the legislative assembly. The governor should be politically neutral, not favouring any one party over another. If the

19 MacKay, *Flight from Famine*, 270–71, 291.
20 Lord John Russell to Earl Grey, August 19, 1849, as quoted in Phillip Buckner, *The Transition to Responsible Government: British Policy in British North America, 1815–1850* (Westport, Connecticut: Greenwood Press, 1985), 7.

council lost the support of the assembly, they would normally resign, and the governor should show equal willingness to grant to their opponents the privilege of forming a government. It is, Grey said, "neither possible nor desirable to carry on the government of any of the British Provinces in North America in opposition to the opinion of the inhabitants."[21]

A MILESTONE IN NOVA SCOTIA: A "REVOLUTION WITHOUT BLOODSHED"

Despite these clear instructions, Sir John Harvey was resistant. Harvey was an experienced colonial governor who had already served in Prince Edward Island, Newfoundland, and New Brunswick before coming to Nova Scotia. He found the innovative idea of a self-governing colony to be a logical absurdity. He also disliked the idea of introducing partisan politics into Nova Scotia.

Behind the scenes, however, Nova Scotia journalist and politician Joseph Howe was doing all he could to promote the change. After the Liberals had clearly won a majority in Nova Scotia's election in August 1847, their Tory opponents refused to resign their places in the executive council, and Harvey had not

Figure 10.3 Joseph Howe (1804–1873).

called upon the Liberals to form a government but rather tried to pressure both parties into a coalition arrangement. At the same time, Howe had struck up a correspondence with Charles Buller, one of Lord Durham's former aides, who was now a British member of Parliament and judge advocate for the colonial office. Buller reassured Howe that Britain's government fully endorsed the idea of responsible government for Nova Scotia and British North America's other mature settlement colonies, and also

21 Grey to Sir John Harvey, dispatch, November 3, 1846, in W.P.M. Kennedy (ed.), *Statutes, Treaties and Documents of the Canadian Constitution, 1713–1929*, 2nd ed. (Toronto: Oxford University Press, 1930), 494–96.

apprised Grey, the Secretary of State for the Colonies, of the true state of affairs in Nova Scotia.[22] Grey wrote again to Harvey to clear up any ambiguity: under responsible government, the governor's duty was not to force his unwilling advisors into a coalition, but to respect the wishes of a majority of the assembly. "Every free government necessarily is a party government," Grey explained, and "I think it is better that Nova Scotia should submit to the evils of party government rather than be without the privileges of freedom."[23]

By the end of January 1848, the Conservative executive councillors who had clung to office were compelled to resign, and Harvey called upon Liberal leader James B. Uniacke to form a government in Nova Scotia. Uniacke's cabinet, including Joseph Howe, was sworn in early in February 1848. Howe wrote excitedly to Buller that "We were conscious of having achieved a Revolution, without bloodshed." He was proud that Nova Scotia should lead the way as the first colony in the empire to achieve self-government.[24] Buller wrote warmly back to Howe, telling him how deeply gratified he was by the news and expressing confidence in his moderation and wisdom. The correspondence was soon cut short, however; Howe learned, when one of his letters went unanswered, that Buller had suddenly succumbed to typhus at the age of 41.

RESPONSIBLE GOVERNMENT IN CANADA

Elsewhere in British North America, the transition to responsible government would not be so peaceful. James Bruce, the eighth Earl of Elgin, arrived early in 1847 to take up his new post as governor of the United Canadas. Only 36 years old, with a young family, Elgin came to Canada with clear instructions from Grey to implement self-government in the colony. Elgin's wife, Mary Lambton, was the daughter of Lord Durham, and Elgin assured her that he would adopt her "father's system" in Canada. Lady Elgin was also the niece of the colonial secretary, Earl Grey, and this family tie perhaps encouraged Elgin and Grey to maintain a frank and open private correspondence about their objectives in Canada.

When Canadian election results in March 1848 showed that the Reformers had toppled the Conservative majority in the legislative assembly, Elgin called upon reform leaders Robert Baldwin and Louis-Hippolyte La Fontaine to form a government. There was no new act passed to inaugurate responsible government in Canada. Instead, it simply became a matter of a new practice: it was now understood that the

22 Chester Martin, "The Correspondence between Joseph Howe and Charles Buller, 1845–1848," *Canadian Historical Review* 6 (1925): 328.

23 Grey to Harvey, draft dispatch on responsible government, in Sir Arthur G. Doughty (ed.), *The Elgin-Grey Papers, 1846–1852*, vol. 3 (Ottawa: J.O. Patenaude, 1937), 1151–55.

24 Howe to Buller, February 12, 1848, Chester Martin, "Correspondence between Howe and Buller," 324.

executive council had to have the support of the elected assembly, and that, under normal circumstances, the governor would act on the advice of his executive council.

Britain's Colonial Secretary, Lord Grey, had been watching Elgin's "great experiment" with some concern, especially given events in the wider world. Europe was engulfed by a wave of revolution in 1848. Republicans in France once again toppled the monarchy, and the spirit of revolution swept through Italy, Germany, Prussia, Galicia, Bohemia, Hungary, and Austria. An abortive 1848 uprising in Ireland threatened British rule. England itself had made modest concessions to reform a few years before, but some sought more profound changes. Chartists in England demanded the extension of political rights to the working classes and collected more than 2 million signatures on a monster petition. Three coaches bore the 500-pound document to the House of Commons. In this inflammatory climate, Karl Marx and Friedrich Engels produced *The Communist Manifesto*, calling upon workers of the world to unite. Grey was increasingly uneasy about the "monstrous absurdities"

Figure 10.4 James Bruce, the eighth Earl of Elgin (1811–1863).

he saw taking place across the channel in France and throughout Europe.[25]

Grey worried that the very survival of the imperial connection in Canada was at stake, that Canadians might opt for what he called "extreme democracy" on the American or French model. But Elgin confidently predicted that the concession of responsible government "slakes that thirst for self Gov[ernmen]t" and offered a system "intrinsically superior to that of the Yankees." Canada's government would retain "the check of the Crown," affording protection to the rights of minorities that might be otherwise trampled by majority rule."[26]

On March 11, 1848, the Baldwin-La Fontaine administration, sometimes known as the "Great Ministry" because of the watershed in constitutional principle that it

---

25 *Elgin-Grey Papers*, I, Grey to Elgin, private, March 22, 1848, 125.
26 *Elgin-Grey Papers*, II, Elgin to Grey, private, December 17, 1850, 775–76.

represented, was sworn into office. When the new legislative session began in January 1849, the governor general's speech from the throne was read in French as well as English. Lord Elgin, having spent much of his youth in Paris, spoke French very comfortably, and he informed the legislature that the imperial Parliament had repealed the offensive provision of the *Act of Union* that had declared English to be the official language of Canada's legislature. La Fontaine had for years made the language issue a central plank in Canada East's reform platform and had insisted on speaking French in the legislature over the jeers and protests of some English-speaking members.

THE REBELLION LOSSES BILL AND THE TORY REBELLION OF 1849

The Baldwin-La Fontaine administration swiftly granted a general amnesty to exiled rebels from 1837 to 1838 who had not yet been pardoned, and many took the opportunity to return to Canada. William Lyon Mackenzie was among them, and he wrote the governor general a contrite letter in which he confessed he had erred in "Worship of the Idol enthroned at Washington."[27] He re-entered active politics, but never achieved his former prominence. Wolfred Nelson had returned earlier from exile with La Fontaine's help and served as a member of the assembly. La Fontaine had also brokered an amnesty in 1845 for the Lower Canadian rebellion leader, Louis Joseph Papineau. Far from being grateful, Papineau returned to the legislature to sneer at *vendus* who had sold out to cooperate with union. Nelson worried that Papineau's attacks on La Fontaine's leadership would split the ranks of French-Canadian reformers and launched a deeply damaging attack on Papineau, accusing him of cowardice for deserting the rebel standard at Saint-Denis on the eve of battle. Nelson bitterly reflected that it was perhaps fortunate Papineau did not have the opportunity to seize power, "persuaded as I am at present that you would have governed with a rod of iron."[28]

The biggest test for the Baldwin-La Fontaine ministry was yet to come. Early in the session of 1849, La Fontaine introduced the controversial Rebellion Losses Bill. The rebellions of 1837–38 had destroyed farms, homes, and other properties in Lower Canada, and the bill sought to compensate their owners. In 1845, property owners in Upper Canada had been compensated for the much more modest damage that occurred there. But the bill to compensate Lower Canadians was controversial for reasons beyond the scope of the damages to be paid. The 1849 bill specified that

27 *Elgin-Grey Papers*, I, W.L. Mackenzie to Lord Elgin, New York, February 14, 1848, 226–234.
28 Wolfred Nelson, as quoted in John Beswarick Thompson, "Wolfred Nelson," *Dictionary of Canadian Biography* (DCB), www.biographi.ca.

those convicted of treason would be barred from receiving compensation, and it was well known that many prominent rebels did not fall into that category, having either received amnesty or fled to the United States. Tory critics of the bill protested that it would compensate many who were known to be treasonous. Wolfred Nelson, for example, was claiming more than £12,000 in compensation.

The debates in the legislature over the Rebellion Losses Bill were deeply acrimonious. The member for Hamilton, Sir Allan MacNab, knighted for his role in helping to suppress the rebellions, vehemently denounced the bill and, warming to his subject, condemned all French Canadians as rebels and aliens. Tory member for Essex, John Prince, who had summarily executed five rebel invaders at Windsor in 1838, joined in the vocal opposition to the bill. Reformer William Hume Blake, solicitor general for Canada West, eloquently defended the Rebellion Losses legislation, criticizing MacNab for his zeal for the Crown but readiness to sacrifice the liberty of the subject. MacNab was a rebel to the constitution and the country, Blake charged.[29] MacNab leapt up in a fury, but Blake refused to retract his words. The house erupted in chaos, with the visitors' gallery a seething riot of fistfights and taunts and ladies having to be escorted to safety. Blake and MacNab had to be held apart by the sergeant-at-arms. When fresh hostilities broke out the following day, John A. Macdonald, Tory member for Kingston, accused Blake of deliberately misrepresenting legal documents from which he quoted and at last challenged Blake to a duel. Perhaps fortunately, Blake did not appear to fight Macdonald. He later admitted that his language had not been as "measured" as it ought to have been.[30]

The bill passed its first critical test. A majority of both sections of the Reform-dominated legislative assembly—predominantly English Canada West and predominantly French Canada East—supported the bill, and it passed by 47 votes to 18. The bill subsequently passed by a vote of 20 to 14 in the legislative council. It remained to be seen if it would pass the second test. Elgin found much about the bill distasteful and had been receiving a torrent of petitions and threats from Tories who demanded that he refuse to grant it royal assent. On the cold morning of April 25, 1849, Elgin travelled in his carriage from his residence at Monklands to Montreal's parliament buildings. Hostile spectators crowded the visitors' gallery, waiting to see what the governor general would do.

Elgin pronounced his assent. He recognized that, under responsible government, his own feelings about the bill were not the issue. This was an internal measure, not a matter that touched upon foreign affairs or any imperial question. Hisses and groans rose up

---

29 As quoted by Donald Swainson, "William Hume Blake," *DCB*.

30 Donald Creighton, *John A. Macdonald: The Young Politician* (Toronto: Macmillan, 1952), 136–38. See also John Charles Dent, *The Last Forty Years: Canada Since the Union of 1841*, vol. 2 (Toronto: George Virtue, 1881), 149–55.

from the visitors' gallery, and the crowd rushed down the stairs to the street where Elgin made his way back to his carriage through a barrage of shouted insults and rotten eggs.

Elgin's acquiescence with his council's policy touched off what he called the "Tory Rebellion of 1849." That evening, a crowd of 1,500 gathered for a hastily organized public meeting at Montreal's Champ de Mars. This was no mob of the poor and disenfranchised; most were well-to-do merchants, the respectable classes whose loyalty to the Crown had always been assured. They pressed through the narrow streets and descended upon the parliament buildings where the legislators were still sitting. The angry protesters lobbed paving stones pried up from the streets through the windows, shattering the gas lamps, and flames began to spread through the building. From the speaker's chair, Augustin-Norbert Morin solemnly pronounced the adjournment of the house before leading the members in an orderly procession from the chamber, and Sir Allan MacNab dashed through the flames to rescue a portrait of his beloved Queen. Meanwhile, a member of the mob declared his own dissolution of "this French house," and another seized the parliamentary mace and paraded it through the streets outside. The fire raged unchecked, with water hoses cut and firemen blocked by the mob. Montreal's parliament buildings were reduced to a smoking shell, and a valuable library of 20,000 books and irreplaceable documents was lost to the flames.

La Fontaine and Baldwin faced threats of assassination, and a mob descended upon La Fontaine's house, smashing furniture and china, tearing up floorboards, burning the stables, and uprooting trees in the orchard. Nor did the rage directed at the governor general quickly abate. Elgin and his household were targeted with hate mail and verbal insults, and late in April 1849, Elgin and his brother, Colonel Bruce, faced a volley of paving stones as they rode in a carriage. The carriage was badly damaged, and Elgin himself was struck by a large rock that hit him in the chest.

Lady Elgin saved the stone that struck her husband, noting its significance in neat writing on the side. The Bruce family has now returned the rock for display in Canada. Elgin's great-grandson, the eleventh Earl, considering the souvenir paving stone while visiting Canada, mused that this was the rock upon which the Commonwealth was founded. It symbolized an important watershed in colonial governance, the shift to colonial self-governance that would later culminate in the Commonwealth of Nations.

Figure 10.5 Paving stone thrown at Lord Elgin during what he called the Tory Rebellion of 1849: the rock upon which the Commonwealth was founded?

ECONOMIC AND SOCIAL DISRUPTION
IN BRITISH NORTH AMERICA

The sense of grievance that had propelled Montreal's merchants into the streets was not only a product of political discontent. Many of the Tory elite who had once enjoyed political ascendancy were indeed dismayed to see their opponents governing the colony and felt abandoned by an indifferent imperial government. This sense of betrayal was deepened further by the staggering economic slump caused by the loss of imperial preference. The 1846 repeal of the Corn Laws left Montreal warehouses, once part of a bustling trade in colonial grain, full of unsold wheat. In a disastrous chain of events, the Americans moved to capture some of the grain trade of Canada West (Ontario), since American-shipped wheat would now face no disadvantage in the British market. In 1845 and 1846 the United States introduced two *Drawback Acts*, which eliminated duties on goods crossing through their borders for re-export. This incentive for wheat producers to ship via the American route was enhanced by the fact that the Erie Canal, linking Lake Erie to the Hudson River and thus to the port of New York, did not face the prolonged freeze that the St. Lawrence did. Wheat producers in Canada West readily began to by-pass Montreal. In 1847, the value of Canadian wheat exported to the United States was £34,000; by the next year it had risen to £374,000.[31] "Peel's bill of 1846," Elgin privately complained to Grey, "drives the whole of this Produce down the New York channels…destroying the Revenue which Canada expected to derive from Canal dues, & ruining at once Mill owners, Forwarders, and Merchants."[32] Elgin continued to write frankly to Grey, letting him know the following spring that property values in most Canadian towns, especially Montreal, had dropped by 50 per cent, and three-quarters of Montreal's commercial men were bankrupt.[33] "I do not think that you are blind to the hardships which Canada is now enduring," Elgin told Grey, but he doubted if Grey was aware of how directly they were traceable to British policy. There were no funds to pay the salaries of public officials, even the governor general himself: "My Ministers have No Money."[34]

Once prosperous merchants and land speculators were not the only ones bearing the brunt of harsh economic times. Many of the main canal-building projects were substantially complete by the late 1840s, and falling traffic because of American competition had dampened enthusiasm for new schemes. At peak times throughout

31 D.L. Burn, "Canada and the Repeal of the Corn Laws," *Cambridge Historical Journal* 2 (1928): 264.

32 *Elgin-Grey Papers*, I, Elgin to Grey, private, November 16, 1848, 256.

33 *Elgin-Grey Papers*, I, Elgin to Grey, private, April 23, 1849, 349.

34 *Elgin-Grey Papers*, I, Elgin to Grey, private, November 16, 1848, I, 256; *Elgin-Grey Papers*, I, Elgin to Grey, February 17, 1848, 124.

the 1840s as many as 10,000 workers at a time had found work in canal construction—usually the newly arrived Irish who lacked the resources to farm. Contractors drew labourers as needed from the crowded shantytowns that sprung up around the canal districts. Authorities in the Niagara district complained that construction sites for the Welland Canal acted "as beacon lights to the whole redundant and transient population of not only British America, but the United States."[35] Merchants and farmers near the canal zone shanties were sometimes the target of thefts of food and firewood by their impoverished neighbours. Canal navvies worked 14-hour days to earn a wage barely sufficient to provide food for two people, leaving families in want even during times of full employment. Some unscrupulous contractors paid workers in scrip only redeemable at contractor-owned stores. With such conditions the norm, the crisis of the 1840s hit especially hard. Diminished traffic at Canadian ports and a glut of timber closed off other opportunities for wage labour.

Harsh economic times exacerbated the existing tensions between rival groups of canal workers that had erupted in occasional violence. Some of the rivalries were ethnic ones; during a strike on the Lachine canals in 1843, Irish workers had fought French-Canadian strikebreakers. There were also violent clashes between Roman Catholics and Protestant members of the Orange Order, between competing Roman Catholic groups, and between Irish workers from the provinces of Munster and Connaught. Nearby residents complained of the drunkenness and senseless brawling that made the canal sites "war zones," according to historian Ruth Bleasdale. One St. Catharines newspaper condemned the canallers as "strange and mad belligerent factions—brothers and countrymen, thirsting like savages for each other's blood."[36]

In New Brunswick, too, economic and social tensions were exacerbated by the decline in the timber industry and surging Irish immigration. In 1849, on the "Glorious Twelfth" of July—the anniversary of the 1690 defeat of the Catholic supporters of James II by the forces of Protestant William of Orange at Ireland's river Boyne—Saint John was convulsed with rioting. Several hundred New Brunswick Catholics turned out to confront a roughly equal number of Protestant Orange Order marchers, under the eyes of British troops. At least 12 were killed in the mêlée, and many more injured.[37]

---

35 Ruth Bleasdale, "Class Conflict on the Canals of Upper Canada in the 1840s," in Michael S. Cross and Gregory S. Kealey (eds.), *Pre-Industrial Canada, 1760–1849.* (Toronto: McClelland & Stewart, 1982), 102.

36 Ibid., 102–07, 111. See also Peter Way, "Evil Humors and Ardent Spirits: The Rough Culture of Canal Construction Labourers," *Journal of American History* 79 (1993): 1397–1428.

37 Scott W. See, "The Orange Order and Social Violence in Mid-Nineteenth Century Saint John," *Acadiensis* 13 (1983): 68–92.

TURNING TO THE UNITED STATES

Disenchantment with the imperial connection led some in British North America to advocate annexation to the United States. The "British American League," which had begun meeting in the spring of 1849, had at first insisted on its loyalty to the Crown while vaguely urging some modification of the political system. By the autumn, however, more radical elements within the league had seized the agenda and were openly advocating a political union of Canada with the United States. On October 11, 1849, the Montreal Annexation Association published an Annexation Manifesto, signed by more than 300, including prominent members of Montreal's business community. John and William Molson, of the prominent brewing family, and John J.C. Abbott, who would later be a Conservative prime minister, signed the manifesto. Perhaps surprisingly, these Tory annexationists, many of whom decried French-Catholic domination, were joined in their cause by radical *rouge* adherents, who evidently believed that the nationalist aspirations of French Canada could be better achieved by a union with the United States.

In time, remedies for some of Canada's economic woes undercut the lure of the United States, and the fierce American internal divisions that would in the 1860s culminate in civil war made that model less and less appealing. In the 1850s, British North America's economy would move in a more determined way toward a continental orientation, with the United States becoming the dominant trade partner. New transportation networks would develop in the railway age to reinforce this economic continentalism.

New political alliances would also develop in the 1850s. The 1848 achievement of responsible government, while a milestone in British North American constitutional maturity, would not resolve every issue. The precarious balance between French and English in the United Canadas at the close of the 1840s would soon be overturned by burgeoning population growth in Canada West. An equal partnership between French and English satisfied English-Canadian reformers when French numbers were greater. But steady growth in the numbers of English Canadians would soon raise crucial questions about political representation and national aspirations.

11 TRANSFORMATION IN BRITISH NORTH AMERICA, 1849–1864

By the middle decades of the nineteenth century, the colonies of British North America were in the midst of a far-reaching transition. The great wave of immigration that began after the Napoleonic Wars had worked a transformation in the colonies. The three Maritime colonies—Nova Scotia, New Brunswick, and Prince Edward Island—had grown to over half a million people from a mere 80,000 at the start of the century. Newfoundland's population had reached 100,000. Newcomer settlement had scarcely touched the westernmost parts of British North America by mid-century, but challenges to the Hudson's Bay Company monopoly in Rupert's Land would change the prairie west, and the gold rush in British Columbia would disrupt the Pacific colony. The most dramatic growth was in Canada. Canada East's population more than doubled between 1825 and 1851, reaching 890,000. Canada West's growth was even more impressive; its population was 952,000 by 1851. With Canada's English-speaking population outstripping the French, demands grew in Canada West for an end to the artificial equality of representation engineered with the 1840 *Act of Union*. Trade patterns also changed: the 1854 Reciprocity Treaty with the United States promoted a continental orientation in the British North American economy, and the railway age enabled the colonies to exploit it.

BLACK IMMIGRANTS AND THE UNDERGROUND RAILROAD

Immigration is always a life-changing experience, but for no population was this more true than for black American immigrants who sought a haven from slavery. Britain had banned the slave trade throughout her empire in 1807 and legislated an end to slavery in 1833. British North America was thus a beacon of freedom to slaves in the United States.

Josiah Henson (1789–1883) was a slave in Kentucky who was deeply influenced by the teachings of Methodist preachers. By 1828, Henson began preaching himself and painstakingly raised the sum of $350 to buy his own freedom. Unfortunately, his master bilked him of his savings and refused to honour his earlier agreement to free him. Henson was ordered to be "sold down the river" to servitude in the deep south—every slave's worst fear. He seized an opportunity to escape, bolting with his wife and four children in October 1830. When his feet first touched Canadian soil, Henson threw himself

Figure 11.1 Josiah Henson (1789–1883).

on the ground, "rolled in the sand, seized handfuls of it and kissed them and danced around, till, in the eyes of several who were present, I passed for a madman."[1]

As a farm labourer in Canada, Henson patiently learned to read by each evening's dim light with his 12-year-old son Tom's tutelage. The gift of reading, Henson recalled in his memoir, opened his eyes to "the terrible abyss of ignorance" in which he had been living and made him feel "more deeply and bitterly the oppression under which I had toiled and groaned."[2] Henson was determined to do something to help those still mired in degradation and ignorance.

In 1841, with the help of American missionary Hiram Wilson and Quaker philanthropists, Henson organized Dawn Settlement, an Upper Canadian community for 500 black fugitive slaves, with a school, farms, a gristmill, sawmill, brickyard, and rope-making facility. The Dawn Settlement was not unique; there were a number of communities in Canada for fugitive slaves. At the nearby Elgin Settlement, the Irish-born Presbyterian minister William King encouraged his black pupils to realize their full potential, and several went on to university studies, three becoming medical

1 Josiah Henson, *Father Henson's Story of His Own Life* (Boston: John P. Jewett & Co., 1858), 126–127.
2 Josiah Henson, *The Life of Josiah Henson, Formerly a Slave, Now an Inhabitant of Canada. Narrated by Himself* (Boston: Arthur D. Phelps, 1849), 65–66.

doctors. Henson himself became the model for Harriet Beecher Stowe's 1852 novel *Uncle Tom's Cabin*, a book that swayed hearts and minds in favour of emancipation.

These thriving communities, as well as Sandwich (now Windsor) and St. Catharines in Upper Canada, became terminal points on the "Underground Railroad," a clandestine network of safe houses and sympathetic friends offering help to runaway slaves. The Underground Railroad brought as many as 30,000 to freedom, especially after the 1850 passage of the *Fugitive Slave Act* in the United States. This Act allowed slave hunters to capture runaway slaves even in free states, ending the tradition of sanctuary north of the Ohio River.

One of the most remarkable "conductors" on the Underground Railroad was Harriet Tubman, born a slave in Maryland. Tubman, who suffered from epilepsy after being struck in the head by an overseer as a child, fled north to freedom in Philadelphia in 1849 and, from a base of operations in St. Catharines, made forays south to escort an estimated 300 from slavery. Tubman's clever tactics and disguises were legendary. Those for whom she ran such risks were given a stern message: even one defector could increase the odds of capture for the rest. She carried a gun and told her "passengers" that they would be free or die; she was proud to have never lost one.

EDUCATIONAL REFORM IN BRITISH NORTH AMERICA

Canada West's surging population triggered a systematic reform of education. By mid-century, Canada West already had more than 2,500 elementary schools, but little sense of system. Some schools received government support, but most charged fees, attendance was voluntary, and standards were lax. Only in 1871 would education be free and compulsory. The remarkable Egerton Ryerson, superintendent of schools in Canada West from 1844 to 1876, made far-reaching reforms. Ryerson was a Methodist minister, a calling he had in common with four brothers, and editor of the *Christian Guardian*, an influential Methodist newspaper. To Ryerson, education was the key to man's achievement of God's purposes, and he saw his appointment as school superintendent as a means to promote Christian virtue in society.

Ryerson compared practices throughout Europe before adopting the model and materials of mass education introduced in Ireland in 1831. In the face of American political and social influences, he hoped a curriculum tailored to the Irish Protestant majority of Canada West would reinforce loyalty to British values. Ryerson copied the Irish system of a strong, centralized authority controlling what was taught and how it was taught, instituting "normal" schools to train teachers.

A vocal Irish Roman Catholic minority in Canada West insisted on preserving separate denominational schools, viewing mixed education as Protestant indoctrination. Their campaign was inspired by Pope Pius IX's fight to win or maintain Catholic education rights around the world, part of an ardent new offensive against secularism. In the 1850s and 1860s, Catholics incrementally won rights to government-funded separate schools in Canada West. The issue could hardly be separated from the rights of Canada East's Protestant minority to maintain a separate system in that half of the colony.

By 1853, Ryerson's work also yielded new legislation for secondary, or "grammar" schools. Secondary schools would now be government-funded, subject to regular inspection, and overseen by headmasters with university degrees. Grammar schools were for a minority: few students continued their education after age 12.

Ryerson also took an active interest in post-secondary education and in 1841 became the first principal of Victoria College, a Methodist college later incorporated into the University of Toronto. The University of Toronto was founded in 1827 as King's College, an elite Anglican institution, but reformers demanded its conversion to a non-denominational institution in 1850. Anglicans responded by creating Trinity College, which remained a separate institution until early in the twentieth century. Queen's University in Kingston was founded in 1841 by the Presbyterian Church.

In older British North American communities, universities had long catered to colonial populations. King's College in Windsor, Nova Scotia—English Canada's oldest university—was established in 1788. The College of New Brunswick (later the University of New Brunswick) was chartered in 1800. Dalhousie in Halifax followed in 1818, Montreal's McGill University in 1821, and two further institutions in Atlantic Canada in the 1830s—Mount Allison in Sackville, New Brunswick, and Acadia in Wolfville, Nova Scotia. St. Francis-Xavier University, established in 1855 in Antigonish, Nova Scotia, catered to the region's Roman Catholics. In Canada East, Bishop's University at Lennoxville was created in 1843 to serve the area's English-speaking Anglican minority. In 1852 the Université Laval was established by the Séminaire de Québec, a college that had begun training priests in 1663. All of these colleges were tiny by modern standards, few serving a student body of over one hundred. University education was the exclusive preserve of a privileged elite.

SHIFTING POLITICS IN THE PROVINCE OF CANADA

Demographic change in the province of Canada also wrought political changes: the 1851 census revealed that Canada West's population now exceeded that of Canada East, and a new party of reformers—the Clear Grits—demanded representation by population, an end to equal representation for each half of the colony. This party was unlike the earlier moderate reform coalition of Baldwin and La Fontaine; they rejected the politics of conciliation and insisted they only wanted "men who are clear grit."[3] Clear Grit reformers also urged universal manhood suffrage, more elective institutions, and "voluntaryism"—that churches ought to be purely voluntary organizations, without government support or political influence. The Clergy Reserves were a case in point— land set aside for the support of Upper Canada's Protestant clergy. An 1840 agreement ended quarrels between Protestant denominations over the reserves, but the Clear Grits demanded that the reserves be withdrawn from church control altogether and placed in the hands of local municipalities.

The Clear Grit reformers had an influential voice in George Brown, an Edinburgh-raised reforming journalist who founded the Toronto *Globe* in 1844 and won election to the assembly in 1851. Brown's emerging leadership of the Clear Grit faction split the ranks of reformers. His adamant stance on voluntaryism, and his eagerness to curtail what he perceived as undue French-Canadian influence in government, ensured that no acceptable compromise could be reached with reformers in the eastern half of the province. The 1853 *School Act*—a concession to Catholic demands for state-funded education in Canada West—was to Brown evidence of the "entering wedge of priestly encroachment," and he was determined to fight back.

Protestant-Catholic Tensions

Events abroad fuelled fears of unwarranted Catholic influence. Italian nationalists Giuseppe Mazzini and Giuseppe Garibaldi made a bold bid in 1848 to unify Italy by wresting it away from the control of the Austrian Empire and breaking the control of the Vatican in the Papal States. While the 1848 Revolution did not succeed, their temporary success in driving Pope Pius IX into exile emboldened anti-Catholic activists the world over. Once restored to the Vatican, Pius IX's vehement anti-liberalism further stimulated international anti-Catholic forces. Orange Order membership in North America surged in this period.

In the summer of 1853, Protestant-Catholic tensions reached a flashpoint in Canada with the incendiary speaking tour of former Catholic priest Alessandro Gavazzi. On the night of June 6, 1853, Gavazzi's anti-Catholic tirade at Quebec's Free Presbyterian Church descended into a mêlée when a mob smashed the windows and burst through the doors. When Gavazzi spoke at Montreal's Zion Church three days later, troops from the local garrison stood by to keep order. But something went badly wrong as Protestants attempted to leave the church through a throng of Catholic protestors. In

---

3 John Charles Dent, *The Last Forty Years: Canada Since the Union of 1841*, vol. 2 (Toronto: George Virtue, 1881), 190, n.

the riotous confusion, troops opened fire. Ten people were killed and dozens wounded. The "martyrdom" of these Canadian Protestants fuelled the already strong anti-Catholic sentiment in Canada West and helped further George Brown's cause.

The Gavazzi riots contributed to a strained atmosphere in Canadian politics, and the old alliance between French and English reformers unravelled. English-Canadian reformer Francis Hincks was driven from office in 1854 when the *Globe* printed allegations of corrupt financial activities. Some moderate reformers, however, opted to cooperate with moderate Tory counterparts, and in 1854 a Liberal-Conservative coalition was formed under the leadership of Sir Allan MacNab and Augustin-Norbert Morin.

This ministry carried out some longstanding reform goals, secularizing Canada West's Clergy Reserves and abolishing Canada East's seigneurial system, with seigneurs compensated for the loss of their traditional privileges. When Morin retired in 1855, Étienne-Paschal Taché filled his place, continuing the proto-federal tradition of having co-premiers, one French and one English. The MacNab-Taché administration took another step toward reform by introducing an elected legislative council, or upper house, in 1856.

That same year, John A. Macdonald replaced the aging MacNab as leader in Canada West. In 1857, George-Étienne Cartier succeeded Taché as Canada East leader of the conservatives or *parti bleu*. The Macdonald-Cartier partnership would ultimately become a dominant force in Canadian politics, but in the meantime, the domination of the Clear Grits kept the Liberal-Conservatives in a minority in Canada West. No one party could capture a majority in the colony as a whole.

A CONTINENTAL ECONOMY

British North America's economy had suffered under the loss of protective imperial tariffs in the 1840s, with some colonists looking longingly to a union with the United States. Others argued that increasing trade ties with the Americans would help the economy recover and hence dampen any enthusiasm for political union. The governor general, Lord Elgin successfully negotiated a Reciprocity Treaty in 1854, which eliminated tariffs on a long list of natural products. Further, fishers from each nation would share access to coastal waters, a powerful inducement to the United States, and access to the St. Lawrence-Great Lakes waterways would also be shared. Exports from Canada to the United States surged—from a value of $8 million in 1854 to $18 million in 1856. Imports into British North America from the United States also rose sharply. Canada's shift from the pound to the dollar in 1857 reflected a growing continental orientation in trade. Other colonies followed suit in the early 1860s.

TECHNOLOGICAL INNOVATION

The mid-nineteenth century seemed an age of technological marvels. Alfred, Lord Tennyson captured the spirit of the times, exhorting Victorians "Forward, forward let us range,/Let the great world spin for ever down the ringing grooves of change."[4] Developments in transportation, communication, and engineering were all hopeful signs of modern progress, and British North America, where distances were great and infrastructure limited, was poised to overcome such challenges with technical innovation.

Nova Scotia-born Samuel Cunard helped to revolutionize steamship navigation through the world-famous Cunard Shipping Line. While the advent of the railway made water transportation seem hopelessly old-fashioned, Cunard recognized that steam power would enable ships to operate as punctually as if on an ocean railway. In 1840, the company's first steamer, the *Britannia*, crossed the North Atlantic in 14 days to carry British Royal Mail service between Liverpool, Halifax, Quebec, and Boston. Cunard also pioneered the use of shipping navigation lights—red on a vessel's port side, green on the starboard, an idea adopted the world over. By 1867, Cunard's service to Halifax ended, however, with commercial considerations dictating that vessels travel directly to Boston and New York. The mid-1850s shift from wooden to iron-hulled vessels also dealt a blow to Maritime shipbuilders and timber producers. The era of wood and wind power was drawing to a close.

The telegraph was also revolutionizing British North America. Launched by American Samuel Morse in 1844, within a couple of years telegraph lines following railway routes connected most Canadian cities. Frederick Gisborne, an English immigrant, was an early promoter of telegraph technology, organizing an overland link from Nova Scotia through New Brunswick to the United States, and then in 1852 an insulated underwater cable between New Brunswick and Prince Edward Island—the world's first submarine telegraph system. Another submerged cable, between Cape Ray, Newfoundland, and Cape Breton Island, followed in 1856. Gisborne's success inspired a far more ambitious plan. After a number of unsuccessful attempts, in 1858 British and American entrepreneurs of the Atlantic Telegraph Company laid a submerged trans-Atlantic cable between Ireland and Trinity Bay, Newfoundland. Unfortunately, excessive voltage damaged the cable and it stopped working within three weeks, but by 1866 the project had been renewed, with cable laid between Valencia, Ireland,

---

4. Alfred, Lord Tennyson, "Locksley Hall," *The Works of Alfred Tennyson* (Philadelphia: Gebbie and Company), 59. Google Books. https://books.google.ca/books?id=Log9AQAAIAAJ&dq=tennyson+locksley+hall&source=gbs_navlinks_s.

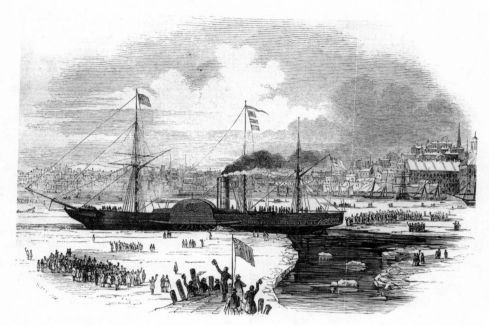

Figure 11.2 The Cunard steamship *Britannia* crossed the North Atlantic in 14 days in 1840.

and Heart's Content, Newfoundland. Within 20 years, more than 100,000 miles of undersea cable linked territories all over the world.

The railway was the most exciting technological change of the era. Thomas Keefer of Montreal in 1849 lamented that Canada's reliance on water transportation suspended most commercial life in the winter: "the life blood of commerce is curdled and stagnant." Thomas Chandler Haliburton of Nova Scotia looked forward to the day when the railway would offer "a safe, easy, and expeditious route to Frazer's River on the Pacific."[5]

In an era before conflict-of-interest guidelines, British North American politicians promoted and profited by railway-building schemes. Francis Hincks reaped handsome profits in railway stocks while overseeing legislation affecting the companies involved. George-Étienne Cartier both introduced the bill to charter the Grand Trunk Railway and acted as the company's solicitor. Sir Allan MacNab acted as director of both the Great Western Railway and the Grand Trunk and supposedly confessed after "one or two bottles of good port" that "all my politics are railroads."[6]

5 As quoted in R. Douglas Francis, "'The Iron Civilizer': T.C. Keefer and T.C. Haliburton, Two Canadian 'Philosophers of Railroads'," in Derek Pollard and Ged Martin (eds.), *Canada 1849* (Edinburgh: University of Edinburgh Centre of Canadian Studies, 2001), 119, 125.

6 As quoted by Peter Baskerville, "Sir Allan Napier MacNab," DCB, http://www.biographi.ca/en/bio/macnab_allan_napier_9E.html.

Figure 11.3 Orange Order Arch, Toronto, 1860.

Canada's railway age began with the 1836 opening of the 16-mile-long Champlain and St. Lawrence Railroad between La Prairie on the St. Lawrence and St. Jean on the Richelieu River. Although there were only 66 miles of railway track in all the British North American provinces by 1850, that number would multiply to over 2,000 miles within 10 years. The Grand Trunk Railway, begun in 1853, was the largest project, incorporating a number of existing smaller lines, including one running from Longueuil, Quebec, to Portland, Maine. To these routes was added track from Montreal to Toronto, and then further west to Sarnia. By 1860, track extended to Rivière du Loup.

To carry railway traffic across the St. Lawrence at Montreal, the 2.7 kilometre Victoria Bridge was built. Billed as the eighth wonder of the modern world, the bridge's tubular steel construction enabled it to withstand rail vibrations, strong river currents, and the pressure of ice jams. The Prince of Wales formally opened the bridge named in his mother's honour in August 1860, presiding over a dazzling spectacle of Victorian self-congratulation that included fireworks, banquets, concerts, and gala balls for several thousand celebrants.

The Prince, making the first official Royal tour to British North America, had earlier toured Newfoundland and the Maritimes,[7] and on September 1, 1860, laid the cornerstone of the new Gothic-revival style Parliament building in Ottawa. Among the other highlights of the Prince's tour was a visit to Niagara Falls, where Charles Blondin, the famous tightrope walker, took a daring aerial walk across the gorge. Tour organizers wisely declined Blondin's offer to wheel the Prince across the gorge in a wheelbarrow. Local Orange lodges constructed triumphal arches for the Prince to pass under, but the divisive Orange Order had been banned in Britain in 1850 and tour organizers hoped to shield the Prince from controversy by avoiding such displays. While the tour bypassed towns where Orangemen insisted on maintaining a

---

7   Bonnie Huskins, "'A Tale of Two Cities:' Boosterism and the Imagination of Community during the Visit of the Prince of Wales to Saint John and Halifax in 1860," *Urban History Review* 28 (October 1999): 31–46.

conspicuous presence, the Order did manage to introduce some Orange symbols into a decorative arch in Toronto without prior detection.[8]

THE CHANGING WORLD OF THE MÉTIS

Change was also coming to Rupert's Land on the prairies, where Métis families lived by means of the buffalo hunt, small-scale agriculture, and seasonal work for the Hudson's Bay Company. Increased missionary activity was one harbinger of the future. Roman Catholic missionary Joseph-Norbert Provencher and two other priests had been working in the Red River Settlement as early as 1818, and Provencher was named the first Bishop of St. Boniface in 1847. In 1844, four Grey Nuns made the arduous journey to Red River from Montreal, travelling with voyageurs using the fur-brigade route. That June, Hudson's Bay Company Governor Simpson at Lower Fort Garry heard boisterous singing on the Red River as a flotilla of canoes approached. The tune was a familiar boatman's song, but the words were different—a song of praise and worship taught to the voyageurs by 38-year-old Grey Nun Sister Marie-Eulalie Lagrave. Within two weeks, the energetic Grey Nuns established an elementary class for girls in the settlement.

Bishop Provencher was initially dismayed by the new priests sent from Montreal: "I have asked for priests, and what do they send me? Children!" But 24-year-old Louis-François Richer Laflèche and 21-year-old Alexandre Taché quickly proved their mettle. "You can send me, without fear, more of these Tachés and Laflèches," Provencher assured authorities.[9] Despite being disabled by severe rheumatism, Father Laflèche, who had Métis heritage, spent 12 years in the northwest, extending his missionary work to Reindeer Lake and Lake Athabasca.

Protestant missionaries followed. In 1820, Anglican missionary John West began work at Red River on the church that would become St. John's Cathedral, but Red River was experiencing strain, and West's program of "civilizing" his parishioners alienated many. He insisted that their "country marriages" were invalid and that these unions should be solemnized. In some instances, this had an unintended effect: men felt at liberty to discard their Native and mixed-race wives. In a changing northwest, Indigenous families were increasingly seen as a social liability. West's successor at Red River, Reverend William Cockran, who arrived in 1825, similarly promoted social divisiveness in the colony. He enjoyed little success in encouraging hunters and traders

8 Ian Radforth, "Arch Rivals: The Orangemen and the Duke," chapter 5 in *Royal Spectacle: The 1860 Visit of the Prince of Wales to Canada and the United States* (Toronto: University of Toronto Press), 2004.

9 Maurice Prud'homme, "The Life and Times of Archbishop Taché," Transactions of the Manitoba Historical Society, Series 3, 1954–55 season. http://www.mhs.mb.ca/docs/transactions/3/tache.shtml.

Figure 11.4 The historic church of St. Andrew's on the Red still stands. It reflects Reverend William Cockran's desire to remake the Red River colony on an English model.

to abandon their ways for a settled agricultural life, but succeeded in constructing St. Andrew's Church on the banks of the Red River in the 1840s. Both St. John's and St. Andrew's still stand today, their English-style churchyards the burial place of many of Red River's prominent citizens.

The Métis of the Red River Settlement would instigate one major change, but would soon have to contend with others. Faced with successive years of poor harvests but strong demand for buffalo hides, the Métis responded by focusing more on trade than agriculture. Buffalo robes were popular in the American market, and industrialists discovered that durable buffalo hides made ideal belting for steam-driven equipment. The establishment in the 1840s of a trading post at Pembina on the Red River, just south of the international border, provided access to the American market. However, Métis exploitation of southern markets violated the Hudson's Bay Company monopoly on the plains, a monopoly that seemed increasingly anachronistic in an era when British policy was shifting to free trade.

In the spring of 1849, HBC Chief Factor John Ballenden arrested four Métis traders for illegal trafficking in furs and liquor. Among the four was Pierre-Guillaume Sayer, whose trial marked a major turning point in Rupert's Land history. The case was heard on Ascension Day, and, after mass at St. Boniface Cathedral, the Métis lingered at the church steps where Louis Riel senior spoke with passion about free trade. That afternoon, the crowd congregated outside the courthouse awaiting the Sayer verdict. The jury found Sayer guilty, but recommended leniency, with charges against the other traders dropped. The turbulent armed crowd and lack of any defence force made Ballenden recognize that the company monopoly was unenforceable. Sayer appeared outside the court a free man. A chorus of celebratory gunfire resounded and a cry rose up from the exultant Métis: "*Vive la liberté! La commerce est libre!*" (Long live liberty! Trade is free!).

With the Hudson's Bay Company monopoly effectively broken, more Red River carts carried buffalo hides south. In 1844, six carts carried cargoes south to St. Paul; by 1855 this had risen to 400, and by 1858 it had doubled again to 800. The steady stream of carting traffic and the more aggressive pursuit of buffalo to the south brought the Métis and their Saulteaux allies into conflict with the Sioux. Cuthbert Grant, Warden of the Plains, brokered a peace with the Sioux Nation after skirmishes in 1844, but new conflicts erupted in 1851. That year, bands of Métis hunters from St. Boniface, St. François-Xavier (White Horse Plain), and Pembina organized a joint hunt in order to be prepared for any confrontation with the Sioux.[10] On July 13, 1851, at Grand Coteau in present-day North Dakota, the Métis clashed with some 2,000 Sioux. The Sioux had captured three Métis scouts the day before and sought to negotiate for their release. But Father Laflèche, chaplain to the Métis, fearing a trap, urged confrontation, even if it meant the captives would be killed. On the eve of battle, Laflèche administered the sacrament so that the Métis fighters might die well. An eclipse of the moon seemed an eerie portent.

The next morning, 77 Métis dealt a devastating defeat to the formidable Sioux. Jean-Baptiste Falcon watched the Sioux approach, a young chief riding at their head. The warrior was "so beautiful," Falcon remembered, "that my heart revolted at the necessity of killing him." He shot the warrior from his horse. One of the captured scouts, Jean-Baptiste Malaterre, made a desperate bid to escape from the Sioux camp but was felled by arrows and musket balls. The Sioux brandished his mutilated body to demoralize the Métis encampment. From amid the circled wagons, Father Laflèche, clad in a flowing white surplice and holding a crucifix high, exhorted the Métis warriors to victory. A Sioux chief was heard to cry that the French had a Manitou (spirit) with them and could not be defeated, and after six hours the Sioux broke off the fight. The next day, the Métis were reinforced by another branch of their hunting party and their Saulteaux allies, bringing their strength up to 700. Fresh hostilities that day ended with some 80 Sioux dead, many more wounded, and 65 horses killed. Malaterre was the only Métis casualty. As the Sioux surveyed the sad spectacle of their

10 Historian David G. McCrady has raised doubts about the identity of the Sioux group that the Métis confronted in 1851. Others have asserted that these were Dakota, but this has not been definitively established, according to McCrady. See David G. McCrady, *Living with Strangers: The Nineteenth-Century Sioux and the Canadian-American Borderlands* (Lincoln: University of Nebraska Press, 2006), 13.

warriors dead on the prairie, a drenching thunderstorm rolled across the coteau. The battle ended the protracted war between the Métis and their Sioux rivals; the Métis, historian William Morton noted, were now "masters of the plain wherever they might chose to march."[11]

Yet, paradoxically, the breaking of the HBC monopoly would bring a change more damaging to the Métis way of life. The population of Assiniboia, including the Red River Settlement, had grown to a modest 6,691 in 1856.[12] Expansion-minded Canadians, such as *Globe* editor George Brown, looked to this fertile farmland as the solution to that colony's diminishing frontiers. The Hudson's Bay Company had long maintained the fiction that Rupert's Land was unsuitable for farming, but in 1857 a British parliamentary committee investigated the company's continued hold over the northwest. HBC Governor George Simpson's bleak picture of the area's agricultural prospects was challenged when a member of the committee flourished Simpson's own ghost-written autobiography, *Journey Round the World* (1847). This work inconveniently enthused about bumper crops of luxuriant wheat and abundant yields of beef, mutton, pork, butter, cheese, and wool. Called upon to explain, Simpson backtracked awkwardly, insisting that he was referring to "merely a few small alluvial points occupied by the Scotch farmers." One committee member remembered that Simpson, "in answering our questions had to call in the aid of incessant coughing."[13]

To shed more light on the area's potential for agricultural settlement, the British government commissioned gentleman adventurer John Palliser to undertake a geological expedition in 1857. Palliser reported that there was indeed a semi-arid, drought-prone area—"Palliser's Triangle"—in the southern prairies, but there was also territory he termed the "fertile belt," the agricultural potential of which was excellent.[14] Canada, too, launched investigations, with geological surveys conducted in 1857 and 1858 by Henry Hind, a chemistry professor from Trinity College. The consensus was that Rupert's Land should be annexed by Canada for future agricultural settlement. This change would be more than a decade in coming, but would confront the Métis with their greatest challenge to date.

---

11 As quoted in William Morton, "The Battle at the Grand Coteau, July 13 and 14, 1851," *Transactions of the Manitoba Historical Society*, Series 3, 1959–60 season. http://www.mhs.mb.ca/docs/transactions/3/grandcouteau.shtml.

12 R. Cole Harris and John Warkentin, *Canada before Confederation* (Toronto: Oxford University Press, 1974), 248.

13 As quoted in James Morris, *Heaven's Command: An Imperial Progress* (New York: Harcourt, Brace, Jovanovich, 1973), 128.

14 Henry Hind also used the term "fertile belt" in his report. For more detail, see entries on "Fertile Belt" and "Palliser's Triangle" in David J. Wishart (ed.), *Encyclopedia of the Great Plains* (Lincoln: Center for Great Plains Studies, University of Nebraska, 2004).

NEWCOMERS ON THE PACIFIC COAST

Newcomer settlement had scarcely begun in the Pacific Northwest by the early 1850s, with only a few hundred non-Natives, most of these on the southern tip of Vancouver Island. There were only a few small and scattered trading posts, such as Fort Langley, on the mainland. The devastating epidemics wrought by first contact had tragically reduced Indigenous populations, but they still vastly outnumbered the newcomers. Few agricultural settlers found Britain's Pacific coast colonies tempting: the journey there required a five-month voyage around Cape Horn or a risky crossing of the Isthmus of Panama, where deadly yellow fever was rife. Those who did venture to the Pacific Northwest found that much cheaper land was available south of the border. With the fur trade in decline in the region, the Hudson's Bay Company had diversified, supplying lumber for California's gold-rush-era building boom, mining coal, and running steam vessels to serve the coast. Since the 1843 establishment of Fort Camosun, the HBC had a foothold on Vancouver Island, and in 1849, the company secured a 10-year lease over the island.

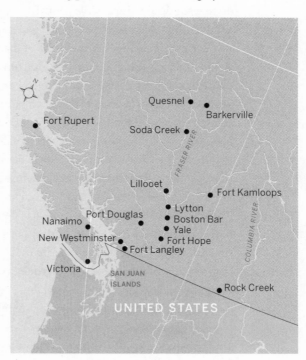

Map 11.1 Mid-nineteenth century Vancouver Island and British Columbia.

The Kwakwa̱ka̱'wakw people in the north of Vancouver Island had long known about the island's coal resources, using the coal primarily as a dye. The Kwakwa̱ka̱'wakw would not permit the HBC to take control of the coal resources but agreed to sell the company the coal they mined themselves. With a growing market for coal, the HBC sought more systematic mining operations, and in 1849 recruited eight experienced Scottish coalminers. These Scottish newcomers to Fort Rupert were dismayed at being thrust into the middle of an emerging dispute with the Kwakwa̱ka̱'wakw, who threatened them and seized their supplies and equipment.

When, in June 1850, the *England*, a vessel bound for California, arrived at Fort Rupert to take on coal, most of the Scottish miners took the opportunity to try California instead. The HBC was alarmed by these defections, since the British population at Fort Rupert was only 30 or 40, and relations with the Kwakwa̱ka'wakw were dangerously strained. Soon, a fresh crisis convinced the newly arrived governor, Richard Blanshard, that he must make a show of force to bolster the company's fragile authority. The *England* had on board four deserters from an HBC ship. When these sailors learned they were about to be apprehended, they slipped away, only to be discovered dead a short while later. Two of the bodies had been hidden in hollow trees, and the third weighted down in the sea. Rumours circulated that they had been killed by the Newitty (Nahwitti), members of the Kwakwa̱ka'wakw Nation who were rivals of the coalmining Kwagiulth. Blanshard conveyed a warning to the Newitty that "white man's blood never dries,"[15] and, in October 1850 and July 1851, took advantage of the presence of British warships to launch punitive raids against their village. The Natives at last offered up the bodies of the three purported murderers, who may have simply been warriors killed in the engagement who could now render greater service by helping to appease the clamour for justice. Blanshard reflected with satisfaction that the act of retaliation had had "a most beneficial effect" in rendering Fort Rupert secure.[16]

Within a year, the company moved its mining operation to the south of the island. Ki-el-sa-kun (Chi-wech-i-kan), or Coal Tyee, while having his rifle repaired at the Fort Victoria blacksmith, told HBC authorities that Nanaimo coal resources were far superior to those at Fort Rupert. The HBC employed Indigenous women to work at their Nanaimo mines, and also recruited two dozen new miners from Britain. The company sold the operation in 1862, but Nanaimo coal remained important, with more than 3,000 coalminers working there by the turn of the century.

The Crimean War against the Russians (1854–56) also prompted new developments on Vancouver Island. British naval crews conducted surveys of the excellent natural harbour of Esquimalt and constructed hospital sheds there in 1855. Within a few years, Esquimalt replaced Valparaiso, Chile, as a coaling base for the navy's Pacific Squadron.

NATIVE-NEWCOMER RELATIONS AND POLICY IN BRITISH NORTH AMERICA

By the mid-nineteenth century, newcomer attitudes toward Indigenous people in British North America were hardening. In an earlier era, cooperation had been essential: fur traders had cultivated valuable trade relations, and sometimes even marital

---

15 As quoted in Robin Fisher, *Contact and Conflict: Indian-European Relations in British Columbia, 1774–1890* (Vancouver: University of British Columbia Press, 1992), 52.

16 See Barry M. Gough, *Gunboat Frontier: British Maritime Authority and Northwest Coast Indians, 1846–1890* (Vancouver: University of British Columbia Press, 1984), chapter 3; quotation, 46.

relations, with the Indigenous people upon whom the trade depended. However, the 1821 merger between the Hudson's Bay Company and North West Company, which shifted the Montreal-based fur-trade network to a maritime-based trade centred on Hudson Bay, reduced the opportunities for this commercial cooperation and undercut Native power by eliminating fur-trade competition.

An era of peace with the United States also brought a shift in Indigenous status "from alliance to irrelevance," as historian J.R. Miller puts it.[17] There was no longer a need to cultivate military alliances with Indigenous nations. In 1830, Britain transferred the administration of Native affairs from military authorities to civilian ones.

Unsurprisingly, agricultural settlers tended not to form the productive partnerships with Indigenous peoples that traders and military officials did. Indeed, the attitude was pervasive among settlers that First Nations were a dying race soon to be supplanted. Mortality from disease meant that almost all Indigenous communities were in sharp demographic decline. In Newfoundland, the Beothuk vanished entirely. Shanawdithit, a Beothuk woman thought to be the last of her people, died of tuberculosis in 1829. Charles Darwin's influential book *The Origin of Species* (1859) contributed to popular perceptions that some peoples of the earth were destined to give way to others.

In the United States, settler expansion precipitated Indian warfare, but British policy dictated that Native land could only be alienated by treaty through the Crown, a policy set out in the Royal Proclamation of 1763. The high ideals of the proclamation were not always met, but by 1836, some 27 substantial land transfers had taken place in Upper Canada under this treaty system. In practice, this usually involved setting aside reserves for those who lived on surrendered territory. In 1830, a more systematic provision for reserves was inaugurated. Paradoxically, the reserves were meant to enable Natives to blend into newcomer society, separating them to protect them from unscrupulous newcomers until they could be inculcated in European ways. Missionaries were at the vanguard of these efforts, educating Natives and aiding them in establishing the houses, farms, schools, and mills that were needed for European-style self-sufficiency.

In Upper Canada in 1836, Lieutenant Governor Sir Francis Bond Head proposed a plan that ran counter to this assimilationist approach. He suggested that all Upper Canadian Natives be relocated to the rocky islands of the Manitoulin area between Lake Huron and Georgian Bay, an area that he believed would be unattractive to newcomers. Bond Head had personally visited many Indigenous communities and his idea seems to have sprung from misguided humanitarianism. Peter Jones ("Sacred Feathers," Kahkewaquonaby, or Desagondensta in Mohawk) was a Mississauga Ojibwe

---

17 J.R. Miller, *Skyscrapers Hide the Heavens: A History of Indian-White Relations in Canada*, 3rd ed. (Toronto: University of Toronto Press, 2000), 103.

chief and Methodist minister who objected to Bond Head's plan. Jones believed that the surest route to success for the Mississauga lay in Christian education and a settled agricultural life. He travelled to London to register his protest against Bond Head's plan and in 1838 was granted an audience with the young Queen Victoria. Bond Head's scheme was abandoned.

A number of pre-Confederation measures had lasting significance for Canadian Natives. In 1839, Britain's *Crown Lands Protection Act* declared Indigenous lands to be Crown lands: the Crown was to be the guardian of the land Natives held in common. It is significant to note that because Natives held their lands in common, and not as individuals, they were barred from voting: the franchise depended upon the possession of property. The 1842 Bagot Commission, led by Governor General Sir Charles Bagot, confirmed the Crown's obligations to Indigenous people but recommended reducing costs. In consequence, the tradition of annual presents to Indigenous nations ended in 1858. (During the era of the War of 1812, when Indigenous alliances were vital, some £50,000 annually was allocated for these gifts.) The Bagot Commission recommended an end to the Native system of communal landholding, but this recommendation had to be abandoned in the face of vigorous resistance by Indigenous people. Bagot's commission set out a plan for residential and industrial training schools for Indigenous children, a well-meaning recommendation that set in motion practices that scarred generations of Indigenous children. A series of enactments in the 1850s sought to define who was an "Indian" in order to limit government obligations.

In the Atlantic region, local officials often bowed to settler convenience rather than respecting eighteenth-century treaty agreements. New Brunswick's 1844 *Indian Act* showed the disastrous consequences of permitting an assembly elected by newcomers to act as wardens over Native land. The Act allowed reserve land to be sold, with the proceeds used to further the goal of civilizing the Natives. In the event, most of the funds were swallowed up in administrative costs, and non-Native squatters often simply occupied Indian land without purchase. Moses Perley, New Brunswick's commissioner of Indian affairs, was a respected advocate for the Mi'kmaq and Maliseet people, who named him an honorary chief. Yet Perley's attempts to win redress for New Brunswick's Natives culminated in his dismissal from his post.

The exploitation of mineral resources added other complications. The northern Ojibwe traditionally mined copper along the northern shores of Lake Superior, with each band controlling distinct areas. As with traditional fishing stations, this was a seasonal activity by bands who lived further inland. In 1845, English mining entrepreneurs formed the Montreal Mining Company, surveyed the region, and obtained mining permits over an area of 180 square miles from Canada's Crown Lands Department. The company's Bruce Mines operation on Lake Huron recovered an encouraging 1,475 tonnes of copper. In the spring of 1846, Natives alarmed by these encroachments confronted provincial land surveyors, and Chief Shinguakouse (Shingwaukonse) of Garden River, near Sault Ste. Marie, appealed to the governor, Lord Elgin, for redress, citing his personal history of service to the Crown, including military service during the War of 1812. To Elgin's disappointment, his executive council dismissed the Natives' claims; the Commissioner of Crown Lands, Denis-Benjamin Papineau, denied that Shinguakouse's people constituted a nation and maintained that they were not the original residents of the area. When a new administration came into office in 1848, Elgin raised the issue again, this time with greater success.[18]

Before matters could be resolved, however, a disturbance erupted at Mica Bay on eastern Lake Superior in November 1849. A force of Natives and Métis, led by a Hamilton lawyer and mining entrepreneur, Allan Macdonell, clashed with mine workers. A force of 100 troops had to be dispatched to restore order. Elgin reported the incident to the Colonial Office, adding the crisp observation that it was regrettable that "steps were not taken to investigate thoroughly and extinguish all Indian claims before licences of exploration or grants of land were conceded."[19]

Elgin himself made a visit to Mica Bay late in the summer of 1850 and extended pardons to the Indigenous leaders of the disturbance. This evidence of the Crown's concern had a reassuring effect. Canada's colonial authorities sent commissioners to investigate a short while later, ensuring that no non-Indigenous intermediary claimed to speak for the Natives. Macdonell's motives were especially suspect. Shinguakouse's son, Chief Augustin, was dismayed to learn that Macdonell had mistranslated Native speeches to Elgin, rendering them discourteous. "An Indian could not speak such words," Augustin declared.[20] In the wake of the commission, the "Robinson Treaties" of 1850 were concluded, alienating 50,000 square miles of territory north of the Great Lakes, establishing 21 reserves, and recognizing Indigenous rights to hunt and fish in ceded territories.

The groundwork for Canadian Native policy was laid with the 1857 *Act for the Gradual Civilization of Indian Tribes*. The goal was to promote Indigenous assimilation into newcomer society, a goal that remained constant through successive post-Confederation *Indian Acts*. Residential schools were to be used to educate Natives who would then surrender Indian status to gain full citizenship rights. Enfranchised

18 Robert J. Surtees, "Treaty Research Report: The Robinson Treaties (1850)," Government of Canada, Indian and Northern Affairs, https://www.aadnc-aandc.gc.ca/eng/1100100028974/1100100028976.

19 Elgin to Grey, dispatch 118, November 23, 1849, Sir Arthur G. Doughty (ed.), *The Elgin-Grey Papers, 1846–1852*, vol. 4. (Ottawa: J.O. Patenaude, 1937), 1486.

20 As quoted in Robert J. Surtees, "Treaty Research Report." See also Alan Knight and Janet E. Chute, "A Visionary on the Edge: Allan Macdonell and the Championing of Native Resource Rights," in Celia Haig-Brown (ed.), *With Good Intentions: Euro-Canadian and Aboriginal Relations in Colonial Canada* (Vancouver: University of British Columbia Press, 2006), 87–105.

Natives would be given freehold tenure over 20 hectares of reserve land and, ultimately, the reserves would be carved up piecemeal among enfranchised Natives who would thus blend into non-Indigenous society. The policy was a dismal failure, with Natives successfully resisting assimilation.

In 1860, Britain transferred responsibility for Native affairs to Canada's colonial administration. This removed Native policy from imperial scrutiny and meant that Canadian politicians elected by settlers would oversee Indian affairs. This, historian David McNab explains, was the "'dark side' of responsible government."[21] Alarmed Natives placed their grievances before the Prince of Wales when he came to North America on his 1860 Royal tour and lobbied in other ways but, with Britain divesting itself of imperial burdens, it was to no avail.

THE BRITISH COLUMBIA GOLD RUSH

On the west coast, where only minor inroads had been made toward colonization, a dramatic change was about to occur. On Sunday morning, April 25, 1858, an American side-wheeler, the *Commodore*, arrived in Victoria harbour with 450 passengers. The newcomers, fresh from California's crowded gold fields, had heard rumours of new finds on the Thompson and Fraser rivers. They bought up supplies in Victoria before making their way across the strait to the mainland. This was only the beginning: before the summer of 1858 was over, some 30,000 flooded north, most bound for the Fraser River between Hope and Lillooet. Tiny Victoria instantly became a booming tent city, with more than 200 buildings springing up in six weeks. Enterprising Natives transported aspiring miners across the Strait of Georgia in cedar dugout canoes, while some impatient travellers even lashed together rafts for the journey.

While most of the first arrivals came via California, not all were Americans. An early visitor to Victoria marvelled that "almost every nationality is represented. Greek fishermen, Jewish and Scottish merchants, Chinese washermen, French, German and Yankee officeholders and butchers, Negro waiters and sweeps, Australian farmers and other varieties of the race, rub against each other, apparently in the most friendly way." Black pioneers in British Columbia established mercantile houses, barbershops, restaurants, and other enterprises and were among the earliest non-Indigenous settlers of Salt Spring Island.[22]

---

21 David T. McNab, "Herman Merivale and Colonial Office Indian Policy in the Mid-Nineteenth Century," in Ian A.L. Getty and Antoine S. Lussier (eds.), *As Long as the Sun Shines and Water Flows: A Reader in Canadian Native Studies* (Vancouver: University of British Columbia Press, 1983), 99.

22 George Woodcock, *British Columbia: A History of the Province* (Vancouver: Douglas & McIntyre, 1990), 100.

The miners worked sandy bars along the riverbanks, using either picks and pans or rocker cradles or sluice boxes. The object of both methods was the same: to churn up sand and gravel in the water so that the heavier gold would be sifted to the bottom. The usual haul was fine dust or small particles, although some found nuggets of up to a half ounce. An average daily yield of three or four ounces had a value of $50 to $65—a considerable sum. Yet isolation made costs high: a bag of flour worth $16 in Whatcom, in American territory, would fetch more than double that in Hope, and as much as $100 in the northerly mining camps.

In response to the gold rush, Britain ended the authority of the HBC on the Pacific coast mainland and created the Crown colony of British Columbia in July 1858. This sent a clear message to the Americans that there was no political vacuum in the Pacific Northwest and presumably forestalled any thoughts of annexation. Governor Richard Blanshard had retired in 1851, and HBC Chief Factor James Douglas was appointed in his stead. Now, with the 1858 gold rush, Douglas relinquished his HBC ties and became the imperial governor. When the HBC lease over Vancouver Island expired in 1859, that colony, too, came directly under British control, with Douglas serving as governor.

Born in British Guiana to a Scottish sugar merchant and a "Creole" mother, who was probably of mixed African and European heritage, Douglas had risen quickly in the fur trade since his beginnings as a 16-year-old apprentice. While stationed at Bear Lake in the wilds of British Columbia, he married 16-year-old Amelia Connolly, the daughter of Chief Factor William Connolly and his Cree wife, Suzanne (Miyo Nipiy). In Victoria, James and Amelia Douglas became the leaders of an inner circle of families—all of whom had HBC ties and mixed-race marriages—who settled there in 1849. The five Douglas daughters were carefully raised to take their places at the very pinnacle of colonial society, acquiring the refined accomplishments expected of such young ladies— dancing, drawing, singing, elegant handwriting, and the art of gracious entertaining.[23]

Celebrated as the "father" of British Columbia, James Douglas faced enormous challenges during the gold rush population boom. Historian Barry Gough describes Douglas as "a master of crisis management."[24] Douglas proclaimed the Crown's authority over all mineral rights, requiring miners to take out licences. Recognizing the value of "gunboat diplomacy," Douglas requested that a Royal Navy vessel be stationed at the mouth of the Fraser to enforce British authority.

---

23 Sylvia Van Kirk, "Tracing the Fortunes of Five Founding Families of Victoria," *BC Studies* 115/116 (Autumn/ Winter 1997–1998): 149–79. Sylvia Van Kirk, "Colonized Lives: The Native Wives and Daughters of the Five Founding Families of Victoria," in Mary-Ellen Kelm and Lorna Townsend (eds.), *In the Days of Our Grandmothers: A Reader in Aboriginal Women's History in Canada* (Toronto: University of Toronto Press, 2006).

24 Gough, *Gunboat Frontier*, 78.

With long experience among Indigenous nations, Douglas had earlier attempted to make provisions for the legitimate acquisition of Native land, but in 1849 Hudson's Bay Company authorities advised him to regard as "waste" any land not actually settled. The Natives were deemed to have only a "qualified Dominion" over their land.[25] Douglas, at his own discretion, concluded a number of small-scale treaties on Vancouver Island before permitting newcomer occupation: 11 of these in the Victoria area, two at Fort Rupert, and one in Nanaimo. Douglas's attitude toward justice also differed from that of his predecessor. Governor Blanshard had believed it was necessary to make a show of force to bolster Britain's shaky prestige with the much larger Indigenous population, but Douglas maintained that Indigenous confidence in British justice could best be won if the rule of law were emphasized; only individuals, and not entire tribes, would be punished for any wrongdoings. Douglas thought Blanshard's punitive actions against the Newitty had been "as unpolitick as unjust."[26] Douglas also took other practical matters in hand. He arranged for American sternwheelers to supplement HBC vessels carrying miners up the Fraser River, and undertook construction of a road along the Harrison River to Lillooet and a track for mule trains from Yale to Lytton along the Fraser.

THE FRASER RIVER WAR, 1858

Historian Daniel P. Marshall has challenged the prevailing historical narrative, which emphasizes Douglas's firm control of gold-rush-era British Columbia. Douglas's own letters have been the source of much of the mythology. He reported to the Secretary of State for the Colonies that he had visited the mining camps in June 1858 and spoke with "great plainness" to the miners, warning them that "no abuses would be tolerated" and that "the Laws would protect the rights of the Indians no less than those of the white men."[27] However, Marshall finds that British control over the area was negligible in the summer of 1858.

Clashes between the miners and Natives culminated in what Marshall calls the Fraser River War. Miners making their way north overland used the old HBC brigade trails in Oregon and Washington, travelling in companies as large as 200 or 300. A German miner among one such party, H.F. Reinhart, was dismayed to see that the

---

25 Dennis F.K. Madill, Department of Indian and Northern Affairs, 1981, "British Columbia Indian Treaties in Historical Perspective," http://www.aadnc-aandc.gc.ca/eng/1100100028952/1100100028954#ft18a.

26 Fisher, *Contact and Conflict*, 53, 55. See also Chris Arnett, *The Terror of the Coast: Land Alienation and Colonial War on Vancouver Island and the Gulf Islands, 1849–1863* (Burnaby, BC: Talon Books, 1991), 43–45.

27 As quoted in Margaret Ormsby, "James Douglas," *DCB*, http://www.biographi.ca/en/bio/douglas_james_10E.html.

object was not merely safe travel, but to "clean out all the Indians in the land." At Okanagan Lake, trekkers helped themselves to a cache of nuts and berries stored at an Indigenous village, dumping the remainder into the lake in order to destroy the Natives' winter provisions. Twenty-five men hid in a gulch and confronted the unarmed Okanagan people when they returned. Reinhart estimated that 10–12 Natives were killed by gunfire and as many wounded: "It was a brutal affair, but the perpetrators of the outrage thought they were heroes, and were victors in some well-fought battle," he reported disgustedly.[28] Native couriers spread word of atrocities throughout the Pacific Northwest, but the Natives' attempts to buy arms and ammunition to prepare for the conflict were thwarted when HBC authorities refused to sell weapons to either party.

Mining activity along the upper Fraser River disrupted age-old traditions in which Indigenous families returned year after year to the same fishing rocks along the river— sites that were optimal for catching salmon at their peak and for positioning drying racks exposed to the canyon's dry winds and sun. The Stó:lō nations of the Fraser River had rituals to pass on fishing rights to a designated spot. The *sia:teleq* (loosely pronounced "see-at-el-uk") was the Stó:lō arbiter of any conflicting fishing claims.[29]

Further up river from Stó:lō territory, the Nlaka'pamux (Thompson) Natives clashed with gold seekers. Miners arriving near the junction of the Fraser and Thompson rivers were dismayed to be thrust into the midst of open warfare, with mutilated and headless corpses drifting down the river past Yale. As many as 36 Natives were killed, including five chiefs, and perhaps the same number of miners. American newspapers circulating in the west fanned the flames, exaggerating the miners' death count and implying that the HBC had incited Native resistance.

By late August 1858, the US Army had reinforced Washington territory, trans-ferring almost all troops in California northward and pursuing a brutal policy of pacification, including the destruction of Native food crops. Volunteer militia, most of whom were miners, marched north to extend conquest above the forty-ninth parallel. One militia company, the Pike Guards, led by San Francisco journalist Captain H.M. Snyder, distributed white flags to Indigenous communities from Yale to Lytton. The threatened alternative to flying the white flag was force: the Nlaka'pamux were warned that, if the white men came again, it would be by the thousands and they would drive the Natives from the river forever.

Historian Keith Carlson notes that Indigenous oral history offers a more positive perspective on these events. A Stó:lō elder, Patrick Charlie, speaking in the 1950s,

---

28 As quoted in Daniel P. Marshall, "No Parallel: American Miner-soldiers at War with the Nlaka'pamux of the Canadian West," in John M. Findlay and Ken S. Coates (eds.), *Parallel Destinies: Canadian-American Relations West of the Rockies* (Montreal and Kingston: McGill-Queen's University Press, 2002), 38.

29 We thank Stó:lō cultural advisor Albert "Sonny" McHalsie for information about the role of the sia:teleq.

reported that Stó:lō chief Liquitem prevented further violence during the dangerous summer of 1858 by holding council with Snyder. Liquitem accepted the offered white flag as a symbol of peace, and then travelled upriver to Spences Bridge to encourage a similar policy of non-violence in neighbouring Native communities.[30]

A short while later, at the end of August 1858, Douglas travelled up the Fraser River to make peace treaties with Indigenous peoples. Again, Douglas's own account suggests that he was the firm master of the situation. He reported to British authorities that he had never seen "a crowd of more ruffianly looking men," but, on his command, they gave three cheers for the Queen "with a bad grace."[31] Daniel Marshall observes that Douglas's official communication failed to mention that British sovereignty had been threatened by foreign newcomers taking the law into their own hands. Moreover, Douglas meted out no punishment to the American adventurers who had usurped British control. Instead, he congratulated Snyder on his restoration of peace to the region.[32]

By the close of 1858, the immediate crisis had passed. Most miners returned south for the winter, and the spring saw far fewer adventurers seeking wealth in British Columbia's gold fields. No doubt the troubles of the previous season, along with disappointing yields and frequent high waters along the Fraser, contributed to the declining numbers.

After the uneasy days of American conflicts with Indigenous nations, greater security was achieved with the arrival of the Royal Engineers in the autumn of 1858 and spring of 1859. The Engineers conducted land surveys and constructed roads, civilian tasks that helped distract from the military purpose of the force and made them less provocative to the Americans. Commanding officer Colonel Richard Clement Moody selected New Westminster, at the mouth of the Fraser, as capital of the mainland colony, and sappers and marines under Moody's command began the arduous work of clearing old-growth timber stands. When their service ended, most of these soldiers accepted land grants and settled in Sapperton, now part of New Westminster. To administer British justice, Cambridge-educated barrister Matthew Baillie Begbie arrived in 1858 to serve as British Columbia's first judge. Begbie approached his duties with a sense of occasion, conducting circuit court sessions in a tent while wearing judicial robes and a wig.

---

30 Keith Carlson, "The Power of Place, the Problem of Time: A Study of History and Aboriginal Collective Identity" (PhD Dissertation, University of British Columbia, 2003), 209.

31 As quoted in Ormsby, "James Douglas," *DCB*, http://www.biographi.ca/en/bio/douglas_james_10E.html.

32 Marshall, "No Parallel."

THE "PIG WAR," 1859

Securing Britain's claim on the northwest proved to be especially important when new cross-border tensions flared in July 1859. An American farmer on San Juan Island, Lyman Cutlar, shot a pig that had broken through the fence from a neighbouring Hudson's Bay Company-owned farm to root in his garden. HBC officials demanded compensation and threatened Cutlar with arrest. The island's 18 or so Americans demanded protection of their rights and were obliged with a contingent of 461 American troops and 14 artillery pieces. Britain in turn dispatched three warships manned by more than 2,000.

Both sides laid claim to San Juan Island. In theory, the matter had been settled when the 1846 Oregon Treaty divided British territory from American at the forty-ninth parallel. But the wording of the treaty was ambiguous and possession of several of the San Juan Islands between Vancouver Island and the American mainland—Orcas, Lopez, San Juan, Shaw, and others—was in question. Despite the sabre-rattling, the pig proved to be the only casualty. By October, an agreement was struck for joint military occupation of the island, a status that remained in place during the tense days of the American Civil War (1861–65), when war between the two countries threatened. In 1871, international arbitration awarded the island to the United States.

CHINESE IMMIGRATION TO BRITISH COLUMBIA

Declining American interest in British Columbia gold mining was offset by a new surge in Chinese arrivals. A visitor reported that Victoria was "crowded with Celestials bound for the...mines." Governor Douglas characterized them as "certainly not a desirable class of people, as a permanent population," but allowed that they are "for the present useful as labourers, and, as consumers, of a revenue-paying character."[33] Almost all these earliest Chinese migrants came from Guangdong province on China's southeast coast, especially the city of Guangzhou (Canton), at the mouth of the Pearl River, or from nearby Hong Kong. Guangdong was suffering under western trade competition and was plagued by overpopulation, unemployment, and famine. The Taiping Rebellion claimed millions of lives in the 1850s and 1860s, disrupting farming and bringing social upheaval. In such an environment, labour contractors readily recruited contract workers: between 1845 and 1873, more than 300,000 contract labourers left the region. An estimated 7,000

---

33 As quoted in Robert E. Ficken, *Unsettled Boundaries: Fraser Gold and the British-American Northwest* (Pullman, WA: Washington State University Press, 2003), 151. Governor Douglas's description of the Chinese as "Celestials" was common nineteenth-century usage. China was known as the "Celestial Kingdom," its emperor the "Son of Heaven."

came to British Columbia by 1860, an almost entirely male population. A thousand Chinese workers constructed the Cariboo Wagon road between Harrison Lake and Williams Lake after 1863. Another 500 strung telegraph wires between New Westminster and Quesnel in 1866. Other Chinese workers found job opportunities in fish canneries, coalmines, laundries, restaurants, and vegetable farming.

THE CARIBOO GOLD RUSH

The waning of the Fraser River gold rush coincided with new discoveries in 1860 in the Cariboo, in British Columbia's wild interior. The discovery of gold on Horsefly River drew thousands to the area. Many miners, however, were discouraged to learn that this was not simple placer mining—the mining of alluvial sand and gravel deposits by a river; instead, it was necessary to sink deep shafts into the rock, using expensive hydraulic systems to direct pressurized jets of water that would wash the rock into a system of sluice boxes. Nevertheless, stories of lucky strikes kept hope alive: Billy Barker, an English canal labourer, for whom Barkerville was named, allegedly made, but then lost, a fortune estimated at $600,000.

Governor Douglas authorized the Royal Engineers to construct a 600-kilometre trail, paved with logs, from Yale to Barkerville to serve the Cariboo gold rush. By 1863 stagecoaches and ox-drawn wagon trains rattled over the high wooden trestle bridges and hairpin turns of the Cariboo trail, and innkeepers offered accommodations along the way. An experiment with using camels to carry freight was not, unfortunately, a success and caused havoc among other animals.

LOWER MAINLAND SETTLEMENT AND DEMANDS FOR SELF-GOVERNMENT

As the Cariboo rush commenced, newcomers were also establishing coalmines and sawmills near the entrance of the Burrard Inlet, the future site of Vancouver. Hastings Mill on the south shore of the inlet and Moody's Mill on the north were steam-powered operations that employed mostly Squamish and Musqueam people living nearby, with teamsters coaxing teams of oxen to drag the heavy logs over greased skids to reach the water.

A growing mainland population demanded political changes. Vancouver Island had had a representative assembly since 1856, although it consisted of only seven members, most of whom had ties to the HBC. Voters had to own 20 acres of land, and the appointed executive council was not responsible to the assembly, so the system on the island was far from democratic. Even so, mainland governance was despotic in comparison. In 1858, Britain's Secretary of State for the Colonies, Sir Edward Bulwer-Lytton, had been mindful of the risk of any form of self-government on the gold rush frontier among "wild" and "transitory" miners, most of whom were American.[34] By 1860, Governor James Douglas permitted the establishment of a municipal council for New Westminster, but mainland colonists demanded more and agitated for responsible government at an 1861 convention at Hope. John Robson, editor of the *British Columbian*, angrily likened their condition to "serfdom" and singled out the despotic Douglas as a special target. So, too, did Amor De Cosmos, a flamboyant Nova Scotia businessman—originally born William Smith—who edited the Victoria-based *British Colonist*. De Cosmos derided the Family-Company-Compact that dominated affairs on Vancouver Island. Douglas denounced the malcontents as a clique of troublemakers, but by 1863 a flurry of colonial complaints about the dictatorial Douglas, and the fact that he had already served as governor for 12 years—about twice the usual term of office—prompted the Colonial Office to relieve him of his posts in both colonies. One of Douglas's last acts was to implement a legislative council for the mainland colony with most members appointed. It first met early in 1864. Douglas, still celebrated as the resourceful "father of British Columbia," was rewarded with a knighthood. His two successors—Arthur Edward Kennedy on Vancouver Island and Frederick Seymour on the mainland—were northern Ireland aristocrats with colonial service all over the globe, and no connection to the Hudson's Bay Company. An era had ended in the Pacific colonies.

MISSIONARIES IN BRITISH COLUMBIA

As HBC influence waned, religious orders were beginning to leave their mark on the Pacific colonies. The settled condition of potential converts facilitated evangelical work. Unlike some Indigenous nations, whose quest for scant resources dictated constant mobility, the more prosperous Natives of the Pacific coast enjoyed abundant salmon, cedar, and berries and occupied permanent sites. Their hierarchical social traditions also enabled the missionaries to claim authority, especially with the loss of traditional spiritual leaders, shamans and elders, through rampant disease. The Roman Catholic Missionary Oblates of Mary Immaculate began work on Vancouver Island in 1849 with a school in Fort Victoria for HBC families. Oblate father Honouré-Timothée Lempfrit's early attempts to extend the reach of his mission further north up the coast faltered when the Cowichan people proved hostile and Douglas had to

---

34 Sir Edward Bulwer-Lytton, as quoted by Ormsby, "James Douglas," *DCB*, http://www.biographi.ca/en/bio/douglas_james_10E.html.

send a rescue party. Despite this inauspicious start, the order ultimately expanded into British Columbia's interior and north. The Oblates' St. Mary's residential school for Native children was established in 1861 at Mission on the Fraser River. Sadly, this hopeful and heartfelt enterprise would culminate in a history of tragic abuse.

The Montreal-based Sisters of Saint Ann began their work on the Pacific coast in 1859, under the management of 22-year-old Sister Mary Providence. Born Eleanor McTucker, Sister Mary Providence left Ireland during the famine, and her English skills were a great asset in the largely Francophone order she entered at age 16. The Sisters of Saint Ann taught children, cared for the poor and orphans, and provided hospital care.[35]

Protestant missionaries—chiefly Anglican and Methodist—were also active in the northwest and competed with Catholics for souls. "Paganism was preferable to the heresy of conversion to the wrong form of Christianity," historian Keith Carlson wryly observes. The Oblate fathers reportedly instructed their converts with an illustration of a "Catholic Ladder," which showed Catholic Indians ascending to heaven while the Methodists went head first into hell. The Methodists fought back with a "Protestant Ladder," in which even the Pope himself was dropped into hell's burning flames.[36]

Among the most famous of the Protestants was William Duncan, an Anglican lay missionary who worked among the Tsimshian people. As a youth working in a tannery, Duncan took evening classes at the Mechanics' Institute and was deeply influenced by social reformer Samuel Smiles, who preached individual self-help through thrift, industry, and a virtuous, orderly life. In 1857, the Church Missionary Society sent Duncan as a missionary teacher to Port Simpson at the mouth of the Nass River. He began to learn the Tsimshian language and was pleased to report that the people had learned to sing hymns and "God Save the Queen." In order to Christianize the Natives and inculcate them in the same Victorian spirit of progress that had shaped his own life, Duncan believed he would have to separate Christianized Natives from corrupting influences. In 1862—providentially just before a devastating outbreak of smallpox swept the coast—Duncan led Tsimshian converts to a new village site, Metlakatla. The fortunate timing seemed to confirm that Divine Providence smiled upon this enterprise.

From 1862 until 1887, when the community moved to a new Metlakatla in Alaska, Duncan and over 900 Tsimshian Christians established a utopian village. It boasted orderly Victorian homes, workshops, gardens, a brass band, a uniformed police force, and substantial public buildings—including a school, museum, jail, and church capable of seating over 1,000 worshippers. Commercial activities at Metlakatla

35 Jacqueline Gresko, "Gender and Mission: The Founding Generations of the Sisters of Saint Ann and the Oblates of Mary Immaculate in British Columbia, 1858–1914" (PhD Dissertation, University of British Columbia, 1999).

36 Carlson, "The Power of Place," 241.

included a salmon cannery, blacksmith, trading post, sawmill, and furniture and soap factories. Residents renounced alcohol and gambling, abandoned traditional face painting and the Potlatch—ceremonial giveaways of property—and vowed to educate their children and to observe the Sabbath.

NATIVE-NEWCOMER CONFLICT ON THE PACIFIC COAST

Advancing newcomer settlement multiplied opportunities for conflict with Natives. The greater prevalence of whisky as an item of trade contributed to outbreaks of violence. At Mission, the Roman Catholic Bishop Louis-Joseph D'Herbomez lamented that "nearly all the Chiefs have been victims of this corrosive destroyer of civilization." Another priest agreed, heaping scorn on the "shameless men…trafficking poisons."[37] Enforcement of colonial law often fell to the gunships of the Royal Navy.

In 1861, the *Forward* bombarded a site near Cape Mudge on Quadra Island to which a Haida party had fled after stealing tools, blankets, rum, and other goods in Victoria. The Natives had also plundered vessels in the Gulf and terrorized settlers on Salt Spring Island. Four Haida were killed in the *Forward*'s attack, and five others taken to Victoria for trial. The *Forward* and three other vessels also launched an attack in 1863 on Kuper Island, where Natives were suspected of harbouring those who had killed Saturna Island settler Frederick Marks and his daughter Caroline Harvey. The naval bombardment destroyed the village of Lamalchi before four men were captured and brought to trial. These prisoners were later executed; a fifth had already been killed by Kuper Island Natives. Another incident involved the sloop *Kingfisher*, which had been involved in illicit whisky trading with Pacific coast Natives; in 1863, colonial authorities seized the vessel, pouring out its contraband alcohol and fining its captain. The very next year, the *Kingfisher* was at the centre of a virtual war between coastal Natives and the Royal Navy. In 1864, the Ahousat of Clayoquot Sound raided the *Kingfisher*, killing its crew of three and leaving the sloop a smouldering wreck. Naval officials at Esquimalt despatched the flagship *Sutlej*, along with the aptly named *Devastation*, to launch a retaliatory attack in which 15 Natives were killed, 9 villages torched, and 64 Native canoes destroyed. Native prisoners taken during the incident were later acquitted by a jury in Victoria.

Not all Native-newcomer clashes stemmed from the whisky trade. The "Chilcotin War" of 1864 was sparked when Natives attacked road crews at Bute Inlet, who were building a route to the Cariboo mines. The road encroached on traditional Tsilhqot'in (Chilcotin) territory, but there were other resentments too. An especially

---

37 As quoted in Carlson, "The Power of Place," 231–32.

devastating smallpox epidemic hit British Columbia in 1862, killing an estimated 20,000 Natives and reducing still further a population that had fallen to about 60,000 by mid-century. In some hard-hit pockets, the mortality rate reached 90 per cent. The Haida, once numbering some 8,000, were reduced to a mere 800 after the 1860s epidemics. The aggrieved Tsilhqot'in lashed out at the road builders, killing 19; some were attacked as they lay sleeping in tents.

Mainland governor Seymour had just hosted some 3,500 Indigenous visitors at a New Westminster celebration of Queen Victoria's birthday; the spectacle included a vast flotilla of Indigenous canoes on the Fraser River, Native songs and drumming, and gifts of Union Jacks and gilt-headed canes to the Natives. On the heels of the celebration, however, Seymour had to accompany a militia force to Bute Inlet to deal with the crisis. The powerful Chilcotin Chief Alexis cooperated in the apprehension of suspects, and after a trial presided over by Judge Begbie at Quesnel, five Native men were hanged. Among these was a Tsilhqot'in chief known as Klatsassin, which translates as "we do not know his name," a man whom Judge Begbie described as "the finest savage I have met with."[38] Questions linger about these punishments for killings that Natives evidently regarded not as murder but as acts of war, and about promises of amnesty allegedly made to induce the fugitives to surrender. The 1993 Cariboo-Chilcotin Justice Inquiry culminated in an apology by British Columbia's government, and the Tsilhqot'in people today celebrate Klatsassin Memorial Day to mark the anniversary of his execution. On the other hand, one road worker's descendant wondered who would apologize for shooting his great-grandfather in the back.

UNION OF THE PACIFIC COLONIES, 1866

Besides contending with Native-newcomer conflict, the colonial governors who succeeded Douglas had the challenging duty of managing their fledgling assemblies. Responsible government had not been conceded, but the assemblies enjoyed the traditional control of the provincial treasury. On Vancouver Island, Arthur Kennedy clashed with an assertive assembly dominated by Amor De Cosmos over that body's frequent refusal to vote for necessary funds. Kennedy, who dourly concluded that Vancouver Island consisted of "those who are convicts and those who ought to be convicts," was dismayed to see his assembly vote to repeal a real estate tax when seven members of the assembly's personal tax bills were in arrears.[39]

---

38 As quoted on "We Do not Know His Name: Klatsassin and the Chilcotin War," Canadian Mysteries, http://www.canadianmysteries.ca/sites/klatsassin/murdersorwar/castofcharacters/727en.html.

39 As quoted in Margaret Ormsby, *British Columbia: A History* (Toronto: Macmillan, 1958), 214, 216.

Financial struggles were only part of the rationale for the decision to merge Britain's two Pacific coast colonies. Just as the Colonial Office was trying to unite the Atlantic colonies, amalgamation of the westernmost colonies seemed to promise more cost-effective colonial governance. Frederick Seymour, the mainland governor, resisted union, but agitation by Amor De Cosmos and other islanders, combined with lobbying by investors alarmed at the perilous state of colonial finances, clinched the decision. In 1866, the two colonies were combined as British Columbia, under Seymour's governorship. A single legislative council, with only 9 of 23 members elected, was briefly located at New Westminster before moving to Victoria in 1868. This half-hearted concession to colonial self-government would not slake the thirst of reformers. In 1871, union with Canada would offer the chance for British Columbia to win responsible government at last.

CONCLUSION

British North American territory west of the Rocky Mountains had witnessed profound and sudden change in the mid-nineteenth century, with the 1858 influx of miners and the end to Hudson's Bay Company control. The Métis of Red River had challenged the company's hegemony in their own territory, but would soon face the even more serious challenge posed by a tide of agricultural settlers. The province of Canada's surging population transformed the political landscape, feeding demands in Canada West for representation according to its greater numbers and contributing to religious sectarianism. Technological change also transformed British North America—the shift from wooden sailing ships to iron-hulled steamers, and the advent of the telegraph and railway. A free trade treaty with the Americans after the loss of imperial protection also reoriented economic life in the colonies. These were formative years in British North America, but even bigger changes were still to come.

12 CONFEDERATION, 1858–1867

E ven Canadians who pay little attention to historical dates probably know one: Confederation in 1867. What exactly Confederation signifies is less clear. Many Canadians imagine that 1867 heralded the start of an independent country, the beginning of our autonomy from Britain. Others may see Confederation as the beginning of new unity, the coming together of colonies that were once separate, and especially the coming together of French and English Canadians. In reality, Confederation was neither. Instead, it was the solution to a number of practical problems, a pragmatic arrangement that has stood the test of time remarkably well.

POLITICS IN THE PROVINCE OF CANADA

One of the most immediate practical problems that made Confederation appealing was chronic political dysfunction in the province of Canada by the 1850s. The artificial equality of political representation for French Canada East and English Canada West that had been put in place with the 1840 *Act of Union* ensured that no one party could reliably capture and keep a majority in the colony's legislative assembly. But the situation was more complicated than a simple English–French dichotomy; there were also substantial divisions *within* each district.

In Canada West, George Brown, editor of the Toronto *Globe* and leader of the Reform, or Clear Grit, Party, fought for "rep by pop" (representation by population) to end the existing equal allocation of seats in a single legislature for each half of the united colony of Canada. The equal representation put in place in 1840 was meant

Figure 12.1 George Brown (1818–1880).

Figure 12.2 John A. Macdonald (1815–1891).

to deny the then-more-numerous French Canadians a majority voice. By the 1850s, however, with the population of predominantly English Canada West outstripping that of Canada East, Brown maintained that this equal representation was an injustice that allowed French Roman Catholics undue influence in the united province. As of 1861, Canada West's population had grown to 1.4 million, as opposed to 1.1 million in Canada East. Brown's Clear Grits commanded the most support in Canada West, but could never hope to sustain a majority in the assembly, as they represented the interests of only one half of the colony.

The other significant party in Canada West were the Liberal-Conservatives, whose leader after 1856 was John A. Macdonald. Originally a coalition of moderate reformers and moderate Tories, this party would later evolve into the Conservative Party. After 1857, Liberal-Conservatives in Canada West formed a coalition with the Conservatives of Canada East, known as the *parti bleu.*

The Liberal-Conservative leader John A. Macdonald would go on to play a leading role in the negotiations to achieve Confederation and in the politics of the country until his death in 1891. The Scottish-born Macdonald left school at age 15, articled as

Figure 12.3 George-Étienne Cartier (1814–1873).

a lawyer with a Kingston firm, and was running a branch law office by the age of 17. By 1844, at age 29, he first won election to the Canadian provincial assembly as a Conservative member for Kingston. Macdonald's longevity in politics was almost certainly attributable to his pragmatic flexibility, his willingness to compromise, and his penchant for delaying unpopular or difficult decisions. However, Macdonald also had remarkable social gifts—a talent for friendship, for drawing others into his orbit. He was on friendly terms with dukes and saloonkeepers, and even over the distance of time, his personal letters radiate charm. Alcohol facilitated many of his social and political connections. Legislative sittings took place in the evening, and members often fortified themselves with strong drink. Even amid this culture, however, Macdonald's habits attracted notice, and at times his drunkenness had real political consequences. Campaigning in his home riding of Kingston in 1872, Macdonald slapped his Liberal opponent's face during a debate and tried to grab him by the throat. He was evidently "much excited," according to a local newspaper, a description historian Ged Martin decodes as "drunk."[1]

George-Étienne Cartier, leader of the *parti bleu* in Canada East, was the other half of the longstanding political alliance formed in 1857; Macdonald called Cartier "my second self." Cartier's family had once been prosperous merchants in Quebec's Richelieu Valley, but fell victim to Lower Canada's agricultural decline coupled with the profligate habits of Cartier's father. Like Macdonald, Cartier made a career in law, beginning work as a clerk for a Montreal law firm at age 17. Cartier had been radical in his youth, even taking up arms with the *patriotes* at Saint Denis in 1837, but his political stance mellowed over time, and he entered politics as a moderate reformer in 1848 before moving to the more conservative *bleu* party. Of short stature, Cartier

1 Ged Martin, *Favourite Son? John A. Macdonald and the Voters of Kingston, 1841–1891* (Kingston: Kingston Historical Society, 2010), 83–94. For an in-depth discussion of the alcohol issue, see Ged Martin, "John A. Macdonald and the Bottle," *Journal of Canadian Studies* 40 (Fall 2006): 162–85.

was handsome and always impeccably dressed. He loved to sing, dance, and socialize and once described "love" as a hobby. Unsurprisingly, he was estranged from his wife and lived in Ottawa with another woman. In an era before conflict-of-interest rules for parliamentarians, Cartier continued to act as solicitor for the Grand Trunk Railway even after becoming a cabinet minister, and used his place in government to advance his client's interests.

Cartier's conservative *parti bleu* drew the support of a majority in Canada East, as well as the approval of the Roman Catholic Church. While Cartier supported policies that would best secure French Roman Catholic interests, he did not believe that it was necessary to break the connection to the British Empire in order to achieve this.

Figure 12.4 Antoine-Aimé Dorion (1818–1891).

By contrast, the *parti rouge* was devoted to sovereignty for French Canada. This more radical party did not garner the wide support in Canada East enjoyed by the *bleus*. The party name had been inspired by the Paris revolutionaries of 1848, whose ideas Louis-Joseph Papineau had admired, and the former rebel leader had been influential in the *rouge* party's formation when he returned to Canada from France. The more moderate Antoine-Aimé Dorion emerged as the *parti rouge* leader in 1851. A Montreal lawyer with a proclivity for philosophy and political theory, Dorion first won election to the assembly of the province of Canada in 1854. Dorion, like Papineau, was an observant Roman Catholic, but the Church did not approve of *rouge* free-thinking liberalism and condemned the party. Many adherents of the *parti rouge* belonged to the *Institut Canadien*, an organization devoted to liberal ideas and open inquiry, which was denounced by the Vatican.

The interplay between these four significant political parties, coupled with tensions over the unsatisfactory system of equal representation for each half of the colony in a single legislature, ensured that no one party could reliably sustain a majority in the province of Canada. The atmosphere was one of instability and even acrimony. An episode in July 1858 exemplifies this.

A ministry headed by John A. Macdonald and George-Étienne Cartier lost a vote in the assembly over situating Canada's capital at Ottawa. Only some adverse votes are understood to be non-confidence votes—votes that imply the defeat of a government. A majority vote against a budget, for example, is understood to be a non-confidence vote. In this instance, since opposition leader George Brown claimed that a want of confidence had been shown in the Macdonald-Cartier government, Macdonald decided to call his bluff: his ministry resigned, leaving the governor general, Sir Edmund Head, no choice but to call upon the opposition to form a government. Elections had been held just a few months before, and Head understandably wished to avoid new ones so soon afterward. Brown asked the governor general for a couple of days to canvass possible supporters, and, perhaps surprisingly, turned to *rouge* leader Antoine-Aimé Dorion to form an alliance. However, Macdonald correctly guessed that a Brown-Dorion ministry would have trouble garnering enough support in the legislature, and he relished the opportunity to humiliate his political opponent; he scoffed that "the fish scarcely waited till the bait was let down. He jumped out of the water to catch it."[2] The Brown-Dorion administration was sworn into office at noon on August 2, 1858, and was defeated in a confidence vote sometime after midnight. Macdonald savoured his triumph, returning to form a new administration in partnership with Cartier once again, but these manoeuvrings resulted in an even more poisonous political atmosphere.

In this chaotic climate of spite and vindictiveness, the governor general, Sir Edmund Head, was among the many who believed that a more systematic restructuring of Canada's political life was desirable. Head busily drew up a plan for federation of the British North American colonies, an idea that had occurred to him earlier when he had been lieutenant governor of New Brunswick. Head mentioned this plan later that year in his speech as he closed the province of Canada's legislative session.

The idea was by no means a new one: as early as 1754—before the American Revolution—Pennsylvania statesman, inventor, and polymath Benjamin Franklin had initiated discussions around a union of all the British North American colonies, which then included the future United States. In 1850, Henry Sherwood, a Tory politician who had earlier been premier of the province of Canada, published a series of letters that outlined his plan for a "Federative Union of the British North American Provinces" and even submitted a draft act to Britain's Parliament. Nova Scotia premier J.W. Johnston endorsed union in 1854, "a dream as old as the English presence in America." Canada East politician Joseph-Charles Taché in 1858 published

2   Toronto *Daily Atlas*, August 6, 1858, enclosure in Sir Edmund Head to E. Bulwer-Lytton, despatch 102, August 9, 1858, Colonial Office Correspondence, CO 42/614, B 230, Library and Archives Canada.

Des provinces de l'Amérique du Nord et d'une union fédérale, which recommended confederation rather than a simple union of the colonies.[3]

In the 1850s, neither British North American politicians nor British policy makers widely embraced any such scheme. In fact, Britain's Secretary of State for the Colonies privately rebuked Sir Edmund Head for supporting the idea, unaware that his predecessor in the Colonial Office had encouraged Head to explore it.[4] Long-range policy planning was not accorded a high priority at the Colonial Office, especially since there was virtually a revolving door to the office of Secretary of State for the Colonies: during Sir Edmund Head's seven-year tenure in Canada, eight successive statesmen filled the role.

In November 1861, a new governor general arrived in Canada to take Head's place. Lord Monck was an affable Irish aristocrat who brought with him an extended family, not to mention a menagerie of family pets: 15 dogs, 7 cats, numerous birds, and even a tame owl made their homes at Government House. Monck was an unpretentious, easy-going man who proved to be remarkably adept at smoothing over political wrangles among warring Canadian parliamentarians.

THE AMERICAN CIVIL WAR AND THE DEFENCE OF BRITISH NORTH AMERICA

In the very month Monck arrived in Canada, a serious military crisis threatened the country's peace. Monck, as governor general, was nominal commander-in-chief but had no military experience and took up his place in a colony that was utterly unprepared to defend itself. The American Civil War plunged British North America into crisis and proved to be another factor that would make the Confederation project appealing. The war was triggered by the secession of the southern Confederate states from the American union in the spring of 1861. President Abraham Lincoln's declared opposition to slavery had threatened the autonomy of the southern states and their continued right to maintain their "peculiar institution." British policy toward the conflict was supposedly neutral. The British had no love of slavery, and had outlawed it in their own realms, but British textile mills depended on the cotton of the American South, a trade that was being disrupted by the Union's naval blockade of southern ports. Despite its avowed neutrality, Britain lent covert aid to the Confederate side, and Anglo–American relations became increasingly strained as the war went on.

---

3 L.F.S. Upton, "The Idea of Confederation: 1754–1858," in W.L. Morton (ed.), *The Shield of Achilles: Aspects of Canada in the Victorian Age* (Toronto: McClelland & Stewart, 1968), 186, 195, 198, 200, 202.

4 Details on this episode may be found in Barbara J. Messamore, *Canada's Governors General, 1847–1878: Biography and Constitutional Evolution* (Toronto: University of Toronto Press, 2006), 78–92.

Should war between Britain and the now fractured United States break out, the likely battleground would be British North America.

In November 1861, Union Navy Captain Charles Wilkes, commanding the frigate *San Jacinto*, intercepted a British mail steamer, the *Trent*, in neutral Atlantic waters and apprehended two Confederate commissioners who were on board. The Southerners were apparently on their way to London to urge British aid for the Confederate cause. The British were indignant at American interference with their freedom of the seas, and the British press demanded that the insult by the "pirate Wilkes" be avenged. British Prime Minister Lord Palmerston drafted a provocative message demanding that the Confederate prisoners be released, and Britain rushed troops across the Atlantic in anticipation of possible war with the United States.

Britain had withdrawn imperial troops from Canada during the Crimean War (1853–56) and there remained only 4,300 imperial regulars in all of British North America, 2,200 of these in Canada itself, supplemented by fewer than 5,000 volunteers in Canada's militia. The urgent reinforcement late in 1861 boosted the number of regulars to 14,000. Unfortunately, the hurried transport of troops was complicated by the onset of winter: only one of the 18 transport vessels could travel up the freezing St. Lawrence to reach the terminus of the Grand Trunk Railway at Rivière-du-Loup. There was no Atlantic coastal railway terminus on British North American soil. The nearest Atlantic terminus was at Portland, Maine, and the Americans would never permit the passage of potentially hostile forces through their territory to reinforce the small garrison in Canada. The troop ships pitched and rolled in a violent gale in the wintry Atlantic before making for Halifax and Saint John. From there, the troops travelled overland by sleigh to Rivière-du-Loup, a time consuming and expensive operation.

Fortunately, the Americans did not invade. Across the Atlantic, Queen Victoria's husband Prince Albert lay desperately ill with typhoid fever. From his deathbed, he prevailed upon Lord Palmerston to soften his ultimatum to the Americans. Similarly, in the United States, Lincoln wisely decided that one war at a time was all he was willing to fight. The Union released the Confederate prisoners and the immediate crisis was averted.

Nevertheless, the emergency sharpened anxieties about the dismal state of colonial defences. The cost to Britain of the last-minute *Trent* reinforcements was a staggering £843,000, and imperial authorities urged Monck to encourage his ministers to make more systematic defence plans. Early in 1862, a Canadian commission chaired by John A. Macdonald prepared legislation to dramatically improve Canada's militia forces. The commission recommended increasing the force to 50,000 active and 50,000 reserve members. The 1862 Militia Bill, Macdonald explained when cautiously presenting it to the assembly, was an "enabling" measure that would permit, but not require, the government to put this plan into effect. But the Macdonald-Cartier ministry hung by a thread when the parliamentary session opened in March 1862, and Macdonald disappeared on a drinking binge rather than shepherding the bill through the house. In May 1862, the ministry went down to defeat.

Monck worried that this evident Canadian disregard for military preparedness would send a signal of weakness that might embolden Union war hawks. He also knew that British taxpayers were growing impatient with shouldering the costs of colonial defence. His most immediate problem, however, was finding a new alternative ministry to take office. George Brown, who had led the Liberal reformers, had failed to win a seat in the last election and was headed to Britain to lick his wounds. Monck called upon Canada West Liberal John Sandfield Macdonald, sometimes called "Sandfield" to distinguish him from the more famous John A. Macdonald. Louis-Victor Sicotte joined Sandfield's ministry as the leader in Canada East.

A controversial *Separate Schools Act* passed by this administration in 1863 granted full provincial funding to Roman Catholic schools in Canada West. The bill was widely supported by the predominantly Roman Catholic Canada East members of the assembly, but only by a minority in the Canada West section of the legislature. Nevertheless, it passed with an overall majority, evidence to Canada West's Protestant "voluntaryists" that French-Canadian Roman Catholics were able to have a determinative effect on policy in the western half of the province and that the union of 1840 ought to be broken. Sandfield Macdonald's government succeeded in passing its education legislation but was defeated a short while later after less than a year in power.

THE MARITIME QUEST FOR AN INTERCOLONIAL RAILWAY

While the province of Canada was preoccupied with endemic political instability, the Maritime colonies had other priorities. Many wished to see an intercolonial railway constructed to link the Maritimes to Canada, and this goal indirectly helped to promote a wider union. Nova Scotia's Joseph Howe had been one of the chief boosters of an intercolonial railway scheme. When earlier overtures to secure British financial assistance for the railway foundered, Howe sought the cooperation of New Brunswick premier Samuel Leonard Tilley. Tilley was mourning the recent death of his wife, but Howe urged him to sublimate his grief in hard work. Within a few months, Tilley secured the agreement of the Canadians for a conference on the intercolonial project. Tilley's colleague, Albert James Smith, opposed any publicly financed railway project, and New Brunswick's Reform party split over the issue. Nevertheless, when Britain at last agreed to guarantee a loan for the purpose, hopes for an agreement between the colonies were high.

Unfortunately, the September 1862 intercolonial railway conference at Quebec, chaired by Canadian politician Thomas D'Arcy McGee, proved abortive. The delegates seemed to reach an agreement about the apportioning of costs, but Sandfield Macdonald's fragile administration could not marshal sufficient support for a publicly financed scheme and was at last forced to concede that the deal was off.

The Maritimers suspected that the Canadians had acted in bad faith and many pinned their hopes on a Maritime union instead as a way to finance the railway. New Brunswick's governor, Arthur Hamilton Gordon, a self-important aristocratic young bachelor whose father, the fourth Earl of Aberdeen, had once been Britain's prime minister, was an active proponent of a union of the Maritime colonies. The Duke of Newcastle, Britain's Secretary of State for the Colonies, encouraged Gordon to press ahead with it.

PRINCE EDWARD ISLAND'S LAND TENURE QUESTION

Prince Edward Island had once been resistant to the idea of a wider union, but during a visit there in the summer of 1863, Arthur Gordon found a more hopeful atmosphere. Gordon was pleased to hear PEI Liberal leader George Coles suggest in a speech that a union might provide the means by which Prince Edward Island could break the power of its monopoly landowners. Coles had been instrumental in the island's quest to gain responsible government in 1851, and now he wished to put an end to the oligarchic system of land distribution. Since 1767, Prince Edward Island had been controlled by a coterie of largely absentee landowners. At that time, the island had been divided into 67 townships of 20,000 acres each, awarded to military officials and other favourites of the Crown. Settlers ever since had rented farms on these vast estates without the security of tenure enjoyed by their counterparts in other British North American colonies. There had been a limited move in the 1840s to provide government assistance to buy out parcels from absentee landlords, but, as historians Rusty Bitterman and Margaret McCallum point out, the issue ran deeper than money alone. The rights of property owners were fundamental, and any move to compel the sale of land violated core British principles; the issue also might have implications for Ireland, where long-standing disabilities against Roman Catholics seemed impossible to redress while still respecting Protestant property rights.[5]

GROWING SUPPORT FOR MARITIME UNION

Buoyed by the climate of support for union in Prince Edward Island, Gordon pressed New Brunswick premier Tilley about the idea. Historian Donald Creighton suggested

---

5   Rusty Bittermann and Margaret McCallum, "Upholding the Land Legislation of a 'Communistic and Socialist Assembly': The Benefits of Confederation for Prince Edward Island," *Canadian Historical Review* 87 (March 2006): 1–28.

that Tilley, a druggist whose fortune had been built on patent medicines, had "something of the counting-house approach to politics." The trim and cheerful Tilley was energetic and practical, treating politics as "a series of concrete, prosaic problems which could best be solved in a matter-of-fact, business-like way." He was not captivated by grand ideas of nation building, but by the opportunities for expanded commerce and improved communications that a wider union would offer.[6]

Events in Nova Scotia had also taken an encouraging turn in the summer of 1863, where a new Conservative ministry took office under Charles Tupper. Tupper, a third-generation Nova Scotian who trained as a medical doctor in Edinburgh, advocated railway building and extolled the advantages to Nova Scotia of colonial union. Both, he believed, would enhance commercial opportunities and make Nova Scotia's influence more widely felt.

Dramatic events south of the border added urgency to the idea of a wider union. Once again, British North Americans were worried about their defences, and no concrete steps had been taken to improve them since the last crisis. In July 1863, Confederate General Robert E. Lee suffered a devastating defeat at Gettysburg, Pennsylvania. A few days later, the Union's capture of Vicksburg, Mississippi, gave the North control of the Mississippi River. The cause of the South turned irrevocably with these two successive defeats, and to the British North American colonies, the prospect of a Northern victory raised the spectre of invasion. Anglo–American relations had not appreciably mended since the tense days of the *Trent* crisis. Among the fresh provocations was Britain's tacit consent for the building and arming of Confederate vessels in British ports. One of these, the cruiser *Alabama*, commissioned in the summer of 1862, proved a devastating menace to Union shipping, capturing 68 prizes of war over two years. Indeed, after the war's end, the Americans pursued damage claims against Britain, with one American statesman proposing that the North American colonies be handed over as compensation.

THE MARRIAGE OF THE CANADAS IN CRISIS

The political instability plaguing the province of Canada continued unabated. In May 1863, the ministry of John Sandfield Macdonald and Louis-Victor Sicotte went down to defeat after only a year in office. The governor general, Lord Monck, called an election and worked behind the scenes to try to mend some of the personal acrimony that prevented political cooperation. Monck recognized that George Brown, while not

---

6 Donald Creighton, *The Road to Confederation The Emergence of Canada, 1863–1867* (Toronto: Macmillan, 1964), 14.

then sitting in the legislature, held the key to a large support base in Canada West. The governor general requested a private interview with Brown and urged him to try to build a coalition once again with Dorion, insisting that Brown had an essential role to play in finding a solution to the deep-rooted dysfunction.

Monck's flattering words possibly pushed Brown into a more conciliatory frame of mind, but personal factors may also have helped. After limping away to Britain in the summer of 1862, suffering electoral defeat, ill health, and financial losses, Brown unexpectedly fell in love at the age of 43. Anne Nelson was the sister of an Edinburgh school friend and, within weeks of meeting, the pair decided to marry. By December, Mr. and Mrs. Brown were sailing home to Canada. Brown's new wife was an intelligent and insightful supporter with whom he could unburden himself about the trials of political life. They had three children, and their happy home became a much-needed refuge for Brown. When business took him away, Brown shared his confidences in affectionate letters, lamenting that he counted the days until they could be together.

After Canada's June 1863 election, George Brown was back in the legislature and a new ministry headed by Sandfield Macdonald had been formed. Monck was gratified when this administration passed a modified Militia Bill that autumn, but other fundamental problems had not been solved. Worse, support for Sandfield's administration ebbed away and it resigned in March 1864, leaving Monck the task of finding a viable alternative ministry. After Monck had consulted a number of prospects, Etienne-Paschal Taché agreed to form a government, with the support of John A. Macdonald and Cartier. This proved a short-lived expedient, and by June 1864, the new ministry was defeated by a margin of only two votes.

Monck stalled when Taché approached him with a request for dissolution of the legislature for an election: four ministries had collapsed within three years, and two general elections during that time had not broken the deadlock. Admitting privately that he was overstepping the strict limits of his constitutional role, Monck appealed directly to George Brown to form a coalition with his rivals. He even brought Canada's political antagonists together socially with lively dinner parties at Government House, one of which featured group sing-alongs in English and in French, with an impromptu solo by Cartier. Brown at last relented, and in June 1864, the "Great Coalition" was formed.

THE GREAT COALITION, 1864

Beyond vice-regal pressure, there were more substantial reasons behind Brown's change of heart. Brown knew that this offered a chance to pursue federation for British North America, something that would break the unworkable union of 1840. He made this goal a condition of his agreement to join the coalition. He further insisted, to satisfy Canada West, that representation by population must be a part of any new formula. His third objective was to pursue the acquisition of the prairie west as an outlet for agricultural expansion.

Besides George Brown, the unlikely partnership included John A. Macdonald, George-Étienne Cartier, Alexander Galt, William McDougall, Thomas D'Arcy McGee, Oliver Mowat, Étienne-Pascal Taché, Hector Langevin, Alexander Campbell, James Cockburn, and J.C. Chapais. The coalition thus brought together all the main political elements of the United Canadas, with the exception of the *rouges*. Étienne-Pascal Taché headed the coalition.

The Great Coalition's plan for federation was helped along by fortunate circumstances. As it happened, the colonies of Prince Edward Island, New Brunswick, and Nova Scotia had scheduled a conference for the beginning of September 1864 to discuss Maritime union. Lord Monck wrote to the lieutenant governors of the Maritime colonies to see if Canadian delegates could be invited to the Charlottetown conference.

In the meantime, during the summer of 1864, a group of other prominent Canadians set out on a tour of New Brunswick and Nova Scotia, led by Canada West politician Thomas D'Arcy McGee. The tour was unconnected to the Charlottetown conference, but did much to build good feelings among the British North American colonies and thus may have helped the Confederation project along. McGee hoped that the visit would help promote the intercolonial railway scheme. "Hold on to the Intercolonial," McGee had written to Tilley that spring. "You have now men in power in Canada who will resume the project with perfect sincerity."[7] Tilley had just introduced legislation in New Brunswick to subsidize railway lines but had been vague about which communities would actually enjoy rail access. One exasperated critic complained in verse: "Mr. Tilley, will you stop your puffing and blowing/And tell us which way the railway is going?"[8]

THE CONFEDERATION CONFERENCES

Seven Canadian delegates arrived at Charlottetown aboard the steam vessel *Queen Victoria* on the morning of September 1, 1864, a day behind delegates from Nova Scotia and New Brunswick. The arrival of so many dignitaries at once, coupled with a long-awaited circus tour that had just arrived in Charlottetown, meant that the island hosts had to deliver some embarrassing news: no accommodations were available, and some of the Canadians had to sleep on board the vessel. Others found rooms at Eckstadt's

7 As quoted by W.L. Morton, *The Critical Years: The Union of British North America, 1857–1873* (Toronto: McClelland & Stewart, 1964), 143.

8 As quoted by Alfred G. Bailey, "The Basis and Persistence of Opposition to Confederation in New Brunswick," in Ramsay Cook (ed.), *Confederation* (Toronto: University of Toronto Press, 1967), 75.

Oyster Saloon.[9] But the other aspects of the conference more than made up for the inconvenience. While the original agenda had been to discuss Maritime union, the Atlantic delegates decided to hear what the Canadians had to say first. The visitors were permitted to lay out a plan, explaining how a broader federal union might work.

The visitors also hosted the Maritimers at a lunch on board the *Queen Victoria*. It was a golden afternoon and the champagne flowed freely, breaking down the delegates' reserves. "Whether as the result of our eloquence or of the goodness of our champagne," Brown wrote to his wife, "the ice became completely broken, the tongues of the delegates wagged merrily." "If any one can show just cause or impediment why the Colonies should not be united in matrimonial alliance" one delegate boomed, "let him now express it or for ever hold his peace." No one objected, Brown reported, "and the union was thereupon formally completed and proclaimed!"[10]

This was only one in a series of social gatherings during that hectic week. A ball at Charlottetown's Government House capped off the events. The event got under way at nine in the evening, with a midnight supper of beef, ham, salmon, lobster, oysters, salad, pastry, fruits, and wine. Toasts and speeches lasted until close to four in the morning. After this contest of endurance, the delegates travelled on to Nova Scotia and then crossed over to New Brunswick, and then to a second Confederation conference in Quebec the following month.

Some delegates brought their wives and families along to take part in the October 1864 Quebec conference, as the 18-day event offered plenty of opportunities for lively socializing. Feo (Frances Elizabeth Owen) Monck, the sister-in-law of the governor general, was shocked by the "drunkenness, pushing, kicking, and tearing" at the delegates' ball; "the supper room floor was covered with meat, drink, and broken bottles." John A. Macdonald "is always drunk now," she noted, and was found "in his night shirt, with a railway rug thrown over him, practising Hamlet before a looking-glass."[11]

NEW TENSIONS WITH THE UNITED STATES

At the height of the Quebec Conference, a new defence crisis erupted to add greater urgency to a scheme for union. On October 19, 1864, a group of Confederate agents launched a raid against St. Albans, Vermont, from their base on Canadian soil.

---

9 P.B. Waite (ed.), *Confederation, 1854–1867* (Toronto: Holt, Rinehart, and Winston, 1972), 80.

10 George Brown to Anne, September 13, 1864, "George Brown Describes the Charlottetown Conference, 1864," Library and Archives Canada, online at https://www.collectionscanada.gc.ca/confederation/023001-7103-e.html.

11 Frances Monck, journal excerpt, October 16, 1864, *My Canadian Leaves* (Toronto: Canadian Library Service, 1963), 79.

One person was killed, and the town's banks were robbed of more than $200,000. Canadian authorities apprehended 14 of the raiders, and Union forces two more. However, when they were tried in Montreal two months later, the defendants were released on a technicality, and some of the seized funds returned to them. Americans were outraged, with the *New York Times* calling for war with Britain. Amid this threatening atmosphere, Canadian officials were alarmed to read news of a sharply reduced British budget for North American defence in 1865. John A. Macdonald wondered aloud if the projected figures had a zero omitted by mistake.[12]

In December 1864, amid an atmosphere of growing hostility, the Americans announced the cancellation of the 1854 Reciprocity Treaty. This was not entirely a product of diplomatic deterioration: American economists argued that the benefits of reciprocity had mainly fallen to British North America. The United States had accumulated a trade deficit of some $30 million over the course of the treaty. For the British North American colonies, the loss of this vital trade connection added an important economic argument to the Confederation proposals: the consequences might be softened if the colonies strengthened their ties with each other.

TERMS OF CONFEDERATION

The delegates at Quebec had hammered out 72 resolutions that formed the basis of the *British North America Act* passed in 1867 by Britain's Parliament. While some Canadians today mistakenly imagine that Confederation heralded a sort of separation from Britain, this is far from the case. The resolutions insisted upon "the perpetuation of our connection with the Mother Country." This was no declaration of independence. Colonial self-government had already been achieved in 1848, with respect to internal matters. Autonomy in foreign policy was still decades away. Executive power would be exercised in the name of the Queen, with the governor general acting as the representative of the Crown in the Dominion government and lieutenant governors filling that role in the provinces.

The Quebec Resolutions called for a federal system, with a general government to deal with matters common to all and local legislatures for each province. The two districts of the United Canadas would thus be able to break out of their unhappy union to become the separate provinces of Quebec and Ontario. While Confederation at first only included Quebec, Ontario, Nova Scotia, and New Brunswick, the resolutions anticipated that Prince Edward Island would later join, along with other British

12 As quoted by P.B. Waite, *The Life and Times of Confederation, 1864–1867* (Toronto: University of Toronto Press, 1962), 31, 33.

North American colonies—Newfoundland, the prairie west administered by the Hudson's Bay Company, and British Columbia and Vancouver Island (united as one colony in 1866).

The terms provided for a bicameral—that is, two-house—central Parliament: an elected House of Commons and an appointed Senate. The seats in the House of Commons were to be apportioned according to population: "rep by pop." Yet the Senate would in theory partly address the domination of central Canada by allowing the Maritime region more seats than would be warranted based on population alone. There would be 24 seats each for Quebec and Ontario, and 24 for the Maritime region (10 for Nova Scotia, 10 for New Brunswick, and ultimately 4 for Prince Edward Island). Besides being a voice of regions, the Senate was also intended to provide a check on the House of Commons. As an appointed body, the Senate was meant to allow for "sober second thought," perhaps to protect propertied interests but also to protect minorities from the vagaries of crude majority rule. Canada's short-lived experiment with an elected upper house, put into effect in 1856, would come to an end.

The apportioning of responsibilities between the dominion and the provincial governments was especially delicate and laid the foundations for longstanding tensions. But in 1864 the goal was to secure substantial agreement for a federation, with the fine points to be worked out later. The "Fathers of Confederation" came from a British tradition of a largely unwritten constitution and undoubtedly took a great deal of constitutional practice for granted. The relationship between government and Parliament, for example, was not spelled out, nor was the role of the prime minister.

John A. Macdonald sought a strong central government and pointed to the bloody American Civil War as an object lesson in what could happen when the individual constituent parts of a union were too powerful. Indeed, he would have preferred a simple union to a federation, but he consoled himself with the belief that the provincial levels of government would eventually wither away, even as he privately acknowledged that it would "not do to adopt this point of view when discussing the subject in [French] Lower Canada."[13]

In the Quebec Resolutions, the dominion Parliament was given powers to "make laws for the peace, welfare and good government" of the federated provinces. By the time these resolutions were translated into the final draft of the *British North America Act*, this phrase became "Peace, Order, and good Government." Some matters specifically assigned to the federal government include criminal law, justice, defence, currency, banking, postal service, Indian affairs, navigation and shipping, fisheries,

13 As quoted by Ged Martin, "Introduction to the 2006 Edition," in P.B. Waite (ed.), *The Confederation Debates in the Province of Canada, 1865*, 2nd ed. (Montreal and Kingston: McGill-Queen's University Press, 2006), xxv.

plus important taxation powers, notably customs, which was then the main source of government revenue. The provinces were to have jurisdiction over such questions as property, civil law, Crown lands, hospitals, and education, as well as matters of "a merely local or private nature." While the provinces thus had control over education, the Act specified that the rights of denominational—that is, religious—schools must be maintained, based on what existed by law at the time of Confederation. This was intended to protect the rights of the Protestant minority in Quebec and Roman Catholic minorities in Ontario.

The general government agreed to assume the debts of the individual colonies at the time of Confederation, based upon a per capita debt allowance. With taxation powers concentrated in the general government, funds would be allocated on a population basis to the provinces for their local expenditures. There was also a clear commitment to construct the intercolonial railway to link Halifax to the St. Lawrence. A separate section of the BNA *Act* provided for the ultimate establishment of a Supreme Court, although this would not be put into place until 1875, and appeals would continue to Britain's highest court, the Judicial Committee of the Privy Council. Canada elected to continue this right of appeal to the JCPC until 1949.

The final draft of the BNA *Act* put under the control of the central government "all Matters not coming within the Classes of Subjects by this Act assigned exclusively to the Legislatures of the Provinces," in other words, "residual" powers. The central government would also have the power to disallow provincial legislation, something that suggests an almost imperial relationship between the Dominion government and the provinces. In theory, the general government would be able to use this power of disallowance to protect minority rights, but in the early years of Confederation the federal government wielded that now-lapsed power quite capriciously. Such provisions as these led some to believe that Macdonald's wish for a highly centralized arrangement had prevailed. *Rouge* critic A.A. Dorion complained that what was ostensibly a federation was really "union in disguise."[14] Others, however, noted that the provinces did indeed have control over substantial matters, including their own constitutions. For example, initially, most provinces opted to have upper houses, or legislative councils, at the provincial level. These provincial senates seemed to imply a substantial, dignified level of government, not something resembling a mere municipality.

Legislation to put Confederation into effect needed to be passed in Britain, but before this could happen, the delegates worked to promote acceptance of the Confederation scheme in their own colonies. It was not precisely a rule that a new constitution would *require* the consent of the colonies affected, but winning popular

14 As quoted by Morton, *The Critical Years*, 165.

support, or at least the appearance of it, was good policy, and British statesmen would be more inclined to hear the proposals colonial politicians put forth if it was understood that they had the support of their constituents.

PRINCE EDWARD ISLAND AND NEWFOUNDLAND ABSTAIN

While Charlottetown was the cradle of the Confederation scheme, Prince Edward Island initially opted against it. Opponents denounced the scheme's risk for increased taxation and expressed fears that islanders would be drawn into defending distant Canada. Historian Peter Waite points out that many islanders feared that they might be *compelled* to join a larger union, as they were mindful that British policy favoured colonial consolidation; a nearby analogy would be the merger of Cape Breton Island with Nova Scotia in 1820. Alexander Anderson, a PEI legislative councillor, probably spoke for many when he voiced his objections:

> I think the offer is something like this: if we will give up to one-half of our revenue to the Canadians, and allow them to tax us as much as they please, they would then take charge of us. We fought hard and contended long for responsible government, and are we now going to give up our constitution and say we are not able to govern ourselves? I do not think that any man or any body of men in Canada can know the wishes or wants of the people of this island as well as we do ourselves.[15]

Prince Edward Island did not join Confederation in 1867, but later would be forced into the union by financial pressures. An overly ambitious railway building scheme made the dominion's offer of release from debts irresistible in 1873.

No delegates from Newfoundland had attended the Charlottetown conference, but, as historian James K. Hiller put it, "in the summer of 1864 the mainland architects of confederation remembered Newfoundland's existence" and invited Hugh William Hoyles' Conservative government to send representatives to the Quebec conference.[16] In the event, however, Newfoundland opted not to join Confederation, and indeed stood aloof until 1949. Hoyles had sent Conservative F.B.T. Carter as a

---

15 Alexander Anderson, Prince Edward Island Legislative Council, April 1, 1865, in Janet Ajzenstat, Paul Romney, Ian Gentles, and William D. Gairdner (eds.), *Canada's Founding Debates* (Toronto: University of Toronto Press, 1999), 62.

16 J.K. Hiller, "Sir Ambrose Shea," *Dictionary of Canadian Biography (DCB)*, http://www.biographi.ca/en/bio/shea_ambrose_13E.html.

delegate to Quebec in 1864, and Carter succeeded Hoyles as premier the following year, but despite Carter's enthusiasm for the scheme, there was too much resistance to Confederation in Newfoundland. Newfoundland had been in the grip of devastating economic decline, with poor fishing and sealing yields, gale force winds, and a blight on the potato crop. A quarter of Newfoundland's revenues were being consumed in poor relief. Critics feared that a protective economic system under Confederation would harm Newfoundland, which was separated from the mainland by hundreds of miles of sea and which depended upon imports to feed its population and upon exports of fish and seals. Newfoundland's orientation was more to the British Isles, something reinforced by the 1866 laying of a trans-Atlantic cable connecting Newfoundland to Ireland. Historian Andrew Smith sees Newfoundland's rejection of Confederation as consistent with the "libertarian, anti-statist streak in Newfoundland's political culture." Newfoundland's per capita debt load, for example, amounted to £1.44 per person in 1864, in contrast to £5.20 in Canada.[17]

Other issues also clouded Newfoundland's consideration of the Confederation proposal, and Carter decided not to press the matter. The 1869 election drove Carter's administration from office, but this was not simply a rejection of a pro-Confederation government. Carter had introduced policies to reduce relief to the able-bodied poor, and Protestant political opponents, disapproving of Carter's Roman Catholic political allies, worked to intensify Orange Order antagonisms and promoted rumours of subversive activities by Irish radicals. Tory anti-Confederation agitator Charles Fox Bennett found it easy to convince Roman Catholics that rule from Canada would be as disastrous for Newfoundland as rule from England had proved for Ireland.[18]

CONFEDERATION DEBATES IN CANADA

Political debate in the United Canadas centred on practical considerations. Thomas D'Arcy McGee painted a vision of "one great nationality…quartered into many communities—each disposing of its internal affairs,"[19] but it would be a distortion to suggest that nation building was the dominant theme.

In Canada East, *rouge* members, who had been left out of the Great Coalition and the Confederation conferences, raised sensible concerns about the proposed scheme. Antoine-Aimé Dorion had favoured some new federal arrangement to break

17 Andrew Smith, "Toryism, Classical Liberalism, and Capitalism: The Politics of Taxation and the Struggle for Canadian Confederation," *Canadian Historical Review* 89 (March 2008): 7, 7n.

18 Ibid., 10.

19 As quoted by David Shanahan, "Young Ireland in a Young Canada: Thomas D'Arcy McGee and the New Nationality," *British Journal of Canadian Studies* 12, no. 1 (1997): 3–4.

the unworkable legislative union of 1840 but found the Quebec Resolutions untenable. "The Confederation I advocated was a real confederation," he insisted. Under the Quebec terms, the provinces would have "the smallest possible amount of freedom of action." He maintained that the idea that an intercolonial railway would improve defence was ludicrous: "a railway lying in some places not more than fifteen or twenty miles from the frontier, will be of no use whatever.... An enemy could destroy miles of it before it would be possible to resist him." It would actually be "a mere trap for the troops passing along it," he argued.[20] Fellow *rouge* member Henri Joly added that the Americans already understood that an attack on any one British North American colony would prompt a spirited resistance by all: Confederation was not necessary to ensure united defence. Moreover, Joly pointed out, expansion to include the west would create "the outward form of a giant, but with the strength of a child."[21]

Cartier defended the Quebec Resolutions, promising that union with the Maritime colonies could help to break the numerical dominance of Canada West. He also maintained that the proposed system would protect the rights of minorities, including Quebec's English-speaking Protestants. Moreover, he claimed that the Roman Catholic clergy, and even the Pope himself, approved of the plan.

English-speaking Canadians were not unanimous in their support for Confederation either, despite John A. Macdonald's skillful management of the 1865 debates and George Brown's considerable influence. Legislative councillor James Currie sensibly pointed out that British North America's limited manpower and pecuniary resources would not multiply under Confederation. Joining with the Maritimes, he said, "was like tying a small twine at the end of a long rope and saying it strengthened the whole line."[22] Yet the prospect of achieving representation by population, and thus breaking the unworkable union of 1840, was appealing in Canada West. The positive votes of Canada West Reformers would ensure the Resolutions' adoption.

By the wee hours of Saturday, March 11, 1865, the Confederation debates in the Canadian legislature were winding down. A Canada West newspaper described the state of the house as "seedy," with members stretched out sleeping on the benches, having exhausted the saloonkeeper's stores of food and liquor, and others expressing their impatience for the division bell by rattling their desks and making birdcalls. At last, at 4:15 AM, the members were called to vote.[23] The yeas prevailed: 91 were in favour

20 A.A. Dorion, in *The Confederation Debates in the Province of Canada*, 62; as quoted in Ged Martin (ed.), "The Case against Canadian Confederation," *The Causes of Canadian Confederation* (Fredericton: Acadiensis Press, 1990), 36.

21 As quoted in Martin, "The Case against Canadian Confederation," 38, 40.

22 Ibid, 40.

23 *Stratford Beacon*, March 17, 1865, as quoted in Waite, *The Life and Times of Confederation*, 156.

of the Resolutions, and 33 opposed. A majority in both sides of the house supported the measure: in Canada West, 54 were in favour and 8 opposed, and in Canada East the vote was 37 to 25.

NOVA SCOTIA AND NEW BRUNSWICK CONSIDER CONFEDERATION

Nova Scotia's support for Confederation was by no means assured. The influential Joseph Howe, who had been instrumental in the fight for responsible government, opposed Confederation. He was not then a member of the legislature but was serving as a fisheries commissioner and so felt compelled to express his objections anonymously. His "Botheration" letters, published in 1865, condemned the Confederation scheme. He ridiculed the clichéd conviction that "something must be done." The one thing that ought to be done, he maintained, was that Nova Scotians, the "freest people on the earth," having won self-government in 1848, "ought all to go down on our knees and thank the Almighty for the abundant blessings he has showered upon us." They ought to resist the serpent in the garden. If the Canadians were in trouble, "let them get out of it; but don't let them involve us in distractions with which we have nothing to do. Are not the Canadians always in trouble? Did not Papineau keep Lower Canada in trouble for twenty years, and McKenzie [sic] disturb the Upper Province for about the same period?"[24] Nova Scotians had no wish to be called from their own homes to defend Canada. Yarmouth merchant, ship owner, and politician Thomas Killam feared that Confederation would limit Nova Scotia's potential markets, would "hedge ourselves in." He saw in Confederation the ruin of Nova Scotia's shipping interests.[25]

Historian Phillip Buckner rejects the idea that those Maritimers who resisted Confederation were inherently conservative or parochial. For some, Buckner explains, the real issue was not a wider union but the specific terms of the Quebec Resolutions.[26] Del Muise has emphasized economic factors, arguing that the old Nova Scotia economy based on wooden ships was giving way to a new continental orientation that depended upon industrial growth, coal, and railway transportation.[27] Those whose interests lay with the latter would be most inclined to support the Confederation

24 "Botheration Scheme," *Morning Chronicle*, January 11, 1865. https://www.collectionscanada.gc.ca/confederation/023001-7135-e.html.

25 As quoted by Smith, "Toryism, Classical Liberalism, and Capitalism," 13.

26 Phillip A. Buckner, "The Maritimes and Confederation: A Reassessment," in Martin, *The Causes of Canadian Confederation*.

27 E.R. Forbes and D.A. Muise, *The Atlantic Provinces in Confederation* (Toronto: University of Toronto Press, 1993).

scheme. As it happened, voters in Nova Scotia would be denied the chance to participate in an election on the question.

Just as Canada's legislature pronounced its support for Confederation in March 1865,
the project faced a reversal in New Brunswick. Tilley's government sought a mandate
on the Confederation issue, and during the election that lasted from February 28 to
March 18, 1865, Albert Smith's anti-Confederation forces ran a lively campaign. Echoing
Joseph Howe's arguments, Smith characterized Canada as convulsed by anarchy and
disquiet, in contrast to the peace and contentment that reigned in New Brunswick. Irish
journalist Timothy Warren Anglin, whose Saint John newspaper the *Morning Freeman*
had long been an influential voice among New Brunswick Roman Catholics, maintained
that Canada, and not New Brunswick, would reap any economic and political advantages. He also rejected arguments centred on defence, insisting that the British North
American colonies were innocent bystanders in Britain's quarrels with the Americans
and thus should not be expected to bear the burden of increased military expenses.
Anglin also argued that New Brunswick's administration was more cost-effective than
that of Canada, and that the residents of New Brunswick enjoyed more free services.
Toll roads and bridges were more pervasive in Canada, he wrote, because the politicians
had spent public money on grandiose parliament buildings.[28] Smith's anti-Confederates
swept Tilley and his supporters from office, a result that some disappointed partisans
blamed on an organized Roman Catholic conspiracy. Lieutenant Governor Arthur
Gordon was compelled to call upon Smith to form a government—a man he personally
despised and had earlier scolded for abusing his position as attorney general. But, within
a year, Gordon would seize a new opportunity to advance the Confederation project.

BRITISH PRESSURE FOR CONFEDERATION

In Britain, the tide had shifted strongly in favour of colonial union or federation by
1865. Consolidated colonies would be better able to defend themselves and would be
less apt to be a burden on British taxpayers. Thus, while Confederation was in no sense
a separation of the colonies from the mother country, it might help the mother country divest itself of onerous obligations. Edward Cardwell, Britain's Secretary of State
for the Colonies, urged his colonial governors to do everything in their power to bring
the Quebec Resolutions to fruition: "I need scarcely assure you that here there is but
one desire—which is to promote to the utmost the work in which you are engaged," he
wrote privately to Lord Monck.[29] London's banking community also lobbied in favour

28 Smith, "Toryism, Classical Liberalism, and Capitalism," 15–16.
29 Cardwell to Monck, private, November 26, 1864, Monck Papers, microfilm A 755, Library and Archives Canada.

of Confederation, seeing in it a means to secure investments in British North America. "Had a group of politically powerful investors disliked the Quebec Resolutions, it is doubtful whether the imperial parliament would have implemented them," Andrew Smith argues.[30]

George Brown had travelled from the Quebec Conference to London where, in December 1864, he had a private conversation with Cardwell about Confederation and about the wish of Canadians to acquire the Hudson's Bay Company holdings in Rupert's Land to provide for western expansion. This idea was also appealing to British policy makers, as it offered the prospect of transferring responsibility for the northwest onto other shoulders. Soon after the passage of the Quebec Resolutions in Canada's legislature in the spring of 1865, Brown returned to London for further negotiations, this time accompanied by fellow members of the Great Coalition government— Macdonald, Cartier, and Alexander Galt. Cardwell attempted to resist arguments that Britain should continue to bear the costs of naval and land defences, but for the most part, British statesmen flattered the visiting colonials with invitations to dinner parties, balls, horse races, and other delights of London society. Macdonald even accepted an honorary Oxford doctorate. The agenda was to promote the Confederation scheme, seemingly at risk with Tilley's electoral defeat in New Brunswick. In London *The Times* proclaimed: "If, in short, these colonies ever wish us to defend their whole soil, they must combine in a general organization…the House of Commons ought to have the courage, if necessary, to enforce it upon the colonies." A later editorial comment put it even more baldly: "We look to Confederation as the means of relieving this country from much expense and much embarrassment….We appreciate the goodwill of the Canadians and their desire to maintain their relations with the British Crown. But a people of four millions ought to be able to keep up their own defences."[31]

THE FENIAN DANGER

In April 1865, Confederate General Robert E. Lee offered his surrender to Union General Ulysses S. Grant at the village of Appomattox Court House in Virginia, ending the American Civil War. Yet, before long, British North Americans would face a new threat to their security, and again, the threat would be based upon a quarrel not truly their own.

30 Andrew Smith, "The Reaction of the City of London to the Quebec Resolutions, 1864–1866," *Journal of the Canadian Historical Association* 17 (2007): 4.

31 *The Times* [of London], April 12, 1865, as quoted in Waite, "Edward Cardwell and Confederation," in *The Life and Times of Confederation;* Ramsay Cook, Craig Brown, and Carl Berger (eds.), (Toronto: University of Toronto Press, 1967), 37; *The Times*, March 1, 1867, as quoted in C.P. Stacey, "Britain's Withdrawal from North America, 1864–1871" in *The Life and Times of Confederation*, 14.

In 1857, Irish republicans who had fled to the United States in the wake of the failed 1848 uprising formed a new society, the Fenian Brotherhood, aimed at securing Irish independence from British rule. American Fenians coordinated activities with their counterparts in Ireland and drew some 10,000 supporters from the ranks of battle-hardened American Civil War veterans. The organization boosted recruitment by offering new enlistees a $100 incentive. Many demobilized soldiers also took advantage of a United States Army offer to buy their own rifles for $6. Much of the Fenians' funding also originated in the United States: Irish expatriates drawn to the republican cause donated almost half a million dollars. Yet some supporters of Irish independence might have shrunk from the terrorist tactics the Fenians employed on both sides of the Atlantic. Threats of political assassinations and bomb attacks kept authorities throughout the British Empire on constant alert, with shared intelligence reporting on secret caches of weapons and the movement of suspects. An 1867 bomb explosion in London killed six and injured many more. A would-be assassin who claimed to be a Fenian shot and wounded Prince Alfred, the son of Queen Victoria, while the Prince made the first ever royal visit to Australia in 1868. Canada's first secret service was established for the purpose of monitoring the Fenian threat, a precursor to a later branch of the North West Mounted Police. Thomas D'Arcy McGee, who had in his youth espoused the cause of Irish republicanism, was despised by the Fenians as a turncoat. In April 1868, as he returned to his rooming house from a late-night parliamentary session, he was assassinated in the streets of Ottawa by a Fenian plotter.

Some Fenians hoped to strike a blow at Britain's North American colonies as a way to exert pressure for Irish independence. Colonial officials had been monitoring rumours of an attack on St. Patrick's Day, 1866, and called out militia units to prepare. The day passed without incident. Then, early in April, reports surfaced that some 1,000 Fenians had descended upon Eastport, Maine, bound for an attack on New Brunswick. British troops and colonial militia, backed by the Royal Navy, put the would-be invaders to flight, leaving, it was said, unpaid hotel bills behind them. In June of that year, fresh assaults came against British North American territory, this time at Ridgeway in Canada West and Missisquoi Bay in Canada East. The Fenian forces overwhelmed Canadian militia, but withdrew when their anticipated reinforcements failed to arrive. Nine militiamen were killed, including three young students from the University of Toronto, and dozens were wounded.

The defence crisis posed by the Fenian raid pushed a wavering New Brunswick into Confederation. Lieutenant Governor Arthur Gordon moved quickly to capitalize on fears about security. He called an election a little more than a year since the previous one, and, as he had hoped, Samuel Leonard Tilley and the pro-Confederation Liberals were swept into office in June 1866, defeating Albert Smith's anti-Confederation administration. Tilley's administration quickly passed a resolution in favour of Confederation.

In Nova Scotia, Charles Tupper had been unwilling to risk calling an election to seek a mandate on Confederation, but he successfully passed a resolution in Nova Scotia for Confederation in April 1866. To Joseph Howe, the timing provoked questions: "the proceedings from beginning to end, were the very best possible to subserve the ends of the Confederates," he pointed out. "The Fenians made their appearance at Eastport, and forthwith the Confederation resolution was tabled in our House of Assembly. A few days after the resolution was carried, and presto! The Fenians had evaporated and gone."[32]

American authorities seemed loath to deal with the Fenian threat. The fact that a society dedicated to terrorist tactics was able to fundraise, recruit, and drill on American soil all pointed to the fact that no administration wanted to alienate Irish-American voters. Some Americans believed that the Fenian raids would merely force the inevitable annexation of Canada, and in this light it is easy to see that, while the military crises themselves quickly blew over, the attacks added urgency to the Confederation project. An American takeover was not an entirely far-fetched notion. In July 1866, a bill was introduced into the United States House of Representatives providing for the admission of Nova Scotia, New Brunswick, the United Canadas, and the western territories into the union. This proposed legislation, denounced as impudent by the Canadian press, did not move beyond the committee stage.

THE LONDON CONFERENCE, 1866–1867

With Confederation approved in British North America, a final step remained: the Quebec Resolutions would have to be drafted into legislation to be passed by Britain's Parliament. Not until 1982, with the "patriation," or bringing home, of the Constitution, would Canada's Constitution be enshrined in Canadian legislation. A change of government in Britain in 1866 brought the Conservatives to power under the Earl of Derby, but support for Confederation did not falter. Lord Stanley, the foreign secretary, privately explained: "The Colonies will remain Colonies, only confederated for the sake of convenience. If they choose to separate, we on this side shall not object: it is they who protest against the idea. In England separation would be generally popular."[33] Enthusiasm for colonial possessions was at a low ebb in Britain by the middle decades of the nineteenth century.

---

32 As quoted in Waite, *The Life and Times of Confederation*, 271.

33 Lord Stanley to Frederick Bruce, March 23, 1867, as quoted in Stacey, "Britain's Withdrawal from North America, 1864–1871" in *The Life and Times of Confederation*, 15.

From December 1866 to March 1867, British North American delegates—including John A. Macdonald, Charles Tupper, and Samuel Leonard Tilley—met with their imperial counterparts at the Westminster Palace Hotel in London. The London Conference hammered out the details of Confederation legislation. Nova Scotia's Joseph Howe was also on hand to make the anti-Confederation case, but the tide in favour was too formidable for him to overcome. The Earl of Carnarvon,[34] Britain's Secretary of State for the Colonies, flattered Howe by seeking out his views, but had no intention of abandoning the project.

Like George Brown a few years before, Macdonald found that his sojourn in Britain involved a whirlwind courtship. While the London conference was underway, Macdonald met the sister of his private secretary, Hewitt Bernard. The 52-year-old Macdonald had been widowed for nine years. Agnes Bernard was 31, a tall, commanding woman, with angular features and an austere manner. Macdonald assured Agnes's brother that he had curtailed his drinking, although rumours persisted that he was frequently "indisposed" during the days of the conference. Nevertheless, Agnes agreed to a speedy wedding in February 1867. Many, not least the bride herself, imagined that she could be a tempering influence on Macdonald, but, as she was forced to admit to her diary, "I was over confident, vain and presumptuous in my sense of power. I fancied I could do too much and I failed signally."[35]

THE *BRITISH NORTH AMERICA ACT, 1867*: A MARRIAGE OR A DIVORCE?

In the same month that John and Agnes Macdonald's marriage was solemnized, Confederation legislation was passed in Britain's House of Commons. The new federated colony was to be styled the "Dominion" of Canada. Tilley wrote to his son that the term occurred to him during his daily Bible reading, when he stumbled upon it in Psalm 72: "He shall have dominion also from sea to sea, and from the river unto the ends of the earth." In March 1867, Carnarvon shepherded the bill through the House of Lords, and the Queen pronounced her Royal Assent on March 29. Macdonald bristled at the fact that British parliamentarians had shown general indifference to the measure, treating it like "a private bill uniting two or three English parishes." Indeed, Governor General Lord Monck's letter to his son describing his plans for July 1, 1867, the day Confederation was to be proclaimed in Canada, speaks volumes. He blandly

---

34 The family seat of the Earls of Carnarvon is Highclere Castle, known to many today as the scene of the popular series Downton Abbey.

35 See Martin, "John A. Macdonald and the Bottle," 171–73.

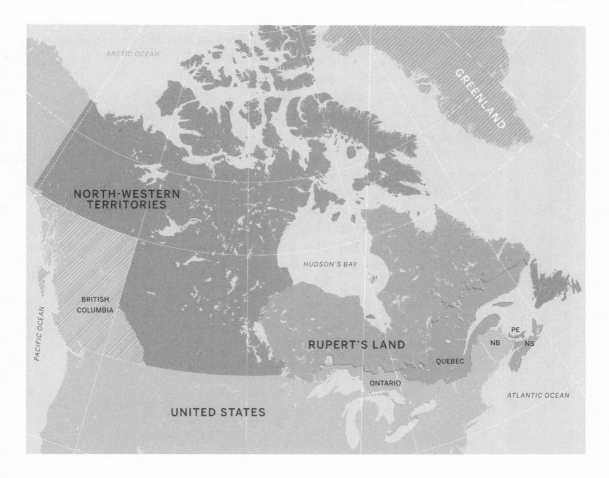

Map 12.1
Canada, 1867.

noted that he would be "obliged to go to Ottawa for a few days for some business."[36] Monck disappointed those expecting a sense of grand occasion: rather than wearing his cocked hat and ceremonial uniform trimmed with gold braid, he simply turned up in his ordinary street clothes. In Halifax, Joseph Howe reported on a Confederation Day crowd of about 600—the number that might be expected for a decent funeral, he said sourly.

For the Maritime colonies, Confederation was a marriage of convenience: there was scant enthusiasm, but imperial pressure and practical considerations all exerted their force. For Canada East and Canada West, united since 1840, Confederation was not so much a marriage as a divorce. The divorce was not from Britain, but rather from each other. Now each section of the once-united colony would be a separate province, able to legislate over questions where autonomy mattered most. If any nationalist

36 As quoted by Martin, *Britain and the Origins of Canadian Confederation*, 288, 290.

agenda was at work, it influenced the breaking of the unworkable union that had bound the Canadas unwillingly together, freeing the provinces of Ontario and Quebec to govern themselves more effectively.

Practical considerations, then, dictated the Confederation arrangements. It would resolve the endemic political paralysis in the colony of Canada and facilitate railway building, trade ties, and defence planning. The Confederation terms spelled out in the *British North America Act* delved into prosaic matters such as provincial debt allowances and the commitment to construct the intercolonial railway. That said, the terms contained numerous ambiguities that would be left to future statesmen and future courts to resolve. Despite Thomas D'Arcy McGee's rhapsodic musings on "one great nationality," that, too, would be decided by the future. A sense of wider national identity could not be forced, but rather would have to be built incrementally as Canadians shared challenges and triumphs in the years to come.

INDEX

SOURCES

Page 9 William D. Finlayson, *The 1975 and 1978 Rescue Excavations at the Draper Site*, National Museum of Man Mercury Series, Archaeological Survey of Canada Paper no. 130, Ottawa, 1985. Drawing by Ivan Kocsis. Page 16 E.R. Degginger/Alamy Stock Photo. Page 57 Archives de la Ville de Montréal. BM007-2-D27-P001. Page 63 Natural Resources Canada. Reproduced with the permission of the Minister of Public Works and Government Services Canada. Source: website (http://atlas.nrcan.gc.ca/site/english/index.html). Page 71 Fourth Edition National Atlas Maps © 2001 (atlas.gc.ca/english/copyright.htmlQ1) Government of Canada with Permission from Natural Resources Canada. Source: website (atlas.gc.ca/english/quick_maps/index_4edition.htmQ2). Page 87 Ron Garnett/All Canada Photos. Page 140 Natural Resources Canada. Reproduced with the permission of the Minister of Public Works and Government Services Canada. Source: website (http://atlas.nrcan.gc.ca/site/english/index.html). Page 163 © Government of Canada. Reproduced with the permission of Library and Archives Canada (2016). Source: Department of National Defense, 17 Wing Publishing Office, *Canadian Military Journal*, 2013/Vol. 13, no. 3, p.18. Page 166 George Simpson, Governor of Rupert's Land, 1857. Archives of Ontario, I0027769. Page 200 La Presse Canadienne, "Dévoilement de Mémorial Louis-Joseph-Papineau". October 21, 2012. Photo by Robert Skinner, La Press. © La Press, ltée. Tous droits réservés. Page 212 D. Gordon E. Robertson/Wikimedia Commons. Page 232 Boy and Girl at Cahera (engraving), English School, (19th century)/Private Collection/Bridgeman Images. Page 235 Nancy Hoyt Belcher/Alamy Stock Photo. Page 247 Portrait of Josiah Henson (1789–1883) 1876 (b/w photo), American Photographer, (19th century)/Schlesinger Library, Radcliffe Institute, Harvard University/Bridgeman Images. Page 253 Ann Ronan Pictures/Print Collector/Getty Images. Page 256 Shahnoor Habib Munmun/Wikimedia CC-Att 3.0.